This book breaks new ground by focusing on the Florentine "super-companies" of the early fourteenth century in their own right. The author closely examines the Peruzzi Company in particular, describing its ownership, family connections, scope of business, organization structure, accounting systems, and its history from 1300 to its dissolution in bankruptcy court in 1347.

From this analysis, the author offers a radical reassessment of the nature and role of these extraordinary organizations. He establishes that although they engaged in all forms of commerce in substantial volume, what made them exceptional was commodity trading, especially in grain, which they conducted on a heroic scale. It was this activity that required heavy capital, sophisticated organization, and an international network. But the author also exposes the limitations of their financial power and explodes the myth that their downfall was caused mainly by bad loans to Edward III to finance his invasions of France.

This book is much more than a business history. It presents the operations of these companies in the context of the swiftly moving political, military, and economic developments in Florence, the Mediterranean, and western Europe during a tumultuous period.

The medieval super-companies

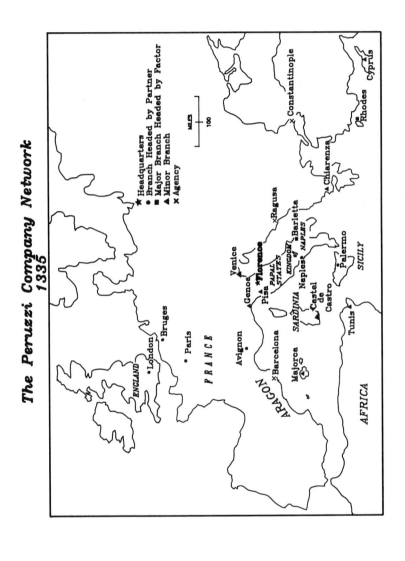

The Peruzzi Company Network
1335

★ Headquarters
● Branch Headed by Partner
■ Major Branch Headed by Factor
▲ Minor Branch
✕ Agency

MILES
100

London
Bruges
ENGLAND
Paris
FRANCE
Avignon
Barcelona
ARAGON
Majorca
SARDINIA
Castel de Castro
Genoa
Pisa
★ Florence
Venice
PAPAL STATES
KINGDOM of NAPLES
Barletta
Naples
Tunis
Palermo
SICILY
AFRICA
Ragusa
Chiarenza
Constantinople
Rhodes
Cyprus

The medieval super-companies
A study of the Peruzzi Company of Florence

EDWIN S. HUNT

University of Cincinnati

CAMBRIDGE
UNIVERSITY PRESS

Published by the Press Syndicate of the University of Cambridge
The Pitt Building, Trumpington Street, Cambridge CB2 1RP
40 West 20th Street, New York, NY 10011-4211, USA
10 Stamford Road, Oakleigh, Melbourne 3166, Australia

First published 1994

Printed in the United States of America

Library of Congress Cataloging-in-Publication Data

Hunt, Edwin S.,

The medieval super-companies : a study of the Peruzzi Company of
Florence / Edwin S. Hunt.

p.   cm.

Includes index.

ISBN 0-521-46156-1

1. Compagnia dei Peruzzi – History. 2. Florence – Commerce –
History. 3. Merchants – Italy – Florence – History. I. Title.
HF416.H86   1994
380.1'06'04551 – dc20   93-40289
                                                    CIP

A catalog record for this book is available from the British Library.

ISBN 0-521-46156-1 hardback

To Iris and Clifford

Contents

Tables, figures, and map

Tables

Figures

Map

Abbreviations

CCR Calendar of Close Rolls
CPR Calendar of Patent Rolls

Introduction

During the last half of the thirteenth and first half of the fourteenth centuries, there emerged a number of very large Italian merchant banking companies. Three of them, the Bardi, Peruzzi, and Acciaiuoli companies of Florence, attained exceptional size, diversity, and geographical reach, but all collapsed in the 1340s. The two largest, the Bardi and Peruzzi, came to grief, according to the chronicler Giovanni Villani, because they advanced loans foolishly and excessively to King Edward III of England to help him finance the opening phases of the Hundred Years' War. Villani claimed that the English king owed the Peruzzi Company the colossal sum of 600,000 Florentine florins when it went bankrupt in 1343, and the Bardi an even larger total of 900,000 florins when it failed in 1346.[1]

Most students and general readers have become aware of the existence of these great organizations from popular political or social histories of the period in which the Bardi and Peruzzi are briefly introduced and promptly dismissed.[2] In such accounts, the firms are characterized as banking houses that naively and greedily overreached themselves in lending huge sums to the king in the vain pursuit of profit. But many other historians have written thoroughly researched works in various languages about particular aspects of the companies' activities, including their role in the history of medieval Florence, or about the operations of individual branches in southern Italy, Sicily, England, France, and the papal courts.[3] In virtually all studies to date, however, the mighty companies have been merely a part, albeit important, of the phenomenon on which each author had concentrated his or her attention. The only exceptions are two

[1] Giovanni Villani, *Storia di Giovanni Villani* (Florence, 1587), Book XII, Chap. 55.

[2] Barbara Tuchman, *A Distant Mirror* (New York, 1978), 81; Paul Johnson, *Edward III* (London, 1973), 71.

[3] For example, Robert Davidsohn, *Storia di Firenze* (Florence, 1956), 7 volumes; Georges Yver, *Le commerce et les marchands dans l'Italie méridionale, au XIIIᵉ et au XIVᵉ siècle* (Paris 1903); E. B. Fryde, *William de la Pole* (London, 1988) and his unpublished Ph.D. dissertation, "Edward III's War Finance, 1337–41: Transactions in Wool and Credit Operations" (Oxford, Bodleian Library, 1947); and Yves Renouard, *Les relations des papes d'Avignon et des compagnies commerciales et bancaires de 1316 à 1378* (Paris, 1941).

old works written in the early part of this century about the Bardi and Peruzzi, but even these are narrowly focused, concerned mainly with the events leading up to the downfall of the companies.[4] There is no literature that considers these unusual firms as complete business organizations, describing how they arose, what they actually did, how they were structured, and why they attained such an extraordinary size. And no scholar has yet published a thorough chronological history of any of these firms. Until such analyses are made, we cannot begin to understand why they collapsed and also why organizations of such proportions never again appeared in medieval Europe. And only then can we free the history of the companies from the simplistic distortions imposed by the chronicler Villani.

This present book is an attempt to begin filling this lacuna by examining one of the three above-named organizations in depth to find out how companies of such exceptional size were able to function in the demanding business environment of the high to late middle ages. Such companies deserve a special title to distinguish them from the many Italian merchant-bankers typical of the early fourteenth century, including some that were fairly large. The word "multinational" is tempting but inappropriate because it inaccurately suggests a similarity to the modern version and because there were no nation-states worthy of the name at that time. "Megacompany" is another seductive term, but is misleadingly pretentious, conjuring up a vision of much greater resources than we will find is the case. I have therefore opted for the relatively simple term "super-company," which connotes an entity both larger than and qualitatively different from other business organizations of that era.[5]

The period with which this book is mainly concerned, that is, the late thirteenth and early fourteenth centuries, coincides almost exactly with the economic "crisis" that has been the subject of much scholarly debate over the past fifty years or so.[6] Stated in its simplest terms, the crisis theory holds that the economic expansion of the

[4] Ephraim Russell, "The Societies of the Bardi and Peruzzi and their Dealings with Edward III, 1327–1345," in *Finance and Trade under Edward III* (London, 1918), 93–115; Armando Sapori, *La crisi delle compagnie mercantili dei Bardi e dei Peruzzi* (Florence, 1926).

[5] The definition of and qualifications for "super-company" status are outlined at the beginning of Chapter 2.

[6] A very useful recent review of this debate appears in Bruce M. S. Campbell, ed., *Before the Black Death* (Manchester, 1991). This collection of essays includes not only some of the latest analysis, but also a thorough historiography on the subject. Barbara Harvey's introduction is especially helpful in articulating the various theses as well as her own views.

two preceding centuries had reversed itself because of population pressure, stagnant technology, and climate change, and that these forces were sufficient to create the conditions for the subsequent long-term recession without the intrusion of the Black Death catastrophe of 1347–50. The super-companies were undoubtedly affected by these developments, especially insofar as the forces contributed to the growth of centers of consumption and centers of production, and thus to the large-scale trade in foodstuffs on which the companies thrived.

It is not the purpose of this study, however, to enter this great debate. For one thing, most of the evidence examined in the controversy concerns the agricultural economics of England and northwestern Europe, whereas the orientation of the super-companies, as we shall see, was more toward the Mediterranean area. For example, they were affected little by the Great Famine of 1315–17 that ravaged northern Europe but very much by the Italian crop failures from the late 1320s onward. More important, the businesses of the super-companies were subject to a wide range of complex overlapping forces – political, military, and cultural, as well as economic – over a wide geographic area. I have therefore concluded that it is more enlightening to bring all of these environmental forces to bear on the story of the super-companies as a matter of relevant information than to attempt to fit them into an evaluation of any general economic argument. As a result, the book is essentially a business history, but permeated with social, economic, and political history.

Three principal and related theses emerge from this study. The first is that although the super-companies engaged in general commerce, banking, and manufacturing in substantial volume, what made them exceptional was commodity trading, which they conducted on a heroic scale. The core of the business was the Florence-Naples axis, wherein the companies controlled most of the export of grain from the Angevin kingdom of southern Italy, while exploiting that market's appetite for textiles of all types. These activities were founded on the need of the growing urban population for imported foodstuffs and industrial raw materials and the need for cash by the rulers who controlled those commodities. It *required* the companies to be big, with substantial capital, sophisticated organizations, and international branch networks, because only such enterprises had the resources to obtain and exploit the necessary licenses from those rulers.

The second thesis is that the much-discussed English wool trade, while eventually very important to the super-companies, was not their principal target nor the reason that they had to be especially large. The Peruzzi Company was not involved in the commerce of wool in a really important way until late in its history, while the Acciaiuoli was never a significant participant. The Bardi Company, the biggest of them all, was unique in being a major player in both grain and wool over a considerable stretch of time, and even that great enterprise had been a super-company in the grain trade of southern Italy long before it became a large-scale buyer and seller of wool.

The third thesis is that the resources of the super-companies have been greatly overstated by historians, possibly to reconcile them with the huge losses purportedly suffered on loans to Edward III. Their resources, although extraordinarily large for their time, were in fact quite limited compared with the demands made on them and had to be deployed with great skill. The managers had to maintain a continuous recycling act with the rulers they served to ensure that there was sufficient money coming out of the system to fund enough new loans to keep those same rulers satisfied and the companies solvent.

Although the Bardi Company was by far the largest and best-known of the super-companies, I have selected the Peruzzi Company as the representative model to study for a number of important reasons. The first is the existence of a wealth of records of this company, which permit an independent analysis of its organizational structure, operating systems, and management philosophy, as well as a plausible reconstruction of its history. The second is that there is a continuous record of shareholder participation of both family and nonfamily members, allowing the examination of the business as a corporate entity distinct from the Peruzzi family. The third reason is the existence of a good set of accounting records depicting the state of the company on July 1, 1335, just nine months before its first significant investments in England. These data make it possible to ascertain what resources the company had available for its English joint venture with the Bardi Company and to isolate the effect of that venture on the company's fortunes. Finally, there is much information available on the key members of the Peruzzi family who were instrumental in conceiving the operating systems and in driving the business forward. It was these creative and energetic people, in the final analysis, who converted the economic and political opportunities presented to them into a spectacular commercial success.

The book is organized in two parts. Part I is designed to provide background information on the origins, business activities, organization structure, and accounting systems of super-companies in general and the Peruzzi Company in particular, along with the economic and political environment in which they operated. Because the family and the company are often confused, the opening chapter has been devoted to exploring the origins and early history of the Peruzzi family and of the company in order to identify the nature of each and the linkages between them. It examines the family's rise in wealth and status and its role in Florentine politics, and provides brief profiles of three key personages. By the end of the chapter, it is clear that while the affairs of family and company were very much intermingled, they remained quite distinct entities. Chapter 2 moves on to the discussion of the super-companies and the nature of their business, dealing with all facets, including their well-known financial activities, but concentrating on the three dominating elements, trade in grain, wool, and cloth. This chapter also reviews the historical background to the rise of the super-companies and the development of their economic and political relationships with the leadership of the kingdoms of Naples, England, and France, and of the papal court. Chapter 3 focuses on the organization structure needed to run a super-company of geographic and product-line diversity, drawing on data mainly from the Peruzzi Company to create the model. Chapter 4 turns to the accounting systems of the period, including a brief discussion of the double-entry controversy and the training of accountants. It then goes on to analyze the Peruzzi accounts in detail, describing the system and what it was and was not designed to achieve.

These four chapters of background and function set the scene for Part II, which presents the chronological history of the Peruzzi Company from its corporate reorganization in 1300 until its final dismemberment in bankruptcy court in 1347. This survey divides conveniently into five chapters, comprising periods covering the company's prosperous years, the beginning of its decline, the attempt to reverse its decline, the events leading to its eventual collapse, and the aftermath of the failure as it concerned both the company and the family. Although the review focuses on the activities of the Peruzzi Company and its personnel, it does so in the context of the political and economic environment in which the company operated. The action moves from place to place where the Peruzzi did business, touching on the great wars and famines that so affected the company in those tumultuous times. In the last two chapters, the scene shifts back and forth between Florence and England, as the events in both places impinged on the fate of the Peruzzi. This chronological history is vital to the thrust of the book, serving more than just to put flesh on the analytical bones identified in Part I. It is needed to reveal how such a company operated in the real world of power politics and repeated calamities in the early fourteenth century.

The conclusions of this study are discussed in a final brief chapter. Probably the most obvious of them is the disposal of the myth that Edward III was the principal agent of the collapse of the super-companies. The losses of the Bardi and Peruzzi in England were not nearly as large as supposed and were only one, and not the most important, of the factors leading to the firms' demise. This myth badly needs disposal, because it continues to be reinforced in otherwise excellent recent works of serious scholars. For example, Sumption's *The Hundred Years' War*, Ormrod's *The Reign of Edward III*, and Waugh's *England in the Reign of Edward III* all blame the bankruptcies of the Bardi and Peruzzi on their loans to Edward III.[7] A less obvious but intriguing conclusion is that after the bankruptcies of the 1340s, no new companies emerged approaching the stature of the super-companies. Even the Medici Bank, large as it became, lacked the reach and dominance of the super-companies of a century earlier. The reasons for this phenomenon are to be found in the reversal of the same forces that caused the appearance of the super-companies in the first place. Although proponents of the "crisis" thesis of the early fourteenth century might take comfort in the fact that all three super-companies failed *before* the Black Death of 1347–50, the nonreappearance of such organizations can most logically be ascribed to drastically reduced population growth following the Black Death and to reduced recourse to borrowing by the rulers who controlled the key commodities.

Included in this volume is a map of the Peruzzi network and several appendixes that I believe are useful references. The first is a genealogy of the Peruzzi family from its known beginnings to the middle of the fourteenth century derived from the monumental study of the nineteenth-century historian and genealogist Luigi Passerini.[8] The charts may look complicated, but they are essential to the understanding of the two main branches of the family and help explain why it is so often necessary to identify an individual by including his father's name. Other appendixes give additional detail on exchange

---

[7] Jonathan Sumption, *The Hundred Years' War*, vol. 1, *Trial by Battle* (London, 1990), 363–4; W. M. Ormrod, *The Reign of Edward III* (New Haven, CT, 1990), 88; Scott L. Waugh, *England in the Reign of Edward III* (Cambridge, 1991), 183.

[8] Luigi Passerini, "Genealogica e storia della famiglia dei Peruzzi," MS folio 41 in the Biblioteca Nazionale Centrale, Firenze.

rates and the accounts of the Peruzzi companies and their shareholders to support comments made in the main text. Finally, I have included a biographical note on Giovanni Villani along with a discussion of the comments of various scholars on his many disputed claims. Villani merits special attention because of the important influence he has had on scholars of the economic history of the early fourteenth century. Whether one agrees with him or not, his is the benchmark against which most numerical estimates for the period are compared.

A word needs to be said here about the main currencies that appear in this work and the symbols used to express them.[9] The symbol most commonly used is "li." for the *lira a fiorino*, which is not a currency at all, but a fictive unit of account employed by the Florentine business community. Local coins, such as the soldi di piccioli, will also be mentioned, but the key Florentine coin used in international trade was the florin (fl.), valued usually at approximately li.1.45. The other main currency encountered is the English pound sterling (£). The exchange rates between the currencies of Florence and England varied considerably, but here we will use a rate close to the standard applied between the super-companies and the English treasury, that is, one florin equals three shillings. This results in a rate of £1 = 6 2/3 florins, which converts to a rate of £1 = li.9.67, which I have rounded to £1 = li.10 for convenience. Several other currencies appear in Tables A2, A7, and A8, but the only ones cited with any frequency in the text are the Neapolitan carlin and ounce (oz.).

This book reflects several years' research of the Peruzzi accounts as well as the secret books of Giotto and Arnoldo Peruzzi and other primary sources.[10] It also owes much to the many scholars whose works I have cited throughout the text. But its unconventional approach comes from my own extensive personal experience in the world of multibranch operations in international business, which perhaps has enabled me to ask questions of the data that might not occur to other historians. This perspective has driven me to enquire how these very large companies with widely dispersed operations could have been organized, managed, and controlled in an essentially hostile environment. I am encouraged in this approach by the conviction expressed by the renowned businessman-turned-historian Raymond de Roover that the medieval businessman faced the same

---

[9] Details are discussed in Chapter 4 immediately following Table 5.

[10] The Peruzzi documents noted here have been meticulously transcribed by Professor Armando Sapori in *I libri di commercio dei Peruzzi* (hereafter, *I libri*) (Milan, 1934). This publication has made a wealth of primary data available to scholars all over the world.

problems of policy and management as do businessmen today – meeting fierce competition, forecasting changing market conditions, and motivating personnel.[11] The similarity of the problems does not mean that medieval super-companies can be regarded as direct ancestors of the modern multinational corporation. The environment and cultures called for very different managerial responses from those developed by today's companies. The book attempts to present those responses in the real-life context of the political, military, and economic events of those very troubled times.

I owe a great debt of gratitude to James Murray and John Brackett of the University of Cincinnati for their many thoughtful and constructive reviews of this study and for their encouragement of my unconventional approach. I am also deeply indebted to Richard A. Goldthwaite of Johns Hopkins University and David Abulafia of the University of Cambridge for their well-reasoned criticisms and constructive suggestions for further research, which have done much to improve the final version of this work. Any errors or omissions that remain are, of course, my own, as are the viewpoints expressed herein. Finally, I am grateful to the editor of the *Journal of Economic History* for permission to re-present some of the material I used in an article published by the *Journal* in March 1990.

[11] Raymond de Roover, "The Story of the Alberti Company of Florence, 1302–48, as Revealed in Its Account Books," *Harvard Business Review* 32 (Spring 1958): 49–50.

Part I

Anatomy of the medieval super-company

1

The company and the family

One of the problems in analyzing the very large medieval Italian merchant-banking organizations that are the subject of this study is that all of them bore the name of a single family that was usually in control.[1] As a result, it is often difficult to distinguish between the activities and motivations of such companies and those of the eponymous families. Historians have compounded the confusion by indiscriminately referring to company and family alike as "the Bardi," "the Peruzzi," "the Frescobaldi," and so forth. This tendency is admittedly difficult to overcome because the affairs of most companies and their family shareholders were indeed very much intermingled.[2] The early companies were in fact largely family associations; the very word *compagnia* etymologically means a family partnership as well as sharing the same bread.[3] But companies that were comprised of a mixture of family and nonfamily shareholders became increasingly common in the later Middle Ages, and some of them became extraordinarily large. In these big "mixed-type" companies, the relationships between firm and controlling family were necessarily less straightforward.

A further complication in the analysis of the very large mixed companies is that although they were usually dominated by certain members of the controlling family, many of their close kinsmen had little or no involvement in the business. For example, the Bardi Company

---

[1] The term "usually" applies here, because, as will be seen in Chapter 2, companies known as the Ricciardi of Lucca and the Frescobaldi of Florence appear to have been really consortia of several firms.

[2] Robert L. Reynolds gives a useful description of this phenomenon in "Origins of Modern Business Enterprise: Medieval Italy," *Journal of Economic History* (Fall 1952), 350–65.

[3] Florence Edler, *Glossary of Medieval Terms of Business: Italian Series, 1200–1600* (Cambridge, MA, 1934), 80. Raymond de Roover adds that although the firms were partnerships, they can be correctly called "companies," because this is the term the companies themselves used. See his "New Interpretations of the History of Banking," *Journal of World History* 2 (1954): 44.

was able to satisfy the Commune of Florence that none of the sixteen Bardi family members who participated in the failed coup attempt in November 1340 was an active partner in the company.[4] The evidence from the Peruzzi Company is that only six to eight family members were shareholders at any one time between 1300 and 1335. They were consistently outnumbered by outside shareholders throughout the period, although they did not lose majority share ownership until 1331.[5] Of course, many Peruzzi kindred served the company in various capacities. Some were salaried employees, called *fattori* or factors, but these were relatively few in number, comprising only 14, or just over 10 percent of the133 factors employed by the company between 1331 and 1343.[6] From the account books it is clear that several other Peruzzi who were neither shareholders nor employees were active in the company's affairs. But thirty-five, exactly half of the seventy Peruzzi adult males identified as living between 1331 and 1343, had no part in the running of the business.[7] Five of them were churchmen. And in the case of the Bardi, less than 3 percent of the 346 factors working for that company between 1310 and 1345 can be identified as members of the huge Bardi lineage.[8]

This evidence casts doubt on the logical assumption that the powerful Florentine merchant-banking lineages were tightly linked to the operation of the family-controlled enterprise, drawing their wealth and cohesion from it. The Peruzzi records show that different members of the family followed different career paths – military, diplomatic, political, ecclesiastical, professional, and entrepreneurial – and many generated their own sources of wealth. This is not to deny the powerful sense of solidarity attributed to medieval Florentine lineages by numerous scholars.[9] On the contrary, the diverse activities of its members inside and outside the company must have had a sym-

---

[4] Sapori, *La crisi*, 127. One of the plotters had, in fact, been a shareholder of the company until the eve of the coup. Sapori rightly treats the termination of his partnership with skepticism, but then goes on to say that the company and family were one and the same, an argument that I challenge at the beginning of Chapter 8.

[5] See Table A4 and discussion in Chapter 6.

[6] A. Sapori, *Studi di storia economica*, Vol. 2 (Florence, 1955), 718–29.

[7] See Figures A1–A3.

[8] Sapori, *Storia economica*, Vol. 2, 730–54. Only 5 employees of the 346 are specifically listed as Bardi, but another 5 are probable kin.

[9] See, e.g., Jacques Heers, *Family Clans in the Middle Ages*, trans. Barry Herbert (Amsterdam, 1976); George W. Dameron, *Episcopal Power and Florentine Society, 1000–1320* (Cambridge, MA, 1991); Carol Lansing, *The Florentine Magnates* (Princeton, NJ, 1991).

biotic effect on the family as a whole. The power and wealth of the company doubtless enhanced the careers of individual members, while their political, military, and diplomatic efforts often redounded to the direct or indirect benefit of the company – all adding to the prestige of the family name. But what is less certain is whether there was a subservient relationship in either direction between the two entities.

A reasonable first approach toward understanding the very large commercial organizations of the early fourteenth century is to take a closer look at some of the people involved in their rise and fall. The Peruzzi Company provides much useful material for a study of this nature. The object of such an examination is not merely to search for commercial geniuses responsible for the firm's success, although the family was indeed blessed with some very able people. The emergence of these exceptional companies is too suggestive of an important economic and social phenomenon to be explained away by the existence of exceptional individuals. The purpose of investigating the Peruzzi family and the careers of certain of its members is to obtain a grasp of the complex relationships among family, business, and the Florentine polity that helped make these extraordinary enterprises possible.

The main source for the data on the family stems from Luigi Passerini's "Genealogica e storia della famiglia dei Peruzzi," which traces the Peruzzi family in great detail back to 1150. As a historian, Passerini is often undiscriminating, not only accepting a great deal of the Peruzzi Company mythology, but also adding some inventions of his own.[10] As a genealogist, however, he is meticulous.[11] The point is worth making because he has argued persuasively against the strongly pressed claims that the Peruzzi originated just outside the earliest walls of Florence near the Porta della Pera and that the family took its name from that location. One source contemporary with Passerini even asserted that the Peruzzi were of Roman descent, which would fit comfortably with Florence's self-image at the time as a daughter of Rome.[12]

---

[10] Passerini, "Genealogica." For example, he claims that the Peruzzi loaned 1,370,000 florins to Edward III, the nonrestitution of which brought the company down in 1338. This amount was more than double Villani's figure and dates the bankruptcy five years early.

[11] Passerini has also constructed a genealogy of his own family, tracing the various branches of both his father's and mother's lines to the eleventh and thirteenth centuries, respectively. See *Storia e genealogica delle famiglie Passerini e de' Rilli* (Florence, 1874)

[12] Conte Francesco Galvani, *Sommario storico delle famiglie celebre Toscane*, Vol. 3 (Florence, 1864), chapter on Peruzzi, 1.

These claims bear the hallmarks of the typical effort of an important family to enhance its status by attempting to establish a pedigree of antiquity and nobility.[13] The family crest and the company logo, consisting of golden pears on a field of blue, build on the della Pera origin and its connection with the pear.[14] But Passerini reluctantly concludes that there is no firm evidence to support the della Pera provenance. He points out that the Peruzzi name is most likely to have evolved from a diminutive of the very common name Piero, buttressing his position with the observation that there were Peruzzi families in several Italian cities that lacked a Porta della Pera. Passerini is probably correct; Giovanni Villani, whose close connections with the Peruzzi company might have biased him in its favor, merely remarks on the existence of the Porta della Pera connection. He is not prepared, however, to confirm that the Peruzzi of his day were descended from that lineage.[15]

A property document in San Remigio dated 1150 is the earliest authentic Peruzzi record presented by Passerini and contains the name of Ubaldino di Peruzzo, indicating his domicile as the village of Ruota in the Valdarno.[16] Early in the thirteenth century the family seemed to gain status in Florence. By 1203, one Guido became a councillor and his name appeared on a peace treaty with Siena. In 1225, one Mazzetto matriculated into the Arte della Seta, the silk guild that was one of the seven major guilds until it was absorbed into the Arte di Por Santa Maria.[17] But the family remained of little significance for some time. Villani compiled a long list of the Guelf and Ghibelline families in each quarter of Florence, when these factions first emerged in 1215. The list included the Bardi described as "of small beginnings," but not the Peruzzi.[18] Nor is there any men-

---

[13] See Gene A. Brucker, *Renaissance Florence* (New York, 1969), 90–1, for further discussion of the claims to antiquity of various Florentine families. Much of the research by families into their past dated from the fifteenth century onward, but efforts on the Peruzzi pedigree must have begun early, because the company logo was already in use in the early fourteenth century and Villani mentioned the Pera Gate connection in his chronicles. Also, Heers, *Family Clans*, 100, notes the early enthusiasm for research into family origins.

[14] According to Passerini, the number of pears in the family crest varied over time and was "indeterminate" in the early fourteenth century. Renouard indicates a company logo at that time with three pears (*Les relations*, 45); Davidsohn indicates that it had "one or three" pears (*Firenze*, Vol. 6, 386).

[15] Villani, *Storia*, Book IV, Chap. 13.

[16] There are references elsewhere to the family dating as far back as 1135 (discussed later).

[17] S. L. Peruzzi, *Storia del commercio dei banchieri di Firenze, 1200–1345* (Florence, 1868), 54, 94; Edgcumbe Staley, *The Guilds of Florence* (London, 1906), Chap. 7.

[18] Villani, *Storia*, Book V, Chaps. 14 and 15.

tion of the Peruzzi among the leading Guelf or Ghibelline families cited by Villani in connection with his various accounts of the Guelf–Ghibelline struggles in the 1260s.[19]

The men who brought the Peruzzi family into prominence were Filippo and Arnoldo, sons of Amideo. Each founded a dynasty with its own distinct characteristics.[20] Arnoldo's was strongly commercial, producing many of the men of "ink-stained fingers" who provided most of the company's leadership and staff. His descendants furnished twenty-eight of the Peruzzi personnel directly involved in the business until its collapse; only nine Peruzzi came from the Filippo branch. Notwithstanding the fact that Filippo was the driving force behind the establishment of the Peruzzi as a super-company, he and his offspring were much more attracted to politics and warfare. He became a knight as did his son Guido. Another son, Chiaro, was a churchman, and a grandson, Simone, of whom we shall hear more, was a celebrated diplomat. But both branches of the family made important contributions to the business and to Florentine politics, and Arnoldo's sons Pacino and Giotto combined business and political skills very successfully.

Initially, the family's progress was held in check by the fact that it, like Florence, was divided into two hostile factions. Filippo was a Ghibelline who participated in the victory over the Guelfs at the Battle of Montaperti in 1260. He was a leader of the Ghibelline party and councillor of Florence and was very influential during the years following the Montaperti triumph.[21] At the same time, the Guelf branch of the Peruzzi was included in a long list of families that opted to stay in Florence while quietly attempting to raise funds for the continuing struggle against the Ghibellines.[22] After the Ghibellines went down to defeat with the Hohenstaufen Manfred at Benevento in 1266 and Conradin at Tagliacozzo in 1268, Filippo disappeared into exile, probably as a soldier of fortune. Passerini tells us that he returned to Florence in 1280 and became one of the Ghibelline signatories to the formal reconciliation between the Guelfs and Ghibellines in that city. We know, however, that he was running a company registered in his name in Florence as early as 1274.[23] Less is known about Arnoldo,

---

[19] Ibid. Book VI, Chaps. 79, 81, and 83, and Book VII, Chaps. 14 and 15. Although not among the leaders, members of the Peruzzi were definitely in business in the 1260s (see Peruzzi, *Storia commercio*, 160–1).

[20] Figures A2 and A3 show each branch in detail.

[21] Filippo's name was included in the list of guarantors of a treaty with Siena in 1261. See Sergio Raveggi et al., *Ghibellini, Guelfi e popolo grasso* (Florence, 1978), 54n.

[22] Davidsohn, *Firenze*, Vol. 2, 701.

[23] Sapori, *Storia economica*, Vol. 2, 656.

except that he too was a decorated warrior, but on the Guelf side, as well as an active businessman.

The social status of the family around 1280 is not entirely clear. One historian regarded the Peruzzi as noble, citing the Villani passage that included the Peruzzi among the noble families that lived in the quarter of the Porta Santa Maria.[24] Another included the Peruzzi in a list of "noble" families along with the Albizzi, della Scala, and Medici.[25] But Villani's disclaimer, as noted, appears to negate such a conclusion. Moreover, the lack of any mention of the Peruzzi family in any of the lists of leading Florentine lineages up to that time implies that it was not an ancient house. Nor was it a "quasi-noble" family by virtue of having one or more consecrated knights among its members. Knighthood, although not necessarily a mark of nobility, was closely connected with it in terms of social status.[26] The earliest of the four Peruzzi knights recorded in Gaetano Salvemini's *dignità cavalleresca* was not consecrated until at least the 1290s.[27] All bore the honorific "messer," reserved for the highest social order in Florence, the knights and judges.[28] Two other Peruzzi, Amideo di Filippo and

[24] Yver, *Le commerce*, 299.

[25] John Larner, *Italy in the Age of Dante and Petrarch, 1216–1380* (London, 1980), 121.

[26] Gaetano Salvemini, *La dignità cavalleresca nel Commune di Firenze e altri scritti* (Milan, 1972), 142–4. See also John K. Hyde, *Padua in the Age of Dante* (Manchester, 1966), 91–2, for a brief but useful discussion of knighthood in medieval Italy and Lansing, *Magnates*, Chap. 8, for a fuller account of the complexities of knighthood status in thirteenth-century Florence.

[27] The four Peruzzi consecrated as knights were Filippo di Amideo (date unknown, but sometime between 1292 and his death in 1303), Ridolfo di Donato (1315), Guido di Filippo (1324), and Simone di Chiaro (date uncertain, probably early 1320s). For the first three, the evidence, although indirect, is convincing, being memoranda in Giotto's Secret Book detailing some of the expenses paid for food, vestments, and retainers for the consecration ceremonies. See G. Salvemini, *La dignità*, 201; Peruzzi, *Storia commercio*, 363; *I libri*, 497–9. For Simone, the evidence is the official record, which describes him as a knight on his election to the office of prior in 1344 (*La dignità*, 146, 175), but Passerini says he was knighted much earlier.

[28] The title *messer* carried a wide variety of meanings in different times and places, ranging from great respect to ridicule. In Venice, it was reserved for the Doge, and throughout medieval Italy, God was "Messer Dominiddio." The *Grande dizionario della lingua Italiana*, ed. S. Battaglia (Turin, 1978), Vol. 10, 216–7, devotes several columns to the word, with a vast number of quotations. From these it appears that, in medieval Florence, *messer* was reserved for judges and knights (*dottori e cavalieri*), but it is unclear which institutions or persons had the authority to bestow the title. We know, however, that Guido di Filippo traveled to Faenza in September 1324 to be dubbed by Count Rugieri of Dovadola di Conti Guidi (*I libri*, 499).

Iacopo di Pacino, also enjoyed that title, but the basis for their award is unknown.

The family's great advance in social status therefore did not occur until the the late thirteenth century. Nevertheless, it is clear from the level of affluence evident in the early 1280s that both branches had enjoyed for several decades increasing wealth and respect in the community, even if not political prominence. The family's line of business was trade in international commodities and luxury goods, considered as "noble and honest, not base merchandise."[29] They were, in effect, members of the class known as the *popolo grasso*, the well-to-do merchants who were shortly to dominate the political and economic life of Florence.

How did the Peruzzi family amass the wealth that enabled it to launch a large-scale enterprise by the late thirteenth century? The usual reasons given for such success are shrewd investments, advantageous marriages, political activity, as well as hard work, drive, and business acumen. Unfortunately, there is little specific evidence on the methods used by Florentine families to acquire their fortunes before the latter half of the thirteenth century. One specifc line of business that has been reported during the twelfth century was the usurious management of monasteries. Peruzzi businessmen were early practitioners of such enterprise when they acted as agents for the nuns of Santa Felicità.[30] One source even suggests that it laid the foundation for the family fortune, but credible support for this view is lacking.[31] There are more likely sources of the family's wealth, however, and it may be productive to attempt certain generalizations based on indirect evidence and on the researches of scholars into other urban families of medieval Tuscany.[32]

A good starting point is the fact that the Peruzzi became important members of the international merchants' and cloth finishers' guild (Arte di Calimala) and the guild of money changers and bank-

[29] P. J. Jones, "Florentine Families and Florentine Diaries in the Fourteenth Century," *Papers of the British School of Rome* 24 (1956): 191.

[30] Davidsohn, *Firenze*, Vol. 1, 1191. The citation is based on two documents dated December 8, 1135, and October 23, 1140, dealing with land transactions.

[31] J. Lestocquoy, *Aux origines de la bourgeoisie* (Paris, 1952), 99.

[32] Sources include Jones, "Florentine Families"; Richard A. Goldthwaite, *Private Wealth in Renaissance Florence* (Baltimore, 1968); Thomas Blomquist, "Commercial Association in Thirteenth-Century Lucca," *Business History Review* 45 (Summer 1971): 157–78; idem, "The Castracani Family of Thirteenth-Century Lucca," *Speculum* 46 (1971): 459–76, and idem, "The Dawn of Banking in an Italian Commune: Thirteenth Century Lucca," in *The Dawn of Modern Banking* (New Haven, CT: 1979), 53–75.

ers (Arte del Cambio), which makes it likely that the early activities
that generated the family's capital following its migration into Florence were concentrated in these two areas.[33] The two types of enterprise were symbiotic, the profit of each providing capital for the other.
Thomas Blomquist's exhaustive studies into the notarial contracts of
thirteenth-century Lucchese money changers reveal a broad range
of endeavor beyond the mere changing of money. They took deposits, made small short-term loans, dealt in precious metals, and eventually financed international commerce.[34]

Typically, the surplus cash generated by commercial activity was
not entirely plowed back into the business; a part was used to acquire rural property by various means. Among the money changers'
favorite loan customers were peasants who borrowed cash to meet
their needs and repaid in kind at an exploitative markup.[35] Such
deals sometimes ended in foreclosure, contributing to the money
changers' large holdings of rural land. Philip Jones goes further, suggesting that in Florence, urban merchants often made loans to land-
lords and peasants in the *contado* (the rural area surrounding the
city) with a view to eventual purchase, commenting that "loans, calculated purchase, and sometimes coercion were combined in developing the estates of merchant families."[36] Prestige was often part of
the motivation, as some of the purchases of rural real estate were
obviously noneconomic.[37] Most of the investment, however, was decidedly economic, and merchant families committed considerable
money and effort in improving their properties to develop produce
for their own consumption and sale. With the rapid growth of the
population of Florence, such properties became very valuable and
generated increasing cash. The Peruzzi family certainly engaged in
similar acquisitions. Giotto di Arnoldo's "Secret Book" is replete with
entries dealing with purchases and improvements in his rural possessions, and even mentions buying a building in Florence for the
storage and sale of the wine from his vineyards.[38] Although this evi-

[33] They also joined a third major guild in 1297, that of the doctors, apothecaries,
    spice importers, and shopkeepers (Medici, Speziali, e Merciai) on account of
    their commerce in spices. See Raveggi et al., *Ghibellini*, 216n, 257n. And later
    they became members of the powerful wool guild (Arte della Lana). See
    Davidsohn, *Firenze*, Vol. 5, 255 n4.
[34] Blomquist, "Dawn of Banking," 60–6.
[35] Ibid., 64.
[36] Jones, "Florentine Families," 188.
[37] Ibid., 200. The Peruzzi were proud to own the ruined *castellare* of Baroncelli
    "for the honor it conferred."
[38] Ibid., 201, and *I libri*, 412, 451, 457, 463, 469, 473, 510.

dence is from the early fourteenth century, it suggests a long-standing interest in such investments.

Marriage does not appear to have played a significant part in the early years of the Peruzzi family's accumulation of wealth. Blomquist has noted that intermarriage occurred among money changers in Lucca, enhancing the interest of each party, and the Peruzzi no doubt entered into similar alliances. There is no evidence, however, that Peruzzi family members obtained wealth by deliberately marrying advantageously. Evidence of marriages into the important houses of Florence occurs only with Filippo di Amideo's children, and these were likely arranged for reasons of prestige and politics rather than wealth, because at that time the Peruzzi were already affluent. The holding of political offices may have made a contribution to the Peruzzi riches, but again it is difficult to say how much. Certainly some family members occupied minor political posts in the early days, but the Peruzzi do not appear to have been frequent holders of significant offices before 1284.[39]

All of these factors may have contributed to the family's wealth in property and revenue-producing assets, but not a great deal to the accumulation of the daunting amount of cash needed for the Peruzzi Company's ambitious overseas expansion. On the contrary, the local property investments of the kind cited above, although income producing, may even have been a net drain on the family's cash reserves. The most important source of cash therefore had to be business itself, that is, well-managed profitable enterprise, along with frugal living habits and a determination to put every spare soldo to productive use. Moreover, the accumulation had to take place over a considerable length of time, given the family's relatively humble origins. Although the earliest evidence of a company appears only from 1274, the family's participation in commerce goes back many years before this date. Davidsohn has noted that the Peruzzi name appeared in French banking affairs as early as 1248.[40] Mazzetto's matriculation into the silk guild in 1225 demonstrates a very early engagement in the luxury cloth business. And, as we have noted, there was probably more than one line of business activity. Filippo and Arnoldo each ran separate enterprises and had achieved considerable success prior to their merger in the 1280s.

The political leanings of the family in the 1280s are not entirely clear. Passerini stated that Filippo converted to the Guelf cause in

---

[39] Raveggi et al., *Ghibellini*, 215–16, includes the Peruzzi in a list of families described as having only "participated sporadically in public offices" before 1282.

[40] Davidsohn, *Firenze*, Vol. 2, 478.

the general reconciliation of 1280, suggesting a family then entirely Guelf in persuasion. But other sources indicate a family retaining Ghibelline sympathies while carefully avoiding extremes. Nicola Ottokar placed the Peruzzi among a number of families that at first tended to Ghibellinism or presented themselves as indifferent, before blending themselves completely into the dominant Guelf category in the 1290s.[41] Another source surprisingly identifies the Peruzzi as Ghibelline throughout the 1290s.[42] Beyond doubt, however, is the fact that the family became united in 1280 and that this event marked a great step forward for the Peruzzi.[43] Two ambitious, rising, well-to-do family units had become one relatively wealthy and politically important entity. The family had not yet "arrived" but was beginning to command respect in Florence's high places. Filippo's political credentials had become such that he was elected a prior in 1284, only two years after the office was first established.[44] And the family's great house, the Palazzo Peruzzi, was built in this period.[45]

Family unity was confirmed in 1283, when the sons of Arnoldo and Filippo formed a special corporation in two equal shares, composed of two separate funds – one to buy land in the *contado* and the other for buildings in Florence, each with common books for accounting.[46] This institution, distinct from the Peruzzi Company, accumulated property for many years. Such corporate arrangements were commonplace in Florence at that time and were created for a variety of reasons and purposes. For example, the four Villani brothers established one in 1322 to provide for their father in his old age.[47] One important motivation for such special corporations was the fact that shareholders of companies were subject to unlimited personal liability to creditors in case of bankruptcy. Shareholders accordingly employed this and other devices to insulate as much family property as possible from the risks of business failure. The Peruzzi Company had reached a size and level of

---

[41] Nicola Ottokar, *Il commune di Firenze alla fine del dugento* (Florence, 1926), 65.

[42] P. Parenti in Raveggi et al., *Ghibellini*, 325.

[43] Sapori, *Soria economica*, Vol. 2, 657.

[44] Under the constitution of 1282, leadership of the commune was vested in six priors, one from each of the six districts into which Florence was divided at the time. All belonged to one of the major guilds. Term of office was limited to two months.

[45] Davidsohn, *Firenze*, Vol. 7, 493, suggests that the house was built "around 1283."

[46] Sapori, *Storia economica*, Vol. 2, 657; *I libri*, 443.

[47] Michele Luzzati, *Giovanni Villani e la compagnia dei Buonaccorsi* (Rome, 1971), 16.

international exposure to risk to make such a precaution advisable.[48]

The nature of the company's early operations is difficult to assess but probably was limited to relatively small-scale commerce and lending, even if on an international basis. There is evidence of a small branch in Naples as early as the 1270s.[49] The union of the family business under the two brothers was timely, as new opportunities for large-scale commodity trading were opening up in the Angevin realm of southern Italy, as will be discussed in Chapter 2. The business prospered mightily, and by 1289 Arnoldo, then manager of the Naples branch, had become a familiar and advisor of Charles II.[50] The company exported grain from Brindisi to Greece in ships of the Templar Order, participated in the salt trade, administering the papal salt flats, and apparently engaged in trade and deposit business in the Levant.[51] During this period, Filippo was the leading shareholder and driving force behind the business, and after Arnoldo's death in 1292, he was paramount, even though Arnoldo's son Pacino briefly headed the company from 1298 until his death in 1299. He mixed business with high politics and community service, setting the tone for the company and for the family. Under his leadership, the company's standing as a model of success and probity was consolidated. It had indeed become an important factor at the court of Naples and was establishing a significant presence in Paris.[52] And in 1294, King

[48] This evidence runs counter to the argument of Heers, *Family Clans*, 218, that the Florentine companies of the "Peruzzi Period" allowed their members little initiative to invest capital outside the companies. This restriction, he says, made it impossible to spread risks over various enterprises, leaving the shareholders vulnerable to bankruptcy. As we shall see in the case of the Peruzzi, there was no lack of diversity in the company's business and much evidence of shareholder investment outside the company.

[49] Yver, *Le commerce*, 292; Davidsohn, *Firenze*, Vol. 6, 838.

[50] Yver, *Le commerce*, 299. Yver added that Arnoldo was also chamberlain to the king, but the reference cited, "*Registro* #6, folio 49," mentions only that Arnoldo was "his Florentine familiar of his house." A familiar to the Angevin king (*familiaris regis*) is normally defined as "an intimate, a familiar resident or visitor in the household, a member of the *familia*, that wider family that embraces servants, confidents, and close associates." See H. Takayama, "*Familiares Regis* and the Royal Inner Council in Twelfth-Century Sicily," *English Historical Review* 10 (April 1989): 357.

[51] Davidsohn, *Firenze*, Vol. 3, 505–6.

[52] Villani, *Storia*, Book VIII, Chap. 63. In discussing the Anagni expedition that led to the seizure of Pope Boniface VIII in 1304, Villani described the Peruzzi as "merchants of the King of France." The company does not seem to have been important to him, however, as Philip IV avoided excessive dependence on any foreign merchant-banker. The relatively modest position of the Peruzzi in France is argued by J. R. Strayer, "Italian Bankers and Philip the Fair," in *Economy, Society, and Government in Medieval Italy*, ed. D. Herlihy, R. S. Lopez, and V. Slessarev (Kent, OH, 1969), 113–21.

James II of Aragon granted Filippo the right to live and practice commerce in his territories.[53] It was acquiring substance and reputation in Florence, attracting nonfamily partners as early as 1292.

One bizarre explanation of the Peruzzi's rapid accumulation of wealth around this time deserves comment. This is Robert Davidsohn's suggestion that they enjoyed a sudden windfall when holders of large deposits perished along with their documents during the destruction of Acre by the Muslims in 1291.[54] Although Davidsohn pointed out that there was only one source for this story, he supported it by alleging a close relationship between the Peruzzi and the Templar Order, principal defenders of Acre.[55] But the case for the claim is weak on two counts. First, the Peruzzi was only one company, a minor one at that, among many from Florence and other Italian cities engaged in commerce at Acre.[56] Why should the Peruzzi, and not others, be singled out for a huge windfall? Second, the deposits had to have been held outside of Acre to be of use to the Peruzzi, in which case they would also have been available to heirs of the depositors. It is very difficult to believe that such supposedly large deposits would have escaped the notice of potential claimants.

During Filippo's dominance in the 1290s, the sons of Arnoldo, except for Pacino, were relatively inactive in the company and may not even have been shareholders. They did, however, along with Filippo, participate energetically in guild and communal politics. Pacino di Arnoldo was especially active. He had already been elected prior twice during the 1280s (1286 and 1288), was chamberlain of the commune in 1290, became consul of the powerful merchants' guild in 1293, and gonfalonier of justice in 1297. Moreover, he was a conspicuous actor in the constitutional debates of 1293, proposing, along with the notorious butcher Dino Pecora, a radical guild-based electoral system.[57] His brother Giotto was prior in 1293 and consul of

---

[53] R. Davidsohn, *Firenze*, Vol. 6, 737, and Vol. 7, 700. Filippo's nephew Giotto, to be discussed in detail later, spent considerable time in Catalonia around 1300. There, he kept a mistress who bore him a son, Donato, who became legitimized and made an active partner.

[54] Davidsohn, *Firenze*, Vol. 3, 505–6, and Vol. 6, 788.

[55] Ibid., 506 n 1. The source cited is the chronicle formerly attributed to Brunetto Latini, 232.

[56] See Abulafia, "Crocuses and Crusaders," in *Outremer* (Jerusalem, 1982), 239.

[57] John Najemy, *Corporatism and Consensus in Florentine Electoral Politics, 1280–1340* (Chapel Hill, NC, 1982), 53–7. Pacino became less radical later and by 1295 had fallen out with Pecora. The latter was sharply rebuked by the chronicler Dino Compagni for slandering Pacino, "a man of good repute." Dino Compagni, *Chronicle of Florence*, trans. D. E. Berstein (Philadelphia, 1986), Book I, Chap. 18.

the bankers' guild in 1297, while another brother, Tommaso, was prior in 1299. Filippo himself held the prestigious post of captain of Orsanmichele in 1294, followed by Giotto in 1297.[58] At the same time, the solidarity of the family was affirmed at Arnoldo's death in 1292, when the two branches established two common funds, one for good works and the other for expenses "in honor" of the group.[59] The latter included contributions toward the costs of the elaborate knighthood consecration ceremonies already discussed, and the settlement of feuds with the Caviciuli and Passerini families, among other things.[60]

Filippo's most remarkable feat was his success in steering the family and company from 1292 till his death in 1303, an extremely violent and dangerous period in Florence's much-troubled history. During that time, the Peruzzi managed to acquire influence as well as increased wealth without exciting the enmity of other families. They were not damaged by the constitutional crisis of 1292 and the consequent Ordinances of Justice, which placed severe restrictions upon some 150 families designated *magnati*. By escaping this designation they almost certainly benefited, because the Ordinances rendered ineligible for important public office a large number of competing candidates. Many of the *magnati* families affected took part in an uprising in 1295 and succeeded in coercing the priors to make changes in the Ordinances in their favor. According to Villani, the *popolo* class was so angered by the action of the Priorate that there

---

[58] Orsanmichele was one of the largest religious confraternities in Florence, charged with the responsibility of distributing alms to the severely poverty-stricken of the city. The Bardi Company distributed some of its charitable donations through this organization, as described by A. Sapori in *Storia economica*, Vol. 2, 854–7. Intriguingly, the square in front of the confraternity hall was the site of the city's main grain market, also called Orsanmichele, since the second half of the thirteenth century. Here a miracle was recorded in 1291, which promptly gave rise to this popular and prestigious confraternity managed by eight, and later six, *capitani*. It is tempting to seek a connection between the Orsanmichele captaincy and the Peruzzi dealings in the grain market, but there is no suggestion of such in any of the literature. Nevertheless, to be a captain was a signal honor, and irrespective of any grain-market association, the post had important commercial and political as well as religious significance. See Luigi Passerini, *Storia degli stabilimente de beneficenza e d'istruzione elementare gratuita della città di Firenze* (Florence, 1853), 404–39, and J. Henderson, "Piety and Charity in Late Medieval Florence: Religious Confraternities from the Middle of the Thirteenth Century to the Late Fifteenth Century" (Ph.D. diss., microfiche, University of London, 1983), Chap. 5.

[59] Sapori, *Storia economica*, Vol. 2, 657.

[60] *I libri*, 497–9, memoranda in Giotto's Secret Book.

was a fresh ordering of the leadership of the *popolo* in Florence. Included among the names of the new leading families was that of the Peruzzi.[61]

Despite their new prominence in Florentine politics, the Peruzzi managed somehow to avoid direct involvement in the Black–White crisis that split the Guelf party into two warring factions. No Peruzzi name can be found among any of the long lists of combatants compiled by Villani or Compagni in their descriptions of the controversy.[62] Logically, the Peruzzi should have been sympathetic to the Whites led by Vieri Cerchi, who, although one of the *magnati*, was a rich, talented merchant-banker, was prepared to live with the Ordinances, and had many friends among the *popolo*. The leader of the Blacks was Corso Donati, the somewhat impoverished head of an ancient noble family who despised guildsmen and was utterly unreconciled to the Ordinances. The Blacks, however, secured the support of Pope Boniface VÌII. The pope, after unsuccessfully demanding that the Cerchi share offices and honors with the Donati faction, sent Charles of Valois, brother of Philip IV of France, to Florence in 1301 with a force of men-at-arms to "restore order." After the dust from this extremely complicated struggle had settled in 1302, the Black party was in full control of the government of Florence, and the Peruzzi were among the leading families supporting that faction.[63] There is no record of the behavior of the Peruzzi during the crisis, or the motivations that drove them to side with the Blacks, but, as Dino Compagni makes clear, the Peruzzi, like all Florentines, would have belonged to a set of social associations and could hardly avoid committing themselves one way or another.[64] Almost certainly their decision was influenced by Filippo's sober assessment of practical business needs, and the current imperative was to cooperate with the papacy and the French. But loyalties tended to fall victim to the pressure of changed priorities, and just one year later Filippo appears to have turned on the pope. If Villani can be believed, the Peruzzi were alleged to have provided drafts "for as much money as may be needed" to help finance Philip IV's expedition in 1303 to kidnap Boniface VIII at Anagni.[65]

[61] Villani, *Storia*, Book VIII, Chap. 12.

[62] Ibid., Chaps. 39–42; Compagni, *Chronicle*, Book II.

[63] Compagni, *Chronicle*, Book II, Chap. 26.

[64] Ibid., Chap. 22.

[65] Villani, *Storia*, Book VIII, Chaps. 63 and 64. There is no corroborating support for Villani's statement, nor any indication of the value, if any, of the drafts cashed by the French. Scholars have accordingly given the comment little attention, and even Davidsohn has little to say (*Firenze*, Vol. 4, 349). This alleged action contrasts with the strong financial support the Peruzzi and other Florentines gave the same pope in helping him defeat the Colonna uprising five years earlier. In Villani's favor, however, is the fact that he was a shareholder of the Peruzzi Company at the time and in a position to have inside information.

During this same period of 1292 to 1303, the Peruzzi Company metamorphosed from an essentially family concern into a multi-shareholder firm with substantial non-Peruzzi representation, but with control retained firmly in the hands of the leading members of the Peruzzi clan. Already in 1292 Filippo brought in three partners from the business community – Banco Raugi, Gianni Ponci, and Bandino Spiglati. In 1300, in recognition of its growth and potential, the company was reorganized along the lines it was to maintain until its collapse forty-three years later. Its capital was set at an impressive li.124,000, equivalent to over 85,000 gold florins, of which just under 60 percent was contributed by the Peruzzi family, split roughly 60/40 between descendants of Arnoldo, and Filippo and his heirs. The remaining 40 percent was held in varying amounts by outsiders representing several families – the Baroncelli, Raugi, Infanghati, Ponci, Folchi, Bentacorde, Silimani, and Villani, an interesting mix of Florentine society of the period. Infanghati was one of the *magnati*; Ponci was the brother of a minor guildsman who was politically influential; Baroncelli and Bentacorde were from powerful *popolani* families; Raugi, Silimani, and Folchi were wealthy investors; and Villani was an ambitious young businessman. And most were prepared to contribute effort and talent as well as capital.

Filippo's leadership during his final years reflects extraordinary political dexterity along with outstanding business vision. He established the Peruzzi family as an important force in Florentine politics while avoiding identification with any of the extreme factions. He structured a family company capable of operating successfully on a vast international scale without tying up an excessive amount of the family's resources. And it has to be noted that despite the significant outside shareholdings, the company capo was always a Peruzzi of unquestioned authority who was usually also head of the Peruzzi family.[66] Credit, however, also belongs to the family as a whole. It seems to have prospered steadily over a century in a violent, arrogant, and unstable society without provoking the serious hostility of other families. To be sure, it had its feuds, most notably with the Adimari, but the family had the good sense to effect a settlement before the situation got out of hand.[67] Overall, the family seems to have acquired a certain *souplesse* in its business, political, and social behavior. There

---

[66] See Raymond de Roover, *The Rise and Decline of the Medici Bank, 1397–1494* (New York, 1966), 78, for an insight on the dominating role played by the "head of the company."

[67] See later in this chapter for a fuller discussion.

is only one recorded instance in which a member of the family was fined for an act of violence.[68]

Both Filippo and Arnoldo produced a substantial number of offspring. As the charts in Appendix I show, many of them survived to engender large families of their own, so that as the fourteenth century progressed, the Peruzzi family was becoming a sizable lineage. In so large a group, it is not surprising that the individuals would engage in a variety of pursuits. Many of the Peruzzi served the company in one capacity or another, but the majority found careers in the church, army, and public service. Of the churchmen, the most notable were Chiaro di Filippo, who received the benefice of Montefoltro directly from the pope, and Zanobi di Giotto, who was dispatched to Avignon to appeal for special prayers for his father on the latter's death in 1336.[69] Three of Filippo's sons – Amideo, Guido, and Biero (also known as Lepre) – served as soldiers at one time or another, and the latter two were killed in Florence's disastrous defeat by Lucca under Castruccio Castracani at the Battle of Altopascio in 1325. Two other Peruzzi, Simone di Chiaro and Pacino di Guido, were captured in that battle and ransomed for 1,225 florins each. In addition, the battle cost the family li.261 s10 for losses of horses, harnesses and traces.[70] However, the Peruzzi clan does not seem to have been very militaristic overall. Aside from Altopascio, the Peruzzi representation in the various campaigns between 1300 and 1340 was very small in relation to the size of the family. To be sure, there are examples of Peruzzi involvement in these conflicts. Arnoldo di Arnoldo was mortally wounded in the campaign of 1312 against Emperor Henry VII.[71] Biero fought in the Battle of Montecatini in 1315 against the dictator of Pisa, Uguccione della Faggiuola.[72] But these are isolated cases, and after Altopascio, the Peruzzi, in common with most other affluent Florentine families, eschewed direct

[68] *I libri*, 15–16. Ottaviano di m. Amideo was fined the very substantial sum of li.546, which the company originally paid in the early 1330s and later recovered, with interest, from Simone, Pacino, Guido, and others.

[69] For Chiaro, see Passerini, "Genealogica"; for Zanobi, see *I libri*, 255–6.

[70] Peruzzi, *Storia commercio*, 402.

[71] Ibid.

[72] *Archivio di Stato di Firenze, Bardi, serie 111 e 88*. Biero's name is included in a long list. This source also indicates that Amideo was among three men nominated as captain in 1309. Peruzzi has reported in *Storia commercio*, 402, an expense of li.237 s7 for fifty foot soldiers who accompanied Giovanni di Giotto Peruzzi in the Battle of Montecatini, but he offers no source and dates the event twenty years later, suggesting that the item may refer to another conflict.

participation in military activity.[73] Most, however, were extensively involved in community or diplomatic endeavors even if very few chose public service as a full-time occupation.

Of the many capable Peruzzi individuals who lived during the first half of the fourteenth century, there were three who so distinguished themselves that they deserve special attention. The careers of these men also serve to illustrate the subtle, symbiotic interconnection among family, company and community. Simone, a grandson of Filippo, had no direct ownership or management role in the company but effectively served it well through his community service and foreign diplomacy. Tommaso, son of Arnoldo, devoted most of his energies to the company, leading it for twenty-eight consecutive years, but he also involved himself to a significant extent in community affairs. Giotto, also a son of Arnoldo, was simultaneously engaged in company and community activities, occupying a series of important political posts while acting as shareholder and officer of the company. And all, in their turn, became family patriarchs.

Simone was the son of Chiaro di Filippo who had entered the church and had little or nothing to do with the business. Simone's career also had no direct connection with the business, but his efforts in diplomacy likely often worked to the company's interests. He was an independently wealthy property owner. He was not a shareholder in the company, but was a substantial investor, having an interest-bearing deposit of approximately li.7,900 with the company and a further li.5,000 jointly with his nephews at the opening of the last company on July 1, 1335.[74] As noted in the following chapter, he owned part of the company's warehouse in Florence, which he rented on a long-term lease.[75] Although he was much more a cavalier than a merchant, he did not entirely lack commercial instinct.

According to Passerini, Simone had already been knighted in 1323 when ordered to Naples to notify Beltrano dal Balzo, brother-in-law of King Robert, that Florence had elected him captain-general of its army. After serving as podesta of San Gimignano and Prato, he fought in the war against Castruccio, and, as noted, was

---

[73] See C. C. Bayley, *War and Society in Renaissance Florence* (Toronto 1961), 3–17, for a useful description of the transition of Florentine forces from mainly local militia to mainly mercenaries between 1260 and 1342. For a more detailed review, see David Waley, "The Army of the Florentine Republic," in *Florentine Studies*, ed. Nicolai Rubenstein (London, 1968), 70–108.

[74] *I libri*, 1.

[75] Ibid., 180.

captured at the defeat of Altopascio in 1325 and later ransomed. Between 1326 and 1333, he was sent several times as ambassador to Siena, once to Avignon to beg John XXII for aid, and finally to the court of Naples to represent Florence at the wedding of Johanna, the daughter of King Robert, to the son of the king of Hungary. In 1335, he headed the delegation to Mastino della Scala, dictator of Verona, to negotiate the purchase of Lucca, and following collapse of the talks he was nominated as military magistrate, responsible for finding money for the *signoria* with which to seek aid from other towns.[76] He then held various offices in Pistoia and San Gimignano until recalled to Florence to serve as prior in 1341. He was deeply involved in the rise and fall of Walter de Brienne as dictator of Florence in 1342-3, and was ambassador to various Tuscan cities. In 1344, he was again elected prior.[77] His last official mission was as part of the embassy to the king of Hungary in 1347, the year before his death from the Plague.

Simone's repeated diplomatic appointments suggest that he was recognized as a man of considerable intelligence, grace, and wit. These attributes and his familiarity with decision-makers throughout Italy clearly did much to enhance the Peruzzi name and to make doing business with the company more respectable for aristocrats. What is most instructive is that he seems not to have been affected by the later misfortunes of the company. Being made prior in the reform regime shortly after the firm's collapse in 1343 suggests either that he enjoyed a personal "Teflon coating" or that the family had somehow managed to distance itself from the ruin of the company. The fact that many members of the family, as we shall see, retained wealth, office, and status after the crash would indicate the latter.

Tommaso served three times as a prior between 1299 and 1321, was consul of the merchants' guild in 1303, and was an official of the mint in 1311. He was also invited in 1312 to be ambassador to Lucca and to seek allies in Lombardy against Emperor Henry VII. Despite these and other public activities, Tommaso devoted most of his energies to the company. He became "chairman of the board" in 1303 on the death of his Uncle Filippo and directed the company with diligence for twenty-eight years until his own

[76] The *signoria* was the collective name given to the top officials of the commune.
[77] The official announcement of the election makes it clear that Simone was a knight at this point (Salvemini, *La dignità*, 175).

death in 1331. Outside the company, he owned large possessions in San Gimignano, where he died and was buried.[78]

Family genealogists and biographers tend to underestimate the skill, discipline, and sheer talent required to manage an organization as large, diverse, and geographically dispersed as the Peruzzi Company in an environment of dreadful communications and virtually no international law. Tommaso may or may not have helped design the sophisticated control system that will be discussed in detail in Chapter 3. There is no question, however, that he made the system work for an extended period of time. It must be remembered that his public service, although essential to the business, was much more than a mere distraction; when he was prior, he would have had to absent himself completely from the business for each two-month term of office.[79] He successfully guided an enterprise that comprised commodity trading in grain and wool; manufacturing and finishing of textiles, fur and leather; general merchanting; and banking, money changing, and transferring funds – all on a grand scale across Europe and the Mediterranean. That success required not only business acumen but the maintenance of satisfactory relations with a number of temperamental rulers, whose favor was essential and who were often at odds with one another. Despite the discretion that had to be allowed to branch managers, given the very slow communications, a modicum of central control had to be established to ensure that the company's overall interests were best served. Tommaso achieved the necessary balance profitably, a feat that proved too demanding for his successors.

Tommaso's brother, Giotto, may have been the most brilliant of the Peruzzi of this era. He was certainly the most colorful, while combining the attributes of both Tommaso and Simone. As a substantial shareholder and treasurer, he was closely involved in the company's affairs. At the same time, he was extremely active in politics, domestic and foreign. He was a prior no fewer than eight times

[78] San Gimignano was a medium-sized town in southern Tuscany most noted for its cultivation of top-quality saffron. This was an important item of medieval trade, valued as a medicine, dye, and condiment, and was exported throughout Italy, France, and especially the Levant, where it was highly prized (see Abulafia, "Crocuses and Crusaders," 227–33). The Peruzzi of Florence (not to be confused with a San Gimignano family of the same name) did not acquire these holdings of lands, houses and towers until 1329, shortly before Tommaso's death. (See Enrico Fiume, *Storia economica e sociale di San Gimignano* [Florence, 1961], 33–40, 214–17).

[79] Ferdinand Schevill, *History of Florence* (New York, 1976), 210. Priors were prohibited from leaving the Palazzo dei Signiori to conduct private business.

between 1293 and 1335. He participated in the reform of the Florentine representative government with the institution of the office of
gonfalonier of justice and other provisions to restrain the magnates.[80]
In addition to his service as captain of Orsanmichele and consul of
the bankers' guild mentioned earlier, he was three times consul of
the merchants' guild. As governor of the mint in 1326, he put the
coinage in order; in 1328 he helped compile the ordinances which
established the commissions of scrutators responsible for determining the eligibility of guildsmen nominated for office.[81] By then, in
partnership with Donato Acciaiuoli and Taldo Valori of the Bardi
Company, he was a formidable power in the city administration.

Giotto was an extremely wealthy man, although, as will be discussed
later, his secret books reveal that he was often short of cash. Most of
the entries in these books deal with acquisitions and disposals of property, many involving large sums.[82] In his palace, reputed to have been
one of the grandest in the city, he was host to King Robert of Naples
in 1310 shortly after the latter's coronation at Avignon.[83] Giotto married twice, both times into prestigious families, the Cavalcanti and
the Donati. With these ladies and the mistress of his Catalonian in-
terlude, he sired a total of twelve children. The family status was now
such that it became involved in a blood feud with the Adimari, an
ancient, powerful, and fractious lineage, which was considered so
serious that the *signoria* felt compelled to intervene.[84] The dispute
was finally settled by Giotto in May 1313, when he gave his daughter

[80] Passerini, "Genealogica," and Peruzzi, *Storia commercio*, 258.
[81] See Najemy, *Corporations*, Chap. 4, for a cogent discussion of the complex electoral reform of 1328. The new system, designed to reduce factional conflict,
provided for the selection of groups of scrutators whose job was to present for
approval lists of potential candidates for high office. The names of the successful candidates were placed in sealed bags for drawing at each bimonthly election.
[82] *I libri*, 419–512.
[83] Villani, *Storia*, Book IX, Chap. 8. See also Davidsohn, *Firenze*, Vol. 6, 534, and *I
libri*, 476–7. In the latter, Giotto's Secret Book details the extension and repair
of the roof and the construction of a special kitchen in preparation for the
visit.
[84] Passerini, "Genealogica." Unfortunately, we do not know the reason for the
feud, but the reason for the intervention of the *signoria* is likely to have been
the need for concord among the city's leading Guelf families in the face of the
invasion of Henry VII. See also Carol Lansing, "Nobility in a Medieval Commune: The Florentine Magnates, 1260–1300," (Ph.D. diss., University of Michigan, 1984), 304–5, for a useful sketch of the Adimari lineage. Described as an
urban–rural hybrid, it became a leading Guelf lineage noted for its propensity
to enter into disputes. Most of the line joined the White faction, but one branch
was Black.

Filippa in marriage to Carlo, the son of Guerra di Adimari with an impressive dowry of 1,800 gold florins.[85] Giotto did not pay the entire dowry, however, as it was regarded as an expense "per onore di loro e de la casa" (for their honor and that of the house) to be borne by the whole family, distributed 60 percent among the heirs of Arnoldo and 40 percent among those of Filippo.[86] Their contributions were actually made to the company, which used the proceeds to buy property and gifts for the happy couple. Interestingly, the main element of the dowry, a property valued at 1,000 florins, was sold for them by the Peruzzi at their request in 1335. The sale price was also 1,000 florins.[87]

In addition to his many other activities, Giotto took over the company chairmanship after the death of Tommaso in 1331. Judging by the increasing disarray in the company's affairs and decline in its fortunes, Giotto was unable or unprepared to devote the attention that Tommaso had given to the business. As will be shown later, the books were not even properly closed at the end of the 1331–5 partnership, and when the results of the period were finally known, they proved to be a substantial loss. Toward the end of his life, he appeared most interested in the prestige of the family and the salvation of his soul, as evidenced by the vast donations to churches that Passerini describes in great detail.[88] His death in August 1336 was marked by lavish ceremony. The expense for appropriate robes, prayers, vigils, and for bringing high-ranking churchmen from Avignon to Florence in connection with his funeral reached the astonishing sum of li.1,465.[89]

The most famous monument to the family's prestige is the artist Giotto's frescoes in the Peruzzi Chapel in the church of Santa Croce. The dating of the execution of the murals, ranging between 1317 and 1335, is the subject of much debate, with the most probable timing being between 1325 and 1328.[90] Interestingly, the initiation of

---

[85] For perspective, Brucker, *Renaissance Florence*, 92, cites 1,000 florins as a typical figure for a dowry among patrician families in 1400. Davidsohn, *Firenze*, Vol. 7, 683–4, describes it as "very high" compared with most dowries at the time.

[86] *I libri*, 426.

[87] Ibid., 348 , 510.

[88] Passerini, "Genealogica," mentions religious institutions in and around Florence, including Santa Croce, where the family had its famous chapel decorated by the artist Giotto (see next paragraph).

[89] *I libri*, 255–6. For perspective, this sum is equal to the combined annual salaries of the six highest-paid employees of the company.

[90] J. F. Codell, "Giotto's Peruzzi Chapel Frescoes: Wealth, Patronage and the Earthly City," *Renaissance Quarterly* 41 (Winter 1988): 585–6. Codell summarizes the views of other scholars, but offers no estimate of her own.

this masterpiece seems to owe little to Giotto d'Arnoldo, although he was undoubtedly consulted on it. The original funding for the chapel itself came from the will of Donato d'Arnoldo written in 1292, which set aside li.200 for its construction in the proposed church of Santa Croce within ten years of his death.[91] The murals for the chapel were commissioned by Giovanni di Rinieri di Pacino, probably in 1325 before the Battle of Altopascio, in which he was captured and held for ransom.[92]

The only reference in the company's extant books is a modest expense of li.27 s10 in fiscal year 1335-6, implying a minor repair or maintenance cost relating to an existing structure.[93] It is very likely that the company would have been involved in financing the original construction, because several entries show that the company had advanced a total of li.807 plus interest to Tano and Gherardo Baroncelli, two of the company's largest outside shareholders, for one of the three chapels that they built at Santa Croce.[94] This work, begun Christmas eve, 1332, and completed in 1338, has been frequently attributed to the surviving chapel painted by Taddeo Ghaddi, one of the artist Giotto's followers. However, Andrew Ladis offers convincing evidence that the chapel referred to in the Peruzzi books did not survive and that the chapel we see today was painted between 1328 and 1330.[95] Given the further evidence that Taddeo's work was strongly influenced by Giotto's Peruzzi chapel, the latter must have been at least partially completed by 1328.[96]

The narrative to this point may suggest a preoccupation with prestige and pride on the part of Peruzzi family members. In the highly competitive social and political atmosphere in Florence at the time,

[91] L. Tintori and Eve Borsook, *Giotto and the Peruzzi Chapel* (New York, 1965), 95, App. A–1.

[92] Ibid., 10, 42 n 39. Borsook suggests that the work may have begun in 1325 and that at least the Baptist cycle was finished before Giotto's departure for Naples in 1328.

[93] *I libri*, 36.

[94] Ibid., 13, 14, 47. There were actually two chapels being completely funded by the company for the Baroncelli brothers at that time, the second being at the church of Sanpiero Scheraggio. The total amount charged to their account for the two projects was li.1,726 plus li.450 accrued interest. Ironically, both brothers died at around the time of the chapels' completion.

[95] Andrew Ladis, *Taddeo Gaddi, Critical Reappraisal and Catalogue Raisonné* (Columbia, 1982), 22. Ladis asserts that the 1332–8 chapel was erected in honor of St. Martin on the now-destroyed *tramezzo* or rood screen. The surviving chapel to the Annunciate Virgin was "built and begun" in February 1328, according to the dedication inscription. See also 89–90.

[96] Ibid., 24–8.

such an attitude among the leading lineages is to be expected. There is, however, a piece of evidence in the Peruzzi chapel which possibly indicates a tendency to understatement lacking in some of the other great families. Borsook refers to "six little heads which gaze toward the altar from the ornamental border," which she believes represent Peruzzi family members. She adds, "Compared to some other Florentines at the time, such as the Strozzi at Santa Maria Novella, who had themselves painted almost life-size being welcomed into Paradise, the Peruzzi were both circumspect and modest by relegating their portraits to the frame."[97]

During the long tenure of Tommaso and Giotto, the political importance of the family continued to grow, as the *popolo grasso* exerted increasing control over the electoral process of the commune. Between 1310 and the reform of 1328, Peruzzi family members were elected as priors nine times, and between 1328 and 1342, the family was represented a further seven times.[98] But this showing, however impressive, needs to be put into perspective. Many other families of the *popolo grasso* equalled or exceeded the Peruzzi representation, and some, such as the Strozzi, Acciaiuoli, Alberti, and Baroncelli-Bandini, did so by a considerable number.[99] The Peruzzi family was undoubtedly an important actor in the political scene in Florence, but only as one member of the business-oriented oligarchy that ruled the city during those years.

A mere count of the number of family members serving in the *signoria*, however, understates the influence of the Peruzzi in the commune, because it ignores the considerable power wielded directly by the company itself. As will be seen in later chapters, the commune's ambitious foreign policy depended heavily on the largest companies for their international connections and their unmatched capability to mobilize cash. As the largest by far of all Florentine companies, the Bardi was enormously influential in city politics, but the Bardi family, having been designated *magnati*, did not have a single representative in the *signoria* from 1293 onward. The largest companies must therefore be understood as political forces in the commune in their own right.

Returning to the business, a new generation took over the leadership of the Peruzzi Company in 1336 and sharply changed its course during its final years.[100] Bonifazio, one of Tommaso's sons, took the

---

[97] Tintori and Borsook, *Peruzzi Chapel*, 23.

[98] Najemy, *Corporatism*, 87, 116–18.

[99] Ibid.

[100] The remainder of this paragraph summarizes briefly what will be discussed in detail in Chapter 7.

helm in that year following Giotto's death. He had been reasonably active in Florentine politics, holding a number of offices,
including that of prior in 1334, and had served the company in
Avignon and for several years in England. The business had been
faltering under Giotto's leadership and was operating at a substantial loss. Bonifazio apparently determined to restore the
company's fortunes by reviving its moribund participation in the
English wool trade. Shortly after taking over, to advance this new
policy, he entered into the ill-fated joint venture with the Bardi
Company to help finance Edward III's war with France. Less than
two years later, probably influenced by his familiarity with the
country, he took the startling step of moving to England to over-
see directly the operations there. Although this attests to the importance that Bonifazio and presumably other shareholders attached to this venture, it was a bizarre decision to leave the center of operations in Florence unattended. This was no short-term
move; company records show that he was in England as early as
March 1338, and remained there until his death in October
1340.[101] In fairness to Bonifazio, it is likely that he appointed his
brother Pacino to take charge in Florence, but a stand-in is never
the same as a leader, so that the business overall continued to
deteriorate.

In any event, Pacino was elected chairman as soon as news of
Bonifazio's death reached Florence (in three weeks, a surprisingly
short time, given the continuing hostilities between England and
France).[102] He had served the company for some years in Bruges
and was familiar with the business, but he was severely distracted
by the demands of the recurring crises in Florentine politics between 1340 and 1343.[103] His main legacy as far as the company is
concerned was his attempt to bring some order into the books.
The surviving Assets Book and Secret Book of the last company
are all in his hand.[104] But he may have one other claim to fame.
The historian S. Peruzzi asserts that annotators of Boccaccio say

[101] *I libri*, 352, records that Bonifazio brought £101 to the English branch on March
1, 1338, although he did not settle there until later in the year. The earliest
English reference is an entry in *Calendar of Patent Rolls,* Edward III (hereafter,
CPR E III), 1338–40, 8, dated June 3, 1338.

[102] *I libri*, 1.

[103] The crises are discussed in detail in Chapter 8.

[104] As discussed in Chapters 4 and 9, much of the writing in the books was probably
not done until after the bankruptcy.

that Pacino is the model for Dioneo, one of the interlocutors in *The Decameron*.[105]

Although the collapse of the company in October 1343 obviously did great economic damage to the Peruzzi lineage, it did not seem to result in social disgrace. To be sure, the family members most closely associated with the company fled the city in November 1343, as will be discussed in Chapter 8. But in addition to the previously noted election of Simone as prior in 1344, no fewer than five family members were appointed as scrutators in that year. This is a remarkable demonstration of the continued political influence enjoyed by at least the Filippo branch of the Peruzzi lineage immediately after the crash, despite the assumption of power by a new popular regime.[106] Nor were the family's economic losses ruinous or lasting. Within five years of the bankruptcy court settlement in 1347, most members of the family appeared to remain affluent. The family shareholders or their descendants "were nearly all in the upper one-fourth bracket of tax assessments in 1352, and some were in the upper one-tenth."[107] Simone di Rinieri, grandson of the brilliant Pacino di Arnoldo, retained some of the Peruzzi business acumen and, as a successful merchant from the 1350s to the 1370s, became one of the wealthiest men in Florence.[108]

The family also escaped relatively lightly from the ravages of the Black Death in 1348. According to Passerini's accounts, seven family members died during that year, one of whom was Simone di Chiaro, possibly a victim of advanced years rather than the pestilence.[109] Given the great size of the lineage at the time, this seems a small number, representing less than 7 percent, much lower than even the most modest estimates of plague losses in that city. Being well nourished and wealthy, the Peruzzi may have had the stamina to survive and the

---

[105] Peruzzi, *Storia commercio*, 259. The annotator is identified as Domenico Manni, an eighteenth-century publisher. Tintori and Borsook in *Peruzzi Chapel*, 41 n18, drawing from this citation, incorrectly identify the Dioneo model as Pacino di Guido instead of Pacino di Tommaso. Another less desirable claim to fame is that Pacino's wife was Alianora di messer Niccolo Gianfigliazzi, of one of the families identified from their coat of arms as usurers by Dante in Canto XVII of *Inferno*. The Gianfigliazzi logo was an azure lion (lines 59–60).

[106] Passerini, "Genealogica." The nominees were Ottaviano di messer Amideo and four sons of messer Guido – Filippo, Giovanni, Alessandro, and Pacino. Two of them, Ottaviano and Pacino, were shareholders.

[107] Gene A. Brucker, *Florentine Politics and Society, 1343–1378* (Princeton, NJ, 1962), 18 n68.

[108] Ibid. Fragments of his Secret Book are published in *I libri*, 515–24.

[109] In Figures A2 and A3, asterisks include the family members who died in 1348.

means to escape to safer areas, but the death rate for the family does seem surprisingly low. Other important families suffered heavy losses, some more than half the male relatives. The Donati, for example, lost nineteen out of thirty-one male members of the family.[110]

Thus, the family continued to prosper but, with the exception of a few like Simone di Rinieri, as landowners and rentiers rather than entrepreneurs. The Peruzzi remained active in politics; several members of the family served in the high offices of gonfalonier of justice and prior into the fifteenth and sixteenth centuries.[111] And although the individual household units of the lineage went their separate ways with regard to their economic status and choice of occupations, they were remarkably cohesive overall. In the fifteenth century they still tended to cluster around the Piazza de' Peruzzi in the San Pier Scheraggio section.[112] And their willingness to accept the imposition of lineage authority is dramatically revealed in a series of documents culminating in a formal self-disciplining agreement drawn up in 1433.[113]

This brief history tells us that the Peruzzi family was wealthy, cohesive, and an important force in Florentine politics during the life of the Peruzzi Company. It also confirms a close and continuing relationship between the company and the family. And it reveals that the chief architects of the company's huge operations were also patriarchs of the family and notables in the community. But there is no evidence that the interests of the company were subordinated to those of the family, despite the fact that the family survived the collapse of the company with so much of its wealth intact. To be sure, the company's resources, as will become obvious in subsequent chapters, were frequently used by family members. But those same resources were also made available to non-Peruzzi shareholders and even to employees. Again, the company often served as a financial intermediary for personal transactions, but the individuals involved, family and outsider alike, were properly assessed for their debts.[114] More-

---

[110] Gene A. Brucker, *Florence: The Golden Age, 1138–1737* (New York, 1984), 43.

[111] Galvani, *Sommario storico*; Passerini, "Genealogica."

[112] D. V. Kent and F. W. Kent, "A Self Disciplining Pact Made by the Peruzzi Family of Florence (June 1433)," *Renaissance Quarterly* 34 (Fall 1981): 347.

[113] Ibid., 337–52, and Thomas Kuehn, *Law, Family, and Women* (Chicago, 1991), Chap. 5, "A Reconsideration of Self-Disciplining Pacts Among the Peruzzi of Florence," 143–56. The pacts were aimed at the containment of a vendetta with a family with which the Peruzzi had political ties.

[114] See, e.g., the dowry for Giotto's daughter, which was arranged by the company and cleared through its books. This expense "for the honor of the house" was eventually prorated among all family members, shareholders and nonshareholders alike. Also, the costs of the Baroncelli chapels, paid by the company, were charged to the Baroncelli brothers.

over, as will be made clear, the company was not the creation of the lineage as a whole. As Lansing has noted, lineage members were normally prepared to act in concert in matters of family prestige and power but were much more pragmatic in commercial undertakings, choosing their partners on the basis of resources and talent rather than kinship.[115] In the case of the Peruzzi, the members of the lineage united to form the property acquistion corporation of 1282 and the charitable foundations of 1292, but company shareholdings were strictly individual and mainly owned by those prepared to work for the company. In short, the company, with its exceptional size and widespread activities, was not a lineage undertaking, but the product of the imagination and effort of a few individuals in the family, especially Filippo and Tommaso, who perceived an opportunity and found the means to act upon it.

Gifted leadership was therefore undeniably a factor in the company's earlier growth and success, but more than raw talent was required to account for the emergence of three Florentine super-companies during the first half of the fourteenth century. A unique convergence of economic forces occurred, creating the conditions that made these improbable companies possible. This study will now turn to an examination of these forces.

[115] Lansing, *Magnates*, 53.

2

The nature of the business

Much of the literature on Florentine economic history of the first half of the fourteenth century has focused on the very large companies, especially those of the Bardi and Peruzzi, perhaps leaving the impression that they were representative of business organizations during this period. Nothing could be further from the truth. The number of companies operating in Florence in the 1330s and 1340s ran to many hundreds.[1] Hundreds more flourished in the numerous commercial centers in Italy and northwestern Europe. But the term "company" encompassed a broad range of enterprises of differing magnitude and complexity, the preponderance of which were small and simple businesses. Some were in manufacturing, others in merchandise trading, others in banking and money changing, and still others in combinations of these activities.

Only a few companies, however, embraced the entire spectrum. Of these, most formed relatively modest-sized organizations, with a small number of partners and limited capital. To be sure, there were many Italian companies of significant size during the late thirteenth and early fourteenth centuries, such as the Ricciardi of Lucca, the Bonsignori of Siena, and the Frescobaldi and Scali of Florence. And of the important non-Italian businesses, William de la Pole's had attained a size that made it a formidable competitor of the Italians in England and northern Europe. But there were a few international companies of such extraordinary dimensions that they deserve to be singled out with the special descriptive term "super-companies."

The medieval super-company is defined here as a private profit-seeking organization operating several lines of business in very large volume in multiple, widespread locations through a network of permanent branches. Super-companies were not distinguishable from

---

[1] As an illustration of the large number of companies in Florence, Brucker cites an incomplete list of 350 companies that failed between 1333 and 1346, presumably only a small part of those extant. See *Florentine Politics*, 16–17.

other important companies merely by their size, which has often been exaggerated to explain the losses allegedly sustained in lending to monarchs, but by what set them apart – a combination of the magnitude, diversity, and geographical reach of their business interests.[2] Above all, it was their high capitalization that enabled them to develop the *volume* of business necessary to support an organization capable of dealing with the complexity of a broad range of enterprise in a widely dispersed branch network. The key to volume was large-scale commodity trading, an activity that required superior resources, sophisticated organization, and political sensitivity and that has been given less attention by historians than the banking, general commercial, and manufacturing aspects of medieval business.[3]

Because statistical evidence is limited and untrustworthy, it is not possible to identify super-companies by means of specific numerical benchmarks. For purposes of this study, therefore, it will be necessary to determine membership in the exclusive super-company club on the basis of certain broad and somewhat arbitrary criteria. These are that the entity must have been, over an extended period of time, a large-scale commodity trader, an international merchant, an important international banker (with the papacy and at least one monarchy as clients), and a manufacturer – all supported by substantial capital and a branch network manned by numerous employees and working partners. As will be shown throughout this study, the Peruzzi Company easily met all of these requirements. Two other companies, the Bardi and the Acciaiuoli, also qualified. Specific data are lacking regarding the number of branches, employees, and the amount of capital subscribed, but from all other measurements, it is probable that the Bardi Company was at least 50 percent larger than the Peruzzi.[4] It was as important as the Peruzzi in the Kingdom of Naples,

[2] See Edwin S. Hunt, "A New Look at the Dealings of the Bardi and Peruzzi with Edward III," *Journal of Economic History* 50 (March 1990): 149–62.

[3] David Abulafia and Georges Yver are notable exceptions. See Abulafia, "Southern Italy and the Florentine Economy, 1265–1370," *Economic History Review* 2, series 33 (1981): 377–88, and Yver, *Le commerce*, Chap. 6, for the importance of the super-companies' involvement in the grain trade. The latter pointedly commented (123) on the part played in this commerce by companies such as the Bardi, Peruzzi, and Acciaiuoli, "que l'on regarde d'ordinaire comme exclusivement vouées aux affaires de banque" (that are normally regarded as exclusively devoted to banking).

[4] For example, the ratio of the companies' share in their English joint venture was 60% for the Bardi and 40% for the Peruzzi. The oft-reported total Bardi assets of li.1,266,775 in 1318 compared with the Peruzzi total of li.742,247 in 1335 (see Table 5) suggests that the size advantage of the Bardi over the Peruzzi was at least 70%. Additional evidence regarding the size and reach of the Bardi will be presented in following chapters.

it enjoyed a greatly superior position in England in wool trading and banking, and it also had a larger general merchandise business in the eastern Mediterranean. France was the only major market in which it trailed the Peruzzi. Although firm information on the Acciaiuoli is scarce, we know that it had major branches in Naples, Sicily, France, Avignon, and England. It was active in most of the same areas as the Peruzzi and was significantly smaller only in England in the late 1330s, when the latter greatly increased its activity there. It had nearly as many factors working abroad as the Peruzzi.[5] It shared the grain monopoly of the Kingdom of Naples and was generally regarded by contemporaries in Florence and Naples as the third member of the "Big Three."[6]

A fourth company, the Buonaccorsi, comes close to super-company status, but falls short because it lacked the capital and personnel to sustain itself at super-company level of activity for more than a brief period of time. Its growth was explosive in the late 1320s and 1330s, but it soon became overextended and collapsed in 1342 for the essentially commercial reasons of too much ambition supported by too little capital and inadequate staff.[7] The earlier great companies, such as the Ricciardi, Frescobaldi, and Scali deserve mention as candidates, but they too are less than super-company rank for different reasons. The Ricciardi and Frescobaldi, as will be discussed later in this chapter, were extremely important in the English banking and wool trade, but were rather narrowly focused, with relatively minor operations in southern Italy and the Mediterranean.[8] The Scali Company was certainly very large and diversified, and its collapse in 1326, with liabilities allegedly in excess of 400,000 florins, sent shock waves throughout the lay and ecclesiastical bureaucracies as well as the commercial world.[9] But there is insuffi-

[5] De Roover, *Medici Bank*, 3. De Roover asserts that the Acciaiuoli had forty-three factors residing outside Florence; the Peruzzi had forty-eight factors abroad (Table 2).

[6] M. Luzzati, *Villani e Buonaccorsi*, 30–3, gives several examples of taxes and contributions as a guide to the size of a company, and the Acciaiuoli was always among the largest companies. See also Yver, *Le commerce*, Chap. 5, and Sapori, *Storia economica*, for various references.

[7] M. Luzzati, *Villani e Buonaccorsi*, 39, estimated the Buonaccorsi capital at only li.15,000 in 1324 and noted that although it grew rapidly thereafter, the firm was relatively undercapitalized (82).

[8] According to Yver, *Le commerce*, 292, the Frescobaldi set up a branch in Naples very early, but nothing seems to have come of it. The Ricciardi are not mentioned at all in Yver's work; neither the Ricciardi nor the Frescobaldi are named in Henri Bresc's massive study of Sicily, *Un monde Méditerranéen; économie et société en Sicile, 1300–1450* (Rome, 1986).

[9] Yver, *Le commerce*, 317. Villani called it "worse than Altopascio," Florence's military disaster of the year before (*Storia*, Book X, Chap. 4).

cient information on the Scali as a going concern to support its candidacy as a super-company. It was not dominant in any line of business or geographical area and did not seem to be in the class of the Big Three for an extended period of time.

It is immediately noticeable that all of the super-companies and even the very large merchant-banker organizations were concentrated in the inland towns of north-central Italy, mostly in Florence. Many reasons have been advanced to explain the preeminence of Italian cities in international trade and finance. The geographical location of Italy between the East and Western Europe has been cited by economic historians such as Renouard and Sapori; and a glance at the map at the beginning of this book is sufficient to confirm the centrality of northern Italy in the medieval commercial world.[10] Other scholars have focused on the genius of the Italian people. Burckhardt stressed their individuality.[11] Peter Burke, in discussing late Renaissance Italy, emphasized its pro-enterprise cultural environment, "where the value-system had been shaped by entrepreneurs."[12] Sapori argued that the supremacy of those entrepreneurs was due to their orderliness, clear thinking, and managerial skill.[13] And in a very recent book, economist Michael Veseth attributed Florence's commercial achievements to a "fifth element" that he called the "creative spark" of the people.[14] But the cultural rationales suffer from their exclusive application to Italians, ignoring the gifted and energetic citizens of Flanders, Catalonia, and Provence, and they do nothing to explain the emergence of super-companies in Florence. Raymond de Roover's "technical" explanation of the Italians' domination of the Commercial Revolution would, if correct, apply even more directly to Venice and Genoa, neither of which produced very large private enterprises, let alone super-companies.[15]

[10] Renouard, *Les relations*, 40; A. Sapori, "The Culture of the Medieval Italian Merchant," in *Enterprise and Secular Change*, ed. F. C. Lane and J. C. Riemersma (Homewood, IL, 1953), 65.

[11] Jakob Burckhardt, *The Civilization of the Renaissance in Italy* (New York, 1954). Burckhardt discusses the individuality phenomenon throughout, but especially in Part II.

[12] Peter Burke, "Republics of Merchants in Early Modern Europe," in *Europe and the Rise of Capitalism*, ed. J. Baechler, J. A. Hall, and M. Mann (London, 1988), 221.

[13] Sapori, "Culture," 65.

[14] Michael Veseth, *Mountains of Debt* (New York, 1990), 19ff.

[15] Raymond de Roover, "The Commercial Revolution of the 13th Century," *Bulletin of the Business Historical Society* 16 (1942): 34–9. In this brief but useful article, de Roover encapsulates many of the views he has expressed in his other works.

The reasons for the emergence of these very large companies must be sought in the effects of the economic expansion in Western Europe during the twelfth and thirteenth centuries and the concomitant development of incipient, but increasingly effective, bureaucratic states. The history of these phenomena is too well known to dwell on in detail here, but a brief review will be useful because the growth of the economy and the emergence of the state bureaucracies during that very busy period have not often been treated together. Both of these developments were important in introducing the circumstances under which the super-companies arose.

The improvement in agricultural productivity across Europe, the attendant surge in population growth, and the exploitation of the Freiberg silver mines led to a concentration of cash among the upper ranks of nobility, lay and ecclesiastical, rural and urban. These developments, in turn, all contributed to the creation of flourishing money economies and greatly increased trade.[16] Mounting demand for fine foods, clothing, and other objects of conspicuous consumption gave rise not only to long-distance trade to the East, but also to substantial indigenous industries – in particular, cloth in Flanders, wool growing in England, and increased viticulture in France and Italy. Commodity markets developed in northern Europe to provide the industries with essential raw materials, such as wool, dyes, and alum, and their urbanized workers with abundant cheap food. In the Mediterranean area, the growing inland towns of north and central Italy began to compete aggressively in these markets as well as in trade in the East, long dominated by Venice and Genoa.

During the twelfth and thirteenth centuries, the trade in important commodities was closely controlled by the rulers of the territories from which the commodities originated. The Venetian state kept a firm grip on its salt trade, the rulers of southern Italy and Sicily on their grains, and late in the period, the kings of England on that country's wool. The growing cash flow from trade in such commodities helped fuel the growth of the rulers' administrative organizations, which, in turn, guided as much as possible of the revenues from these sources into the royal treasuries. In some cases and at some times, the rulers' bureaucracies directly managed the commodity trade; in others, they exercised their monopolies through export controls and customs duties, subcontracting the actual sale of the goods to certain of the private merchants who paid the export duties

---

[16] The early chapters of Peter Spufford's *Money and Its Use in Medieval Europe* (Cambridge, 1988) give an excellent analysis of the interaction of all these dynamics.

and taxes.[17] But such subcontracting rights were granted only to favored merchants in return for services rendered. The service most appreciated was the advance of ready money, of which the rulers became increasingly in need. They required cash for luxury goods and impressive buildings not merely for personal gratification, but also for enhancement of prestige in a court society where ritual was an important indicator of power. Monarchs also needed cash to improve their bureaucratic control over their subjects and, above all, to finance their territorial and dynastic ambitions.

Merchants throughout western Europe prospered in this period of economic growth and bureaucratic order, most finding profitable niches in segments of enterprise – local and regional trade, long-distance trade, or various facets of manufacturing and banking. They formed associations to regulate commerce and to protect their interests and they generally stayed within their own specialty. By the end of the twelfth century, foreign merchants, primarily Italians, found themselves increasingly involved with rulers whose needs, especially for foreign adventures, could no longer be satisfied by native businessmen.[18] Thus, what Sapori calls the "first emigration" of Italian merchants to England occurred after the Third Crusade in which Richard I incurred huge expenses abroad, not the least of which was his ransom.[19] From the middle of the thirteenth century onward, larger merchant companies, especially from the Italian cities, became increasingly involved in financing princely objectives, such as the papal struggle against Emperor Frederick II, Charles of Anjou's campaigns to conquer southern Italy, and the unsuccessful attempt of England's Henry III to install his son Edmond on the throne of Sicily. Businessmen thereby crossed enterprise as well as geographic boundaries, becoming buyers and sellers of wool, lenders to princes, and transfer agents of the papacy, in addition to being general merchants. As will be discussed later in this chapter, firms such as the Bonsignori of Siena and the Ricciardi of Lucca became substantial well-capitalized partnerships, capable of providing finance to rulers on an unprecedented scale.

[17] Venice provides an example of direct management of commodity trade. France and England occasionally exercised direct control but usually used indirect methods. Naples under the Angevins is the best example of a kingdom with the consistent use of indirect controls through merchant monopolies.
[18] Among the foreign merchants were southern French, Catalan, Flemish, and German as well as Italian. And in southern Italy and Sicily, the many Italian merchants from the north were regarded as foreign.
[19] Sapori, *Storia economica*, Vol. 2, 861, n39.

Meanwhile, Florence had begun to emerge as the prime industrial and financial center of Italy, despite its lack of natural advantages. The city was landlocked and located off the main north south routes connecting Rome and Lombardy.[20] As a route from the sea, the Arno River was reliably navigable only partway to Florence, and passage depended on peaceful relations with Pisa and Lucca.[21] And the town was situated in hilly country that was both unsuitable for large-scale grain cultivation and lacking in mineral or timber resources in the immediate area.[22] But it was well suited to the development of the cloth industry. It had abundant, rapidly flowing water nearby for cleansing, fulling, and dyeing wool, and while not on important trade routes, it was easily accessible to them and to large population centers. Until the second half of the thirteenth century, the Florentine cloth industry was a modest local enterprise using inferior local wool, but as population and the market for its products increased, it sought better wools from more distant places and improved the quality of its product. Meanwhile, its merchants were selling increasing quantities of textiles of all kinds and qualities, including top-quality woolens obtained from Flanders and Brabant, and had become expert in finishing imported northern gray goods to suit the preferences of the Mediterranean market. All of these textiles achieved wide distribution in the major markets of Italy, southern France, and the Mediterranean, although woolens manufactured entirely in Florence did not begin to compete with the best of the northern fabrics until the 1330s.[23] This profitable business and the international trading network that accompanied it generated a great

[20] Florence was situated on the Via Cassia, but the main north-south route was the Via Francigena, which crossed the Arno west of the city. Another main route, the Via Flaminia, passed east of Florence on its way to Bologna.

[21] Davidsohn, *Firenze*, Vol. 6, 526, notes that full boatloads of grain and other commodities could get as far as Signa, or even Empoli when the water level was high, but only lighter boats could reach Florence.

[22] Brucker, *The Golden Age*, 67, notes that Tuscany's forests were depleted and its iron deposits were insignificant, so that ore had to be imported from Elba. Sufficient timber for smelting iron occurred only in the higher slopes of the Appenines, the nearest being beyond Pistoia to the northwest. See also Richard A. Goldthwaite, *The Building of Renaissance Florence* (Baltimore, 1980), 280–1.

[23] There is some controversy over Florence's importance as an industrial center. Villani's assertion that more than 30,000 persons obtained their livelihood from working in just the wool industry (*Storia*, Book XI, Chap. 93) would place Florence as a leading industrial city. But Hidetoshi Hoshino, *L'Arte della lana in Firenze nel basso medioevo* (Florence, 1980), 132 and elsewhere, disputes Villani's production estimates and argues that Florence was never an industrial city in the same sense as the great towns of Flanders.

deal of capital, a crucial element in making Florence a center for
international finance. But, as we shall see, cloth manufacturing and
trading could be successfully managed by moderately capitalized
firms; a further ingredient was necessary to create the need for super-companies – large-scale grain trading.

By the end of the thirteenth century, the expansion of agricultural
production and population in Europe had run its course, but the
population of towns continued to grow to meet the needs of industry
and trade. The Italian cities, especially Florence, attracted large numbers of industrial workers with the result that they had greatly out-
run the agricultural resources of the surrounding areas. Already in
1258 the commune of Florence forbade the export of grain from its
contado, and in 1274 it created an office at Orsanmichele to control
and distribute grain in the city.[24] By the early fourteenth century, the
Florentine *contado* could supply food for the city only about five
months of the year, so that Florence had to import food grains on a
massive scale to maintain its industrial and commercial well-being.[25]
Further supplies were obtainable from nearby Romagna or from
Sardinia to the west, but the principal centers of reliable surplus grain
production were Puglia in southern Italy, Sicily, and the Crimea. These
sources of food energy, especially the nearer ones, were to cities like
Florence what the oil-rich countries of the Middle East are to today's
industrial centers of Europe.[26]

Accordingly, the businessmen who dominated Florentine politics
had a strong economic interest in acquiring the ability to influence
the power structure in southern Italy. It was the desire to gain access
to the granaries of Puglia and Sicily, aside from any religious or political convictions, that prompted the Florentine Guelfs to support

[24] Dameron, *Episcopal Power*, 144. Further details will appear later in this chapter.
[25] Domenico Lenzi, *Il libro del Biadaiolo* (hereafter, *Il Biadaiolo*), G. Pinto, ed. (Florence, 1978), 317. Although Lenzi, the chronicler of *Il Biadaiolo*, actually made
the statement in the famine year 1329, he obviously intended it as a generalization. The editor agreed with Davidsohn's contention (*Firenze*, Vol. 5, 238) that
the comment referred to "normal" times. Lenzi also asserted that food prices in
Florence were always higher than anywhere else in Italy, presumably because of
its heavy reliance on imports.
[26] The concern for provisioning medieval cities was not unique to Italy. Flemish
towns faced similar problems in the fourteenth century when the climate in
northern Europe became increasingly inhospitable to grain growing and grain
supplies had to be imported from northern France up the Leie River. Ghent
adapted to this situation by reorienting itself from a predominantly industrial
basis to a mixed economy of grain and trans-shipment, as well as textiles. See
David Nicholas, *The Metamorphosis of a Medieval City* (Lincoln, NE, 1987).

the papacy in its efforts to install Charles of Anjou as king of Naples
and Sicily. After a long and expensive struggle, Charles' project was
crowned with success following the Battle of Tagliacozzo in 1268.
The Florentine businessmen duly followed in his wake, as Charles,
like the Normans before him, welcomed foreign merchants. They
brought wealth and could be controlled or ejected, whereas native
merchants might one day pose a threat to the monarchy.[27] Furthermore, the use of foreign merchants fit comfortably with the Angevin
system of government, which drew its administrators from outside
each region to ensure that officials were beholden to the king and
his regime.[28] Hence, partners and employees of the Florentine merchants also began to occupy important positions in the Neapolitan
bureaucracy.[29] At the same time, the Angevins possessed the military
strength that Florence often needed. The result was a relationship of
mutual advantage.

Initially, the pickings for the Florentines were not very rewarding,
as Charles and his court continued trading with Provence, which had
been under Charles' suzerainty since 1247.[30] More important, the
king maintained tight control over the grain trade, requiring licenses
for export and setting prices or imposing duties that left little room
for profit for the merchants.[31] He managed this feat with the help of
secret agents who kept his government posted on current cereal prices
in the main importing markets.[32] Charles' financial independence,
however, was short-lived, as the Sicilian revolt erupted in 1282, supported by King Peter of Aragon. This reverse denied Charles a rich
source of income and cost him huge sums in fruitless efforts to re-

[27] D. Abulafia, "The Crown and the Economy under Roger II and His Successors,"
   Dumbarton Oaks Papers 37 (Washington, DC, 1983), 1–13. Abulafia concluded
   that the Norman rulers of Sicily saw foreign merchants as "suppliants in search
   of the vital necessities Sicily and Apulia produced." The Angevin successors
   likewise preferred merchants they could control.
[28] Steven Runciman, *The Sicilian Vespers* (Cambridge, 1958), see especially
   Chap. 8.
[29] Yver, *Le commerce*, 325–7.
[30] Ibid., 291–4. Yver suggests here that preference for French fashions was the
   main reason for the continued trade with Provence. But this trade did little to
   enhance the position of the port of Marseilles, also under Charles' sway since
   1252. See J. Pryor, "Foreign Policy and Economic Policy: The Angevins of Sicily
   and the Economic Decline of Southern Italy, 1266–1343," in *Principalities, Powers and Estates* (Adelaide, 1978), 45.
[31] Michel de Boüard, "Problèmes de subsistances dans un état médiéval: Le marché
   et les prix des céréales au royaume angevin de Sicile (1266–1282)," *Annales
   d'Histoire, Économique et Sociale*, 53 (September 1938), 483–501.
[32] Ibid., 491.

cover the island. He died in 1285; his son, who became Charles II, had been captured during an ill-conceived naval expedition in 1284 against the Aragonese–Sicilian fleet and was not ransomed until 1289.[33] By 1293, the Angevin kingdom was desperately fending off invasions of the mainland from Sicily. Charles II's normal source of financing, the papacy, had declared a crusade on his behalf, but typically the income from clerical tenths and other levies flowed in very slowly while the Angevins spent very quickly. The Italian merchants were willing to advance funds to the papacy only to the extent that they could secure their loans with near-term papal revenues.[34] They held back in lending money directly to Charles until he was prepared to share his monopolies and set aside part of his revenues to repay his debts.[35] Despite these precautions, some of the lenders failed, most notably the Bonsignori of Siena after 1298.[36] The stronger and better-managed companies – the Bardi, Peruzzi, and Acciaiuoli – survived to enjoy the fruits of the risks they had taken. The Sicilian war finally ended with the Peace of Caltabellotta in 1302, but the Angevins remained dependent on the merchants, as they embarked on a spending spree, rebuilding Naples and indulging themselves in prestige-enhancing conspicuous consumption. Thus, the lucrative grain trade, delivered to the Florentines through the exigencies of war, became transformed into a long-term quasi-monopoly for them as a result of subsequent Angevin profligacy.[37]

[33] Runciman, *Vespers*, 247.

[34] N. Housley, *The Italian Crusades* (Oxford, 1982), 238–9. The word "Italians" rather than "Florentines" is used here despite the fact that the latter became dominant in southern Italy, because non-Florentine firms were important players there in the thirteenth century. Although Siena was for many years a Ghibelline stronghold, the Bonsignori of that city were key papal bankers, holding the distinction of being the longest serving (twenty-five years) of the companies designated Mercatores Cameres Apostolice by the popes of the latter half of the thirteenth century. During that period, such companies were entrusted with the bulk of the financial operations of the papacy. See Renouard, *Les relations*, 570, and E. D. English, *Enterprise and Liability in Sienese Banking, 1230–1350* (Cambridge, MA, 1988), 23–40.

[35] Charles of Anjou operated all export trade as a state monopoly. Rights to export goods, especially food grains, were granted to merchants sometimes for specific amounts and sometimes for limited periods of time – and always in return for loans. See Abulafia, "Southern Italy."

[36] The failure of the Bonsignori, which was not complete until 1310 in some branches, had multiple, complex causes, but the principal one was inept management in its later years (English, *Sienese Banking*, 55–78).

[37] In fairness to the Angevins, it should be noted that they also invested considerable sums in productive assets such as shipping and port facilities. See Yver, *Le commerce*, 155–70; Pryor, "Foreign Policy," 48–9.

With few exceptions, historians, drawn by Villani's account of the collapse of the super-companies, have tended to see the English wool trade and banking as the vital components of those firms' business, relegating their southern Italy operations to a role of secondary importance.[38] To be sure, English trade and finance played a key part in the spectacular rise and fall of the important earlier companies, such as the Ricciardi and the Frescobaldi, and also loomed large in the considerations of the super-companies, especially in their declining years. But it was the special relationship between Florence and the Kingdom of Naples, especially the two-way trade of grain and cloth, that enabled a select group of Florentine merchant-bankers to evolve into super-companies. It is no coincidence that the Big Three super-companies of the early fourteenth century, the Bardi, Peruzzi, and Acciaiuoli, were all strongly represented in the Angevin kingdom over several decades. The qualitative difference in these companies from other merchant-bankers arose from the challenge of organizing the grain monopoly, which launched them into a quantitative level of operations beyond anything previously experienced by private firms. For example, Florentine exports of Puglian grain in 1311 were recorded at the astonishing total of 45,000 tons, "enough to fill fifty of the largest Genoese ships of the fifteenth century."[39] And between 1327 and 1331 the total annual volume of grain exports controlled by the super-companies averaged a more normal but still very impressive 12,300 metric tons.[40] It is important to recognize that these tonnages were far in excess of Florence's needs, so that the shipments of grain were destined not just to Florence, but to a great number of locations throughout Italy and the Mediterranean, especially Tunis

---

[38] Villani, *Storia*, Book XI, Chap. 88, and Book XII, Chap. 55. The huge English losses reported by Villani (1.5 million florins) dwarf the 200,000 florins allegedly suffered in Naples. As noted earlier, Yver and Abulafia are among those historians who have recognized the importance of southern Italy to the Bardi and Peruzzi.

[39] Abulafia, "Southern Italy," 382.

[40] Abulafia, "Sul commercio del grano Siciliano nel tarda duecento," *La società mediterranea all'epoca del Vespro: XI Congresso della Corona d'Aragona, Palermo–Trapani–Erice, 25–30 aprile 1982*, Vol. 2 (Palermo, 1983), 5. The figure cited was actually 110,000 *salme*, which is converted at about .112 metric ton per *salma*. Unfortunately, these data do not include the destination of the grain exports, so that we do not know how much of the total went to Florence. Villani in his famous panegyric on Florence (*Storia*, Book XI, Chap. 93) gives a rough partial estimate of grain consumption, from which I will attempt to estimate grain imports in Chapter 5.

and other North African ports.[41] And there was much more. The super-companies enjoyed preferential trade in the region's other abundant raw materials, such as edible oil and wine, which were much appreciated in the northern Italian markets. In return, they exploited a virtual monopoly in the Angevin market for the better grades of cloth, as local manufacture was limited to the lower end of the market and the nobility became admirers of the merchandise offered by the Florentines.[42] They increasingly penetrated the economic life of the kingdom, practicing all manner of trades, major and minor, farming the gabelles, and operating the mints. In 1316, the Bardi, Peruzzi, and Acciaiuoli formed a syndicate (enlarged in 1330 to include the Buonaccorsi) that collected taxes, transported cash, paid bureaucrats' salaries and troops' wages, managed military stores and, of course, the grain and wine trade.[43] They dealt with government officials as equals, many of whom, as already indicated, were fellow Florentines, and they did not hesitate to approach the king with complaints whenever they encountered difficulties with them.[44]

The grain markets as they affected the super-companies need to be examined on two distinct levels – international and local. In the international markets, the super-companies operated somewhat like the modern great commodity dealers Cargill and Archer-Daniels-Midland, negotiating with governments for the acquisition of huge quantities of grain while attempting to distribute advantageously these surpluses among clients in need.[45] The companies leased ships from Venice, Genoa, and other maritime cities to transport these bulk cargoes of up to 2,500 *salme* (approximately 280 tons) each to destinations throughout Italy and the entire Mediterranean area.[46] With regard to Florence, some of the grain was shipped from Naples to Pisa, Genoa, or even Talamone, but most of it moved from the Adriatic ports of Manfredonia, or Barletta, where the super-companies formed

[41] David Abulafia, "A Tyrrhenian Triangle: Tuscany, Sicily, Tunis, 1276–1300," in *Studi di storia economica toscana nel Medioevo e nel Rinascimento in memoria di Federigo Melis* (Pisa, 1987). See also M. de Boüard, "Problèmes de subsistances," 491.

[42] Charles I and his successors actively fostered the establishment of a woolen industry, luring Florentine workers to Naples with concessions, but were only modestly successful (see Pryor, "Foreign Policy," 47).

[43] Yver, *Le commerce*, 308.

[44] Ibid., 305.

[45] See the *Economist* (June 1, 1991): 71, for an account of the international commodity operations and government dealings of Archer-Daniels-Midland.

[46] For a comprehensive listing of loading ports, destinations, and sources of ships, see G. Yver, *Le commerce*, 123–5.

an exclusive colony. Northbound ships from Barletta often stopped at Ragusa (now known as Dubrovnik), some to unload cargo, others to transact business en route to their final destinations of Venice, Ancona, or other ports along the Adriatic.[47] The final leg of the journey to Florence from such ports was overland, although from Venice goods could be shipped by river transport at least as far as Bologna via the Po River and a canal.[48]

The super-companies' customers for grain supplies were local grain dealers, local governments, and sometimes their own branches. Some markets, such as Florence, with its constant need for foreign grain, were regular. Others, such as Siena, were sporadic customers, importing only in times of scarcity. But destinations were often ad hoc. Contracts for ship leases from Palermo reflect several alternative destinations with tonnage fees for each, allowing the owner of the grain the option to wait until the last possible moment for intelligence on market conditions.[49] At the other extreme, for grain shipped under export tax exemption from the Angevin kingdom, the destination was predetermined and had to be strictly observed.[50]

The local markets, particularly in the heavily populated towns of north-central Italy, came under increasing regulation from the third quarter of the thirteenth century. The attitude of the local government toward food supplies was pragmatic; it determined to fill the commune's needs at lowest possible cost, because to do otherwise would invite dangerous social upheaval, especially in times of scarcity.[51] In Florence, the control of the distribution of cereal grains was assigned to the "Six of the Biada" from about 1274 onward. The cereals covered included four main types of wheat and several other grains including barley, rye, sorghum, and millet. The officials were

[47] B. Krekic, "Italian Creditors in Dubrovnik (Ragusa) and the Balkan Trade, Thirteenth through Fifteenth Centuries," in *Dawn of Modern Banking* (New Haven, CT, 1979), 246. The Peruzzi were very active in Ragusa, with as many as nine agents there who not only dealt in grains and other merchandise, but also acted as temporary custodians of cash being remitted from southern Italy to Florence via Venice.

[48] Davidsohn, *Firenze*, Vol. 6, 527.

[49] Abulafia, "Commercio del grano," 12–13, cites an example of the Peruzzi in 1299 contracting to ship 2,500 *salme* of wheat to Pisa, Genoa, Tripoli, Tunis, or Gabès, with rates agreed for each option.

[50] Yver, *Le commerce*, 119. Certificates of discharge were required from the consular authorities of the port of debarkation for the exemption to be honored.

[51] William M. Bowsky, *The Finance of the Commune of Siena, 1287–1385* (Oxford, 1970), 37–8, reports that in April 1329, during the great famine, mobs rioted in Siena, killed four officials, and made off with the grain stores.

elected under a complicated system for periods ranging from two to six months and were assisted by notaries, official weighers, messengers, police, and spies.[52] The "Six" oversaw the managers of the only market in which grain could legally be bought and sold, the Orsanmichele, and they regulated the importation of grain. In times of scarcity, they induced the commune or any of the major guilds to import grain, stockpile it, and offer it at fixed prices below cost, assigning the loss to the commune.[53]

How did the super-companies fit into this local regulated scene? Family members would have sold some of the produce from their farms in the *contado*, and the companies would have marketed imported grains directly to millers and other customers in the Orsanmichele. They may also have sold to other grain dealers and certainly to the commune from time to time. They were not in the business of milling grain, although the Peruzzi did own at least three mills that were leased to third parties.[54] Whatever their activity in the grain market, they were clearly affected by its regulations. Profits were frequently constrained in times of plenty by the competition of supplies from nearby sources and in times of dearth by the political necessity to "do the right thing."[55] But the super-companies were in a position in normal times to make reasonable, if not excessive profits. Their Puglian wheat consisted mainly of the hard preferred *grano ciciliano*, which commanded a higher price than the local varieties.[56] There was also opportunity for profit in the wildly fluctuating prices caused by variations in availability.[57] And the companies could turn the regulatory system to their advantage, being closely

---

[52] Davidsohn, *Firenze*, Vol. 5, 240–1. The spies were employed to track down hoarders and rule breakers.

[53] Ibid., 241.

[54] John Muendel, "The 'French' Mill in Medieval Tuscany," *Journal of Medieval History* 10 (December 1984): 245 n15.

[55] In good harvest years, Siena and its *contado* had surplus to sell to Florence. See William M. Bowsky, *A Medieval Italian Commune: Siena Under the Nine, 1287–1355* (Berkeley and Los Angeles, 1981), 201–9. From 1329 (the year of the great famine) onward, the Florence Commune intervened increasingly in the market in poor harvest years, enforcing a "political price" significantly below the free market price. See *Il Biadaiolo*, 62. This governmental intervention will be treated more fully in Chapter 6.

[56] According to *Il Biadaiolo*, wheat in Florence was graded into four main types. The most expensive was *grano calvello*, a very soft grain used in the best bread and cakes; next was *grano ciciliano*, then *grano communale*, and, last, *grano grosso*.

[57] See *Il Biadaiolo*, 63–70, for a useful set of tables summarizing monthly prices of all grains in Florence from 1320 to 1335.

connected to it, occasionally even as poacher turned gamekeeper.[58]

It is not possible to estimate the profitability of the grain business with any degree of accuracy, given the constantly changing variables of market prices in the growing areas, the Angevin export tax, transport costs, and market prices at the destinations. It is, however, possible to obtain a very rough idea of the profit potential of shipments to Florence from the detailed price data that appear in *Il libro del Biadaiolo*. These prices are expressed in *soldi di moneta piccola* per Florentine bushel, and by converting the export tax and transport costs into that measurement, we can judge how much room for maneuver the companies had in selling to the Florentine market. The export tax, as will be shown later, could vary widely, but the typical rate was twelve Neapolitan ounces per 100 *salme*. As shown in Table A7, this converts to a range of 2.5 to 3.4 soldi per bushel. Marine transport costs were of course highly variable, but data on ship leases from Sicily to Pisa suggest a range of s1.5 to s2.2 per bushel.[59] Adding transfer, demurrage, port fees, insurance, and overland cartage, the total transport cost to Florence is unlikely to have been less than s2.5 to s3 per bushel.[60] To break even, therefore, the companies would have had to buy the grain in Puglia at a price at least s5 to s6 per bushel less than the market price in Florence. The Florentine price ranges for *grano ciciliano* are shown in Table 1.

Clearly, during those extensive periods when prices ranged between s8 and s12 per bushel, profit margins on imported Puglian wheat would have been thin to nonexistent. Even in some of the years of higher prices, margins might not have been great if widespread scarcities had also driven up the cost of grain in southern Italy. As a result, the super-companies probably did not consistently earn a very large markup in shipping grain to Florence, although they no doubt did better in other cities where they were able to seek out the best prices. But given the huge volumes involved, the business required

---

[58] Ibid. Taldo Valori and Gherardino Gianni of the Bardi and Guccio Soderini of the Peruzzi were elected to the Six of the Biada in 1328 and 1329 (304n), as was Bonifazio Peruzzi in 1335 (523).

[59] D. Abulafia, "Commercio del grano," 12–13, gives a range of 2.1 to 3 tari per *salma* of eleven bushels from Sicilian ports to Genoa and Pisa.

[60] Per bushel overland transport costs are fiendishly difficult to estimate because of variations in terrain and differing availability of river transport, types of vehicles, and traction animals. For the most recent study of medieval grain transport costs, see James Masschaele, "Transport Costs in Medieval England," *Economic History Review* 2, series 46 (May 1993): 266–79. The author has courageously constructed ton per mile averages from wide variations of data, but it would be risky to apply them to the very different conditions of Tuscany and Romagna.

Table 1. *Price ranges for grano ciciliano in Florence, 1309–35*

Years	Soldi per bu.	Years	Soldi per Bu.
1309–10	10–12	1325–7	11–14
1311–13	13–18	1328	18–20
1315–16	9–12	1329	NMF[a]
1320–1	8–10	1330	20–32
1322	12–18	1331–2	11–18
1323–4	18–23	1333–5	17–22

[a]No meaningful figure; prices were very volatile in this famine year.
Source: Il libro del Biadaiolo, 160–542.

only a small operating margin after direct costs to generate enough income to carry the companies' overheads and leave a generous profit. For example, a margin averaging a mere .25 of a soldo per bushel on the Peruzzi's share of the Angevin grain monopoly (30,000–40,000 *salme* or 330,000–440,000 bushels) would yield around 80,000–100,000 soldi or 13,000–17,000 florins per year. This, in turn, converts to li.20,000–25,000 per year, which would have covered the Peruzzi's annual salary bill of approximately li.9,000 and made a major contribution to the profits reported in Table A3.

Overall, therefore, the international grain trade – vast, fluctuating, subject to risks of tempest, piracy, war, and arbitrary government action – was lucrative in the hands of these astute managers. It had to have been very rewarding to justify these risks and the enormous cash investment needed to participate in this business. For the super-companies' privileged position with its chief supplier, Angevin Italy, did not come cheaply. It had to be sustained by continuous advances of sums, large and small, to meet the king's needs, both public and private. The most regular of the large loans was for the payment of part or all of the substantial annual *cens* to the papacy.[61] Other large advances were for military operations, as in 1310, when the companies contracted to pay 24,000 ounces of silver carlins to pay Robert's troops stationed in Romagna.[62] Still other big loans covered major personal expenses of the king, such as the cost of his visit to Provence

[61] Yver, *Le commerce,* 303. The king of Naples held his kingdom as a vassal of the Holy See, to which he was obligated to pay an annual fee, or *cens,* of 40,000 florins. The Bardi, Peruzzi, and Acciaiuoli advanced part or all of the *cens* to the papacy virtually every year between 1309 and 1330.
[62] In 1310, this sum would have been equivalent to about 110,000 florins. At 60 silver carlins per ounce and an exchange rate of 13 carlins per florin quoted in P. Spufford's *Handbook of Medieval Exchange* (London, 1986), 63, a Neapolitan ounce was valued 4.6 florins.

and Avignon in 1309–10.[63] Most of the smaller advances related to routine royal household expenses, including the liveries and salaries of household servants and men-at-arms and even the king's charitable donations. The mechanism of funding varied according to the amount and purpose of the credit provided. The small routine sums for household expense were disbursed by requisitions issued directly on the companies, an arrangement that may have given rise to the questionable claim that the Peruzzi had opened unlimited credit to the monarch.[64] The large payments by the companies were covered by specific loan agreements for each advance, giving detail as to how, where, and when the money was to be handed over, and the means and timing of reimbursement.[65]

Repayment was achieved mainly by diverting to the lenders certain revenues of the crown designated in the loan contracts, such as general tax receipts from a city, province, or the whole kingdom, or from gabelles or customs.[66] Frequently, repayment was made through the waiver of the export tax on grain. The companies' expectation of profit on the loans came not from charging interest, which was contrary to Angevin, as well as canon law, and there is no evidence that any was paid.[67] Nor were "damages" for late payment seen as a collusive form of disguised interest, because the regime continually put pressure on its officers to pay on time to avoid late-payment penalties.[68] The companies looked to currency exchange and fees for transporting cash for some profit but obtained most of their earnings in the form of "gifts" from the king.[69] These were frequent and significant and were formalized in certain loan contracts. Sometimes the gifts were in cash, but mostly they were in the form of tax exemptions, franchises, and valuable privileges, the most coveted of which was the right to export grain.[70]

By helping to satisfy Florence's need for grain while providing a

---

[63] Yver, *Le commerce*, 369–70. Here, Yver provides a month-by-month schedule of advances made by the Peruzzi during the trip.

[64] Ibid. The "unlimited credit" comment was made by Yver on 297.

[65] Ibid., 371.

[66] Ibid., 380–6.

[67] Ibid., 376.

[68] Ibid., 388. Yver concluded that the pressure for timely payment and the penalties for late payment induced frequent errors by the primitive Angevin bureaucracy, usually in favor of the super-companies.

[69] Fees for currency transport and exchange could be significant in the case of large loans of Florentine florins requiring military escort. Davidsohn refers to charges for *portagium* of as much as 12% and for exchange of 6% or more (see *Firenze*, Vol. 6, 418–22, 792–8).

[70] Ibid., 380.

large secure market for a variety of manufactured goods, the Angevin connection was immensely profitable for the companies that were large enough to take full advantage of it. The relationship conferred the additional benefit of providing a platform for expanded trade throughout the Mediterranean. B. Z. Kedar has suggested that the medieval trading area had an "inner core" comprising Catholic Europe and the lands around the Mediterranean and Black seas. By the late thirteenth/early fourteenth century, this inner core, he argues, had become commercially settled, with intense competition leading to greater efficiency, rational weighing of chances, and focus on long-term operations.[71] This "routinized" business climate was made to order for the large Florentine companies with their quasi-permanent corporate structure and well-trained factors available to act as foreign representatives. With trade in grain and cloth as a base, they established branches in strategically located markets throughout the Mediterranean that in themselves may have been too small to warrant the expense and complexity of permanent organizations for general trading. By setting up their subsidiary structures in such locations, they avoided confronting the great maritime powers of the Mediterranean – Genoa, Venice, and Catalonia. Thus the Peruzzi had branches in Majorca, Sardinia, Tunis, Chiarenza, Rhodes, and Cyprus, but not in the major centers of Constantinople, Alexandria, Ragusa, or Barcelona, where they dealt primarily through agents. Moreover, the companies made themselves useful to Genoa and Venice by directing maritime trade their way and establishing small branches in their cities.

Sicily was a special case where the Florentine companies prospered despite their close association with the detested Angevin regime in Naples and the fierce economic rivalry in that area between Florence and Catalonia.[72] Probably, by the time of the Sicilian rebellion in 1282, the Florentine presence had been too slight and too recent to have generated the hatred of the Sicilians.[73] Moreover, in spite of its close links with Catalonia, the Kingdom of Sicily was independent.[74] In any event, the new government welcomed all foreign merchants

---

[71] B. Z. Kedar, *Merchants in Crisis* (New Haven, CT, 1976).

[72] See Carmello Trasselli, "Nuovi documenti sui Peruzzi, Bardi e Acciaiuoli in Sicilia," *Economia e Storia* 3 (1956): 180. Here, and in his *I privilegi di Messina e Trapani* (Palermo, 1948), Chap. 3, Trasselli argued that the War of the Sicilian Vespers was really an economic struggle between Florence and Catalonia over Sicily's important textile market.

[73] As noted earlier, Charles I had given the Florentines only limited scope between 1266 and 1282. See de Boüard, "Problèmes de subsistances," 482–501.

[74] Trasselli, "Nuovi documenti," 182.

without distinction except those deemed "enemies of the king." As Henri Bresc puts it, the government proclaimed *"liberté, égalité, fiscalité"* to keep the ports open for sale of its wheat on which the kingdom relied for its tax revenues.[75] All three super-companies had important branches in Sicily. The Peruzzi's branch manager in Palermo, Francesco Forzetti, served a remarkable forty-two years from 1299 to 1341 and became a partner in the company from 1331 onward.[76] Here was no monopoly of any sort, and the quantities traded by the super-companies, while substantial by normal standards, paled to insignificance against those in the Angevin kingdom. For example, Bresc reports that the Bardi shipped 7,073 *salme* (about 800 tons) of wheat over the period 1307–9, which was useful business, but not really big.[77] Nevertheless, Sicily was a worthwhile operation with a significant home market. Palermo was a very large city and an important transit port for the western Mediterranean. In addition to wheat, the companies exported wine, cheese, and salted tuna and they imported cloth from Florence and elsewhere, trading not merely between Sicily and Florence, but selling Sicilian products all over the Mediterranean and north-west Europe, transported in ships chartered from Genoese, Catalan, Sicilian, and Tuscan owners.[78]

For Florence, Sicily seems to have been a backup source for wheat in case of severe need, and the normal destination port was Pisa. Villani mentions the importation of Sicilian wheat by the Florence Commune during the famine of 1329, landed in this instance at the small port of Talamone, well south of Pisa. This route then entailed long, expensive cartage overland, illustrating the problem of importing comestibles when the nearest port is hostile.[79] The Tuscan share of Sicilian wheat exports fluctuated greatly, ranging from 71 percent during the period 1300–9 to 6 percent during 1319–29.[80]

A word should be said about cotton. It was cultivated widely in southern Italy and Sicily, as well as other parts of the Mediterranean, and in theory should have been a logical target for large-scale exploitation by the super-companies in both its raw and finished forms.

[75] H. Bresc, *Un monde*, Vol. 1, 371.
[76] Ibid., 382. Forzetti was a rare type of branch manager, neither factor nor partner, but an influential local. Due to gaps in documentation, we cannot be sure that he represented the company continuously for the entire period, but there is no reason to suggest that he did not (see Trasselli, "Nuovi documenti," 186). He first appears on the list of partners in the 1331 company, the one in which "outsiders" theoretically became a majority. See Chapter 6.
[77] Ibid., 549.   [78] Ibid., 433, 285.·
[79] Villani, *Storia*, Vol 10, Chap. 118.   [80] Bresc, *Un monde*, 549.

As Maureen Mazzaoui points out, "cotton manufacture stands out as
the only major export industry geared to the output of low-priced
goods for popular consumption with profits heavily dependent upon
volume of turnover."[81] And certainly, the super-companies dealt in
cotton. Pegolotti's *Pratica* contains numerous references to cotton,
cotton thread, and cotton wool.[82] There is also evidence that
Florentine companies, including the Peruzzi, were active in the cotton trade in Armenia and probably also in Cyprus.[83] But this commodity seems to have been of slight interest to the super-companies,
possibly because its cultivation and manufacture were so widely dif-
fused.[84] There is not a single mention of cotton in the entire Peruzzi
accounts.

Turning to northern Europe, the commodity of greatest interest
to the Italians, as already noted, was wool, and its primary source was
England. Like Apulian grain, English wool was very big business.
During the last half of the thirteenth century and the first half of the
fourteenth, exports of wool ranged between 20,000 and 33,000 sacks
per annum, with two peak years in excess of 40,000.[85] It was wonderfully profitable; merchants are estimated to have earned more than
£2 sterling per sack on an investment ranging between £8 and £10
per sack for wool sold to cloth manufacturers in Flanders.[86] The trade
had been dominated by Flemish merchants until the second half of the
thirteenth century when their influence declined as a result of repeated
embargoes and confiscations by the English government as well as increasing competition from English and especially Italian merchants.[87]
The position of the latter was enhanced by the opening of the Atlantic

[81] Maureen F. Mazzaoui, *The Italian Cotton Industry in the Later Middle Ages, 1100–
1600* (Cambridge, 1981), 60.
[82] Francesco B. Pegolotti, *La pratica della mercatura* (Cambridge, MA, 1936), see
index, 417.
[83] Mazzaoui, *Cotton Industry*, 39.
[84] Ibid., 61–2. In northern Italy, manufacture was confined mainly to the Po Val-
ley.
[85] E. M. Carus-Wilson and Olive Coleman, *England's Export Trade, 1275–1547* (Oxford, 1963), 122. The sacks reported were of standard customs weight of 364
pounds (13).
[86] E. B. Fryde, "The Wool Accounts of William de la Pole," *St. Anthony's Hall Publications* 25 (1964): 14. These are very rough estimates but are based on a reasonably broad array of data during the late 1330s and early 1340s. Depending on
the quality of the wool, Fryde calculated profit at between £1 10s and £3 sterling (equivalent to about li.15 to li.30) per sack after all transport and storage
expenses.
[87] For discussion on the Italian competitors, see later this chapter.

sea routes by Genoese and Catalan shippers in the 1270s.[88] Here it must be noted that the attraction for the Italians was the profit to be made in buying and selling wool, especially of high quality, to Flemish and Brabantine textile manufacturers. As will be discussed more fully in Chapter 5, English wool as a raw material for the Italians' own cloth manufacturing did not begin to flow into Italy in quantity until the early fourteenth century, and then in mostly inferior grades. Top-quality English wool did not become an important ingredient in Florentine cloth until the 1320s and 1330s.[89]

In England the Italians had to deal with a monarchy that was different in many respects from that of the Angevins in Italy. The latter were conquerors determined to exploit their newly acquired possessions; their aristocracy were beholden to the king and the king to the papacy and the Florentine financiers. The king had direct power over the country's resources and was able to put their management in the hands of the select foreign merchants on whom he relied, rather than local merchants whom he considered neither adequate nor trustworthy. By contrast, the English monarchy in the latter half of the thirteenth century was long established, but with a powerful, independent-minded baronage that over time had hedged the king round with restrictions on his ability to raise revenue.[90] The Italian merchants, although active in the wool trade and banking, faced strong competition from well-entrenched local and Flemish merchants. Moreover, they were reluctant to become heavily involved in financing the monarchy, given the fluctuating and uncertain nature of its income.

The advent of Edward I changed the situation dramatically. Like the Angevin kings, he had a penchant for expensive display as well as costly territorial ambitions, and had already become significantly indebted to the Ricciardi Company of Lucca during a leisurely return from his crusade to the Holy Land after Henry III's death in 1272.[91] Looking to the bountiful wool crop for a source of cash that he could claim as his own, he succeeded in establishing in 1275 a

---

[88] Robert S. Lopez, "Majorcans and Genoese on the North Sea Route in the Thirteenth Century," *Revue Belge de Philologie et d'Histoire* 29 (1951): 1163–79, puts the earliest recorded Genoese arrival at an English port at 1277. Lopez' argument that Majorcan ships may have been even earlier is disputed by David Abulafia in "Les Relaciones commercials i polítiques entre el Regne de Mallorca," *XIII Congress of the History of the Crown of Aragon, Palma, 1989–90*, Vol. 4, 69–79.

[89] Hoshino, *L'Arte della lana*, 115–30.

[90] J. R. Lander, *The Limitations of English Monarchy in the Later Middle Ages* (Toronto, 1989).

[91] Richard W. Kaeuper, *Bankers to the Crown* (Princeton, NJ, 1973), 81–2.

customs duty of 6s 8d per sack on virtually all exports of wool.[92] Almost immediately, Edward turned over much of the management of the customs to the Ricciardi Company of Lucca, which was expected to provide him with advances on the security of the anticipated duty revenue. The "Ricciardi system" described by Kaeuper, which was designed to help the monarchy match income and expense flows more closely, involved the king's other revenue sources and included a multitude of services, especially money transfers to and from the continent. The system was sustained by adequate cash flows from collections and profit until 1294, when Edward revoked the Ricciardi's authority to collect customs and imprisoned members of the firm.[93]

The Ricciardi has the appearance of at least an incipient super-company. It had multiple shareholders and was engaged in substantial international financing and commercial enterprise, including an extensive papal deposit and money transfer business, a sizable share of the wool trade, and widespread merchandising activities in England and France.[94] But its business was limited essentially to northern Europe and Italy, it was only a significant rather than a dominating factor in the wool trade, and it had no manufacturing activity. It was really a very large merchant-banking organization, with emphasis on the banking. Moreover, its status as a company is unclear. Richard Goldthwaite notes that only two of the partners can be identified as Ricciardi and suggests that the "company" may well have been a consortium of Lucchese merchants.[95] This view is reinforced by the curious fact that it was the London "branch" that declared bankruptcy in 1301, whereas the Lucca "company" simply faded away several years later without a formal liquidation procedure.[96]

The next big company to become entangled in the web of English wool was the Frescobaldi. This was a substantial organization, with branches in Naples and London dating back to the 1260s and 1270s,

---

[92] Carus-Wilson and Coleman, *Export Trade*, 1. Exceptions to liability for duty on wool and cloth were "insignificant" (2).

[93] Kaeuper discusses the Ricciardi system in detail in *Bankers*; see especially Chap. 3, "The Control of the Customs, 1275–1294."

[94] Ibid. This book is the source of most of the information in this paragraph.

[95] Richard A. Goldthwaite, "Italian Bankers in Medieval England," *Journal of European Economic History* 2 (Winter 1973): 765–6. Here a consortium would have been a group of independent companies conducting the specific English and papal businesses, much like the English joint venture of the Bardi and Peruzzi of the late 1330s.

[96] Kaeuper, *Bankers*, 244ff.

respectively.[97] It was also one of the papacy's official bankers from 1291 to 1293.[98] By the beginning of the fourteenth century, it had lost ground to the Big Three in Naples as it concentrated its efforts in England. In 1299, it became a leading banker to Edward I and by 1302 was appointed the king's principal banker, with control of customs to ensure repayment of its advances.[99] In short, the Frescobaldi occupied roughly the same position as the Ricciardi before it. Unfortunately for the Frescobaldi Company, its reign was brief. Edward I's heavy reliance on Italian bankers was one of the major grievances of the English aristocracy, and when weak-willed Edward II continued the system after his succession in 1307, he quickly enraged his barons. The resultant "Ordainers' Revolt" of 1310 included the Frescobaldi among its victims, causing the main partners and employees to flee the country.

Not much is known about the size of the Frescobaldi business except that on its own it was probably not very large. The resources sufficient to finance lending to the English crown at an average of £15,300 (over 100,000 florins) annually from 1302 to 1310 were made possible by working through a consortium of companies.[100] Moreover, it seemed incapable of maintaining large-scale operations elsewhere at the same time.[101] The loss of the English business eventually drove it into bankruptcy in 1315, but the repercussions in the community of Florence seem to have been mild. The family remained influential and certain of its members resumed active business, albeit on a modest scale.[102]

Following the expulsion of the Frescobaldi, Antonio Pessagno of Genoa was Edward II's principal banker until 1319.[103] The Bardi also became a lender of increasing importance until the end of the civil war of 1321, when Edward II began to amass considerable treasure and used this company more for depositing surplus than for borrowing.[104] As regards the borrowing, the amounts involved were well

[97] Richard W. Kaeuper, "The Frescobaldi of Florence and the English Crown," in *Studies in Medieval and Renaissance History*, ed. W. M. Bowsky (Lincoln, NE, 1973), 44; Yver, *Le commerce*, 292.
[98] Renouard, *Les relations*, table (570).
[99] Kaeuper, "Frescobaldi," 62–3; A. Sapori, *Storia economica*, Vol 2, 872–7.
[100] Goldthwaite, "Italian Bankers," 765–6.
[101] Kaeuper, "Frescobaldi," 71–2.
[102] Ibid., 92.
[103] Natalie Fryde, *The Tyranny and Fall of Edward II, 1321–26* (Cambridge, 1979), 22. This man is often also referred to as Anthony Pessaigne.
[104] Ibid.; see Chap. 7, "Royal Finance, 1321–6."

within the capacity of this enormous firm. The other super-companies did very little royal lending; the Peruzzi's main connection to the crown was indirect, through its business dealings with the king's favorite, Hugh Despenser the Younger, a substantial depositor.[105] During Edward II's reign, the Bardi had become the major factor in the English wool trade, but the Peruzzi and the other super-companies were also able to participate, although on a more modest scale.

The accession of Edward III to the throne in 1327 brought a return to the pattern of large loans to the monarch as the price of admission to the wool trade, even before he began to rule in his own right in 1330.[106] Edward III never granted exclusivity to any of the merchant-bankers, but as his needs grew, he narrowed his dealings to a few select firms, to which he gave large segments of tax revenue and wool trade in exchange for loans. The Bardi became Edward III's principal banker from the beginning of his reign, but the Peruzzi did not become seriously involved until late in 1336, while the Acciaiuoli did not become royal lenders at all. This complex story will be discussed at greater length in subsequent chapters.

One important fact is clear: The super-companies did not owe their emergence to their involvement with the English kings or domination of the English wool trade. The Bardi and Peruzzi had become super-companies long before they had developed their intimate relationship with the English crown, and the Acciaiuoli became a super-company with virtually no association with English kings at all. That company's only involvement with Edward III occurred in the summer of 1341, when it played a small part in the unsuccessful attempts to obtain ransom for the release of Henry of Lancaster.[107] Wool trading and cloth merchandising were clearly very important parts of their businesses throughout most of their histories, but domination of their sources of wool supply was not essential to success.

The third important political and commercial relationship of the super-companies was with the papacy. In terms of actual size and profitability, this business was not a significant segment of the super-companies' operations. The Curia had used Italian merchant-bankers for loans and deposits during the latter half of the thirteenth century,

[105] E. B. Fryde, "The Deposits of Hugh Despenser the Younger with the Italian Bankers," *Economic History Review* 2, series 3 (1951): 344–62.
[106] E. B. Fryde, "Loans to the English Crown, 1328–31," *English Historical Review*, 70 (1955): 198–211.
[107] See T. H. Lloyd, *The English Wool Trade in the Middle Ages* (Cambridge, 1977), 188. The problems of the Bardi and Peruzzi in connection with the ransom are discussed in Chapter 8, this volume.

but Clement V, the first Avignon pope, suspended formal relations with them early in the fourteenth century, influenced by the collapse of the Bonsignori and Ricciardi companies. Pope John XXII resumed the employment of the merchant-bankers in 1316, but restricted them largely to money transfer operations.[108] The bankruptcy of the Scali Company in 1326 made the Curia even more cautious, causing it to spread its risks among several of the leading firms, including all three super-companies.[109] The amount of money involved in transfers handled by these merchant-bankers was modest, relative to the size of their overall business. Collections and transfers within most of France were handled internally by the papal treasury, and although those in the British Isles were substantial, they were not really big business. For example, the total transfers from England to Avignon between 1332 and 1337 averaged only 13,000 florins per annum handled by the Bardi and 12,000 florins by the Peruzzi, not very great sums compared with the transactions of these firms with the English crown.[110] The papacy did not place deposits with or borrow money from the merchant-bankers during the first half of the fourteenth century so that its total business with them was neither large nor very lucrative.

Papal business nonetheless was extremely important to the super-companies. As already described, papal influence as suzerain of the kingdom of southern Italy was vital to their operations in that country. In all parts of Europe, their formal relationship with the papal treasury and their personal contact with the princes of the church gave those select companies an entry into the vast ecclesiastical transfer business outside the Curia as well as a cachet that was of inestimable value in dealing with their aristocratic clients. The transfer system in itself was very useful to the companies' operations throughout Europe, especially in England, where it was helpful to have papal collections available to pay for wool purchases. And finally, the papacy frequently used its good offices to recommend the companies to potential clients and to intervene, or threaten to intervene, on behalf of the companies against recalcitrant debtors.[111]

Finally, a further word needs to be said about the merchandising operations of the super-companies. As mentioned earlier, they were important and normally very lucrative but not essential to the super-

---

[108]   Renouard, *Les relations*, 420–2.

[109]   *I libri*, 94, reveals a case, however, wherein the Bardi and Peruzzi made good on one Scali default to the Curia. See Chapter 3, this volume, for details.

[110]   Renouard, *Les relations*, 137.

[111]   Ibid., 541–6.

companies' evolution. Merchandise sales did, however, profit from the economies of scale resulting from the super-companies' domination of the rich market of southern Italy and their deep penetration of other Mediterranean markets through their branch system. Their power, market knowledge, and creditworthiness improved merchandise profits in two ways. The first is that these factors enabled the super-companies to pick and choose among suppliers throughout the known world to achieve optimum landed costs. The second is that the large volumes and steady business generated through their market penetration helped them reduce unit transport costs by means of consolidation of shipments and repeated use of selected carriers.[112]

The references to market penetration suggest that the super-companies were highly competitive, and indeed they were. They competed aggressively for trade against the merchants of other cities and for the favors of princes and prelates against all comers. Commercial rivalry often manifested itself at the political level, as firms vied for privileges that played out in the marketplace, But within Florence, competition among businessmen appears to have been muted in some respects, with a guild-oriented tendency to share certain markets rather than to drive single-mindedly for market penetration. Clearly this was the case in the joint monopolies in southern Italy and England. Within these market-allocation arrangements, however, there was likely to have been considerable jockeying for position. And although competitive pressures do not appear to have been mainly responsible for the major bankruptcies of this period, they will have played a part. In the scramble for survival in 1342–3 described in Chapter 8, there was little evidence of cooperation among Florentine companies. Finally, despite the many friendly arrangements, price competition was a powerful force in medieval business, as is shown in the discussions of wool and grain markets throughout this book.

This long preamble leads at last to the nature of the super-companies' business. The length and range of this analysis has been necessitated by the great scope and complexity of the super-companies. To focus only upon specific aspects of the businesses produces results like those of the fabled three blind men trying to understand the nature of an elephant. A study limited to the spectacular dealings with the English crown and the papacy concludes that the companies

---

[112] Transport costs were a significant and increasing proportion of total costs in the early fourteenth century. See J. H. Munro, "Industrial Transformations in the North-west European Textile Trades, c. 1290–c. 1340: Economic Progress or Economic Crisis?" in *Before the Black Death*, ed. B. M. S. Campbell (Manchester, 1989), 120–130. See also later in this chapter for further discussion of carriers.

were primarily bankers and wool traders. One that emphasizes Mediterranean commerce suggests that they were just very large general merchants; and one that is restricted to Florentine operations pictures these firms as mainly manufacturers and traders. They were all of these, but the core of their businesses was commodity trading, principally grain and wool, and the marketing of cloth. The core marketing axis was Florence–Naples, wherein the latter ensured adequate supplies of foodstuffs of all kinds to the working population of Florence, which, in turn, provided manufactured goods, especially cloth, to the Angevin kingdom of southern Italy. Beyond that core there was significant trading of products of all kinds in the major markets of northern Europe, Italy, and the Mediterranean, but this, while important and profitable, was peripheral to the main enterprise.

Knitting these businesses together was the financing power of the super-companies. There has been much scholarly argument on whether the Italian companies exposed themselves to the high-risk financing of monarchies for its inherent profitability or for the lucrative privileges that such lending made possible. The probability is, as usual, some of both. Financial operations in general were expected to turn a profit, and certain forms – such as cash transfers, currency exchanges, drafts, and commercial loans – were clearly structured to do so. The companies also may have aimed to earn a profit on royal lending, and negotiated cash "gifts" and "damages" as euphemisms for interest in their contracts. But realistically, they expected to do no better than break even on such business, that is, to recover the money advanced and perhaps their own interest costs, because experience had taught them that cash "gifts" were elusive and that repayments were subject to lengthy delay. The gifts that really mattered were those that came in the form of tax exemptions and privileges to trade in valuable commodities and manufactures. Certainly, few of the important companies were prepared to undertake royal lending on its own merits; there are no known examples of large-scale continuous financing of monarchs unaccompanied by important commercial privileges. Exceptions such as the advances made to Edward III in the late 1330s by Flemish and German merchants were isolated cases of stand-alone pawnbroker-type loans at the pawnbroker rates of interest approximating 1 percent per week, secured by hard assets such as jewelry or hostages.[113] Most evidence

---

[113] E. B. Fryde, "Financial Resources of Edward III in the Netherlands, 1337–40," *Revue Belge de Philologie et d'Histoire* 45 (1967): 1188–90.

concerning the huge high-risk loans to monarchs that comprised the bulk of the super-companies' financing suggests that they were considered more as facilitators of lucrative trade than as important purposeful generators of profit. For example, even at a time when the Bardi Company was said by Fryde to have earned an excellent profit on large loans to Edward III, the preponderance of the company's earnings for the period 1330–2 stemmed from wool, cloth, grain, and general trading, with wool alone accounting for 43 percent of the total profit.[114]

Seen in this light, finance was a business in its own right but for the most part remained ancillary to trade. Nevertheless, it was vital to the companies because it made possible the political favors that were very much a part of the nature of the business. We have observed from the dramatic examples in southern Italy and England that financial power was essential to enable the companies to negotiate with the governments for a favorable environment for their enterprises. Without that financial power, the great trading operations would have been impossible.

Cash flow and its control were thus the central problems of the super-companies. Their early successful management of those problems created the basis for attaining much of their size and power, just as their later failure to control cash did much to destroy them. The substantial amounts of money advanced to monarchs were only part of the cash problem. The companies had to pay market prices for the grain and wool; these commodity investments were not recovered until the products were sold in the export markets some considerable time later. In the case of grain to Florence or wool to Flanders, the delay was sometimes only a month or two, but often, especially when wool began to be imported into Italy, the immobilization of cash could last many months.

The extent of this deferral of payment is vividly illustrated in Francesco Pegolotti's *Pratica della mercatura,* which details the expense and the multitude of steps involved in transporting wool by the sea–land route from London to Florence.[115] In London, customs and export tax had to be paid, along with tips to officials, wine for the clerks, fees to the customs weigher and broker, charges for porters, haulage, customs porters, and shipping to Libourne in Gascony, near Bordeaux. There the wool incurred innkeeper charges for the per-

[114] Robert S. Lopez and Irving W. Raymond, *Medieval Trade in the Mediterranean World* (New York, 1955), 370–1. This earnings analysis is discussed in further detail in Chapter 6, this volume.
[115] Pegolotti, *La pratica,* 256–8. The alternative all-sea route mentioned earlier was also important during the early fourteenth century.

sonnel and temporary storage, carriage and turnpike fees for the overland trip from Libourne to Montpellier and then on to Aigues-Mortes, where it was transferred to the port and loaded on a ship for Pisa. In Italy there were porter, warehousing, carriage, and notarial fees to pay, followed by tolls at three different locations, unloading at Signa, carriage from Signa to Florence, and customs in Florence. Assuming all went well, the entire trip would take several months; we know from the papal records that the time allowed for money transfers just from Avignon to Florence was thirty to forty-five days.[116] But often all did not go well. The many transfers and formalities afforded almost unlimited opportunities for delays. Ships that turned back to ports in England to escape piracy or bad weather were sometimes held up for customs examination all over again. On such occasions, the king had to intervene with letters of authentication to satisfy the officials that appropriate duties had already been paid.[117]

Even before the transport began, there were problems of delay. The *Calendar of Close Rolls* and the *Calendar of Patent Rolls* of Edward III are studded with examples of the agonizing slowness in securing permission to export wool already bought and held by the companies. There is also much evidence that the companies paid wool growers, especially monasteries, well in advance of delivery, sometimes years in advance, to ensure availability and attractive prices.[118]

The case illustrated here deals with wool from England, an important source of supply from the 1320s onward, but the Florentines, as noted earlier, obtained their wool from a variety of sources in western Europe and the Mediterranean.[119] Once the wool had safely landed in the company's warehouses in Florence from whatever source, the company would gradually sell it off to the hundreds of *lanaiuoli*, the petty capitalist entrepreneurs of the wool guild.[120] Only a small amount will have been kept for the company's

[116] Renouard, *Les relations*, 476. This convention applied during the reigns of John XXII, Benedict XII, and Clement VI.
[117] See, e.g., *Calendar of Close Rolls* Edward III (hereafter, *CCR* E III), 1339–41, 93, 429, and E III 1337–9, 570. The latter entry shows that London customs even had to be ordered to release wool for export on the basis of the first lading, ignoring the extra weight caused by the "damp" when the ship carrying the wool returned to port after a storm at sea.
[118] Eileen Power, *The Wool Trade in English Medieval History* (Oxford, 1941), 43; M. M. Postan, *Medieval Trade and Finance* (Cambridge, 1973), 10.
[119] See Hoshino, *L'Arte della lana*, 115–30.
[120] Ibid., Table 35, 226, gives data on the number of enrollments in the guild during the first half of the fourteenth century. There were 626 members in 1332.

own manufacturing. Cloth production was organized on the "putting-out" system, whereby the entrepreneurs oversaw operations as the the goods that they owned passed from specialist to specialist in the long process of turning wool into finished product.[121] This is a system that does not lend itself to economies of scale or high profitability, with the result that the super-companies did not participate in cloth manufacturing in a large way.[122] Nevertheless, they did enter manufacturing on a small scale, just as they did in other lines of endeavor.[123]

Although a super-company's commitment of cash to in-process goods was minimal, it did have a significant investment in intermediate textiles imported for finishing. And it had a large capital outlay tied up in finished product acquired both from Florentine *lanaiuoli* and foreign producers, especially those from Flanders and Brabant. The finished goods, like the raw wool, immobilized cash for a long time. Some were disposed of quickly, through local sales from an annex to the company's main warehouse or to its employees in Florence or abroad.[124] Most of the cloth, especially the finest materials, had to be shipped to the markets in southern Italy, the Mediterranean, and northern Europe. The entire process from purchase of wool in England to final sale in foreign markets resulted in a cumulative immobilization of cash over an extensive period of time creating a severe burden for the super-companies.

No discussion of the movement of goods is complete without a reference to insurance. The super-companies sometimes acted as insurer, sometimes as insured. In situations such as the sea–land transport of wool, they assumed the risk for their own merchandise, and often provided insurance for others for a fee.[125] And occasionally they

---

[121] The specialist processes included combing/carding, spinning, weaving, fulling, tentering, raising, shearing, and dyeing. J. H. Munro describes these steps in detail in "Textile Technology," in *Dictionary of the Middle Ages*, Vol. 11 (New York, 1988), 693–710. See also Brucker, *Renaissance Florence*, 60–6, for the functioning of the putting-out system.

[122] Hoshino, in *L'Arte della lana*, 201, asserts that the wool industry was essentially artisanal, with little capital (500 to 2,000 florins) needed to compete and with low but secure profit expectations. Production output of each entrepreneur ranged between 50 and 150 bolts per year and in no case exceeded 300 bolts per year.

[123] The Peruzzi Company's manufacturing activity is briefly described in Chapter 3.

[124] *I libri*. There are numerous references in the Peruzzi accounts to advances to overseas partners and factors being made in the form of cloth in lieu of cash.

[125] For example, the Bardi charged a premium of 8 3/4% of the value of the goods to insure a shipment from Paris to Pisa via Genoa. This and other information in this paragraph is derived from Davidsohn, *Firenze*, Vol. 6, 429–36.

insured marine shipments, such as the Peruzzi coverage of a consignment of silk from Sicily to Tunis in 1337. But more often, especially in the case of marine transport in the Mediterranean, the super-companies were the insured parties, with insurance usually arranged as part of the overall financing of the venture. The risks covered varied, sometimes very broad for overland shipments, but often very narrow for maritime transport, limited to acts of piracy. Logically, the role of the insurer tended to go to the party best situated to assess or even influence the risks. Overland, it went to the super-companies, which were able to use their political connections, innkeeper network, and close oversight – at sea, to the shippers who could call upon the intelligence and power of their home ports to manage the threat of pirates.

Because cash was the central problem, the super-companies had both to mobilize the cash and to deploy it judiciously. With regard to the former, Sapori makes much of the "myriads of small investors" as major sources of financing through their participation in specific ventures (*accomandigia*) and their advances on merchandise ordered (*depositi*).[126] These were unquestionably important in helping to fund the buying and selling of the raw materials and finished products of all kinds in markets throughout Europe and the Mediterranean. But they were essentially short-term devices suitable for providing the money for general trading operations, not for financing the large sums tied up in the loans to monarchs, in the transport of wool, and in the manufacture of cloth. To meet such needs, the companies required a strong capital commitment from partners both inside and outside the immediate family. As discussed in the previous chapter, the Peruzzi's record of profitability and probity during the 1280s and 1290s provided the incentive to attract a number of wealthy outsiders as shareholders. As a result, the 1300 company, the first for which corporate details remain, raised a capital of li.124,000, of which li.54,000 (nearly 44 percent) were contributed by ten outsiders. This impressive capital stock was supplemented by interest-bearing deposits, initially at 8 percent, later 7 percent, from shareholders and wealthy individuals.[127] There are no data for the early years, but the deposits in the final years, even in a period of decline, were large

---

[126] Armando Sapori, *Studi di storia economica medievale* (Florence, 1947), 278.

[127] Davidsohn, *Firenze*, Vol. 3, 556, misleadingly asserts that depositors received a share of profits in addition to fixed interest. Participants in the *accomandigia* contracts might share in the profits of those specific ventures, but only shareholders were entitled to a distribution of profit (or loss) of the company as a whole.

enough to suggest that they were an important source of funds.[128]

Although obtaining cash was important, husbanding it was even more so. The super-companies took sensible steps to ensure the most effective use of their capital for the essential needs of the business – loans and inventories – avoiding investment in fixed assets. They did not own ships or wagons; they hired them along with the necessary personnel, including soldiers to protect the cargoes. The Peruzzi Company did not even own its main warehouse and subsidiary shops in Florence.[129] This is not to suggest that the companies shunned real estate ownership altogether. As will be shown in Chapter 3, the Peruzzi seemed to have had a branch of its organization that specialized in the purchase and sale of property, largely on behalf of family members, shareholders, or even employees. But overall, the guiding principle of the Peruzzi Company was to run its operations with as little investment as possible in real estate and business-related fixed assets. In addition, by having such property in noncompany hands, the companies avoided the risk of its seizure to satisfy creditors in case of bankruptcy, apparently a common motivation.[130]

Armed with ample capital, a system for conserving cash, and as will be shown, a solid organization, Florentine super-companies such as the Peruzzi were prepared to move aggressively into Angevin Italy at the beginning of the fourteenth century when opportunities arose there to share in large-scale trading monopolies in exchange for loans.[131] They found further resources in wealthy local depositors. The extent of these deposits has been the subject of much debate because the evidence is patchy and largely anecdotal, but it is known that the Peruzzi received permission to establish a bank in Naples in 1302.[132] Local deposits were almost certainly recorded in the branch books, as there are few instances of deposits from outside Florence

[128] Deposits in the Peruzzi Company by both partners and outsiders were significant in 1335, but declining between 1335 and 1343. See Tables A1 and A6.

[129] *I libri.* Numerous leases are recorded in the expense section of the Peruzzi Book of Assets, 180. Here may be seen several examples of lease arrangements for shops, stables, and warehouses, including three- and four-year leases on the main Santa Cecilia warehouse, part of which was owned by Simone di Chiaro Peruzzi, a man with no company ownership connections.

[130] Luzzati, *Villani e Buonaccorsi*, 12. Luzzati notes that the Peruzzi put Giovanni Villani in charge of its Palazzo Alessi in Siena after he had left the company in 1308, citing this as a common device to protect important property because of the ever-present risk of bankruptcy.

[131] Abulafia, "Southern Italy." The opening pages of this article give numerous examples of large-scale business opportunities being offered by the Angevin kings in exchange for loans.

[132] Davidsohn, *Firenze*, Vol. 6, 280–1.

appearing in the surviving central accounts of the Peruzzi.[133] Anecdotal evidence is usually problematic, but there is enough of it to suggest that over time the amount of local deposits is likely to have been substantial.[134]

Finding money to advance to the king in return for lucrative privileges was only part of the super-companies' problems. The imperative was to ensure that a significant portion of the loans was recycled back to the company with reasonable promptness, because medieval companies, unlike modern corporations, had few resources on which to fall back in an emergency and certainly no banks of last resort. Recycling was not difficult in the case of those loans that merely anticipated export taxes due on grain sales that the companies would have paid anyway at a later date. But most other advances that were to be recovered directly or indirectly required skillful negotiation to obtain adequate means of repayment or privileges worth at least as much as the loans extended. As discussed earlier, Yver's analysis of the Angevin kingdom's records reveals a well-conceived system of loan recovery, reinforced by tenacious follow-up to ensure prompt collection of the money sources assigned to the loans. Examples of the fierce pressure exerted by the companies on government agencies for repayments included recourse to the king himself as a potent tactic against dilatory debtors.[135] Indirect recoveries were more complex, consisting as they did of money-generating rights or offices. Abulafia cites direct control over port taxes (including taxes on grain exports) in the Adriatic provinces of the Kingdom of Naples and control of the Neapolitan mint as the most remunerative privileges granted to the super-companies.[136]

Timing of effective repayment was as important as the amount of repayment. Although the super-companies were well capitalized, they

---

[133] *I libri.* Examples appear on 12 and 185, apparently representing deposits of the Hospitalers and an individual in Palermo, but these are rare cases. There is no direct evidence of local deposits in the Peruzzi branches because those records did not survive, but surviving Datini books of its Barcelona branch in 1399 reveal the existence of local deposits at that time. See Raymond de Roover, "The Development of Accounting Prior to Luca Pacioli According to the Account-books of Medieval Merchants," in *Studies in the History of Accounting*, ed. A. C. Littleton and B. S. Yamey (Homewood, IL, 1956), 142–3.

[134] Luzzati, *Villani e Buonaccorsi*, 86–95, offers one example, the case of a Provençal lady who sold her chateau and unfortunately deposited the proceeds with the Buonaccorsi in Naples shortly before that company's bankruptcy.

[135] Yver, *Le commerce*, 388, reports that Charles of Calabria, King Robert's son, warned his justiciars in a letter to take care and pay up, lest the Peruzzi withdraw its credit from "my lord and father."

[136] Abulafia, "Southern Italy," 380.

soon found that the sums requested by the Neapolitan monarch would quickly milk them dry. They also recognized that if they ran out of lendable funds to the king, they would promptly lose their privileges. This meant that with indirect payment, the super-companies had to evaluate not only the intrinsic worth of the privileges granted, but also the rate of cash flow that they produced. The management of the royal loan portfolio thus entailed the effective recycling of cash so that fresh funds would be continuously generated for relending to the monarchy, for financing the business, and for an adequate return to the shareholders in Florence. The handsome dividend distributed by the 1300 Peruzzi Company in 1308 and the maintenance of its privileged relationship with the Neapolitan government for over forty years testify to an early and continuous success in this complex juggling act.[137]

The importance of politics extended to all facets of the super-companies' business. As has been shown in the previous chapter, strong company leadership was essential at headquarters in Florence to protect both company and family from rival intramural factions. Abroad, the companies were constantly struggling to win position with the ruling class of one polity while trying to do the same in another polity that was an antagonist of the first. Despite Kedar's claim of relative stability in the Mediterranean and northern Europe in the early fourteenth century, the term "relative" needs to be emphasized.[138] As mentioned, the Peruzzi had a very large branch in Aragon-associated Sicily and loaned money to its government, which remained hostile to the Kingdom of Naples and the papacy even after the Peace of Caltabellotta. King Robert of Naples launched six expeditions against Sicily during his long reign and one serious invasion attempt in 1314 to punish King Frederick for offering aid to Emperor Henry VII.[139] It also maintained a branch in Majorca, an autonomous kingdom, but under loose Aragonese overlordship at the time.[140]

France and England presented a special problem to the super-companies. They were frequently at loggerheads, even between the actual wars of the first, second, and fourth decades of the fourteenth century, but the Peruzzi maintained active, if modest, operations in both countries. During the reign of Edward II, when relations be-

---

[137] A history of dividend distributions of the Peruzzi Company is given in Table A 3.
[138] Munro, "Industrial Transformations," 121–9, argues against even relative stability.
[139] Runciman, *Vespers*, 278.
[140] See D. Abulafia, "The Problem of the Kingdom of Majorca (1229/76–1343): 2. Economic Identity," *Mediterranean Historical Review* 6 (June 1991): 35–61.

tween England and France were reasonably amicable, the Peruzzi Company capitalized on this good will and even used the good offices of the King of France on two occasions to support its defense against claims of the English government.[141] But the animosity of France toward England, as well as its repeated conflicts in Flanders, where the super-companies also had important branches, eventually forced the Bardi and Peruzzi to make a choice. The decisions were made easier by the French government's lack of steady assured revenue and its record of harsh treatment of foreign merchant-bankers on several occasions.[142] Early in the fourteenth century, the Bardi opted for England, accepting a negligible role in France. The Peruzzi Company deferred its decision until the eve of the Hundred Years' War when it began financing Edward III's war preparations and reduced its presence in Paris.[143]

Papal politics, as usual, were complex and problematic, but largely continued to be aimed at curbing the power of the Empire in northern Italy and the Angevins in southern Italy, while increasing the papacy's own temporal holdings in central Italy. The Holy See attempted to play the role of peacemaker between France and England, but after its transfer to Avignon in 1305, it tended to favor France in its diplomacy, despite Philip IV's brutal attacks on the Order of the Templars.[144] The super-companies were, by and large, comfortable with these politics, especially after the cessation of the Sicilian crusade, which allowed them to keep their valuable close connections with the papacy without serious offense to the various monarchies with which they did business. The Bardi, and especially the Peruzzi, built good will with the papacy by providing substantial financial aid to the Knights Hospitalers after that Order's conquest of Rhodes in 1309.[145] The Hospitalers was among the earliest of the crusading orders of chivalry recognized by the pope and became particularly important to the papacy as heir to many of the Templars' estates after the suppression of that order. The Peruzzi's assistance also gave them an important branch in Rhodes, a useful market in itself as well as a transit point for trade in the Levant and Asia Minor.

Finally, the commune of Florence had its own political agendas

---

[141] *CPR* E II 1307–13, 515; *CCR* E II 1318–23, 303.

[142] Strayer, "Italian Bankers," 113–21.

[143] These events are discussed fully at the beginning of Chapter 7.

[144] Joseph R. Strayer, *The Reign of Philip the Fair* (Princeton, NJ, 1980), 285–95. Philip's persistent harassment and property seizures led eventually to Pope Clement V's decision at the Council of Vienne in 1312 to suppress the order.

[145] See Chapter 5 for details of this loan.

that further complicated the companies' relationships with the foreign rulers. Florence's disastrous wars with neighboring communes during the 1320s, 1330s, and 1340s, which the leading families strongly supported, clearly demonstrated the city's military incompetence and its continuing reliance on the support of the Kingdom of Naples and the papacy, putting its super-companies at a disadvantage in their dealings with those and other polities.[146] Unlike the Venetian and Genoese merchants, the super-companies had no flag to follow, no armed force to carve out their markets. As private businesses headquartered in a militarily weak city-state, they could bring only indirect pressure to bear on the rulers of the territories in which they operated through the need of those monarchs for the companies' resources.

Given the international financial and political aspects of the super-companies' operations, an important part of their business activity was intelligence gathering. Timely information was vital to their financial dealings in which predicting monetary flows and rates of exchange was crucial to profitability. Information from their far-flung networks also made the companies' representatives welcome at courts, where news and gossip of any kind were much appreciated. The intelligence came mainly in the form of letters that accompanied business instructions and transaction data. An excellent example of this is to be found in a letter from the Ricciardi firm in Lucca to its London representatives in 1303, which included news on the Pope's movements, the conclusion of the French–English war, the status of the struggle between Black and White factions in Florence, along with local news of a sensational murder.[147] But intelligence services to royal patrons could go much further. *The Wardrobe Book of William de Norwell* includes a large payment made to the Bardi and Peruzzi for the expenses of their spying activities on French military preparations in Normandy.[148] The Bardi Company ingratiated itself with Edward III in 1333 by capturing the traitor Thomas de Gourneye in Sicily and delivering him to the king.[149] It also aided that king in Au-

---

[146] The disadvantage to the companies of Florentine politics became increasingly evident in the 1330s and 1340s, as will be discussed in Chapters 7 and 8.

[147] George A. Holmes, "A Letter from Lucca to London in 1303," in *Florence and Italy: Renaissance Studies in Honour of Nicolai Rubenstein*, ed. P. Denley and C. Elain (London, 1988), 227–33. Although the Ricciardi's London branch was technically in bankruptcy from 1301, the representatives remained there for several years.

[148] Mary Lyon, Bryce Lyon, and Henry S. Lucas, *The Wardrobe Book of William de Norwell, 12 July 1338 to 27 May 1340* (Brussels, 1983), 60.

[149] *CPR* E III 1330–4, 483.

gust 1336, when his diplomatic mission to France, fearing that important letters to him would be intercepted by the French, used the Bardi to send duplicates to England.[150] But the companies' own survival often depended on a swift courier service such as that which could get the news of Chairman Bonifazio's death in London to the Peruzzi headquarters in Florence within three weeks.[151] If a political patron could be served as well, so much the better.

To sum up, what set the super-companies apart from the typical merchant-banker was their focus on large-scale commodity trading, which, in turn, necessitated the large-scale financing of political potentates to obtain permission to exploit such trade. The super-companies' size and political power opened up opportunities for economies of scale in marketing widely distributed products such as textiles, but these were a bonus, rather than an essential ingredient differentiating super-companies from other firms. Said the other way around, it was the rulers in control of exploitable surpluses and in need of large and efficient sources of cash who made the super-companies possible. And when these rulers developed other means of raising cash, as in England, or found their commodity less exploitable, as in southern Italy, the need for the medieval super-companies disappeared.[152]

The super-companies sustained their size and reach through their ability both to accumulate very large amounts of capital and to keep that capital circulating profitably. By astute management of their cash flows, the super-companies were able to provide a vital service to powerful but cash-short rulers, to attract additional investment from private individuals with surplus funds, and to maintain diverse prosperous businesses in Europe and the Mediterranean. This latter activity – buying and selling raw materials and merchandise, overseeing manufacturing, financing trade, lending money, exchanging currencies, and the attendant paperwork – was the companies' raison d'être, but it could not be carried out gainfully on a large scale without close attention to the political and cash control underpinnings of the business. Successful management of the kind of business dis-

---

[150] Malcolm Vale, *The Angevin Legacy and the Hundred Years' War* (Oxford, 1990), 258.

[151] *I libri*, 1.

[152] In England, it was the vastly improved administration of royal income and expense that released the monarchy from the grip of private financiers. In southern Italy, the demand for its main export, wheat, collapsed as a result of the catastrophic drop in population following the Black Death of 1348. These factors are discussed in greater detail in the Conclusions.

cussed here called for a sophisticated organization structure that would enforce tight central control while recognizing the necessity for local independence of action in an environment of widespread operations, very poor communications, and political opportunism. Such a structure required skillful, dedicated, and loyal managers at all levels to make it function effectively. An examination of the Peruzzi Company will provide some insights into how these organizational challenges were met.

3

The structure of the Peruzzi Company

The medieval super-companies, like most companies of significant size, were organized legally as quasi-permanent multiple partnerships. They were quasi-permanent in that they did not dissolve with the death or retirement of a partner, and even upon "dissolution" of the partnership they were immediately renewed. Each partnership lasted as long as it suited the partners; some were closed and profits distributed after two years, while others continued for as many as twelve years. The main purpose of closing a partnership was to effect a new alignment of shareholdings, usually, but not always accompanied by a formal distribution of profit. Whatever the reasons for closure, the business continued without interruption. Partnerships were multiple, with as many as twenty-one partners in the 1331 Peruzzi Company, each contributing a specific amount of money. The money values constituted share ownership, which entitled each owner to a share of profit or loss prorated to the percentage of his contribution to total company capital. Thus, the word "shareholder" can be used interchangeably with the word "partner." The companies were partnerships in the sense that each shareholder was subject to unlimited liability against all of his personal possessions in case of bankruptcy. Any distribution of profit was therefore tentative, subject to subsequent positive or negative adjustments years or even decades after the original distributions.[1]

The super-companies' intended permanence is attested by the fact that none was terminated voluntarily. This sense of permanence was enhanced by the use of a company logo, such as the golden pears on a blue background in the case of the Peruzzi and the diamond-shaped heraldic design of the Bardi. The very conservative papal treasury apparently found the logos to be especially reassuring.[2] Each com-

---

[1] Several examples of long-deferred adjustments to profit are shown later in this chapter and in Chapter 4.

[2] Y. Renouard observed that the logos were necessary to create a sense of permanence for clients located abroad who would distrust companies that they saw were frequently dissolving and reconstituting themselves (*Les relations*, 45).

pany also had its own seal, kept by the chairman. It seems to have been used sparingly, as there are only three instances of its employment reported in the Peruzzi accounts, all of which were to confirm the signature of a partner on formal documents.[3] The company style was based on the name of the chairman of the company and was changed not with each partnership renewal, but only with a change in the company's leadership. Thus the legal title of the Peruzzi Company was Tommaso de' Peruzzi e compagni from the date of Tommaso's assumption of the chairmanship in 1303 until his death in 1331, when it became Giotto de' Peruzzi e compagni upon Giotto's election to succeed Tommaso as chairman.

The earliest clearly defined Peruzzi Company was that of 1292. It was formed on November 1, after Arnoldo's death, and ran until May 1, 1296. Probable shareholders included Filippo as chairman and the four sons of Arnoldo – Pacino, Tommaso, Giotto, and Arnoldo – and at least three outsiders. The next company, with similar shareholders, existed from May 1, 1296, to May 1, 1300. Filippo was chairman except for a brief period (1298–9), when Pacino d'Arnoldo headed the company. Unfortunately, little is known about the size of the shareholdings or the structure of the companies. It is only the companies from 1300 onward that provide sufficient information from which to construct an analysis of the organization of the company's business.

There is no direct evidence from which to determine whether any of the large multibranch companies commonly drew up formal divisions of responsibility and lines of authority. It is certain, however, that organization structures did exist, whether formal or implied, because the scope of their businesses demanded them. It is well known that the chairman had complete authority, that many of the partners were active managers both at headquarters and in foreign branches, and that well-trained factors were given important sedentary and traveling assignments. But what has been lacking is a picture of how they all fit into a coherent organization plan in a very large company. Fortunately, in the case of the Peruzzi, a reasonable idea of structure can be gleaned from a careful study of the surviving account books, the *Libro dell'asse sesto* and the *Libro segreto sesto* of the last company, that of 1335–43.

These account books indicate that, from the 1300 company at least, the Peruzzi had adopted a bilevel form of organization that permitted a degree of decentralization at the operating level, but that re-

<hr>

[3] *I libri*, 105, 217, 221.

served important areas of decision making to the chairman's central office in Florence.[4] Thus, all partners, whether in Florence or abroad, participated in the company's management, but they deferred to the man they chose as their chief. The chairman was a powerful, dominating figure whose tenure, in the case of the Peruzzi, was ended only by death or bankruptcy.

The organization chart that follows in Figure 1 shows that there were several subsidiary "companies" in Florence controlled directly by the chairman or his delegate, in addition to fourteen foreign branches, each with a manager reporting to the chairman.[5] The fact that some branches were headed by a partner and others by a factor is important, and the reasons for this distinction will be addressed later in the chapter. What a chart of this type cannot reveal is the inevitable relationships that cut across organization lines – branch to branch, branch to subsidiary, and subsidiary to subsidiary. These relationships will be brought into the discussion of each of the segments of the business.

Florence Edler has characterized the *tavola* as comprising the banking business and the *mercanzia* as including all segments of medieval business except banking.[6] This is correct in the sense that the description covers the primary functions of these two main subdivisions. And certainly there is evidence that the *tavola* was a distinct section of the company with its own leader.[7] But it is a serious oversimplification of corporate structure for the larger entities, especially the super-companies. First, Figure 1 reveals that in addition to the *compagnia della tavola* and the *compagnia della mercanzia*, there existed a distinct *compagnia della drapperia* which isolated at least part of the cloth business. The Bardi company went even further; as noted in Chapter 2, it not only separated its wool and cloth businesses, but also treated them as distinct profit centers. Second, the super-companies had a well-developed foreign branch system, with each branch responsible for

---

[4] Although the surviving account books deal mainly with the 1335–43 period, these, the Secret Book of Giotto, and other sources provide evidence that the bilevel form of organization had been in place from virtually the beginning of the century, as will be made clear from Chapter 5 onward.

[5] In fact, there were sixteen branches, but two of them, Genoa and Chiarenza, are not shown in the table because they were very small and did not have resident managers

[6] Florence Edler, *Glossary of Medieval Terms of Business* (Cambridge, MA, 1934), 176.

[7] Davidsohn, *Firenze*, Vol. 6, 280 n1, refers to the company of 1308 showing the banking affairs of Tommaso de' Peruzzi & Co conducted by the *cambiatori della tavola* under Giotto Peruzzi as chief.

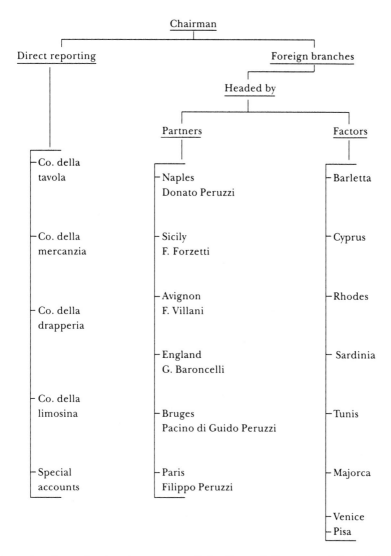

Figure 1. Organizational structure of the Peruzzi Company, July 1, 1335. The Bruges branch was led by a factor from 1336 onward. The Paris branch was led by a factor from 1337 onward, on the death of Filippo Peruzzi.

its own results.[8] It must also be remembered that the Florence-based subsidiary companies and the foreign branches were really departments, organically part of the main company and not legally distinct entities, as in the case of the Medici a century later.[9] But each branch was required to maintain a complete set of accounts and report its balances periodically to Florence, especially at the close of each partnership, and was subject to the laws of the polity in which it was located. The fact, as will be demonstrated in Chapter 4, that the systems of reporting differed from branch to branch suggests a degree of independence at the local level, or conformity to local practice.

Third, the central office in Florence had direct manufacturing, trading, and banking businesses of its own for which it needed the branches as outlets, limiting branch independence. Furthermore, under certain circumstances the central office overrode the principle of branch responsibility entirely. These exceptions generally related to the resolution of unfinished business left over from previous companies, such as past-due collections, lawsuits, and conflicts with local authorities, which were handled by the central *tavola*. Merchandise and real estate claims appear to have been the province of the *mercanzia*. The *tavola*, however, was the only mechanism used to route the adjustments in profit of previous companies to the shareholders of those companies.[10] Beyond such "cleanup" issues, there were inevitably situations in which the interests of the branch clashed with those of the company as a whole. In such cases, the concerns of the central office were paramount. The most outstanding instance is Chairman Bonifazio's startling decision to take personal command of the company's relations with the English monarchy in 1338.

There are, however, less dramatic but equally instructive examples

[8] The surviving fragment of the Bardi account of 1318 reveals balances for eight branches. Sapori, *La crisi*, 216. The Peruzzi branch balances will be discussed in detail in Chapter 4. The fact that balances were reported, however, does not necessarily mean that each branch was controlled as a profit center, as there is no evidence to support such an assumption. Some of the large companies below super-company rank had substantial branches, but others, such as the Alberti in the early fourteenth century, had only factors resident abroad (R. de Roover, "Alberti Company," 20).

[9] De Roover, *Medici Bank*, 76–8. De Roover argued that the Medici's holding company system gave the shareholders better protection against risk of losses by errant branches. The virtue of this arrangement in the medieval environment is questionable, as it entailed entrusting the fate of each branch to long-term local minority shareholder-managers. Even the Medici dropped the system in 1455.

[10] *I libri*, 280–3, provides some of the many examples of debit or credit allocations to the shareholders of the 1324–31 and 1331–5 companies.

of the kinds of situation in which the Florence office took charge. One was a lawsuit against the 1324–31 company *tavola* by the heirs of a Landuccio Mazetti, a Florentine concern, for a large sum due in Bruges. The claim caused Donato di Pacino de' Peruzzi, a shareholder, to journey to Bruges in 1333 to take charge of the litigation over the head of the branch manager and fellow-shareholder Pacino di Guido di Filippo de' Peruzzi. Donato was actually named by the plaintiffs in the suit, which was to be brought before the count of Flanders.[11] The expenses reported for Donato's trip included the cost of horses and four bolts of velvet, which had been made in Florence and brought to the countess of Flanders as a gift. Other expenses for the suit were relatively minor, consisting mainly of the costs of making presentations to the count's lawyers and clerks to obtain a favorable judgment, which apparently was finally received in 1338.[12] The latter costs were paid by the Bruges branch, charged to the 1324–31 *tavola* and eventually allocated to the shareholders of the 1324–31 company.[13]

A second example involved the *mercanzia* which was ordered to transfer to the 1331–5 company 2,333 1/3 florins in October 1336 to compensate for the return of a deposit by Filippo Villani's Avignon branch to the Abbot of Samichele delle Scluse (now known as St. Michele della Chiusa) in August of that year. The abbot had originally made deposits totaling 7,000 florins in 1312, split one-third each among the Bardi, Peruzzi, and the Scali companies. Also in October 1336, the company authorized the Avignon branch to pay the abbot a further 583 1/3 florins. After the Scali Company had gone bankrupt in 1326, the Curia had only obtained 50 percent of the Scali's share of the deposit through the bankruptcy court. The Bardi and Peruzzi agreed to reimburse the Curia 583 1/3 florins each to make up for the Curia's 50 percent loss of 1,166 2/3 florins.[14] This is an obvious case where the branch took the action, but strictly on direct orders from Florence. It may also be a medieval example of the controversial practice of reimbursing the investment losses of really important clients![15]

The *compagnia della drapperia* appears to have encompassed only

[11] Donato, the previous manager of the Bruges branch who also served as the count's general receiver, was obviously well placed to deal with the count's court. See Chapter 6 for more details on Donato's activities in Bruges.

[12] *I libri*, 101, 28, 158.

[13] Ibid., 158.

[14] Ibid., 94.

[15] Renouard, *Les relations*, 542, has noted that the companies were contractually obligated to make the reimbursement, but the record is not entirely clear on this point.

the manufacture of cloth and its sale in Florence. This unit is not mentioned in connection with the sale of cloth abroad, and it probably did not deal with the product of other manufacturers in Florence. There are numerous entries in the Peruzzi accounts covering cloth transactions, but only two of them refer to the *compagnia della drapperia*.[16] Two of the Peruzzi Company's factors were assigned to the *drapperia*, but in what capacity is not indicated.[17] A third factor, Giovanni di Berto Ruggieri, wrote up the accounts for the 1331–5 *drapperia* and traveled to Bruges and Paris on behalf of that unit.[18]

The manufacturing operation seems to have been quite small. It likely included the finishing of cloth imported from Flanders, in view of the long association of the Peruzzi with the Calimala guild, which specialized in finishing, and of the already-mentioned journey of the accountant to Bruges. It probably also engaged in complete cloth manufacturing as a logical extension of its wool business. Reference is made to two men, Tano Chiarissimi and Gherardo Rustichi, who are described as "compangni a la drapperia."[19] These men were not employees of the company, and apparently paid part of del Bene's salary.[20] It is probable, therefore, that they were entrepreneurs who ran the cloth manufacturing shop for the Peruzzi Company, even though the latter was represented in the wool guild. It should be noted that the company also employed a full-time shearer, but there is no evidence to connect him with the *drapperia*. Instead, he seems to have been used for special assignments, some involving lengthy transfers abroad, rather than for routine manufacturing.[21] All things considered, the *drapperia* appears to have been a clearly defined but small manufacturing arm of the company.

The final "company" shown in Figure 1 is the *compagnia della limosina*, really an account through which the Peruzzi Company do-

[16] *I libri*, 240, refers to a single bolt of cloth sent to a factor in Barletta in 1338; Giotto's Secret Book also contains an entry on 462 that includes several bolts supplied to his family by the *drapperia* in 1329.

[17] Ibid. The factors were Dono Berci (6, 46, 237) and Lorenzo di Bettino del Bene (82).

[18] Ibid., 102. The entry referred to the "ragione della drapperia vecchia da Santa Cicilia." Santa Cicilia was the Peruzzi's main warehouse, rented from Simone Peruzzi.

[19] Ibid., 82.

[20] Ibid. The entry includes a note that part of del Bene's salary was due "aside from that which Tano Chiarissimi and Gherardo Rustichi, our partners in the *drapperia*, assigned him."

[21] Ibid., 65. The shearer, Giovanni di Iacopo, resided in Naples between July 1335 and May 1337 and spent time on company business between July 1338 and July 1339 in Milan and Pisa.

nations to charities were channeled. It was common for the super-companies to set aside 1 to 2 percent of their shareholdings for "God's work," from which the *limosina* received appropriate allocations of profit and loss.[22] The Bardi designated its charity shareholding *Messer Domeneddio*, that is, God. Because of the irregularity and uncertainty of profit distributions, the *limosina* was also funded within the company, with charitable allocations being made routinely, usually in January or February of each year for the fiscal year commencing the following July 1. The money was destined not only directly to the poor, but to unnamed religious organizations and hospitals that served the poor. Such gifts no doubt enhanced the company's reputation in a general way as a good corporate citizen, but there is no evidence that they were specifically directed at furthering the company's political and social interests in Florence. Between 1335 and 1338, the Peruzzi gave over li.300 per year; from 1338 to 1341, the payments declined to an average of a little over li.125 per year and dried up thereafter.[23] The donations of the Bardi to their charities were very large, averaging close to li.3,000 per year during those same years, suggesting that the Bardi Company was much larger, more profitable, or more generous than the Peruzzi.[24] It is risky, however, to draw too many conclusions from this difference, because the two companies may have accounted differently for their donations. For example, it is likely that the foreign branches had charitable obligations, which may have been included in the Bardi, but not the Peruzzi totals.

The final segment of the business shown in Figure 1 as reporting directly to the chairman is a collection of individual foreign loans or deposits controlled from Florence, called, for convenience, "special accounts." These include the Hospitalers' important account, a large deposit in Palermo, and accounts held by certain church dignitaries.

The company units discussed so far were all under the control of the office of the chairman. The management of the foreign branch system was more decentralized due to the sheer length of time required for coherent round-trip communication. The organization of the super-companies' sprawling branch systems must have been one of the most serious problems facing their managements, given the environment of primitive and often dangerous communications. To be sure, they developed excellent internal courier arrangements, as earlier attested by the prompt receipt in Florence of the news of

[22] Ibid. Surprisingly, the *limosina* charity fund was also charged with its share of company losses, like any other shareholder. For examples, see 119 and 319.
[23] Ibid., 30–1.
[24] Sapori, *Studia economica*, Vol. 2, 853.

Chairman Bonifazio's death in London. The Peruzzi spent over li.1,000 between 1335 and 1341 on the dispatch of correspondence and in one famous instance paid li.203 to charter a fast ship to send an urgent message to Rhodes.[25] Such provisions permitted some consultation with the head office in Florence on decisions of exceptional import to the company, but clearly, most commercial decisions had to be made on the spot by local managers. They would have been given the legal tools to do their job, that is, powers of attorney to bind the company.[26] At the same time, their freedom of action had to be circumscribed by firmly applied internal controls. Unfortunately, there is no evidence of the precise form of such controls, but it is inconceivable that a branch manager would have had the authority to take unlimited deposits or make unlimited loans.[27] At the very least, his power to obtain deposits from or lend money to individuals or institutions outside his territory would have required the concurrence of the Florence head office.

The presentation of the probable Peruzzi organization structure in neat chart form should not beguile the reader into viewing the super-companies in the simplistic terms of a modern business-school case study. As far as can be discerned, each of the super-companies had its own philosophy. For example, the Bardi Company, possibly by reason of its enormous size, appears to have been somewhat more decentralized than the others, carrying on a large and continuous business with the monarchies of England, Naples, Cyprus, and others from its local branches. Its approach was to put its ablest and most politically adroit people in such branches, giving them a fairly loose rein. For example, the head of the London branch for many years was Taldo Valori, who became a powerful political figure back in Florence in the 1330s.[28] And Francesco Pegolotti, the Bardi's highest-paid factor, was given a virtually free hand to negotiate arrangements with the rulers of Cyprus and Armenia.[29] The Buonaccorsi,

[25] *I libri*, 181. This long entry includes a collection of disparate expense items covering several years. The charter of the ship to Rhodes, which has drawn comments from Sapori, Fryde, and S. L. Peruzzi, will be discussed in detail in Chapter 7.

[26] De Roover, *Medici Bank*, 79. He notes that the Calimala guild statutes of 1332 specified that anyone, whether factor or partner, representing a trading company abroad had to be armed with a power of attorney.

[27] The need for prompt authorization for the stream of large loans necessitated by the business in England was an important reason for Bonifazio's decision to move to London.

[28] Passerini, "Genealogica," in an essay on Simone Peruzzi.

[29] Pegolotti, *La pratica*, xx–xxii.

although not quite a super-company, is of interest because it seems to have been very centralized for a large firm, having the reputation of employing inferior people and shifting them from branch to branch, especially between Naples and Avignon.[30]

With regard to the Peruzzi, it appears that the Florence management centralized policy but was prepared to decentralize *execution* within the constraints established by policy. As a result, each branch was operated pragmatically and, therefore, differently, depending on the character of the business and the personality of the branch manager. For the complex and lucrative branch of Naples, both policy and execution called for close coordination with Florence. The business was obviously of great importance and therefore deserving of attention. But equally important, as will be shown in subsequent chapters, was the close political connections between the kingdom and the commune which called for coordinated actions by the company in both centers. Moreover, reasonably rapid overland courier communication was possible, permitting relatively frequent consultation. At the other end of the spectrum was the English branch. Here, until 1336, judging from the company's actions, the policy was that the branch could carry on normal commerce but could engage in large-scale lending, especially to the monarchy, only with prior approval of Florence. It granted loans to ecclesiastical establishments, especially the Hospitalers, but the accounts were controlled in Florence even though the branch advanced the funds.[31] It acted as a deposit bank for Hugh Despenser the Younger and possibly other of Edward II's favorites, but otherwise steered clear of royal entanglements.[32] Between 1300 and 1321, its lending was limited to a trifling £900 sterling to Edward II and nothing at all to Edward I, putting it in the lowest rank of Italian merchants in this regard.[33] The Peruzzi had the resources to be a more aggressive lender in England, but policy seems to have dictated otherwise, possibly out of Tommaso's apprehension over the Ricciardi and Frescobaldi disasters, and possibly also for fear of prejudicing the company's important French business.[34]

There were two main types of branches, one headed by a share-

---

[30] Luzzati, *Villani e Buonaccorsi*, 71.

[31] The Hospitalers loans will be dealt with more fully in Chapters 4 and 5.

[32] Fryde, "Despenser."

[33] W. E. Rhodes, "The Italian Bankers in England and Their Loans to Edward I and Edward II," in *Historical Essays by Members of the Owens College,* ed. T. F. Tout and James Tait (London, 1902), 168. Two minor loans that were made in Edward II's reign after 1321 will be discussed in Chapter 5.

[34] As will be discussed in Chapters 5 and 7, the Peruzzi had strong connections and ambitions in France.

holder and one headed by a factor. The criteria for determining the level of manager assigned to the branch were clearly related more to the political demands of the post than to the economic importance of the business conducted by the branch. As can be seen in Figure 1, shareholders managed those branches where close, continuous, and diplomatic contact with the ruling elite was essential to the success of the business. There, the managers had to have the social status, social graces, intelligence, and authority in the company to deal with demanding prickly noblemen. Thus, we see shareholders managing the politically sensitive branches of Naples, Sicily, England, Avignon, Paris, and Bruges. We also see the downgrading of Paris to a factor-led branch after the death of Filippo di Pacino de' Peruzzi in May 1337 and the decision to enter the joint venture with the Bardi in England. The business had become low-level and low-profile. The Bruges branch was also relegated to management by a factor in 1336. In one sense this is curious, given the increased activity in that city regarding the financing of the English king. However, it is likely that the political aspects of the Bruges operation came under the chairman's office, especially after Bonifazio's presence in Flanders and London from March 1338.

The leadership of the English and Sicilian branches deserve additional comment. In England, the level of the managers changed with the fortunes of the branch. For several years in the 1320s, Bonifazio led the branch. At that time, he was neither shareholder nor factor, but as the son of Chairman Tommaso, he was clearly an important figure. But with the fall of Edward II, the Peruzzi connection with Despenser put the company in bad odor, and Bonifazio departed the country, leaving a factor as his proxy.[35] The Sicilian business was run from its inception in 1299 by Francesco Forzetti, a permanent resident. Whether he was originally a factor or whether he had some special status, he did not become a partner until 1331. It is worth noting that the branch had a series of loans outstanding to King Federigo III reported separately from the branch trading accounts and apparently under the control of Florence.[36]

Branches headed by factors were those where the presence of a high-status manager was not vital to the conduct of the business. The branches in Venice, Genoa, and Pisa dealt primarily in logistics and legal problems rather than buying and selling for the local market, and in any case were close enough to Florence to enable sensitive

---

[35] CPR E III 1327–30, 372.

[36] I libri, 195. Some peculiarities of these loans will be discussed in Chapters 4 and 5.

political problems to be handled from there. Barletta was a very large branch, but its business was essentially technical trading and logistics, best suited to the talents of a well-trained factor. Moreover, it was located away from the seat of power in Naples, where the shareholder-manager could look after all the company's political interests in the kingdom. The branch at Rhodes was also substantial and involved contact with ruling nobility, in this case the Knights Hospitalers. In its early start-up years, it was managed by a partner, Ruggeri di Lottieri Silimanni.[37] However, it was remote, its business was largely trading, and control of the very large loans and deposits rested in Florence. Nevertheless, it was important enough to warrant being run by some of the company's highest-paid employees. Cyprus, Majorca, Sardinia, and Tunis, being useful but relatively small and remote operations, did not warrant the attentions of a full-time shareholder-manager. In particular, although Cyprus was a significant market and entrepôt in the first half of the fourteenth century, the Peruzzi branch there was modest compared to that of the Bardi presence.[38] It was managed by a low-level employee, while the Bardi had Francesco Pegolotti, its highest-paid and most valued factor in charge for several years. In Genoa and the port of Chiarenza on the west coast of Greece the Peruzzi had what were described as branches, but with no resident manager. Chiarenza, which did not even seem to have a permanent factor, may have been run out of Naples, whose king bought the port in 1307.[39] Finally, there were important locations such as Ragusa, Constantinople, and Barcelona in which the companies' interests were represented only by independent agents.

The basic structure that emerges is about what should be expected of an enterprise of this size and type – a clear vertical line of quasi-autonomous units reporting to the office of the chairman, supplemented by horizontal connections among the units. Each of the companies in its own way would have adapted this structure to strike the balance between central control and local autonomy most suited to its needs. Rigid centralization requiring head office approval of all significant transactions would have made it impossible to operate in lucrative markets that happened to be distant and politically complex. Excessive decentralization, in contrast, would have placed the head office in the position of helplessly having to deal with faits

[37] Ibid., 439.

[38] Cyprus's role as an entrepôt owed much to the papal ban against direct trading with Alexandria and other Islamic ports. See Peter W. Edbury, *The Kingdom of Cyprus and the Crusades, 1191–1374* (Cambridge, 1991), 150–3.

[39] Peruzzi, *Storia commercio*, 318–20.

accomplis by local managers. The Ricciardi seem to have suffered from this problem in England, as did the Bardi and Peruzzi companies. But the fact that the super-companies flourished for so many years indicates that at least for a time, they had found a satisfactory balance.

Having adopted the branch system and having accepted varying degrees of decentralization, the most serious challenge facing the companies was the need to overcome the negative aspects of such an organization structure. The emergence of independent-minded satrapies was a serious threat, especially in locations where the branch manager was in constant contact with the ruling aristocracy and exercised the control over monopolies that had been granted to the company. Branch managers enjoyed personal privileges and money grants, which put considerable strain on their loyalty to the company's interests. For example, in England, the king promised substantial sums to the wives of Peruzzi managers there, and 500 marks to Bonifazio's daughter for her marriage, suggesting that even the chairman was not free from temptation.[40] At least two Bardi employees were granted significant parting gifts by the same king, implying that they had done a good job on his behalf.[41] We cannot be sure that the sums were actually paid to these individuals, but the existence of such promises indicates serious potential for conflict of interest.

With regard to factors, the most serious threat was outright corruption. Temptations abounded, and there is evidence that a few employees did succumb. In 1330, the company accused Silimanno Bottieri, a factor who had worked for sixteen years in Bruges and England, of defrauding the company of 5,000 florins out of the 50,000 he had managed.[42] In 1336, the Peruzzi Company had Iacopo di Tuccio Ferrucci seized and thrown into Florence's jail, the notorious Stinche, for having "made much damage to us while staying in Naples and Avignon."[43] And Bartolo Gherardini confessed on his deathbed in 1340 that he had embezzled a sum from the company.[44]

The Peruzzi Company recognized that these problems required continuous attention and used four principal means of dealing with them. The first was the maintenance of a strong control group at

[40] *CPR* E III 1338–40,195, 392. The sum of 500 marks was equivalent to about 2,250 florins. For perspective, the dowry given in the marriage of Giotto's daughter to settle the feud between the Peruzzi and Adimari families in 1312 was 1,800 florins, considered a very handsome sum.

[41] *CPR* E III 1340–43. 412 (200 marks to P. Bini) and 469 (£1,000 to Filippo Bardi).

[42] Davidsohn, *Firenze*, Vol. 6, 390.

[43] *I libri*, 107.

[44] Ibid., 96.

Florence headquarters. Unfortunately, we have no direct information on the composition of the "office of the chairman," which may well have been an informal group with changing membership. Nor is there any evidence of any formal delegations of authority to group executives. What is certain is that the chairman, even one as diligent as Tommaso, required a trusted support group to help him hold the reins of such a large diverse organization. One member of this group is likely to have been his brother Giotto, who was his treasurer for many years and who eventually succeeded him.[45] His sons Bonifazio and Pacino almost certainly worked for him at the center of operations in Florence, which made them acceptable to the shareholders as successor chairmen. Bonifazio also gained branch experience by serving in Avignon from 1319 to 1321 and in England during much of the 1320s, as did Pacino from 1322 to 1325 in Avignon and from 1334 to 1335 at the Bruges branch. In addition, there is abundant evidence from the 1335–43 accounts that several shareholders were actively engaged in monitoring the company's business, both in Florence and abroad. For example, between December 1336 and December 1338, Giovanni Soderini lived for ten months in England, made a trip to Paris, returned to Florence, and then stayed three months in Venice.[46] Baldo Orlandini traveled to Flanders and Brabant on behalf of the English branch in 1339, then worked in England from July 1339 to December 1341, when he returned to Florence.[47] Geri Soderini worked in Naples in 1336 and 1337, and his brother Ghuccio worked in Sicily from May to August 1338.[48] Donato di Pacino Peruzzi seemed to be a high-level troubleshooter in matters requiring good connections with the French court. In addition to his involvement in the Bruges claim discussed earlier, he participated in a very important Paris lawsuit as well as various affairs in Burgundy and Avignon.[49] In short, many of the shareholders and their sons were actively engaged in helping the chairman control the business.

The second important key to the proper functioning of this organization structure was staffing, which was kept strictly under the control of the Florence office. All branch employees were carefully selected Italians, usually trained in Florence and given tours of duty at the home office and various foreign locations.[50] Professor Sapori has

---

[45] Ibid., the *libro segreto di Giotto*, 419–512. [46] Ibid., 254–5.

[47] Ibid., 259. [48] Ibid., 249–50.

[49] Ibid., 251–2.

[50] All companies attached great importance to the selection and control of employees. See, e.g., de Roover, "Alberti Company," 49–50. But misconduct occurred nonetheless, as noted earlier.

prepared a useful analysis of 133 factors who worked for the Peruzzi Company from 1331 to 1343 drawn from the Peruzzi account books.[51] Of this number, 14 were from the Peruzzi family and 9 were from the families of other shareholders, altogether slightly over 17 percent of the total. The vast majority of factors were outsiders, including a host of impressive family names – Strozzi, del Bene, Guicciardini, Alberti, but notably no Bardi nor Acciaiuoli. Attractive remuneration was obviously of vital importance in luring quality employees and sustaining their loyalty, and the salary information available for 110 of the factors shows that, for the most part, they were well paid. Table 2 gives the number of factors in each salary range. This is an approximation because the data cover a twelve-year period (the information being too fragmentary to be useful for any single point in time), and salaries of course increase over time through seniority and promotion. The table shows the highest-attained salary of each individual, giving the data an upward bias but permitting a satisfactory generalization of the range of factor salaries.

One advantage in showing the highest-attained salary is that it indicates the level to which an ambitious young Florentine white-collar worker might aspire – somewhere between li.100 and li.150 per year, a very handsome income.[52] It should be noted that all salary figures reported here are in *lire a fiorino*, the unit of account used in the bookkeeping of the super-companies and should not be confused with the lire di denari piccioli, the unit in which most living expenses are measured. The relationship of the lira a piccioli to the *lira a fiorino* varied over time, as can be derived from Table A7, ranging from 1.72 to 2.28 between 1300 and 1340.[53] In 1338, the *lira a fiorino* was equivalent to over 2 lire a piccioli. The salaries shown here should therefore be doubled before comparing them with living costs cited by most economic historians.[54] The highest-paid individual earned li.290, giving him parity with the salary the Bardi paid the famous Pegolotti

---

[51] Sapori, *Storia economica*, Vol. 2, 718–29.

[52] De Roover, "Alberti Company," 24–6, notes that the highest-paid employees (li.200+) "could afford a large house, one or two servants, and a horse or mule in the stable." He also reports that Bardi and Peruzzi salaries were significantly higher than those of the Alberti and most other companies.

[53] This relationship is derived by dividing the soldi figures in Table 2 by 29, the number of *soldi a fiorino* per florin.

[54] For examples of Florentine data expressed in lire a piccioli, see Charles M. de La Roncière, *Prix et salaires à Florence au xivᵉ siècle, 1280–1380* (Rome, 1984), or Henderson, "Piety and Charity." The multitude of figures reported by Henderson, including citations from archival sources and de La Roncière's many works, are reported in lire a piccioli.

Table 2. *Salary ranges of Peruzzi Company factors, 1331-43*

Annual Salary lire a fiorino	Non-Peruzzi	Peruzzi	Total
Below 60	27	1	28
60-79	15	7	22
80-99	7	–	7
100-119	17	3	20
120-149	18	1	19
150-199	5	–	5
200+	9	–	9
Total	98	12	110

referred to earlier. The salaries of Peruzzi family members, clustering at the lower end of the scale, suggest that the company did not offer sinecures, at least highly paid ones, to its kinfolk.

In addition to salary, a factor might earn a bonus under special circumstances: for example, Giovanni Bonducci was granted li.40 given "of our good will" for well representing the company in Puglia.[55] The manner in which factors were paid, especially those on foreign assignment, was to provide advances for all their living expenses, while their salaries were accrued in another account. This was a perfectly logical practice, enabling the branch to fund factors in local currency while keeping their actual salaries confidential and under the control of the central office. What is curious is that each account could carry on for years, running to extraordinary size, including accrued interest, euphemistically described as *dono di tenpo,* before being settled, suggesting a breakdown in accounting procedures.[56]

Although most, if not all shareholders, along with several sons of shareholders, worked actively for the company, none received any apparent remuneration other than their pro rata share of profit. The repeated use of the phrase *dono* or *donamento di tenpo* has confused some historians into deducing that the company was compensating partners for time devoted to the business. Even as astute a business historian as Raymond de Roover fell into this error, incorrectly citing a credit as a salary equivalent that on close examination was sim-

[55] *I libri*, 304.
[56] Ibid., 303–18. An analysis of the interest credits in the salary accounts shows that salary was considered due at the end of each year, so that interest at 7% was calculated from the beginning of the following year.

ply another of the many euphemisms for interest.[57] There is no evidence anywhere in the accounts of salary compensation to shareholders; the single example cited by de Roover is questionable.[58] Such compensation might have been paid by the branches, but this is highly unlikely in a firm that controlled all other salaries, domestic and foreign, in Florence. But if all were contributing effort, possibly rough justice was served by only the pro rata profit distribution. Other companies sometimes apportioned their profit allocations to recognize the "industry" of certain partners, but there is no evidence of such practice by the Peruzzi. Shareholders did, however, have ready access to company cash, goods, and services through expense advances for personal as well as company needs. Each had what amounted to a running tab on the company's books in which were logged advances of cash, cloth, grain, or horses and other livestock for reimbursement of travel and living expense on company business, but also for such obviously personal outlays such as acquisition of property, payment of dowries, luxury items, taxes, and funeral expenses. As noted in Chapter 1, even the Baroncelli Chapel in the Santa Croce was financed through the company. In another instance, the company paid 60 florins to bring a certain *mastro* Alberto from Bologna to treat Bonifazio for a malady of the throat.[59] A useful way to demonstrate

---

[57] De Roover, *Medici Bank*, 80. He cites Donato di Giotto as a good example of "time and efforts" compensation during the period December 9, 1332, to June 30, 1335, from 160 (actually 260) of *I libri*. The entry concerns not Donato, however, but his son Giottino, a factor who earned a salary of li.160 s16 d8 for the period. Giottino was also awarded *donamento di tenpo* of li.115 up to July 1, 1343. This is interest at the standard rate of 7% per annum, which when compounded for the eight years equals 71.8%; applied to the unpaid salary, this yields exactly the li.115. The *donamento di tenpo* is simply an acknowledgment of delinquent payment, of which there are many examples in the salary accounts, all of which test out arithmetically as interest at 7% per year. The application of interest is evenhanded, as it is also charged on the accumulation of expense advances. Elsewhere, de Roover describes *dono del tempo* as salary (*Money, Banking and Credit in Medieval Bruges* [Cambridge, MA, 1948], 32) and the interest liability as "bonus" (44nn 28, 29).

[58] De Roover, "Luca Pacioli," 129, cites salary awarded to Pacino di Tommaso Peruzzi for his service in Bruges in 1334–5 (*I libri*, 378) as evidence of a stipend to a branch manager-partner. But it is unlikely that Pacino was a partner at that time. The entry cited was one of a group of salary adjustments to five of the late Tommaso's sons, four of whom never became partners. The name of Bonifazio, Tommaso's senior scn and heir, is conspicuous by its absence. And the branch manager of Bruges was a different Pacino, Pacino di Guido. See n62, this chapter, for further comments.

[59] *I libri*, 261.

the flavor of these accounts is to present a rough translation of an entry made in the account of one of the shareholders:

> And debit Donato . . . li.439 s13 d5. . . . . The said moneys were taken and posted to his account from July 1, 1338 to July 1, 1339: li.8 s5 d4 we gave for him to Bettone Cini and Company, tax collectors, for the tax on his own possessions for the years 1337 and 1338; and li.76 s5 d1 for house expenses and two bales of flax that had come to him from Naples and for amber prayer beads and capers that came to him from Venice and to reclothe his bastard son Tommasino in Pisa where he had been ill; and li.61 s17 d3 for bolts of cloth taken from our warehouse for clothing for himself and his family in that year; and li.224 s8 d9 for 28 ounces 15 teri of silver carlins converted at li.7 s17 d6 per ounce that Ruberto de' Peruzzi and our Naples company paid . . . for the needs of Francesco, son of the said Donato; and li.68 s17 for 9 ounces of silver carlins converted at li.7 s13 per ounce, which our above-mentioned company of Naples gave for him to Puccio Duti of Florence. . . . And they add up in total to the above sum.[60]

This was not an unusual or exceptionally lengthy entry. Conversely the shareholders and sons made deposits to their accounts in the form of cash, goods, and property. To the balances the company meticulously applied interest at the usual 7 percent per annum. In most cases, it is possible to work out the interest calculation precisely, but in some instances the numbers cannot be traced satisfactorily because the amounts to which interest is applied are accumulations over time.

The system described here confirms the comment made earlier that the affairs of the company and its shareholders were very much

---

[60] Ibid., 253. "E dè dare Donato . . . lbr.439 s.13 d.5. . . . I detti danari a presi e sono posti a sua ragione da kalen luglio anno 1338 a kalen luglio 1339: le lbr.8 s.5 d.4 a fior. demmo per lui a Bettone Cini e compangni ghabellieri per la ghabella delle posesioni sue per l'anno 1337 e per l'anno 1338; e lle lbr.76 s.5 d.1 a fior. tra per spese di chasa in Firenze per due balle di lino che gli venneno da Napoli e per paternostri d'anbra e chapperi che gli venneno di Vinegia e per rivestire a Pisa Tommasino suo figliuolo bastardo ch'era la malato; e lle lbr.61 s.17 d.3 a fior. per panni avuti dal fondacho nostro per vestire di lui e di sua famiglia in dett'anno; e lle lbr.224 s.8 d.9 a fior. per once 28 teri 15 di carlini d'argento, a ragione di lbr.7 s.17 d.6 a fior. l'oncia, che Ruberto de' Peruzzi e compangni nostri di Napoli pagharono per lui . . . per bisongnie di Francescho figluolo del detto Donato; e lle lbr.68 s.17 a fior. sono per once 9 di carlini d'argento 60 per oncia, a ragione di lbr.7 s.13 a fior. l'oncia, che'detti nostri compangni di Napoli dierono per lui a Puccio Duti di Firenze. . . . E montano in tutto la sopradetta somma."

intermingled. But the data also indicate that a shareholder facing the risk, family disruption, and expense of a foreign posting received no more compensation than a shareholder who remained in Florence. This is unreal and provokes the question of whether the shareholder accounts in *I libri* represent normal practice or whether they reflect changes made by the auditors of the bankruptcy court to maximize assets available to the firm's creditors. This and other anomalies will be discussed more fully in Chapters 4 and 9.

From the Peruzzi accounts it is clear that there was a sharp distinction between factors and managing shareholders, countering any notion that in the big companies a young man would join as an apprentice factor, work his way through the ranks, and become a partner or even chairman one day.[61] The evidence from the Peruzzi Company, with one exception, is once a factor, always a factor.[62] The genealogical tables in Figures A2 and A3 identify the Peruzzi factors and show that often factors were sons or brothers, and even heirs, of family shareholders but never attained that rank. The relatively small number of employees from the large shareholder families is surprising, given the propensity in family oriented cultures to provide "jobs for the boys," and suggests that management and employee positions were filled on the basis of qualifications rather than patronage or social status. Another employment criterion appears to have been that a factor must not be a member of the family controlling another super-company. As noted earlier, no members of the Bardi, Acciaiuoli, or Buonaccorsi families were on the Peruzzi payroll.[63] Furthermore, in the list of 346 employees of the Bardi Company between 1310 and 1345, there were no Peruzzi, Acciaiuoli, or Buonaccorsi.[64] Thus, although these firms often collaborated to exploit markets, they were indeed competitors who jealously guarded their proprietary information.

[61] Although there may have been exceptions (see later this chapter), they were rare. De Roover, *Medici Bank*, 80 confirms this, as does Sapori, *Storia economica*, Vol. 2, 704. In the case of the Bardi, 5 out of 346 factors rose to partner status between 1310 and 1345, but four of the promotions occurred in 1320, suggesting an exceptional deviation from normal policy.

[62] The possible exception is Pacino di Tommaso de' Peruzzi, who was credited with a salary while working in Bruges in 1334–5 (*I libri*, 378), which strongly indicates that he had been a factor. But Sapori does not include him in his list of factors. Francesco Forzetti was not an exception. He was a special case, a long-term resident branch manager who, before he became a partner in 1331, was probably compensated by commision because there is no evidence that he was ever paid a salary.

[63] Sapori, *Storia economica*, Vol. 2, 718–29.

[64] Ibid., 730–54.

Table 3. *Deployment of Peruzzi Company factors – outsiders and family members*

| | July 1335 | | | 1331-43 | | |
	Non-Peruzzi	Peruzzi	Total	Non-Peruzzi	Peruzzi	Total
England	3	2	5	21	6	27
France	4	—	4	7	—	7
Avignon	2	2	4	8	4	12
Flanders	3	1	4	15	3	18
Naples	5	1	6	13	4	17
Sicily	6	—	6	9	—	9
Barletta	5	—	5	12	1	13
Other[a]	13	1	14	30	3	33
Total	41	7	48	115	21	136
Florence	39	1	40	[b]	[b]	[b]
Grand Total	80	8	88	NMF	NMF	NMF

[a] Rhodes, Majorca, Sardinia, Cyprus, Tunisia, Pisa, Venice.
[b] Not possible to quantify, but most factors spent some time in Florence during this period, resulting in no meaningful figure (NMF) for the grand total.

The third means of control was rotation of personnel from location to location, including sojourns in Florence, to keep them from becoming too closely associated with local interests. From the Sapori data we learn that 98 out of the 133 factors, and all Peruzzi family member factors, worked in at least one foreign location between 1331 and 1343. We also discover where they worked, which helps give a rough sense of the size of each branch. These data are presented in two ways in Table 3 – estimated factors on hand July 1, 1335, and factors employed over the 1331–43 period. Both are approximations, but close ones. The former is probably slightly understated because specific dates are not always clear. In the latter presentation the totals are higher than the number of factors involved because the data give all the "transfers in" to each branch over the twelve-year period, without subtracting the "transfers out." Also, the branch numbers are affected by differing rates of turnover. Despite these limitations, the additional presentation gives a sense of the intensity of activity in each branch over a period rather than a static situation at only one point in time. Note how "busy" England, Naples, and Avignon are compared with France and Sicily.

Staffing decisions in the branches required a delicate balance of assigning a long enough tour of duty in any location so that the factor would be knowledgeable and effective in the local market, but not so long that he became too enmeshed with local society. Factors of proven loyalty might be left for extended periods in branches where their expertise was vital to the business, but even as trusted an employee as the Bardi's Pegolotti was given a number of different assignments. Managing partners, on the other hand, were not deliberately rotated. Their loyalty was reinforced by occasional sojourns at Florence headquarters as evidenced by travel expense entries such as "spese del camino a venirsene a firenze" (travel expense to Florence) for Francesco Forzetti, the long-serving branch manager of Sicily in 1337.[65] In addition, numerous visits were made by shareholders to the main branches as shown earlier.

A smoothly functioning central office, quality staffing, and rotation of personnel all contributed to the cohesiveness of the company, but the fourth and most important means of holding the company together was the dedicated, tenacious attention of the chairman. Raymond de Roover has aptly underscored the significance of central management control, especially of foreign branches in an age of slow communication, citing the Alberti Company and Francesco Datini as examples of successful "stern and difficult" employers.[66] In contrast, he attributed the downfall of the Medici Bank largely to the relaxed grip of Francesco Sassetti, the general manager for an underinvolved Lorenzo de' Medici.

The Peruzzi Company was very fortunate in having two very able, single-minded chairmen over a period of more than forty years. The talented and enterprising Filippo dominated the company from its inception until his death in 1303. His successor, Tommaso, was characterized by Sapori as a strong, prestigious governor, of great honesty and ability during his uninterrupted tenure from 1303 to 1331.[67] Filippo built the company structure and Tommaso maintained it rigorously, but after Tommaso's death in 1331, the tight central control weakened. Giotto became chairman in the early to mid-1330s, when he was already an old man distracted by family and political priorities. The company was losing money, but it was years before anyone knew how much. At around the same time, the company was losing a large reservoir of senior-level experience, as Amideo, Filippo, Ridolfo, and Guido de' Peruzzi all died in the mid-1330s, along with Tano

[65] *I libri*, 248, 253.
[66] De Roover, "Alberti Company," 49–50.
[67] Sapori, *Storia economica*, Vol. 2, 681.

and Gherardo Baroncelli and Geri Soderini. In addition, three outside shareholders of long standing – Catellino di Manghia degli
Infanghati, Gherardo di Gentile Bonaccorsi, and Piero di Bernardo
Ubaldini – dropped out at the closing of the 1331–5 company, possibly indicating worsening conditions and loss of confidence in the
company's ability to deal with them. Bonifazio's brief stewardship, as
already noted, was marked by his long absence in England, further
eroding central control. It should be noted, however, that the *structure* remained intact, as Giovanni Baroncelli remained as manager of
the English branch. Bonifazio had merely changed the locus of his
office from mainstream Florence to peripheral London.

Raymond de Roover has made the point that one of the drawbacks
of the multiple partnership system of the fourteenth-century companies was that "in case of losses or difficulties, quarrels among partners about policy and appropriate remedies were likely to make matters worse instead of better." He went on to say, "Discord of this kind
. . . may have played a part in causing the collapse of the Bardi and
Peruzzi companies by alarming the depositors at a critical juncture."[68]
Discord was certainly possible after 1335 and even probable during
Bonifazio's extended absence in England. Although direct evidence
is lacking, the departure in 1335 of three outside shareholders could
be construed as indirect evidence of conflict. As a point of interest,
de Roover and Sapori have drawn attention to the fact that outside
partners had acquired the majority of the shares in 1331, implying
that the Peruzzi family had lost control of the business.[69] With the
withdrawal of the three outside shareholders and the addition of the
heirs of Ridolfo di Donato, however, the Peruzzi family was almost
certainly again in the majority from 1335 onward. Possibly this indicates a rallying of the Peruzzi clan to the aid of the company, but it
could also indicate failure to recruit additional outside shareholdings.
The Peruzzi majority could also explain the prompt election of Pacino
to the chairmanship immediately after the news of Bonifazio's death
reached Florence.[70]

A word should be said about the number of people involved in the
company's operations. In total, there were many more than normally
indicated by historians. Table 4, based only on the evidence of the
accounts, shows the number of people effectively working for the
company in July 1335.

[68] De Roover, *Medici Bank*, 78.
[69] Ibid., 78; Sapori, *Storia economica*, Vol. 2, 678. But as is made clear in Chapter 6,
  this volume, effective control remained firmly in the hands of the Peruzzi.
[70] *I libri*, 1.

Table 4. *Personnel effectively working for the Peruzzi Company, 1335*

	No. of people
Shareholders	21
Shareholder sons	8
Factors related to shareholders	18
Unrelated factors	70
Drapperia "partners"	2
Total	119

In modern terms, this is a small number for a business organization, but bearing in mind that these were mostly "white-collar" personnel, it represented a very large establishment by medieval standards. For perspective, the largest single bureaucracy of the period was the papal court at Avignon; excluding the guards, ceremonial officers, and palace staff, the total number of personnel is estimated at around 250.[71]

What did all these people do? Of course, many of them were engaged directly in doing the company's business – overseeing the manufacturing and movement of goods, trading, banking, and preparing the transactional paperwork. As shown in Chapter 1, the shareholders and their sons also often held official positions with the Florence Commune, which indirectly impinged upon the business. But a large number were involved in seeing to the proper function of the company's internal controls. The surviving Peruzzi Company accounts, running to 390 printed pages, are literally the tip of the iceberg. The task of painstakingly recording thousands of transactions, logging them in the books of original entry, analyzing them, and ensuring follow-up kept many of these people busy both in Florence and in the branches. Letter writing also occupied the senior members of management, who spent over li.1,000 between 1335 and 1341 on dispatching correspondence. To illustrate the magnitude of the recording function, the reported purchases of materials between 1335 and 1341 included seventy-eight reams of paper, eleven account books

[71] Yves Renouard, *The Avignon Papacy: 1305–1403* (Hamden, CT, 1970), 83–7. Renouard calculated the total staff at the papal court including the cardinals (but not their retinues) at about 500. This total comprised 200 guards and ceremonial officers and probably 50 palace staff serving in the kitchen, pantry, buttery, stables, and almonry.

identified by different colored covers (white, black, red, yellow, orange, and green), one book of income and expense, one assets book, and seven notebooks for memoranda and writing letters.[72]

Aside from the company personnel already listed, there was an unknown but significant number of people who were dependent on the company for at least part of their livelihood. In Florence these included carters and "putting-out" system workers engaged in the manufacture of cloth, such as carders, spinners, weavers, fullers, and dyers.[73] Abroad, people employed by the company included marine shippers, overland carters, correspondents, and innkeepers (*oste*). Many of these people would have worked regularly with the same company, which tended to do repeat business with the same contractors of proven reliability. The innkeepers were in a special category, usually working regularly with the same one or two companies; for example, the Peruzzi and Alberti employed the same *oste* at Nice.[74] The innkeepers did much more than supply food and lodging for men and horses. They offered temporary warehousing and porter services along the trade routes, and the Peruzzi used them in places such as Libourne and Montpellier on the wool route through southern France described in Chapter 2. The innkeepers also assisted factors accompanying the trade goods with formalities required by local authorities and advanced funds to such factors and to couriers.[75]

Historians have tended to focus more on the commercial functions of factors, agents, and correspondents in foreign locations than on the responsibilities of the branch managers. It has already been established that the most important Peruzzi branches were headed by partners and that their role was political and diplomatic, as well as commercial. In effect, they represented the company at the courts of Naples, Sicily, Paris, London, Flanders, and Avignon, often assisting the rulers in their administration. Donato di Giotto de' Peruzzi, branch manager at Naples, was well connected in that court, as were the heads of the branches of other super-companies.[76] In Flanders, as we have seen, Donato di Pacino served as Count Louis' general receiver between 1326 and 1329.[77] At Avignon, much of the manager's effort was directed toward seeking papal influence to secure favors,

---

[72] *I libri*, 181.
[73] The Peruzzi Company did have in its direct employ, however, one stable hand, as well as the shearer mentioned earlier.
[74] Renouard, *Les relations*, 52.
[75] *I libri*, 72, 74, 127.
[76] Yver, *Le commerce*, 326.
[77] Ellen Kittell, *From* Ad Hoc *to Routine* (Philadelphia, 1991), 142, 207.

redress injustices, or pursue delinquent clerics.[78] And in England, as is well known, the company's business from 1337 onward was predominantly government related. Thus, the success of the company overall depended to a large extent on the skill of the shareholder branch managers in obtaining trading and banking privileges at an acceptable cost.

As has been demonstrated here, the organization and control systems of these large diverse businesses were sophisticated and, by and large, effective. The super-companies were successful for a considerable length of time because they operated under a coherent set of principles directed from the center by a strong-willed chairman who was supported by intelligent working associates, along with competent and loyal employees both in Florence and abroad. The system, however, was fragile, because in an environment of volatile politics and poor communications, it demanded a degree of consistent excellence that could not be sustained indefinitely. The system also had a price, as the controls required a significant number of people engaged in unproductive paperwork and communications, which constitued a substantial overhead burden not faced by smaller enterprises.

The use of the word "unproductive" in association with paperwork is not meant to be disparaging, but merely descriptive of effort that does not directly contribute added value. Well-designed and executed paperwork was, as de Roover has aptly pointed out, an essential adaptation to the changes in business organization.[79] Because medieval accounting has been the subject of so much controversy, the following chapter will be devoted to a detailed description and analysis of the Peruzzi accounts, which will illuminate both their surprising sophistication and their limitations.

[78] Renouard, *Les relations*, 105.
[79] De Roover, *Medieval Bruges*, 13.

4

The accounting of the Peruzzi Company

The Peruzzi Company has often been cited in the long-standing controversy over the origin of double-entry accounting, and because of this it is worthwhile to digress briefly to review medieval bookkeeping systems and their relevance to the business world in which the Peruzzi and other companies operated. This review will not attempt to deal with the arcane arguments of Weber, Sombart, Schumpeter, et al. regarding the role of systematic bookkeeping in defining profit and depersonalizing business, thereby creating the essential ingredients of capitalism.[1] These concepts not only are outside the scope of this study, but also relate to developments largely beyond the era of the super-companies. Nor will it delve into disputes, such as that between Lane and Yamey, over the influence of double-entry accounting on the transition of merchant-entrepreneurs from an itinerant to a sedentary mode of operation.[2] The super-companies were rooted firmly in Florence as far back as can be determined and do not appear to have passed through an itinerant phase. Yet, although the

---

[1] For a discussion of these theories and a guide to further reading on them, see Basil S. Yamey, "Scientific Bookkeeping and the Rise of Capitalism," *Economic History Review* 2 series 1 (1949): 99–113; and J. R. Edwards, *A History of Financial Accounting* (London, 1989), 59–63.

[2] Basil S. Yamey, "Notes on Double-Entry Bookkeeping and Economic Progress," *Journal of Economic History* 35 (Winter 1975): 717–23, and Frederic C. Lane, "Double Entry Bookkeeping and Resident Merchants," *Journal of European Economic History* 6 (1977): 177–91. In essence, Yamey argued that double-entry accounting made no contribution at all to the resident merchant's control over the activities of distant factors, agents, or partners. Lane allowed that Sombart had exaggerated the role of double-entry accounting in the emergence of capitalism, but he maintained that this new form of bookkeeping did play an important part in the "revolution" in commercial practices in the thirteenth and fourteenth centuries. The Yamey article is perhaps too abrupt in dismissing the double-entry contribution outright; Italian businessmen would not have developed it if it had had so little value. But Yamey in his many other commentaries has served us well by consistently puncturing the mystique around which economic historians in the past have tended to wrap a simple record-keeping system.

importance of evolving accounting systems may have been exaggerated by some authors, the invention of a number of new techniques did take place in the period of the super-companies and undeniably helped them evaluate and control their businesses.

Early in their histories, before the companies grew large enough to need a comprehensive system for accounting, they would have already encountered single-entry bookkeeping, also known as charge and discharge or stewardship accounting. Feudal manors and governments registered income, expense, and the settlement of obligations, sometimes in narrative form with figure references, sometimes in separate lines for each category, and sometimes in separate lines with figures in columns.[3] Merchants used single entry in managing individual ventures and were faced regularly with the system in their many transactions with various governments. Although rudimentary, this form of accounting had the virtue of providing the basis for rational decisions at lowest cost, given the needs of such institutions at the time. It did not provide profit measurement routinely (although it could do so on an ad hoc basis, especially in merchant ventures), and it did not distinguish between capital and revenue. Most important, it made the concealment of fraud easy, resulting in the need for frequent audits. Governments continued to use the charge and discharge method long after the Italian companies moved toward double entry with the result that audits were a continuing feature of the relations between the Bardi and Peruzzi and government treasurers, especially those of the English monarchy.[4]

For companies, the charge and discharge method broke down when trading activity began to entail numerous complex transactions in numerous locations, creating disorder and loss of control. The concept of double entry evolved slowly as one of the means of meeting the problems of expanded international business. This evolution may have begun when Italian accountants noticed that receipt of cash from a debtor resulted in two entries, a discharge in the record of the debtor and a charge in the record of the cashier, prompting the establishment of crossreferences.[5] By 1300, the prefixes *dove avere* and *dove dare* were used to distinguish positive entries (cash receipts) from negative entries (cash payments). One advantage to companies of the evolving double-entry method over single entry was the greater care and accuracy it demanded of the clerks, fostered in part by the arithmetic check that arose from periodic balancing, which increased the difficulty of falsifying records. Another was that the new system

---

[3] Edwards, *History of Accounting*, 35–41.
[4] To be discussed in detail in Chapters 7 and 8.
[5] Edwards, *History of Accounting*, 50–1.

made it easier to divide accounting duties safely among a number of people as the business expanded. But the primary value of double entry to the *management* of the business was its role as an *aide memoire* and as a much improved system of control. It had no advantage, then, as now, over single entry as an aid in assessing the merits of a business proposition.

Double entry is defined in Webster as "a method or system of bookkeeping that recognizes both the receiving and giving sides of a business transaction by debiting the amount of the transaction to one account and crediting it to another account, the total debits in the system always equaling the total credits." On the basis of this simple definition, it can be said that the Peruzzi Company employed this method. But accounting historians are much more demanding in setting qualifications for double-entry status. Melis and others, finding business and household transactions jumbled together in medieval accounts, insisted that they be separated to qualify as double-entry systems, describing some of them as "lame" double entry because of their failure to meet this standard.[6] But mingling business and private affairs has nothing to do with accounting systems and everything to do with the predilections of the owners and managers. Even today there is no shortage of examples of such mingling in the accounts not only of closely held companies, but also of public corporations.[7] Other scholars have stressed the importance of separating capital from revenue accounting, striking trial balances, producing balance sheets, making columnar presentations, and so on. De Roover listed three criteria for double entry – (1) each transaction must be recorded twice so that the books will balance; (2) the accounts must be complete; and (3) they must lead up to a comprehensive financial statement showing assets and liabilities and profit and loss.[8] Given these restrictions, most scholars involved in the subject have concluded that the Peruzzi accounting system, while complex and sophisticated, fell somewhat short of double-entry technique.[9]

[6] Lane, "Double Entry Bookkeeping," 187.
[7] The savings and loan scandal of the late 1980s revealed countless cases of company assets appropriated by owners and associates. Occidental Petroleum financed and provided operating funds for a museum to house chairman Armand Hammer's art collection. For examples of company managers making personal use of company assets, see B. Burrough and J. Helyar, *Barbarians at the Gate* (New York, 1990), an account of the takeover of the RJR/Nabisco Corporation.
[8] Raymond de Roover, "The Organization of Trade," in *Cambridge Economic History*, Vol. 3 (Cambridge, 1956), 92.
[9] See De Roover, "Luca Pacioli," 114–74; Richard Brown, ed., *History of Accounting and Accountants* (1905; London, 1968); Federigo Melis, *Storia della ragioneria* (Bologna, 1950), Part III, Chaps. 3 and 4.

A careful analysis of the surviving Peruzzi books by and large confirms these conclusions, but whether or not the system qualified completely as double entry is of little significance and was certainly unimportant to the Peruzzi Company's owner-managers. While it lacked some of the necessary refinements, it definitely was not single entry, as it used debits, credits, and multiple crossreferences throughout. Moreover, as we shall see, it produced a set of balances from which a comprehensive balance sheet might have been discernible, had the surviving documents been those of a going concern rather than of a failed company in bankruptcy court. In any case, the system satisfied the needs of the company's owners for a considerable number of years. The main weakness in its design was the substantial continuing effort and organization required to keep it functioning effectively, so that when this effort began to flag, the control began to crumble.

Along with a coherent system of bookkeeping, the companies needed qualified personnel trained in arithmetic to cope with the enormous number of complex calculations involved in a large business dealing in multiple currencies. Adding to the complexity is the fact that all figures were required to be reported in roman numerals, a mathematically cumbersome system, although the more supple arabic system was well known and understood.[10] One solution to this problem was an ancient device, the abacus, a counting board of squares and columns, on which computations could be made based on the roman system, using *quarteruoli* or counters of various sizes, shapes, and colors.[11] Another was to make calculations in arabic, but post the results in the books in roman numerals. Either solution was possible, because students of commerce were trained both in the abacus and the arabic system.

Young students preparing for a career in commerce received train-

[10] The acceptance of arabic numerals, then called *algorismus*, in record keeping was slow due to their perceived susceptibility to fraud by adding, removing, or changing a single figure (Edwards, *History of Accounting*, 47). Arabic numerals were specifically prohibited for use in account books in the 1299 statutes of the Arte del Cambio in Florence. See W. Van Egmond, "The Commercial Revolution and the Beginnings of Western Mathematics in Renaissance Florence, 1300–1500" (Ph.D. diss., Indiana University, and University Microfilms, Ann Arbor, MI, 1976), 320–1.

[11] Frank J. Swetz, *Capitalism and Arithmetic: The New Math of the 15th Century* (La Salle, IL, 1987), 29, asserts that the abacus mathematics used the Roman system. See also 29–33 for a brief history of the evolution of the abacus in medieval Europe. Sapori, *Storia economica*, Vol. 1, 74–8, provides useful details of the layout of the abacus and the use of the counters, drawing upon examples from the Bardi Company.

ing in mathematics from private tutors or, more likely, after 1300 in the so-called abacus schools (*scuole d'abbaco*).[12] Such schools taught not only the use of the abacus, as their name suggests, but all kinds of computational skills needed in the practical business world and, in particular, the system of arabic numerals.[13] By the 1330s, according to Villani, there were six schools in the city teaching the abacus and algorism (the arabic system) to 1,000 to 1,200 children.[14] The teaching methodology was one of practical problem solving, establishing rules for specific problems that could be applied to similar problems, rather than examining the logical foundations of the problems and their solutions.[15] In other words, the approach was "learn the answers to the problems, not why the methods are true," emphasizing learning by rote and developing a retentive memory. The brighter graduates from such schools might then become apprenticed to a super-company such as the Peruzzi and trained in the intricacies of that company's specific accounting system.

The Peruzzi system was unquestionably complex. Although only two of the important books, the Sixth Assets Book and the Sixth Secret Book, have survived, they contain numerous entries from subsidiary books, which reveal an enormous accounting undertaking. Unfortunately, aside from the Book of Bad Debtors, all of the missing books have singularly uninformative titles, determined by the size of the book or the color of its cover. Thus, it is tantalizingly difficult to divine the specific purpose of each of them, requiring careful examination of the postings to seek clues as to their nature.

Some generalizations can be made about these lost books. According to the page numbers in the postings, they were large, running to several hundred pages, in one case as many as six hundred. They are also numbered consecutively, apparently as they were filled up, but from what starting point is unclear. The latest White Book was the eighteenth, the Red Book the eleventh, while the Orange Book was still on the first. In contrast, the two surviving main books were numbered in accordance with the company concerned, starting with the

[12] Van Egmond, "Western Mathematics," 72. The earliest documents indicating the existence of abacus schools, one in Florence and one in Milan, are dated 1316, but their content makes it clear that the schools had been in operation for some time. Van Egmond places their origin at around 1300. See also P. F. Grendler, *Schooling in Renaissance Florence* (Baltimore, 1989), 6–11.
[13] Richard A. Goldthwaite, "Schools and Teachers of Commercial Arithmetic in Renaissance Florence," *Journal of European Economic History* 1 (1972): 419.
[14] Villani, *Storia*, Book XI, Chap. 93.
[15] Van Egmond, "Western Mathematics," 234.

1300 company. Thus, the Fifth Assets Book deals with the 1331–5 company and the Sixth Assets Book with the 1335–43 firm.[16] This book-numbering system suggests that the subsidiary accounts were continuous and corporate, whereas the main Assets and Secret Books were periodic, that is, specific to each partnership.

The accounting period by which records were kept was not the calendar year, which at that time in Florence commenced on March 25, but a fiscal year that began on dates suited to the company's convenience. That convenience must have changed over time, because the earliest company in 1292 started its year on May 1, while those from 1300 through 1324 opened on November 1, and the last two companies commenced on July 1. The Bardi Company, in contrast, consistently started its year on July 1 at least as far back as 1318. The cause of these changes is obscure, but they suggest changes in the nature of the business, because companies typically close their accounting years at an appropriate point between the end of an active period and the beginning of a slack one, when inventories are low and there is opportunity to "take stock" in every sense of the term.[17] Possibly the November date was influenced by the completion of the harvest, while July may have been appropriate for the wool trade, or even because it marked the onset of the summer doldrums, but these can only be speculations. In any event, coincidence with an "official" new year's day was unimportant, because throughout the territory served by the company there was a variety of such dates, including January 1, March 25, Easter, July 15, September 1, and Christmas Day.

Among the subsidiary books, the easiest to discern are the Libro Grande and the Red Book. The former was the merchandise trade register that was the source of the balances in the foreign branches, reflecting accounts payable by the branch and good receivables from debtors. Bad debts were taken over by the Florence office for follow up and attempted collection, including the use of lawsuits where appropriate. Curiously, there is no report of merchandise balances for Florence, which there had to be, because there were obviously sales and purchases in the Florentine area. In addition, a large portion of

---

[16] There were actually seven companies from 1300 onward, but the books designated "First" covered the first two companies, those of 1300–8 and 1308–10.

[17] De Roover points out that inventory valuation was less important than today, because venture accounting still prevailed. Separate accounts were opened for each lot of merchandise, and balances were transferred to profit and loss only after the goods were sold. Inventories were therefore not totaled separately for balance sheet presentation or revalued, as in modern accounting. But obviously, they had to be counted periodically and revalued to account for loss or damage. See de Roover, "The Organization of Trade," 93.

the accounts payable had to be for intercompany transactions, because most of the branch sales were of imported goods and some were from the company's manufacturing operations in Florence. These balances must have been carried elsewhere, most likely in the White Book or Black Book discussed later in this chapter.

The postings from the Red Book make it clear that it was primarily a holding account for expense advances to partners and employees and their families throughout the company. The disbursements of cash and kind were made both in Florence and the branches, cleared through the Red Book for control, and then routed to the individual accounts in the Assets and Secret Books. It also was the channel for miscellaneous but significant expenses such as brokerage commissions, accounting supplies, dispatch of couriers and letters, entertainment, warehouse fixtures, and losses on wool contracts, to name a few.[18] A "holding" or "conduit" account of this kind has two purposes – a place to accumulate certain expenses until they can be posted in their final destinations, and a control device for identifying and totaling such expenses. An account of this type leaves no open balances at the closing of the books. Similarly, the Orange Book had no balances, but its purpose was much less clear. From the few postings to the main books, it appears to have been a conduit for odds and ends of expenditures and receipts that did not fit anywhere else.

The purpose of the Yellow Book is relatively easy to determine. It dealt primarily with the legal claims of the entire company. The numerous entries from the Yellow Book describing lawsuit expenses and receipts relating to Sicily, Genoa, Majorca, and England attest to the company's procedure of controlling legal matters centrally.[19] This book also received the charges for the rent of the company's warehouses, shops, and stables, along with the expense of maintaining the horses. At July 1, 1335, there were balances reflecting a modest number of open cases, forty-four receivables and "several" payables.

The two remaining subsidiary books, the White Book and the Black Book, are quite important and large, but very difficult to interpret. They both appear to be books of original entry for disbursement and receipt transactions of all kinds in Florence and for nonmerchandise transactions abroad that were controlled by Florence. For example, a major property purchase in Rhodes and a loan to the prior of the Hospitalers in England were entered in the White Book.[20] Although there is no evidence of merchandise transactions

---

[18] *I libri*, 181. [19] Ibid., 104, 108, 152.
[20] Ibid., 23,195.

passing through these books, the volume of entries and the lack of Florence office merchandise account balances elsewhere suggest that some merchandise dealings were recorded in them. The only discernible difference between the Black Book and the White Book is that most, if not all, Black Book postings dealt with indirect transactions – that is, cash or goods received or given by someone on behalf of someone else. As shown in Table 5, both books had large balances on July 1, 1335, made up of 192 open entries for payables and 226 for receivables in the White Book and 107 for payables and 112 for receivables in the Black Book. No information is provided on what these open entries represented, although, as discussed later, the shareholders' capital contributions were probably recorded in both books.[21]

The Assets Book and the Secret Book combine to produce something that at first glance appears broadly similar to the consolidation account of a modern multinational corporation. They contain what look like the opening balances of the new company carried forward from the old company, and they deal with certain items of income and expense, especially interest, not carried in the subsidiary books. But their primary function is to house the individual accounts of depositors and borrowers controlled by the Florence office, mainly nonshareholders in the Assets Book and shareholders in the Secret Book.

The Assets Book, and probably the Secret Book, opens with a brief prayer for the profit and safety of the company and its employees.[22] Each main section of both books is headed by the phrase, "Al nomen di Dio amen." These pious invocations in mundane account books may seem incongruous, perhaps even cynical, to twentieth-century eyes. Partly they attest to the pervasiveness of the Christian faith among medieval businessmen, about which much has been written.[23] But also they may perform a legal function. A. P. Usher has commented that bankers in Mediterranean countries were required to swear that their journals were a true record of transactions so that entries were made in more detail than needed for purely accounting purposes, a characteristic borne out by the Peruzzi documents.[24] He also suggested persuasively that the pious phrases appearing on bills of exchange and account books were designed to give additional sanction to otherwise informal documents, enhancing their enforceability.[25]

[21] Ibid., 11, 12, 195. The notes accompanying the balance merely give the number of entries and the number of pages.

[22] The opening pages of the Secret Book are missing.

[23] See, e.g., Brucker, *Renaissance Florence*, 101–9, 172–212.

[24] Abbot P. Usher, *The Early History of Deposit Banking in Mediterranean Europe*, Vol. 1 (Cambridge, MA, 1943), 11.

[25] Ibid., 77–8. Usher cited as authority the constitution of emperors Arcadius and

Before describing the mechanics of these books in detail, it is worth commenting on two features in them that attest to sophisticated accounting conceptualization. The first relates to the manner in which the outstanding balances in the previous company are carried forward into the new company. At the beginning of the debit and credit sections of the Assets Book, a series of entries have been posted, which, to the unwary scholar, might appear to be a restatement of the balances brought forward from the old company. In fact, they are mirror images of those balances, necessitated by double-entry accounting procedures to provide the offsets to the opening individual account balances in the new company. This device is needed because the books of the previous partnerships were never really wound up as long as the corporate entity continued to exist.[26] Simply stated, then, the debits shown in the opening pages of the new company's books represent not the assets of the new company but the liabilities of the old company.[27] Those liabilities are carried forward into the new company through offsetting entries into the individual accounts. Likewise, balances shown in the opening pages of the credits section of the books represent assets, not liabilities. As a result of these entries, the new company's books start out with exactly the same individual account balances as those with which the old company ended, ensuring smooth continuity.

The second feature is that all debit and credit entries to the individual accounts are constructed logically, with signposts clearly informing the reader of the whereabouts of the offsetting entries. As a result, it is possible to trace the evolution of each account over the life of each partnership. The Peruzzi books may not qualify as double-entry accounts, but, as discussed earlier, they do reflect considerable double-entry thinking.

Honorious of A.D. 395, which provides that any bare agreement in which the name of God is invoked should be enforced by the courts. In addition, the authority of the New Testament was invoked, usually Paul's Epistle to the Colossians (3:17), "Whatsoever ye do, in word or deed, do all in the name of the Lord Jesus."

[26] As we have seen, numerous adjustments were made to the balances of superseded companies many years after their "closure." I will continue to use the word "closing," however, when referring to the settlements of accounts at the end of each partnership. The term is appropriate, even if not technically correct.

[27] For example, in *I libri*, 8, the entry giving the balance of the Naples branch shows it as an asset in the new company but describes it as money assigned to pay 88 creditors. This is obviously a liability of the old company. Conversely, the balance for Naples shown in *I libri*, 193, as a liability of the new company is described as money receivable from 137 good debtors, clearly an asset of the old company.

Unfortunately, it is impossible to determine precisely how final balances and profit and loss calculations were made, because, as we have seen, these two surviving books deal not with a going concern closing in a normal way, but with a company sliding into bankruptcy. It is obvious that the company suffered losses during the 1335–43 period, but to what extent remains a mystery. The bankruptcy court eventually settled with Florentine creditors at the rate of 7 soldi 3 denari on the lira, or 36.25 percent, but the total amount owed the creditors is unknown, as is the amount raised from the private resources of the shareholders.[28] Nor do we know whether there were significant numbers of unpaid creditors in the branches.

The structure of the Book of Assets is well known from the detailed descriptions of Sapori and de Roover.[29] Very briefly, the first section deals with debit accounts, starting with the balances carried forward from the old company, picturesquely described by Sapori as its "living remains," although, as discussed, they were really the reverse of the living remains. These are followed by over two hundred pages of individual accounts and then by forty pages of expense debits, mainly interest. The second half of the book is devoted to credits, adopting the same pattern as the first part – "credit" balances carried forward from the old company, followed by individual accounts and lastly by income credits, again mainly interest.

The term "Secret Book" conjures up to twentieth-century minds the idea of a repository for the recording of nefarious or illegal actions. In fact, its content is entirely innocent, and it would be more aptly described as "confidential" or "private." It completes the Assets Book with information on the balances carried forward, individual account transactions, and expense and income for shareholders and their heirs, again with debits in the first part and credits in the second. It also contains the company's articles of association, interim year-end balances (although none were calculated during the period 1335–43), and the salary accruals for all employees. Finally, it includes the allocations of adjustments to profit or loss of previous companies to the shareholders of record for those companies, or their heirs. These allocations are reminders that the shareholders were subject to unlimited liability and that they could be assessed with gains or losses years or even decades after the books were closed. Mostly, the adjustments were positive, reflecting eventual collection of deemed bad debts, indicating a conservative attitude toward accounts receiv-

---

[28] Sapori, *La crisi*, 174. The settlement is discussed in detail in Chapter 9, this volume.

[29] *I libri*, Introduction; de Roover, "Luca Pacioli," 129–30.

able as well as a tenacious collection policy.[30] There were, however, occasional allocations of losses, such as a thirty-year-old Paris lawsuit that failed, which no doubt was greeted by the relevant shareholders with dismay.[31]

There are extensive lacunae in the Assets Book, especially toward the end of the second half, which create serious problems of analysis. The Secret Book also has gaps, but these are less troublesome, and many of the missing pages can be reconstructed from data available elsewhere. Despite these deficiencies and lack of a complete picture of the methodology, it is possible to achieve a reasonable comprehension of what the surviving accounts mean. A useful way to start is to construct an estimated balance sheet and profit or loss statement from the data available as of July 1, 1335 (see Table 5).

Before discussing what these figures mean, a word needs to be said about what the figures are. They are *lire a fiorino*, a fictive money unit of account that all Florentine businesses used to measure their operations and represented throughout this book by the symbol "li." The lira was divided into 20 *soldi a fiorino* and 240 *denari a fiorino*. All "real" currencies, Florentine and foreign, were translated into these lire for record-keeping purposes, although the cash used in transactions or sitting in the till would be gold florins, silver grossi, quattrini, and denari piccioli in Florence and the local currencies in each of the branches. The basic intermediary currency was the gold florin which was initially established at a rate of 1 florin = 1.45 *lire a fiorino* (usually expressed as 29/20).[32] This conversion rate could change from time to time, and many actual conversions of florins into lire were at rates as high as 1.55, although never lower than 1.45. In translating a foreign currency, the conversion was sometimes made in a two-step procedure, first from the foreign money to the florin and then from the florin to the lira, but just as often directly to the lira. Whatever the procedure, the system was extremely useful for the management of the business, as it reduced a hodge-podge of coin-

[30] For example, in Table 5 there is a credit to the 1331–5 shareholders recognizing accumulated collection of debts of that company up to November 1341. Several additional examples will be seen in this chapter and in Chapters 5 and 6. And evidence of other forms of conservative accounting policy will appear later in this chapter.

[31] The rejection of the Peruzzi position by the Parlement of Paris in 1336 was an important event affecting the company's business plans in both France and England, and will be discussed in detail in Chapter 7.

[32] For a helpful brief commentary on units of account, see Spufford, *Handbook of Medieval Exchange*, xx–xxi; also Carlo Cipolla, *The Monetary Policy of the Fourteenth Century* (Berkeley and Los Angeles, 1982), 20–3.

Table 5. *Account positions at July 1, 1335* (lire a fiorino)

Item	Assets	Liabilities	Balance
Advs. to/borrowed from			
Shareholders	27,260	66,375	(39,115)
Factors	1,638	6,841	(5,203)
Others[a]	*30,712*	*104,219*	*(73,507)*
Subtotal	59,610	177,435	(117,825)
Accts. receivable/payable			
Previous companies	11,755	8,725	3,030
White Book	179,464	101,027	78,437
Yellow Book	44,618	14,285	30.333
Black Book	115,390	96,317	19,073
Branches[b]	*328,871*	*382,421*	*(53,550)*
Subtotal	680,098	602,775	77,323
Fixed Assets	2,539	–	2,539
GRAND TOTAL	742,247	780,210	(37,963)
Unidentified, net			(715)
1331–5 loss at July 1, 1335			*(38,678)*
Special "gift" charge from 1335–43 company			(20,550)
1331–5 loss allocated to shareholders			*(59,228)*
1331–5 late collections credited to shareholders			
November 18, 1341[c]			4,560
Net final reported 1331–5 loss			*(54,668)*

[a] See Table A1 for details.
[b] See Table A2 for details.
[c]Although dated 1341, the entry was clearly made in 1343, following two other entries dated July 1, 1343.

ages of constantly changing relationships into a statistical measure of value common to all the company's operations.[33] Finally, as indicated earlier, all units were reported in roman numerals, although for convenience they are shown here in arabic. It is worth pointing out at this time that the computations were remarkably accurate; in all of the surviving Peruzzi documents, Sapori was able to detect only a few minor errors.

[33] For an indication of the diversity of coinages, see Spufford, *Medieval Exchange*, and for a useful discussion of money units of account, see Frederic C. Lane and Reinhold C. Mueller, *Money and Banking in Medieval and Renaissance Venice*, Vol. 1, *Coins and Moneys of Account* (Baltimore, 1985).

Returning to Table 5, the first section shows the balances in the shareholders' accounts. Here, assets reflect money owed by partners to the company, and liabilities money owed by the company to partners. Stated from the standpoint of the shareholders, the asset balances represent their borrowings from the company, and the liabilities represent their deposits, described as *sopraccorpo*, in excess of their capital contribution. The large negative balance indicates that partners kept more deposits in the company than they borrowed from it, a situation that changed significantly by 1343 (see Table A6). These figures also reflect the enormous variety of transactions described in the previous chapter – money, goods, and property for personal use. All balances, positive or negative, attracted interest at 7 percent per annum. Regarding the factors, the open balances are due to the fact that the salary records were kept in the Secret Book in Florence and that employees working in foreign branches were granted living expense advances instead of being paid their salaries. In his examination of the Alberti Company, de Roover has commented that receivables from factors included merchandise entrusted to them for trading, but there is no evidence of this in the case of the Peruzzi.[34] The assets here represent only the accumulation of unsettled expense advances and the liabilities the accumulation of accrued unpaid salaries. It is interesting to note that in a largely cash-based society, the company was familiar with the concept of accruals. Also, interest at the usual rate was calculated on open balances.

The "others" balances are long-term deposits or borrowings from other than shareholders, as shown in Table A1. The balances reflect mainly deposits by members of the Peruzzi family not involved in ownership, former shareholders, and clergymen. The largest single item for both assets and liabilities at July 1, 1335, was the Florence control account for the Order of the Hospitalers. The assets and liabilities virtually netted out, as deposits were largely offset by borrowings, especially in England. As in the case of the shareholders, all balances were credited or charged with interest at 7 percent per annum.[35]

The likely content of the balances in the colored books has already been discussed and the "due to and from" previous companies is self-explanatory. The branch balances, however, deserve detailed examination. The first point to note is that the closing dates reported from the branches vary significantly. As shown in Table A2, many,

---

[34] De Roover, "Alberti Company," 22.

[35] A possible exception is the Hospitalers. Its balances were carried in a special account, which has not survived, so that we cannot be certain whether interest was applied.

such as Venice and Pisa, are within a few months of July 1, 1335, but others, such as Tunis and England, came in over a year later. Whatever the date, however, the balances of all branches were those as of June 30, 1335. Another point to note is that several of the branches reported receivables as being from "good debtors," not just debtors, attesting again to conservative accounting. In the cases of late-reporting branches, the good debtors at June 30, 1335, would have been factually established as such because they had actually paid up by the time the positions were submitted to head office.[36]

A striking characteristic of branch reporting is its individuality, suggesting a degree of independence from central office control. In addition to the timing variations noted above, each branch reported its results in a somewhat different way. According to accounting historian Federigo Melis, there were two ways of presenting balances – *a croce*, that is, the total assets and liabilities reported separately; or less common, *a bilancio*, that is, the net balance of assets and liabilities.[37] Most of the Peruzzi branches used the *a croce* system in one way or another. Some merely gave total values with little added comment; others listed the number of debtors and creditors; still others gave indications of other assets such as cash, household goods, and merchandise. Of those using the *a bilancio*, Venice helpfully included the number of debtors and creditors and the money totals applicable to each in its report. England, Bruges, and Majorca, however, merely showed the net balance, with no indication of what it represented. Such netting is confusing to scholars because it makes it impossible to make a rational assessment of the size of the branch. Bruges, for example, shows a balance of only li.593, a grotesque understatement of its importance.

The figure for fixed assets looks ludicrously small and represents only business-related land and buildings in Rhodes. Elsewhere, including Florence, the company rented premises and had no capital assets in connection with manufacturing or transport operations. Furniture and fixtures were expensed.[38] As a matter of accounting interest, the concept of depreciation was understood during the fourteenth century, but as is obvious here, the Peruzzi had little reason to apply it.[39]

The large special "gift" item that appeared at the very end of the Sixth Secret Book is puzzling at first glance, but can be explained.[40]

---

[36] Supporting this interpretation is an entry from the Rhodes branch dated April 12, 1336, reporting a balance of li.2,820 representing "fifty more good debtors" in addition to the 114 debtors reported previously (September, 1335). *I libri*, 193.

[37] Melis, *Ragioneria*, 503. [38] For an example, see *I libri*, 181.

[39] De Roover, "Luca Pacioli," 144. [40] *I libri*, 390.

According to the total balances reported in Table 5, there was a loss on operations of li.34,118 (li.38,678 less the credit for subsequent collections of li.4,560). But the shareholders of the 1331–5 company were not charged with the burden of the loss until July 1, 1343, so that they owed interest to the 1335–43 company on the loss for the seven years from July 1336 to July 1343. The special "gift" was unquestionably an interest charge from the 1335–43 company to the 1331–5 company at the standard rate of 7 percent. Compounded over seven years this amounts to a rate of over 60 percent, which would yield the "gift" charge of li.20,550. It is not possible to be sure that the Peruzzi accountants used this method of calculation, but it seems as likely an approach as any.

Finally, the small unidentified number of li.715 is simply what it takes to get from the total of the reported balances to the reported loss of li.59,228 that was allocated to the 1331–5 shareholders.

One crucial liability in the "living remains" of the 1331–5 company has been left unidentified – the capital account. The company owed its shareholders their capital contributions of li.88,500 and the charity contribution li.1,500, and this large sum had to be reflected somewhere. De Roover's analysis of the Alberti partnerships from 1302 to 1329 clearly labels the owners' equity as one of the companies' liabilities.[41] De Roover also asserts that profit or loss was determined by deducting total liabilities and invested capital from total assets.[42] But there is no evidence of the equity investment in the individual shareholder balances in the Secret Book where one would expect to find it. Moreover, interest was consistently applied to all of the shareholders' balances, positive or negative, whereas interest is never applied to equity. Sapori was also puzzled by this peculiarity and concluded that the capital of the company was recorded in the book of the accounts, not the Secret Book.[43] The most likely answer to this problem is that the capital subscriptions were posted to two accounts, one for residents of Florence and one for residents abroad. One White Book entry specifically refers to money relating to shareholders outside of Florence, which would include li.21,000 in capital contributions.[44] The capital account for the residents of Florence must have been entered in the Black Book, because no other single liability entry was large enough to encompass the li.67,500 owed to those shareholders.[45]

[41] De Roover, "Alberti Company," 51–9.
[42] De Roover, "Luca Pacioli," 125. [43] Sapori, *La crisi*, App. II, 240.
[44] *libri*, 9. The entry, dated May 17, 1335, was for a total of li.56,249 s3 d9.
[45] *I libri*, 11. The Black Book entry was for a total of li.96,317 s8. There were two entries from the White Book, the li.56,249 already noted and li.44,777 s11 d5 on 12.

It is worth noting here that there was also a "gift" charge to each of the shareholders of the 1335–43 company, immediately following the charge previously described, which added up to li.32,408. It is impossible to determine how the calculations were made, but clearly some sort of formula was used, judging by the amounts levied. Again, these were obviously additional interest charges to these shareholders relating to an equity shortfall, either because of inadequate initial capital contributions or because of accumulated losses over the 1335–43 period. This and other evidence suggest that the 1335–43 company was never recapitalized. It should be understood that equity shortfalls were not unusual in medieval companies, as will be discussed more fully in Chapter 5; Giotto di Arnoldo Peruzzi reported delinquencies in his capital contributions over extended periods of time and was accordingly charged interest on the deficiency.[46]

The accounting techniques revealed here, while impressive with regard to record keeping and controls, were not adequate to manage such a complex business. Unlike the Bardi, the Peruzzi made no evident attempt to assess the profitability of any of the company's enterprises or product lines. Nor do these results provide any more than a rudimentary feel for the operating effectiveness of any of the branches, as they reflect only merchandise activity, ignoring even direct personnel costs, let alone an allocation of central-office overheads. The wide variations of positive and negative balances among the branches and the colored books lead to deep suspicions about the representativeness of the individual balances. It is certainly possible that a chairman such as Tommaso and some of his branch managers kept informal data for operating profit analysis. In the last decade of the company's existence, however, events were moving so much more rapidly than the flow of accounting information that timely analysis would have been impossible. Sapori claims that the collapse of the Peruzzi in October 1343 came as a complete surprise to the Florentine business community.[47] An examination of the accounts in the final years of the

---

[46] *I libri*, 459–62. Giotto appeared to be consistently in debt to the company from about 1315 onward. In 1324, he finally settled a very large "overdraft" by means of crediting the company with his share of the dividend from the preceding period and paying his share of capital due. This seems to have been a "window-dressing" maneuver, as he immediately went into debt to the next company.

[47] Sapori, *Storia economica*, Vol. 2, 686. Here he refers to G. Villani's chronicles, Book XI, Chap. 88, for support. But Luzzati in *Villani e Buonaccorsi* speculates that the Peruzzi were among the last to abandon Walter of Brienne in 1343 because, knowing that the company was close to collapse, they appreciated the protection the dictator had been giving them against their creditors (54–5). The question of "surprise" is discussed more fully at the beginning of Chapter 9.

company exposes a situation sufficiently confused to lend credence to
this assertion, but the events that unfolded during 1342 and 1343, as
discussed in Chapter 8, let alone the lack of a dividend since 1324, must
have created doubts about the company's viability in the minds of at
least some Florentine businessmen.

There is no way of judging whether the subsidiary books were properly maintained during the final years, but it is probable that they were
kept reasonably well. The company did continue to operate, and the
data needed for eventual entry in the Assets and Secret Books seem to
have been available for posting years after the events. The Assets and
Secret Books were clearly not kept current. At the head of each page is
written the year in which the entries were supposedly made and to which
they supposedly refer, but many pages contain anomalies that bring into
question the date on which they were really written.

According to Sapori, the Assets and Secret Books were compiled
simultaneously in their entirety by Pacino di Tommaso, the chairman of the last company.[48] It is possible that he started writing the
accounts at the inception of the company in July 1335, but this is
questionable both because he had just returned from his assignment
in Bruges and because control of these books, especially the Secret
Book, normally rested with the chairman. At the opening of the company, Giotto di Arnoldo was still chairman, albeit very old, and when
he died in 1336, he was succeeded by Bonifazio. Pacino may have
written entries earlier, but it is unlikely that he took charge of the
books until Bonifazio left for England in the spring of 1338.

Irrespective of when Pacino started posting, there is much evidence
to show that entries were made long after the transactions concerned.
Several are clearly of a catch-up nature. One example is the multiple
posting regarding Donato quoted in the previous chapter, but there
are several of much greater length, including a catchall entry of a
long series of unrelated expenses incurred between 1335 and 1341.[49]
The expense and salary sections of the Secret Book are especially
suspect, where the dates of entry are frequently at variance with the
year indicated at the head of the page. Moreover, the preponderance of the salary entries was made on pages designated 1343, with
many relating to earlier years.[50] As mentioned previously, expense

[48] *I libri*, XXV.
[49] Ibid. The "catchall" referred to is on 181, but there are many others, such as on
140, 151, 255–6, 269, 363.
[50] Ibid., 302–18. Entries were few in the years 1335–42 (none in the years 1336, 1340,
and 1342), but there were eighty in 1343, suggesting a postbankruptcy cleanup.
They cover salaries through previous years and are often confusing. For example,
under the heading 1339, all but one entry deals with salaries up to 1341.

advances to factors often accumulated to very large sums, while accrued salaries did the same. Clearly no attempt had been made to balance accounts for years.

The most serious anomaly in these books is the fact that the 1331–5 accounts were not actually finalized until well after July 1343. This is more than merely a matter of the allocations of the loss to the 1331–5 shareholders being delayed until July 1, 1343. The fact is that the loss was not finally determined until that time. The special "gift" charge already discussed was calculated as of that date. Moreover, the Sicily branch balance was not struck until after April 9, 1343, the effective date of the exchange rate used to convert a large account receivable from King Federigo III of Sicily from local currency to lire.[51] This anomaly is further evidence to support the view that the 1335–43 company was never recapitalized.

The long delays in posting might be excused on the grounds that these books were intended for summarizing data well after the events strictly for shareholder accounting. But the eight-year delay in finalizing the results of the previous company hints at a virtual collapse of the company's information systems. It is entirely within the realm of possibility that the settlement of the 1331–5 company did not take place until after October 1343 under the aegis of the bankruptcy court. Between July and October of that year, Florence was suffering the upheavals of the overthrow of the dictator, Walter of Brienne, and the revolution of the lower-order guildsmen against the regime of which the Peruzzi were a part – hardly the time for orderly concentration on arcane accounting issues.

There are three additional accounting anomalies which add to the impression that at least part of the Peruzzi accounts were dictated by the bankruptcy court. The first is what must have been a most wel-

---

[51] Ibid., 196. This very large (li.62,434) entry was for a series of loan contracts made with the court of King Frederick up to July 1, 1335. It is curious on two counts. The first is that it came through the Libro Grande, suggesting that the advances were in the form of merchandise, not cash. The second is not only the very late date for the establishment of the exchange rate, but the rate itself, which reflects a devaluation of the Sicilian currency from the rate showing in the other balances of 1335. But Spufford's tables in *Medieval Exchange*, 65, point in the opposite direction, a relative devaluation of the florin. This peculiar rate suggests that either the king actually paid the debt on that date at a negotiated rate, or the company was using an exchange rate mechanism to write down the receivable. Neither of these alternatives is very plausible, especially the first, because Trasselli's research into the Palermo archives indicates that much of the debt was still owed after 1342, a fact he believed may have contributed significantly to the failure of the company (see Trasselli, "Nuovi documenti," 194).

come receipt in April 1345 from Warden Abbey in Bedfordshire, England, of £900, equivalent to li.9,787. This money was credited to the shareholders of the 1324–31 company, which had made a loan to the abbey back in the 1320s.[52] Entries into the individual accounts of those who were also shareholders of the latest company made the point that the special "gift" charge of July 1343 did not take this allocation into account as it occurred after that date. But entries dated July 1343 followed these 1345 entries using the word *sopradetti* (abovementioned) indicating that the 1343 entry was made *after* the 1345 entry.[53] What this suggests is that most of the closing entries, irrespective of date, were made at one time, possibly as late as the end of 1345.[54]

The second anomaly is an inexplicable aberration from the normally meticulous allocation of income or expense to shareholders. One of the 1331–5 shareholders, Gherardo di Gentile Bonaccorsi, is not mentioned anywhere in the accounts, simply disappearing without trace. He is not given an allocation of his share of the 1331–5 loss or of any of the adjustments made to any of the other companies of which he was a shareholder dating back to 1310. What is especially curious is that allocations were made to all the other shareholders as though his share remained in place; where his portion went is a mystery. It is possible that he was involved directly in the Buonaccorsi Company, which collapsed under questionable circumstances in 1342 and that his share of the adjustments went to the bankruptcy settlement of that company.[55] This seems unlikely, as there is no evidence that he was part of the Buonaccorsi Company, and some activity should have been registered in his personal account between 1335 and 1342. The most probable answer is that he died before 1335 and his account was cleared in the missing Fifth Secret Book, but still left dangling is the question of what happened to his allocations.

The third anomaly is the fact that expenses paid for shareholders

[52] The only loan recorded in England was on April 3, 1323 (*CCR* EII 1318–23,195) for £1,330 6s 8d. It may have been a long-term advance, which was common practice among Italian companies to ensure availability of an abbey's wool production for years ahead at attractive prices. But see Chapter 5 for some curious aspects of Warden Abbey's relationship with the Peruzzi Company.

[53] *I libri*, 362. Moreover, the balances of entries posted at the foot of this page "as of July 1, 1343" include the 1345 item.

[54] Ibid. The latest entries in the book are dated around the end of 1346, when a few of the former shareholders no longer associated with the firm had their accounts cleared by bankruptcy court, as discussed later.

[55] See Luzzati, *Villani e Buonaccorsi*, 46–60, regarding the unusual circumstances surrounding the Buonaccorsi bankruptcy.

on company business, including travel and living expense abroad, were meticulously recorded and charged to their personal accounts. For factors, charging living expenses was logical, since these represented advances against the salaries that were being accrued in Florence. But for the shareholders, there is no evidence of any such offset. It is utterly unrealistic to expect that certain of these hard-headed businessmen would accept this considerable extra expense for service to the company over a period of years without some form of appropriate compensation. Either they did receive it in some hidden way off the books, or the expenses had in fact been absorbed originally by the company and later charged back to the individuals under instructions from the bankruptcy court auditors. The latter seems the most probable explanation for two reasons. The first is the interest of the court to increase the assets of the bankrupt company by any means possible. The second is that most of the charges to the individuals occur in the larger "catchall" types of entry, suggesting a concerted effort to root out expenses that could be legitimately attributed as personal to the shareholders.

Finally, there are three declarations of discharge written into the Secret Book by the company chairman, Pacino di Tommaso, in the presence of officials of the Florence Commune and the bankruptcy court. The first concerns two of the minor family shareholders, the brothers Salvestro and Donato de' Peruzzi on March 27, 1346.[56] The second and third declarations are for two former outside shareholders, Chatellino di Mangia degl' Infanghati on October 19, 1346, and Piero di Bernardo Ubaldini on November 16, 1346.[57] Possibly there were others in the missing pages. These discharges appear to be settlements of the individuals' obligations to the company.[58] The significance of these declarations is that they are direct evidence of bankruptcy court intrusion into the Peruzzi Company's innermost accounts. The addition of this anomaly to all those already cited produces the strong impression that important parts of the surviving accounts of the Peruzzi Company represent not the activities and status of a going concern but the creation of the court auditors of a bankrupt firm as dictated to its chairman, Pacino di Tommaso.

[56] *I libri*, 275. Salvestro was a former shareholder. Donato's name appears on the list of the 1335–43 company shareholders but for some reason was paired with his brother, and the two were discharged together.

[57] *I libri*, 284, 290.

[58] The declarations make no mention of the fate of the men's capital contributions. Donato's was presumably forfeited, because he remained a shareholder of the final company. But the capital of the other dischargees may also have been lost, because there is no evidence that it was returned to them at the close of the 1331–5 company.

Returning to the July 1, 1335, balances in Table 5, a word needs to be said on the meaning of asset totals. The total assets figure of li.742,247 is the Peruzzi equivalent to the total of li.1,266,756 reported by the Bardi Company in 1318.[59] This Bardi figure, sometimes cited in its equivalent of around 875,000 florins, has been frequently quoted and almost universally misunderstood by historians of every kind. Brucker, for example, erroneously called it turnover, a very different value and, in any case, a meaningless one in a mixed manufacturing, trading, and banking business.[60] Most have correctly recognized the figure as a total of assets but have simply marveled at it, some trying to grasp its significance by making inappropriate comparisons. Brucker related the Bardi total to the 120,000 florins that the king of France paid for the Dauphiné, and Renouard to the 80,000 florins Pope Clement VI paid for the purchase of Avignon from Queen Johanna of Naples in 1348.[61] Fryde went so far as to compare the Bardi number with the annual revenue of the king of England, a completely unrelated statistic, from which he drew horribly unreal conclusions.[62] Bolton and Kaeuper have echoed Fryde's comparison.[63]

The Bardi Company was indeed a very large and powerful company, in a class by itself, but the total of its assets must not be construed as being convertible into deployable ready cash. The fragment from which this total is obtained shows it as the sum of accounts receivable, merchandise, and other goods. The document also includes an incomplete schedule of the balances of eight branches, totaling li.424,000, which means that probably one-third of the assets were scattered among various foreign locations. The Peruzzi branch totals for 1335 shown in Table 5 amounted to 44.3 percent of all assets. What the fragment does not contain is a statement of total liabilities. Judging from the Peruzzi balances – and Sapori confirms that they are comparable to those of the Bardi – the assets are likely to have

[59] Sapori, *La Crisi*, 216.
[60] Brucker, *Florence: Golden Age*, 88–9.
[61] Ibid., 89; Renouard, *Les relations*, 60.
[62] E. B. Fryde, "Public Credit, with Special Reference to North-Western Europe," in *The Cambridge Economic History of Europe*, Vol. 3, ed. M. M. Postan, E. E. Rich, and E. Miller (Cambridge, 1963), 455. Here Fryde writes, "In 1318, at a time when the ordinary revenues of Edward II probably did not surpass £30,000 per year, his main bankers, the Bardi of Florence, possessed total assets of 875,000 florins (£130,000). Italian firms of this stature could afford to be easygoing in their relations with royal clients."
[63] J. L. Bolton, *The Medieval English Economy, 1150–1500* (London, 1980), 390; Richard W. Kaeuper, *War, Justice, and Public Order* (Oxford, 1988), 44 n84.

been financed to a large extent by small deposits and accounts payable directly linked to much of the merchandise and receivables making up the assets.[64] The means of financing is crucial to understanding the significance of asset totals; very large assets supported by even larger liabilities spell weakness, not strength. There are many familiar examples in bankruptcy courts today. The Peruzzi Company, despite its impressive asset totals in 1335, was en route to collapse.[65]

One more point needs to be made in evaluating asset totals. Notwithstanding the expert opinions that the companies did not quite attain double-entry bookkeeping, they were close enough to it to have employed double-entry balancing procedures. As made clear earlier, for every debit there was an offsetting credit, for every asset a liability. The nature of this accounting often results in reporting gross instead of net positions, thus inflating both asset and liability totals. Three examples from the Peruzzi balances will illustrate this point. Total assets include li.1,638 receivable from factors, but these are merely advances made against salaries owed and accrued on the liability side. Similarly, "advances to others" includes li.25,233 receivable from the Hospitalers, but this asset is more than offset by a liability of li.28,636 borrowed from that order. Finally, there can be a huge difference in the total of branch assets, depending upon whether, as discussed, the balances are rendered gross (*a croce*) or net (*a bilancio*). England, Bruges, Venice, and possibly Majorca elected to report net; if all branches had done so, the total branch assets would have dropped from the li.328,871 reported to li.101,803.[66] From an accounting point of view, the method that the Peruzzi chose to disclose these assets and liabilities is entirely valid; but an equally valid method would have resulted in a more realistic assets total of less than li.500,000, only two-thirds of the total actually presented.

Part of the reason for delving so deeply into the accounting aspects of the companies is to emphasize the risk of erroneous interpretation of events from an examination of only the surface numbers. Historians of business seem too easily beguiled by large figures and rush to deduce relationships where none exist. An example common today is the tendency to compare the net sales of a company with the gross national product of a country, equating the "power" of a corporation with that of a country when the only relationship between the two statistics is that they are numbers expressed in U.S.

[64] Sapori, *Storia economica*, Vol. 2, 688.
[65] See Tables 8 and 9 for a more detailed analysis of the Peruzzi balances of 1335.
[66] The li.101,803 is the total of all the positive balances submitted by the branches. See Table A2 for details.

dollars.[67] For medieval companies, the accounting "living remains" need to be studied with special care because they were designed not for twentieth-century scholars but for the enlightenment of contemporary management or law courts regarding the conduct of the business. The closer we come to understanding the purpose of these constructions, the closer we come to interpreting accurately the nature and progress of the enterprises and the men who managed them, free of the hyperbole of chroniclers' reports.

Some of the statements in this chapter have been perhaps too critical of the Peruzzi bookkeeping and information systems because most of what we know about the company comes from the questionable accounts of its dismal final years. The company was in fact very successful throughout most of its existence, and the accounting procedures undoubtedly played their part in that success by reinforcing the management and control structure described in Chapter 3. It should also be understood that these procedures were not unique to the Peruzzi but were widely used by other Florentine companies of that period. Moreover, the accounting scheme, whether double entry or otherwise, was not a forward-looking management tool for decision making. Its value was primarily in maintaining order and broadly measuring the performance of the various parts of the organization. But it was a cumbersome system, and when the organization began to crumble, so did the reporting function.

The first four chapters of this book have been devoted to an analysis of the medieval super-company phenomenon, using the Peruzzi Company as a model. The study has focused on the relation of the firm to the family that dominated it, the nature of the business and why such business required a company of exceptional resources, the organization of the enterprise, and finally, the accounting systems. This background is essential to understanding the chronological history of the Peruzzi Company, the ingredients of the company's success through the years, and the sources of its ultimate failure – the subject of the remaining chapters.

[67] See Edwin S. Hunt, "A Critique of the Anthropological literature on the Multinational Corporation" (M.A. thesis, University of Cincinnati and Microfilms International, Ann Arbor, MI, 1984), Chap. 4, 53–9.

Part II

History of the Peruzzi Company from its reorganization in 1300

5

The prosperous years, 1300–1324

The year 1300 was a good year for pause and reflection. Pope Boniface VIII had declared it a Jubilee Year, granting full remission of sins to those who spent a stipulated amount of time at the churches of the Blessed Apostles of St. Peter and St. Paul in Rome during the course of the year.[1] This declaration prompted a host of pilgrims to visit that city, bringing with them rich offerings for the church and lucrative business for Roman merchants. Giovanni Villani joined the pilgrimage to the Eternal City and claimed that it was this experience that moved him to begin his famous chronicle of the history of Florence.[2] And Dante, of course, set his *Divine Comedy* in this year.

Although tensions remained throughout western Europe, 1300 was also a year of relative calm after a decade of political instability. Florence's staunchest ally, Charles II of Naples, had become firmly established and was winding down the long and fruitless struggle to reconquer Sicily. Another important ally, Philip IV of France, had overcome an uprising by his vassal, Count Guy of Flanders, in 1297 and occupied all of the county in 1300. Philip's war with England over Aquitaine had given over to protracted diplomacy following the preliminary peace agreement at Montreuil-sur-Mer in 1299.[3] Harvests had been good, and the general prosperity that gave rise to the super-companies in the thirteenth century seemed ready to be extended comfortably into the fourteenth.

In this somewhat benign atmosphere, the leadership of the Peruzzi Company decided that the company must undergo a thorough reor-

---

[1] According to Villani (*Storia*, Book VIII, Chap. 36), a Roman was required to visit these churches for thirty days and a non-Roman for fifteen days to qualify for remission.

[2] Ibid. The purpose of his sojourn in Rome is believed to have been Peruzzi business as well as spiritual edification. See Louis Green, *Chronicles into History* (Cambridge, 1972), 11.

[3] Strayer, *Philip the Fair*, 323. The final peace, including the restitution of Aquitaine to Edward I, did not take place until June 1303 (see Vale, *The Angevin Legacy*, 224).

ganization. The exact nature of the restructuring is not known, because there is very little information available on the antecedent companies of the 1290s. The most important change was probably the introduction of a large number of outside shareholders bringing with them significant amounts of fresh capital. Although there is an indication of outside participation in the 1292 and 1296 companies, only three non-Peruzzis appear to have been partners in each of these companies, and the amount of their capital contribution, if any, is unknown.[4] Again, there is no basis for comparing the capital of the 1300 partnership with that of its precursors, but the amount of capital in the new company, li.124,000, was so enormous by the standards of the time that it probably represented a significant increase from previous levels. Certainly, it was a breathtaking figure for what had been a small family business barely a generation earlier. This much is clear: in the eyes of its owners, the 1300 company was something new and different, a departure from all that had gone before. It was recorded as the "First Company," and all subsequent organizations were numbered in relation to it, suggesting a completely new set of company statutes. Details of shareholdings in the 1300 and subsequent companies are given in Tables A4 and A5.

The reasons for the reorganization are unknown, but some intelligent speculations can be advanced. The driving force behind the change was almost certainly Filippo di Amideo, the company's cofounder and chairman. He was getting old. His cofounder and brother, Arnoldo, had died in 1292. Arnoldo's eldest son, Pacino, had briefly run the company (1298–9), but he too had died, and apparently none of his brothers had sufficient experience to take charge at that point. Filippo's own sons seemed to have had little interest or aptitude for business management. In resuming leadership in 1299, Filippo must have felt the need to place the company that he helped create on a sound footing to assure its importance, its permanence, and its maintenance under Peruzzi control. By making it a more "public" company with a large number of shareholders, but with the majority of shares in Peruzzi hands, he achieved all three objectives. The outside shareholders contributed to his aims in three ways. First, their infusion of fresh capital enabled the company to take advantage of the magnificent opportunities opening up in the Angevin

---

[4] *I libri*, 210, 215, 228, 232, give the names of Banco Raugi, Gianni Ponci, and Bandino Spiglati of the 1292 company and Raugi, Spiglati, and Ugo Aldobrandini of the 1296 company as being credited with late collections due those companies, implying that they were partners. Raugi and Ponci also became shareholders of the 1300 company.

kingdom of Naples. Second, they brought much-needed talent to help run this diverse and geographically dispersed business. Finally, their wealth and prestige increased the company's influence in the community, helping to steer it through the factional strife that was so much a part of social and business life in Florence and that was surfacing again in 1300, this time as the Black–White controversy.[5]

Whatever the motivations for its formation, the 1300 company emerged full-blown, like Athena from the brow of Zeus, endowed with sufficient strength to take advantage of its opportunities and to overcome the hazards of the turbulent years immediately ahead. The main features of its branch system were already in place, with permanent representation in Naples, Barletta, the Papal Court of Rome, Pisa, Venice, Paris, Cyprus, and Tunis. The Sicilian branch was already established, headed from 1299 by Francesco Forzetti who would eventually serve the company there for forty-two years.[6] The company was also active in Bruges, where the young shareholder Giovanni Villani was soon to reside briefly, and in Catalonia, where Giotto di Arnoldo was in residence.[7] Only two locations that were to become important to the Peruzzi, England and Rhodes, were insignificant business centers for them in 1300.[8]

This powerful new company soon had to face a series of crises in its home territory. In 1301, Boniface VIII sent Charles of Valois to Florence to intervene in the Black–White controversy in favor of the Blacks. As discussed in Chapter 1, there is no information on the part that the Peruzzi and their associates played in this struggle, but the fact that nothing untoward happened to them suggests that they at least avoided antagonizing the triumphant Blacks. When violence erupted anew in 1303 and again in 1304, they appear to have been more involved. The original leader of the Blacks, Corso Donati, formed a new faction in 1303 with a group of Whites headed by the

---

[5] Villani, *Storia*, Book VIII, Chaps. 38 and 39. Here Villani describes the origins of the dispute, which engaged most of the important families of Florence during the first decade of the century.

[6] Bresc, *Un monde Méditerranéen*, 382, 400; Davidsohn, *Firenze*, Vol. 6, 822. The company was already shipping large quantities of cereal grains from Palermo in 1299.

[7] As noted in Chapter 1, Giotto lived in Catalonia at that time (actually in the northern inland town of Gerona). The company never established a branch there, but later set up one in Majorca.

[8] T. H. Lloyd, *Alien Merchants in England in the High Middle Ages* (Sussex and New York, 1982), estimates that the Peruzzi started trading in England in 1303 "at latest" (172). By 1306, the company is recorded as having two employees in that country (193).

Cavalcanti family and provoked so much violence that the new pope, Benedict XI, sent Cardinal Niccolo da Prato to Florence to restore peace. When the mission failed in June 1304, the cardinal left the city, placing it under interdict and excommunicating its citizens.[9] The new party, now headed by the Cavalcanti and others, backed the cardinal and attempted to take over the city. In this endeavor they obtained the support of several leading businesses and families, including the Peruzzi and Baroncelli, according to Villani.[10] They may have participated in the fighting that followed and probably suffered losses in the huge fire that was started by the combatants and gutted a large part of the city, destroying much merchandise. It is even possible that they were among the *popolani* who later joined the plot to take the city with the help of exiled Whites but then defended it when they perceived that a large part of the exile force was Ghibelline.[11]

There were other big problems for the company, both at home and abroad. The fourteenth century opened with a series of cold, wet years that resulted in harvests so poor that scarcities were reported in seven out of the ten years between 1301 and 1310.[12] Villani described 1303 in particular as a year of famine and extraordinarily high grain prices only partially relieved when the commune arranged large imports of grain from Sicily and Puglia in Genoese ships.[13] For the decade 1300–9 Tuscany took more than 70 percent of recorded Sicilian exports of grain.[14] On another front, the Flemish revolt against France interrupted the supply of both finished and unfinished cloth, especially between 1302 and 1305. Finally, in the midst of these crises, the company lost the steady hand that had guided it for so many years. Filippo died in September 1303 and was succeeded by his astute but less experienced nephew Tommaso.

The Peruzzi's business with France and the papacy also suffered later in the decade. In France, the Peruzzi had been one of the most prominent Italian merchants and appeared to work closely with Philip IV's principal bankers, the Franzesi firm headed by Albizzo and Musciatto Guidi, better known as Biche and Mouche, respectively. As

[9] Excommunication was a serious practical matter to the city merchants, as it sanctioned the expropriation of their goods and the voiding of their contracts.

[10] Villani, *Storia*, Book VIII, Chap. 71.

[11] Ibid., Chap. 72. Villani notes that the change of heart by these *popolani* families was prompted more by fear that victorious Ghibellines would dispossess them than by loyalty to the city, although they naturally cited loyalty as the reason. Villani makes a point of saying that he was a witness to these events.

[12] La Roncière, *Prix et salaires*, 716.

[13] Villani, *Storia*, Book VIII, Chap. 68.

[14] Bresc, *Un monde Méditerranéen*, 549.

is well known, Philip had become engaged in a bitter controversy with Pope Boniface VIII over the taxation of clergy in France, among other things.[15] This dispute culminated in the notorious French expedition in 1303 to Anagni, a small town south of Rome, where Boniface was eventually taken from his papal palace and briefly held. The Peruzzi, as noted in Chapter 1, may have helped finance the enterprise by providing Mouche with credits "as much as may be needed."[16] Villani added that the Peruzzi managers were unaware of the purpose of the funds, a reasonable comment because the attack on the pope apparently was an improvisation following long negotiations, not the original plan of the expedition.[17] The Peruzzi may have gained some short-lived advantage from its cooperation, being given control of the mints of Paris, Troyes, Tournai, and Sommières in 1305.[18] But Philip became increasingly disinclined to depend on any foreign bankers and gradually squeezed them out, although the Peruzzi fared better than most.[19]

The Peruzzi's commerce with the papacy appeared to make no headway and probably went into reverse. The company had a branch in Rome that did transactions with dignitaries of the papal court, but it was not one of the official bankers or transfer agents of the papal treasury. When Clement V was elected pope in 1305 and moved his court to southern France, he disrupted what little official business the Peruzzi had with the court. His decision in 1306 to discontinue the policy of using designated Italian firms to manage the finances of the Curia closed off any chance the Peruzzi may have had of achieving a direct commercial relationship with the papacy.

Despite these various afflictions, the first decade of the new Peruzzi Company proved to be reasonably profitable. At the first closing in 1308, the company declared a dividend of 100 percent, that is, li.124,000. Subsequent collections of doubtful accounts, mostly during the next ten years, resulted in additional distributions of about li.71,500 so that the total payment to the shareholders over the first eight and one-half years was li.195,500.[20] Sapori attributes an annual

[15] For a concise account of this argument, see Strayer, *Philip the Fair*, 251–81.
[16] Villani, *Storia*, Book VIII, Chaps. 63 and 64.
[17] Strayer, *Philip the Fair*, 277–8.
[18] Strayer, "Italian Bankers," 119 n12. In effect, the Peruzzi became successor to the Franzesi (Davidsohn, *Firenze*, Vol. 4, 432).
[19] Strayer, "Italian Bankers," 117. Note also *I libri*, 435, which shows large uncollected debts from the king of France and several of his barons at the close of books in 1308. These were recovered by 1313.
[20] The eight and a half years is due to the fact that the company started on May 1, 1300, and closed November 1, 1308.

rate of return of 15.4 percent to these figures on the basis that part of the later dividend remained with the company for a number of years.[21] He cites this as an excellent rate of return, nearly double the typical interest rate on loans. But this figure is not nearly as good as it looks because Sapori, like many other historians analyzing business profits, ignores the time value of money in all his rate of return calculations.[22] The Florentine businessmen were aware of this concept because they could easily compare what they earned on their shareholding with what they received on loans to the company. At that time, the interest offered by the Peruzzi was 8 percent per annum, which, compounded over eight and one-half years would have yielded them 92 percent, not much less than the first dividend the shareholders received. The two main subsequent distributions came five and eleven years later, so that their effect on the rate of return would be modest. Overall, the real rate of return for the first eight years was likely not more than 11 percent, a far-from-handsome reward for the time and effort most of the shareholders put into the management of the business. But it was not a bad yield for such a hazardous period, and the shareholders must have felt gratified at the close of the books. Besides, the perquisites associated with being a shareholder, such as access to company merchandise, facilities, services, and finance, were not inconsiderable, as will be seen toward the end of this chapter.

The next closing of the books completed the accounts of the First Company. For an unknown reason, the 1308 company, despite a slight change in capital and shareholders, including the replacement of Giovanni Villani by his brother Filippo, was regarded as a continuation of the First Company. The capital was increased to li.130,000, with the Peruzzi share dropping to li.71,000 or 55 percent of the total from li.74,000 or 60 percent. The dividend declared at the end of 1310 was li.52,000, or 40 percent of the capital, an annual rate of return of truly handsome proportions. This closing marked the apogee of Peruzzi Company fortunes; although subsequent companies

---

[21] Sapori, *Storia economica*, Vol. 2, 673. His explanation for the 15.4% figure is maddeningly vague and does not include any calculations.

[22] See Table A3 for a comparison of Sapori's figures and real rates of return for all of the Peruzzi companies. The use of the word "profit" in this table may be questioned here because the figures represent distributions to shareholders rather than reported earnings. They closely approximate profit, however, because they reflect not only the initial dividends, but also the subsequent allocations right up to the final years of the firm. The only exception is the 1331–5 loss, which, as indicated in Chapter 4, was clearly established within the company's books.

were profitable, none attained the level of the 1308–10 business.

These results suggest that the company suffered setbacks in the first half of the decade but recovered strongly in the second half. What accounted for the conversion of the ill winds described into such good results? One important factor was the return to relative stability within Florence. To be sure, conflict continued, but much more of it was directed outside the city toward the conquest of Pistoia and Prato. Another reason was the fact that the repeated scarcities of grain, while deleterious in their effect on the Florentine economy, were not entirely bad news to a company active in the grain trade. It may not have made much profit on sales controlled by the commune, despite rumors of profiteering reported by Villani, but it must have enjoyed the generally higher price levels prevailing between 1305 and 1310.[23] Yet another reason was because the unrest in Flanders was only temporary, and while it may have reduced textile sales and finishing activity, it may have also given further impetus to full-scale cloth manufacturing in Florence. Finally, although the Peruzzi Company was not an important factor in the English wool trade at this time, its involvement was showing signs of increasing. The earliest Peruzzi Company entry to appear in the English *Calendar of Patent Rolls* is dated November 1306 and relates to the shipwreck involving a consignment of the company's wool destined for Flanders.[24]

These developments, while useful, contributed little to the well-being of the company. The predominant source of its success lay in its expansion in the Mediterranean and, in particular, the Kingdom of Naples. Peace was finally established with rebel Sicily in 1302, after the failure of the final papal-organized campaign led by Charles of Valois. The Angevin rulers now directed their energies into building projects and political ventures in northern Italy. These activities consumed more money than ever and brought the Angevins into increasingly close contact with the Florentines, who, in turn, had increasing need for their military support. The Peruzzi Company carefully cultivated the king and his court and by 1304 was an important lender, advancing the equivalent of approximately 90,000 florins over a thirteen-month period.[25] In 1306, it loaned a further 45,000 florins

---

[23] Villani, *Storia*, Book VIII, Chap. 68, mentions demands to examine the commune's accounts on the grain traffic. For grain price levels, see La Roncière, *Prix et salaires*, 716.

[24] *CPR* E I 1301–7, 538.

[25] Abulafia, "Southern Italy," 380. The figure cited is actually 18,280 gold ounces. According to Spufford's *Handbook*, 62–3, the Neapolitan ounce at that time was equivalent to about 5 florins.

that seem to have been repaid, with profit, fairly promptly.[26] Peruzzi credit helped King Charles II purchase the port of Chiarenza in the Morea, where the Peruzzi promptly set up a branch.[27] The king showed his appreciation of the company's help in various ways. In 1302, he granted the company permission to establish a bank in Naples. In 1306, he bolstered the Peruzzi's power and prestige in Florence by petitioning the authorities there to permit Peruzzi personnel to bear arms.[28] Two years later he gave the Peruzzi control of the taxation of grain exports from the Abruzzi.[29] And in 1309, the newly crowned King Robert gave the company the right to have civil cases in which it was involved put before the Court of Appeals, not the ordinary tribunals.[30]

Robert was a special friend of the Florentines and of the Peruzzi in particular. As duke of Calabria, he had taken part in the siege of Pistoia in 1308 and later, as king, he led the Guelf League against the incursion of Emperor Henry VII. While in Florence, he resided at the palace of Giotto Peruzzi. This cozy relationship naturally rested on the ability of the Peruzzi and the other super-companies to mobilize the cash that the king needed and on the king's willingness to let these firms monopolize his export trade and manage much of his administration. The two-way trade of grain, edible oil, and other materials for textiles and other manufactured goods was wonderfully lucrative and produced the bulk of the Peruzzi's profits.

The company expanded elsewhere in the Mediterranean, building substantial businesses throughout the western half from its branches in Sicily, Tunis, Majorca, and Sardinia. Its presence in the eastern half consisted only of small branches in Cyprus and Chiarenza, and agency arrangements in Ragusa, Constantinople, Alexandria, and the Levant. The firm's most important action in that area was its aid in financing the conquest of Rhodes by the Knights Hospitalers in 1309. Although the initial advances were probably small (the large loans were to come later), the influence of this association was to become extremely important to the company. In addition to the direct commercial advantage of securing a privileged position on the island and in the region with the new masters, the Peruzzi gained the prestige of associating with an institution that enjoyed substantial assets and public goodwill in western Europe. The Hospitalers were very much a part of the alliance of the pa-

---

[26] Abulafia, "Southern Italy," 380.

[27] Peruzzi, *Storia commercio*, 318–20.

[28] Ibid., App. 12, which includes an excerpt from Reg. 154 folio 141 of the kingdom.

[29] Abulafia, "Southern Italy," 380.

[30] Yver, *Le commerce*, 302.

pacy, the Angevins, and Florence, and supported Charles II in his Sicilian campaigns.[31] And the papacy would have especially appreciated the Peruzzi's assistance to the Hospitalers in their hour of need, especially in the wake of Philip IV's campaign to demolish that other great crusading order, the Knights Templar.[32]

The Second Company came into being in 1310 and lasted until 1312. Capital was augmented further to li.149,000, the highest level ever attained by the Peruzzi. The Peruzzi family increased its contribution to li.79,000, while that of the outsiders rose to li.68,000, or 46 percent of the total, mainly through the addition of two new shareholders. This company also produced an amazingly good return, given the disruptions in and around Florence resulting from Henry VII's campaign in the area. Henry had invaded Italy in 1310 with the apparent approval of Pope Clement V, who wanted to check the expansion of Angevin power in Italy. The emperor received the Iron Crown of Italy in Milan in 1311 and planned to move on to Rome for his imperial coronation. The Black leadership of Florence rebuffed Henry, amnestied a number of less conspicuous Whites, called upon Robert of Naples for help, and feverishly resumed construction of the city's third circle of walls. After long negotiations and his coronation in Rome in June 1312, Henry determined to crush Florence. He failed in this endeavor, lifted the siege in the autumn, regrouped his forces over the winter for a drive on Naples, but died before he could mount a serious offensive.

The Peruzzi's part in this struggle was mainly financial, as, together with the Bardi and Acciaiuoli, the company financed the cost of Robert's troops in the Romagna.[33] But it was also personal, as Arnoldo d'Arnoldo, one of the prime family shareholders, died in battle before the city in September 1312.

The Second Company was short lived, closing in 1312 after only two years. The main reason for the early dissolution seems to have been the untimely death of no fewer than four shareholders. In addition to Arnoldo, three outside partners died in 1312 – Banco Raugi, Gianni Ponci, and Uguccione di Bonaccorso Bentaccordi.[34] Neither

---

[31] A. J. Forey, "The Military Orders and the Holy Wars against Christians in the 13th Century," *English Historical Review* 104 (January 1989): 1–24.

[32] For details on Philip's attack on the Templars, see Strayer, *Philip the Fair*, Chapter 4, and Peter Partner, *The Murdered Magicians: The Templars and Their Myth* (Oxford, 1982).

[33] Yver, *Le commerce*, 304. The three companies contracted for a total of 24,000 Neapolitan ounces, equivalent to about 120,000 florins.

[34] Sapori, *Storia economica*, Vol. 2, 674. No indication is given as to whether any of these men were killed in action.

the men nor their capital contributions were replaced, so that the Third Company began business with a capital of li.118,000, down li.31,000, or over 20 percent from the previous company. The Peruzzi share fell by li.11,000, but that of the outsiders dropped even more, by li.20,000 to li.48,000, raising the Peruzzi family ownership to nearly 60 percent. Especially remarkable is the fact that not one of the four shareholders seems to have had brothers, sons, or nephews with the aptitude or interest to maintain his share in the business.

A second possible reason for the fleeting existence of the Second Company is the severe business depression that struck Florence between 1310 and 1315 as a result of the costs and trade disruptions associated with the invasion of Henry VII, followed by the war with Pisa in 1314–15. This depression nearly ruined the Alberti Company, which was obliged to suspend crediting interest to depositors between 1312 and 1314 in order to stay afloat.[35] It no doubt also contributed to the collapse of the Frescobaldi Company in 1315. And the effect of the financial crisis on the Peruzzi shareholders' other interests may have caused them to cash in part or all of their Peruzzi holdings. But the Peruzzi Company sailed through the storm (including the years beyond 1312) virtually unscathed, very likely because the most profitable part of its business was concentrated in the south.

The first significant contraction of ownership of the company represented by the 1312 reorganization was not occasioned by any reduction in opportunities for the use of cash. On the contrary, as will be shown later, the Peruzzi became involved on an ever-increasing scale with the Angevin kingdom. Of immediate import, the company apparently negotiated in 1312 a very large loan to the grand master of the Knights Hospitalers, reportedly in the amount of 191,000 florins repayable in four equal annual installments on the feast day of St. John the Baptist.[36] The money was to be used to finance the construction of buildings and fortifications for the Hospitalers on the security of all the order's possessions in all countries.[37]

It is worth digressing to consider this alleged loan in detail as an example of the exaggerated accounts of the super-companies' ability

[35] De Roover, "Alberti Company," 44–5.
[36] Peruzzi, *Storia commercio*, 254. This report is questionable not only for the reasons discussed in the text, but also because it attributes the instigation for the loan to John XXII, who did not become pope until 1316. Of several possible dates for the feast of St. John the Baptist, the most likely is June 24, his birthday in the calendar of the Roman church. St. John the Baptist was the patron saint of Florence, and his birthday was the traditional date for the annual payment of rents in the diocese (see Dameron, *Episcopal Power*, 119).
[37] Davidsohn, *Firenze*, Vol. 5, 759–60.

to lend huge amounts of money at short notice. The Peruzzi connection with the Hospitalers' conquest of Rhodes may have begun as early as May 1306, when a certain "Fulco" of that company reportedly participated in a meeting in Cyprus with Fulkes de Villaret, grand master of the order, and the Genoese corsair Vignolo di Vignoli to plan the invasion.[38] The timing and amount of lending, however, are far from clear. Anthony Luttrell asserts that the Hospitalers had contracted huge loans "with the pope and his bankers" by 1310, the year the conquest was completed.[39] But as we have seen, Pope Clement V had discontinued the practice of having designated bankers, and in any case, the Bardi and Peruzzi were already heavily engaged in lending to King Robert in connection with Emperor Henry VII's invasion of Italy in that year. Moreover, the Hospitalers Order was a terrible credit risk after its expulsion from Syria in 1291 and even more so during the trial of the Templars, when rulers throughout Europe were casting covetous eyes at the Hospitalers' assets in their territories. It is therefore unlikely that the Peruzzi committed significant funds before 1312, the year in which the pope granted the Hospitalers the lucrative Templar properties in Cyprus.[40]

As for the figures, the earliest cited ones are not of the sums originally loaned by the companies, but the amounts alleged to be due to them several years later. Luttrell states that the Hospitalers owed the Bardi and Peruzzi "at least 500,000 florins" in March 1320.[41] Delaville le Roulx cites an amount of 575,900 florins at that time, but *owed to all lenders.*[42] But all seem agreed, based on papal records, that in 1321 the Peruzzi were owed 191,000 florins and the Bardi 133,000.[43] Therefore, let us consider the 191,000 figure and its significance. This

---

[38] Anthony Luttrell, "Interessi fiorentini nell'economia e nella politica dei Cavalieri Ospedalieri di Rodi nel Trecento," *Annali della Scuola Normale Superiore di Pisa: Lettere, storia e filosofia*, 2d series, 28 (Pisa, 1959), 317–26. "Fulco" was presumably Bencivenni di Folco Folchi, a shareholder of the Peruzzi Company at the time.

[39] Ibid.

[40] The Peruzzi and the Bardi probably did not feel entirely comfortable in advancing serious funds to the order until the following year, when formal transfer of the Templar assets took place (see A. Luttrell, "The Hospitallers in Cyprus after 1291," *Acts of the First International Congress of Cypriot Studies* 2 [Nicosia 1972]: 161). In that year also, the threat to Florence had evaporated with the death of Henry VII and the agreement of King Robert to become protector of that city.

[41] Luttrell, "Interessi fiorentini," 318.

[42] Jean Delaville le Roulx, *Les Hospitaliers à Rhodes (1310–1421)* (Paris, 1913), 23–4, 53–5. In addition, he said that the order owed £10,000 Genovese.

[43] Renouard, *Les relations*, 542; Davidsohn, *Firenze*, Vol. 6, 547 (in addition to the others cited).

amount, equivalent to li.275,000, would have tied up more than twice the company's capital in one risky venture. But the company probably never loaned anything like this total. First, the 1321 figure would have reflected not only accumulated interest since the inception of the loan, but also a sizable markup for arranging and managing the debt.[44] Second, although the commitment may have been made in 1312, realistically the cash would have been advanced in tranches as needed, rather than all at once, and charged to different priors of the order.[45] The main sources of funds would have been depositors, lay and ecclesiastical, very likely in Naples and elsewhere in the Mediterranean, given the shortage of cash in depression-ridden Florence at that time. Possibly the Peruzzi syndicated part of the loan as a separate venture, parceling it out among various individuals and institutions with a political, moral, or economic interest in aiding the Hospitalers.[46] And while interest was theoretically illegal, the depositors no doubt expected and received a return at the then going rate of 8 percent per annum, which the Peruzzi would have been obliged to recover from the borrower. Thus, after subtracting the interest, fees, and amounts allocated to other investors, the cash outlay of the Peruzzi would have been considerably less than the stated amount due. The company's share of the loan was clearly not too burdensome, because it was able to award its shareholders a handsome dividend in 1319 while acknowledging that the Hospitaler loans and the Rhodes branch accounts were still open.[47] The company's confidence in eventual repayment turned out to have been well placed, perhaps helped by the intervention of Pope John XXII.[48]

At the beginning of this digression, the word "alleged" was used with reference to the Hospitaler debts to the companies because there is another possible explanation for these extraordinary loans. It is that the principal lender may not have been the super-companies, but the papacy itself, using the super-companies as agents of the pa-

---

[44] If the money had been advanced in 1312, the cumulative effect of interest alone over nine years at the then going rate of 8% would have been 100%, so that the original loan would have been less than half the amount cited.

[45] *I libri*, 439. Giotto's Secret Book names several Hospitaler chapter priors as debtors, including those of Venice and Avignon as well as Rhodes.

[46] While there is no evidence that the Peruzzi syndicated the loan, there was a precedent for such action in the consortia operated by the Ricciardi and Frescobaldi in their financing of the English monarchy (see Chapter 2).

[47] *I libri*, 439. But Giotto noted that "we expect great profits, God willing."

[48] Renouard, *Les relations*, 542; Davidsohn, *Firenze*, Vol. 6, 548. Repayment was scheduled in eight semiannual installments beginning in 1321, but it became necessary to extend the term a further two years.

pal treasury. There are three reasons for suggesting this alternative. The first is that the order, besides being financially unstable, was headed by a grand master, Foulkes de Villaret, who by 1312 had proved to be extravagant, incompetent, and corrupt, alienating his leading brethren.[49] Under such circumstances, the super-companies would have been wary of lending large sums to that organization without the explicit support of the papacy. The second reason is the Peruzzi Company's apparent lack of concern mentioned earlier at its interim closing in 1319, which gives the decided impression that this was a lucrative arrangement, with little company money at risk. Finally, the popes appear to have regarded the Hospitalers' repayment installments as indirect income to the papacy even when they continued after the debt had been extinguished in 1335.[50]

The point in discussing this loan in such detail is to emphasize the need to question the inflated amounts involved in so many of the financial transactions attributed to the super-companies. The fact that historians have rarely challenged the reports of very large loans (which later become astronomical in the Peruzzi's English dealings) has helped create a mystique around the super-companies that has obscured the reality of their business. They were indeed big organizations for their time, and they made use of the available instruments of cashless transfer, such as bills of exchange and bank debits and credits.[51] But in an economy where *creation* of credit through fractional bank reserves was insignificant, such devices had only limited application, and larger payments had to

[49] Luttrell, "The Hospitallers in Cyprus," 288. The leading brethren later pressed for his resignation and even tried to assassinate him in 1317. He was eventually replaced in 1319 by a more responsible leader, Hélion de Villeneuve.

[50] Luttrell, "Interessi fiorentini," 319. The payments after 1335 were described as "deposits" to the super-companies, accumulating to 360,000 florins by 1343. This figure is based on a note dated 1382 in the accounts of the Hospitalers at Malta, which mentions the existence of a document showing that the Bardi, Peruzzi, and Acciaiuoli owed this sum. Luttrell associates these purported deposits with the unsuccessful attempts to recover with the pope's help sums owed by the Peruzzi in June 1345 (Sapori, *La crisi*, 198). But the Hospitalers' muted efforts to obtain satisfaction from the bankrupt Peruzzi (discussed further in Chapter 9) lead to the suspicion that most payments had been passed along to the papacy, leaving a relatively modest balance really owed the order by the company.

[51] Spufford in *Money and Its Use*, 255–9, gives a useful description of these financial instruments and their widespread use in medieval Europe. Lane and Meuller in *Money and Banking*, 61–4, 69–89, provide additional data and an excellent overview of medieval banking systems.

be made in hard cash.[52] Therefore, either the sums reportedly loaned by the super-companies were greatly overstated or the super-companies found ways to lay off large parts of both the cash and the risk entailed in such loans. There is no evidence in any of the surviving company books to support the existence of "megaloans." To illustrate, the Peruzzi had reportedly lent very large amounts up to 1308 to the king of France, the Hospitalers, the papacy, and above all, to the king of Naples. But at the close of books in 1308, the balances due from the first three of these debtors totaled a mere li.26,000. The amount due from all other debtors was li.40,000, and the king of Naples was not even mentioned.[53] This suggests that the company's system for managing its cash flow in that kingdom, discussed in Chapter 2, was working very well indeed.

The Third Company lasted a remarkable twelve years from 1312 to 1324, with an interim accounting and dividend distribution in 1319. It was the last of the prosperous Peruzzi companies driven by unparalleled success in its most important market, the Angevin kingdom of southern Italy. Yver cites the period between the death of Henry VII in 1313 and the arrival of the duke of Calabria in Florence in 1325 as the apogee of the super-companies' fortunes in that country.[54] Two developments greatly enhanced their position. The first was the very close liaison that came about between Florence and Naples following Henry VII's invasion. To ensure its protection, Florence in 1313 granted King Robert overlordship of the commune for five years, albeit with limited powers, and renewed it in 1318 for a further five years. Under these circumstances the leading merchants became virtual ambassadors between Naples and Florence.[55] The sec-

[52] Spufford, *Money and Its Use*, 255, acknowledges that the commercial credit system he describes was inadequate to handle large international political payments or even smaller payments where there was an imbalance of trade. The problem of credit is discussed more fully in Chapter 7, this volume, in connection with Peruzzi loans to Edward III.

[53] *I libri*, 435. The Secret Book of Giotto reports for the closing of the 1308 company, "rimase a partire del guadagnio fatto infin'a quel die de quelo ch'era scritto lbr. 26,236 e d3 in fior., i quali si riserbaro a partire per cagione de la ragione di parigi che no si potè metere in saldo per li molti danari che si dovea ricevere da Re di Francia e d'altri baroni d'intorno de la Corte del Re; e rimase a metere in saldo la ragione di Benciveni Folchi ch'avea tenuta intorno del Maestro de lo Spedale, e quella di Corte di Papa, e quela d'Inghiliterra del cambio che non si pottero fare; e rimasero er apuntati e i pendente, che non si contaro per alcuna cosa, da lbr. 40,000 a fior. che si deono ricevere da molte gienti."

[54] Yver, *Le commerce*, 308.

[55] Ibid., 306.

ond was Robert's quarrel with Venice between 1311 and 1314, marked by his seizure of Venetian goods. Even when peace was finally concluded in 1316, the Venetians had lost their old privileges, and the Florentines exerted great pressure to ensure that they stayed lost. In 1316, the Bardi, Peruzzi, and Acciaiuoli companies formed a syndicate and succeeded in getting the grain export monopoly formalized under their control. As a result, as Yver commented, "the Adriatic was plowed by Venetian ships loaded by Florentine merchants who transported to Venetian possessions and even to Venice itself grains bought from growers or royal estates, as well as oil, wine, cheese, and other agricultural products."[56]

It is worth emphasizing once more the size and importance of the grain trade. Recorded Florentine exports of Apulian grain in 1311 reached the remarkable total of 45,000 tons.[57] A few calculations may be helpful in putting this figure into perspective. The 45,000 tons are roughly equivalent to 400,000 *salme,* or 4.4 million Florentine bushels.[58] Drawing on various sources, including chroniclers Villani and Lenzi, Giuliani Pinto has calculated annual grain consumption of 150,000 *moggia* for the combined city and *contado* of Florence, versus a total production of 120,000 *moggia* in "normal" crop years.[59] The shortfall of 30,000 *moggia,* equivalent to 720,000 Florentine bushels per year, would have been the normal import requirement in the early decades of the fourteenth century.[60] An unknown amount would have been supplied from the Romagna nearby and from Sardinia, leaving normal annual requirements from the south of perhaps 400,000 bushels. These estimates, as crude as they are, make it clear that the supplies available from the Apulian grain monopoly significantly exceeded Florence's normal needs. Admittedly, 1311 seems to have been an atypical year, and the normal amount of grain available for export was probably more like that in the years 1327–31, that is, 110,000 *salme,* or around 1.2 million bushels.[61] Also admittedly,

[56] Ibid., 310.

[57] Abulafia, "Southern Italy," 382, mentioned in Chapter 2, this volume.

[58] One *salma* of wheat grain weighs about 112 kilograms (see Yves Renouard, "Une expédition des céréales des Pouilles en Arménie par les Bardi pour le compte de Benoit XII," in *Mélanges d'Archéologie et d'Histoire* [Rome, 1936], 813) and is equivalent to about eleven Florentine bushels (see Edler, *Glossary,* 256).

[59] *Il Biadaiolo,* 77–9.

[60] Conversion from *moggia* to Florentine bushels is tricky, as the ratios vary according to time and place. Lopez and Raymond, *Medieval Trade,* 73, cited 16.59 bushels as the conversion factor, but the figures used here are based on twenty-four bushels per *moggio* as applied by Pinto and confirmed by Edler, *Glossary,* 187.

[61] David Abulafia, "Sul commercio del grano siciliano nel tardo duecento," *La societa, mediterranea all'epoca del Vespro* (Palermo, 1983), 5.

Florentine crops fell well below normal in several years; as Pinto points out, a relatively modest reduction in Florentine grain production would have had a dramatic effect on import requirements.[62] In most years, however, the super-companies would have directed the sale of substantial quantities of this valuable commodity to other cities in Italy and the Mediterranean.

Prices of grains were generally high throughout the 1312–24 period, although years of actual reported scarcity were rare.[63] As Abulafia points out, however, years of scarcity were not always good for Apulian grain because, being of higher quality and more expensive than the local product, it was less affordable to the poorer segments of the population.[64] But Apulian wheat had the advantages of being preferred both for its superior quality and its remarkable keeping properties.[65]

Trade between Florence and the Angevin kingdom, as already noted, consisted of much more than the exchange of cloth for grain, but these two commodities formed the heart of the commerce between the two polities. Until the early 1320s, virtually all the luxury cloth sold in Naples was of Flemish, Brabantine, or French origin, and companies such as the Peruzzi either bought the finished product for reexport, or imported semiprocessed material for finishing.[66] Their direct manufacturing was limited to a bewildering variety of lighter and cheaper grades of cloth. According to Hoshino's careful study of Florentine customs and wool guild documents, English wool began reaching Florence in quantity during the second decade of the fourteenth century, primarily in inferior grades, such as *agnellina* and *boldrone*.[67] More typically at that time, however, Florentine manufacturers made cloth from wools originating in various parts of Italy,

---

[62] *Il Biadaiolo*, 78. For example, a crop reduction of 25% would double import needs to 1.4 million bushels.

[63] La Roncière, *Prix et salaires*, 716. Scarcities were reported only in 1317 and 1322.

[64] Abulafia, "Southern Italy," 385.

[65] De Broüard, "Problèmes de substances," 484, citing archival sources, noted that the best quality of Sicilian wheat, properly stored, could keep "10, 15, 20 ans et plus."

[66] Rules of the Calimala Guild, to which the Peruzzi belonged, forbade its members to finish cloth manufactured in Florence. See Staley, *The Guilds of Florence*, 131.

[67] Hoshino, *L'Arte della lana*, 116–17. For a discussion of the varieties of cloth produced in Florence and sold throughout the Mediterranean, see 123–30. Hoshino's research calls into question the contention of earlier scholars that most Florentine cloth production was made from English wool by the early fourteenth century (see Lopez "Majorcans and Genoese," 1168).

including the south, as well as Spain, North Africa, and Burgundy. The Peruzzi reportedly used both English and Burgundian wool between 1322 and 1325.[68]

A word should be said at this point about the composition and manufacturing processes involved in luxury cloth, as opposed to the cheaper grades.[69] In medieval Europe, the finest short-staple wools from which luxury fabrics were made came from the Welsh Marches, the Cotswolds, and Lincolnshire in England, shorn from mature, preferably live sheep. Such fine wools produced relatively weak yarns, with the result that cloth woven from them had to be compressed and strengthened by the process of fulling. Moreover, it had to undergo several shearings to achieve a satisfactorily smooth finish and texture. In contrast, the lighter, coarser cloths, such as worsteds, or local varieties woven from worsted warps and woolen wefts, were made from cheaper, tougher, longer-staple wool.[70] Such fabrics required little or no fulling or shearing. Thus, luxury cloth was expensive because of costly raw materials, a long, complex manufacturing process, and the meticulous attention to detail required to satisfy a discriminating clientele.

The lighter and cheaper woolen goods made in Florence found a ready market in southern Italy, sold in fairs and in the lesser cities throughout the kingdom, but in the early 1320s the penetration of the luxury cloth market by Florentine manufacturers was modest. The Peruzzi cloth sales in southern Italy would, up to 1324, have consisted of lesser-quality goods fabricated by itself or other manufacturers from Italy and various parts of Europe for the "mass market" and luxury cloths mostly made in northern Europe, possibly including a small quantity of Florentine production. There is no evidence to suggest that the Peruzzi had the capability of making luxury textiles at this point.

Other sales outlets for Florentine-made cloth were, of course, Florence itself and its *contado*, as well as cities throughout Italy. As Hoshino emphasizes, Florence was a major distribution center for textiles, and merchants from other cities came there to buy, rather

---

[68] Hoshino, *L'Arte della lana*, 118.

[69] The source for the statements in this paragraph is Munro, "Textile Technology," 694. For those interested in further details on this subject, the entire article (693–711) is most helpful. For a discussion of the various types of northern European cloths sold in the Mediterranean area, see H. C. Krueger, "The Genoese Exportation of Northern Cloths to Mediterranean Ports, Twelfth Century," *Revue Belge de Philologie et d'Histoire* 65: 4 (1987): 722–50.

[70] The local varieties had their own names, such as serge, *saye, saye drappée,* and *baye.*

than having Florentine merchants take their wares to those cities.[71] It is worth noting that the Peruzzi lacked significant branches in any of the cities in north and central Italy except Pisa, Genoa, and Venice, where company employees worked mainly in forwarding operations rather than local selling.[72] But like most Florentine merchants, the company no doubt bought merchandise in other Italian cities for sale in Florence and elsewhere. Certainly, cloth manufactured in other cities, especially Milan, competed successfully both at home and abroad with the Florentine product. In the western Mediterranean and Sicily, Tuscan merchants marketed Florentine and Lombard cloth as well as a wide range of draperies from the Low Countries, because local manufacture had not been successful.[73] Documentation from Sicily covering the first half of the fourteenth century is too scarce, however, to judge the market penetration of the various makers, particularly the Catalans, who must have been fierce competitors in the western Mediterranean.[74]

Unfortunately, data on quantities sold are so sparse that it is impossible to make a rational estimate of the size of the Florentine textiles business. Given the limited range of product quality and the stiff competition for the available markets, Villani's estimate of annual Florentine production of 100,000 pieces early in the century seems high.[75] If it is anything close to accurate, however, this figure underlines the tremendous importance of the captive market in southern Italy to Florence's well-being.

The Angevin connection was also important in the eastern Mediterranean, as the grain monopoly and the demand of the court for luxuries helped to justify the establishment of branches in Cyprus

---

[71] Hoshino, *L'Arte della lana*, 69, 72.

[72] The company reportedly did have representation in Milan (from 1309) and Bologna (from 1323), which Davidsohn described as "branches" (*Firenze*, Vol. 6, 883, 853), but there is no evidence of formal branch accounts nor reference to such branches in the surviving Peruzzi books.

[73] Ibid. Hoshino notes on 82 that various attempts to implant wool manufacturing in Palermo by Genoese artisans were unsuccessful. In southern Italy, local manufacturing was modest and limited to low-quality goods. It should also be remembered that early in the fourteenth century, exports of Flemish cloth still included a range of cheaper goods that did not disappear from the Mediterranean market until the 1330s (see Munro, "Industrial Transformations," 110–11).

[74] Bresc, *Un monde Méditerranéen*, 476.

[75] Villani, *Storia*, Book XI, Chap. 94, cites 1336–38 annual production as 70,000–80,000 pieces, compared with 100,000 pieces thirty years earlier. Hoshino, *L'Arte della lana*, 131–2, argues strenuously that the 70,000–80,000 estimate is vastly overstated, but his presentation lacks coherence. See Appendix V on Villani for further details.

and Rhodes. Once such a branch was in place, it could be used as a base of operations for the Levant, the East, and Africa for the buying and selling of a vast range of goods. The Peruzzi accounts contain numerous references to the variety of materials and products in which the company dealt, including wool, cotton, silk, cloths, alum, dyes, rope, precious metals, jewelry, and spices of many kinds. Some of the goods and commodities purchased there were for company use, but most were for resale in Italy and northern Europe. The branches also engaged in local and regional trade, and served as distribution points for forwarding merchandise of the company and other merchants to further destinations. In short, the company seemed prepared to enter any kind of commerce, however minor, that would turn a profit. These myriad small transactions helped carry the considerable overhead costs of the company's permanent organization, a subject that will be discussed more fully in Chapter 6.

The company's branch in Bruges was undoubtedly a very active one despite the lack of documentary evidence and the tiny account balance registered in 1335. As indicated in Table 3, there were four permanent employees in Bruges under the management of a family-member partner, a sizable operation by medieval standards. Moreover, the branch was a "busy" one, with many employees coming and going between 1335 and 1343. There is every reason to believe that the branch was at least as active during the first quarter of the fourteenth century, because Bruges was the marketing and financial center for the nearby industrial cities of Flanders and Brabant. Here was the prime, if not the only, source of luxury cloth so vital to the company's southern trade. From here, too, Peruzzi factors could market the English wools acquired from the company's London branch or elsewhere to the entrepreneurs from whom it bought finished product. Finally, from here company employees would have engaged in financial operations, arranging credit with both buyers and sellers as well as transfers of funds through letters of credit and bills of exchange.

The Bruges branch's intercompany links were not limited to Florence. Although most of the finished goods would have been shipped to the headquarters warehouse, a considerable volume of product would have been destined to the customers of the company's branches in Paris, Avignon, and London.[76] The branch also could provide

[76] There is only limited direct evidence of interbranch commerce within the Peruzzi Company because of the lack of detailed branch accounts. But the fact that such business was a logical part of the branch system is supported by the accounts of the Barcelona branch of the Datini Company, which showed significant debit and credit balances with other Datini branches (see De Roover, "Lucca Pacioli," 142–3).

financial services to clients unrelated to the company's merchandise business.

The peace following the disruption of the Flemish revolt of 1302–4 was uneasy, but it lasted throughout most of this period, despite a serious flareup in 1314.[77] The French victors levied huge indemnities, falling mainly on the towns, but eventually received only a small amount. Nonetheless, the relative calm and the threat of action on the indemnities gave those towns both opportunity and motivation to increase their production. The end of hostilities between England and France also assured the uninterrupted flow of English wool. The city of Bruges nevertheless needed financial help and was able to borrow from the Italian companies, given its importance to them and its respectable credit rating. The Peruzzi Company acted as a collector of Flemish indemnities for the king of France and occasionally granted loans to help make the payments possible. The only loan to Bruges for which there is direct evidence in the Peruzzi accounts did not take place until 1328, but it is unlikely to have been the first of its kind.[78]

The Paris branch was also considered important, even after the company's involvement in royal financing had all but petered out. According to Strayer, in the latter part of the reign of Philip IV it remained responsible for the receivership of Carcassonne, the collection of the Flemish indemnity, and technical assistance in the mints, and it made a minute contribution to Philip's preparations for a Flemish war in 1314.[79] The fact that the company had to work both sides of the Flemish dispute exemplifies the awkward situations into which a super-company could be drawn by political rivalries. But the size of the Paris market, with its large population of elites and its nearby industries and fairs, seems to have been sufficient in itself to warrant a substantial permanent branch. In 1335 it had the same number of factors as Bruges and was also headed by a Peruzzi partner. Given its government activities in the early years of the century, it may have been even larger then.

The work of the branch is most likely to have been of a marketing nature, selling merchandise of all kinds drawn from the Mediterranean and the Levant as well as from the north. Marketing of course

---

[77] See Strayer, *Philip the Fair,* 337–46. There was also the very serious maritime revolt starting in 1323, which will be discussed in the following chapter.

[78] De Roover describes this loan (*Medieval Bruges,* 84–5) as well as another smaller, but still sizable loan of 1330 (281). Details of the 1328 loan will be given in Chapter 6.

[79] Strayer, "Italian Bankers," 117 and n32, 121.

included any necessary credit and financing arrangements to conclude the sales. The branch also may have provided raw materials for the industries in the suburbs. Paris was an important transit point; company travelers from Florence to Bruges or London would often pass through Paris. The branch must have been profitable or useful to the company in many ways. Despite the many arbitrary fines, levies, and even imprisonments at the hands of the French authorities, the Peruzzi, like other Italian companies, continued to operate in Paris, presumably treating such hazards as a cost of doing business there.

The company's business in Avignon was also conducted by a well-staffed branch, led by a partner, Filippo Villani, brother of the chronicler. Although a small city, Avignon was large in potential, with the papal court, cardinals and their retinues, hangers-on, and petitioners from abroad all bent on gaining prestige with conspicuous consumption, a market made in heaven for traders. The branch took deposits from prelates and loaned money to them, but the papal treasury remained aloof from the Italian merchants until the accession of John XXII in 1316.[80] The new pope approved a contract in January 1317 with the Bardi and Peruzzi, giving them the authority to transfer to Avignon sums gathered by the collectors in England, Italy, and the East.[81] Later that year, the contract was extended to include Scotland and Ireland.

The business was important for the prestige it brought even though the companies were not designated as "official" apostolic bankers. It also brought financial flexibility, because the companies were able to meet their obligations by delivering funds from locations most convenient to them, instead of from the actual collection points. Thus, papal funds collected in England could be kept there to buy wool, and the cash due to Avignon could be remitted from Florence by the dates agreed. The companies charged fees for the service to reflect distances and risk, but since the papal treasury was aware of the usefulness of the business to the companies, it could negotiate them to a low level. The amount of money transferred was modest because the greatest source of papal revenues, France, was excluded from the arrangement. Thus, the much-discussed papal transfer business, while attractive to the companies, was not a very profitable one.

[80] There was, however, a deposit of 7,000 florins in 1312 by the Abbot of Samichele della Scluse divided one-third each among the Bardi, Peruzzi, and Scali companies. The deposit, while ostensibly the abbot's, was registered by the notary of Clement V's chamberlain, and the complicated eventual reimbursement in 1336 appeared to involve the administration of Pope Benedict XII. *I libri*, 94.

[81] Renouard, *Les relations*, 127–31.

The English branch was also an important one by 1335, with five employees managed by the son of a partner, but it was probably much smaller in the first two decades of the century. The company seemed determined to keep clear of royal entanglements. Its presence in the English wool trade was accordingly overshadowed by the Frescobaldi, the Bardi, and others who were prepared to lend money to the king. The only loans made by the Peruzzi to an English monarch prior to 1336 were for £700 in 1311, £200 in 1315, and 1,000 marks (£667) in 1322.[82] Some indication of the Peruzzi's level of activity in England can be obtained by examining the *Calendar of Patent Rolls* and the *Calendar of Close Rolls* and comparing the entries with those of the Bardi, known as a very active firm there. During the period 1301 to 1321, the Peruzzi Company was cited in eight entries in the *Calendar of Patent Rolls*, most dealing with minor issues, while the Bardi appeared in eighty-four entries, many of significant importance. In the *Calendar of Close Rolls* for the years 1307 to 1323, the numbers were five and sixty-five, respectively.

This modest level of market penetration seems to have been satisfactory to the conservative chairman Tommaso, and must have given the company adequate access to its wool requirements for Flanders and Florence. In the early 1320s, however, the Peruzzi suddenly became more active in England with the arrival of Bonifazio, son of Tommaso, as branch manager. In June 1322, he signed a ten-year lease with the Bishop of Durham for the manors of Hoveden and Richall, York. The purpose of these manors is not known; most likely they were collecting points for wool. What is remarkable about the lease was its confirmation nearly two years later in a ceremony at Westminster that appears to have been attended by no fewer than five of the company's shareholders.[83] The presence of so many senior representatives of the company in England's capital cannot be explained by a minor lease agreement. Rather, it attests to a decision by the company to become an important player in the English mar-

[82] *CPR* E II 1307–13, 399, E II 1313–17 254, and E II 1321–24, 198. The 1322 loan, along with one for £4,000 from the Bardi, was needed for Edward II's Scottish campaign of that year. It was the last time that Edward II was to borrow significant sums in England from the Italian firms. See N. Fryde, *The Tyranny*, 93. The Peruzzi did, however, advance 3,951 gold florins to the constable of Bordeaux in 1324. See Vale, *The Angevin Legacy*, 237.

[83] *CPR* E II 1321–24, 401. The entry is dated March 20, 1324, but refers to a lease dated June 21, 1322. It is not entirely clear from the English translation in the *Calendar* whether all the Peruzzi notables listed were present or represented by proxy, but such an array of names would be extraordinary for a lease of this type unless the people happened to be on the spot.

ket, in particular in the wool trade. The timing of this event suggests that the change in attitude was motivated by the company's determination to supply the manufacturers of higher-quality textiles in Florence for which English wools of the better grades were essential.

Two entries in the *Calendar of Close Rolls* provide evidence of serious investment in the English wool trade. The first is a loan in April 1323 of £1,330 to Warden Abbey, an early wool-producing Cistercian establishment in the county of Bedford.[84] This is an enormous sum to advance to an abbey with an annual income of little more than £200, which planned to use at least part of the money to rebuild its church on a lavish scale.[85] The abbey seems to have had both resources and influence, because the loan was recorded as repaid in full, probably in 1340.[86] This was no more than two years after having been excused by reasons of extreme poverty from having to pay the latest clerical tenth.[87] The Peruzzi apparently made a further large loan sometime between 1324 and 1331 for which records are missing, because the company received payment of £900 sterling from Warden Abbey in April 1345, eighteen months after its bankruptcy, and credited the receipt to shareholders of the 1324–31 company.[88]

There seems to be no commercial rationale for such large investments in a minor producer of middling-grade wool.[89] Possibly, the abbey served as an important collection point for the surrounding area and used some of the funds to buy wool for the Peruzzi. But the

[84] *CCR* E II 1318–23, 705.
[85] The Victoria History of the Counties of England *Bedfordshire*, Vol. 1, 362–4. The very costly ceramic tile floors of the church, similar to those in Prior Crauden's chapel at Ely Cathedral of 1324–5, have survived and are described by Evelyn Baker in "Images, Ceramic Floors, and Warden Abbey," *World Archaeology* 18 (February 1987): 363–81.
[86] *CCR* E II 1318–23, 705. The entry was noted "cancelled on payment acknowledged by Peter Dini and Henry Accursi, merchants of the aforesaid society." Dini served in England only from March 18, 1339, till his death in July 1340 (see Sapori, *Storia Economica*, Vol. 2, 727).
[87] *CPR* E III 1338–40, 46. The entry states, "Pardon, out of compassion for their recent depressed estate, to the abbot and convent of Wardon of their contingent of the last three-yearly tenth granted to the king by the clergy of the province of Canterbury." This pardon was confirmed on February 1, 1341, in *CCR* E III 1341–3, 7. Pleading poverty may not be proof of poverty, but getting excused from taxes is persuasive evidence.
[88] *I libri*, 272. This is one of several similar entries on various pages relating to this receipt from the "abate di Guardona in Inghliterra."
[89] Pegolotti, *La pratica*, 262. The prices quoted for wool from Guardona fall in the lower middle range of producers listed. Annual production is shown as twenty-five sacks, which is in the upper middle range.

incongruity of these transactions suggests a more compelling logic, the intervention of an anonymous powerful benefactor. This man could well have been Henry Burghersh, bishop of Lincoln, who is recorded as staying at Warden Abbey in 1323 when he granted the abbot and convent an indulgence to aid in the rebuilding of the church.[90] Burghersh, as bishop of a great wool-producing diocese, would have been well worth cultivating by a company ambitious to advance its position in the higher-quality wool trade. Also, as a consistent opponent of the Despensers and the king, he enjoyed the special protection of Pope John XXII and could be a useful friend in court in case of a change in the regime. Later, when he was chancellor, treasurer, and councillor to Edward III, Burghersh would have been in a position to continue his assistance to the abbey's building project by arranging the tax exemption already noted. For the Peruzzi, he would have been an invaluable contact, although there is no evidence that he ever intervened on the company's behalf.

The second *Close Rolls* entry, dated March 1324, is the acknowledgment by the prior of the Hospitalers in England of a debt of £1,303, with lands and chattels in Bedford, Essex, and Hertford as collateral.[91] This is the first of many entries relating to the Hospitalers in England and appears to reflect the parceling-out of the liability of loans made by the company to the grand master of the order in Rhodes.[92] A further entry in February 1326 confirmed that there was an apportionment of the loans granted to the order for the conquest of Rhodes and commanded the prior to pay its debts to the Bardi and Peruzzi, notwithstanding a prohibition the king had imposed on the export of currency.[93] Interestingly, the text of the writ gave credit to the Hospitalers, and by inference their financiers, for conquering Rhodes from the Saracens. In fact, the island was taken from the Christian Byzantines, showing once again how easily and conveniently history can be distorted.

Further evidence of quickening interest in England is the 1322 loan to the crown. More important, the Peruzzi became principal deposit banker for Edward II's favorite, Hugh Despenser the Younger. Starting in January 1321, Despenser maintained an active account that attained a balance exceeding £3,000 on November 1, 1324.[94]

---

[90] E. Baker, "Warden Abbey," 364. Baker cites M. Finch's translation of Bishop Burghersh's memoranda as the source for this statement.

[91] *CCR* E II 1323–7, 170.

[92] These are part of the loans discussed earlier in this chapter.

[93] *CCR* E II 1323–7, 545.

[94] E. B. Fryde, "The Deposits of Hugh Despenser the Younger with Italian Bankers," *Economic History Review* 2 series, (1951): 360.

Fryde comments that between 1321 and 1326, Despenser was a more important source of funds to the English branches of the Bardi and Peruzzi than were the papal collectors in England, a tribute to the importance of this account and the often unappreciated smallness of the papal transfers.[95]

During the early 1320s, then, the Peruzzi's English business seemed set fair. It had acquired a valuable relationship with the most powerful man in the kingdom aside from the king himself, holding money for him rather than having to lend it. In this case, the Peruzzi Company was even more favored than the Bardi, which began to hold only a lesser amount of the Despenser cash from 1324 onward.[96] The company's papal connection, while not especially lucrative, greatly enhanced the company's status in England. And even its good relationship with the French monarchy was helpful during this period. On one occasion, the French king intervened on behalf of the Peruzzi to relieve the firm's English branch of a fine of 500 marks for alleged violation of the wool staple charter.[97]

Overall, the twelve-year term of the Third Company was one of solid achievement, with stability in its major markets in the Mediterranean and new growth in the papal and English businesses. Even the retrenchment in France was not a serious matter, and the company maintained a significant commercial position in that country. Profit averaged a respectable, if not outstanding, li.18,000 per year, and the real rate of return for those shareholders who were fully invested throughout the period was 11 percent for the first seven years and a very good 14.5 percent for the later five years. The shareholders wished to close the books in 1319 but could not do so because of the open accounts with the Hospitalers and the Rhodes branch, but they felt sufficiently confident of the soundness of these accounts and the prospect of profit to distribute an interim dividend of 100 percent.[98] Their confidence was eventually justified, as the final closing in 1324 yielded a further dividend of 90 percent.

There were, however, disturbing signs of trouble ahead. Political problems were emerging in the second decade of the fourteenth century that would distract and eventually overwhelm the *popolani* leadership, of which the Peruzzi Company shareholders were very much a part. Following the successful defense of the city against Henry VII

---

[95] Ibid., 348.
[96] Ibid., 347. The Bardi, however, was the king's main deposit banker. See N. Fryde, *The Tyranny*, 93.
[97] *CCR* E II 1318–23, 303.
[98] *I libri*, 439.

in 1312, Florence became involved in a series of wars with its neigh-
bors over the next thirty years that proved disastrous, thanks to a
remarkably consistent demonstration of military incompetence.

The first phase of these new local struggles began when Uguccione
della Faggiuola took over as dictator of Pisa and sacked Lucca in
1314. He then attacked the Guelf League of Tuscany and adminis-
tered a crushing defeat on its forces at Montecatini near Pistoia in
1315. Biero di Filippo was the only Peruzzi family member involved
in the battle, although there is a questionable claim that Giovanni di
Giotto also served there.[99] In 1316, Uguccione was overthrown by
Castruccio Castracani, who secured Lucca's independence. There
followed a long period of inconclusive skirmishes between the mercenaries of Castruccio and those of Florence.[100] In 1318, Florence
felt sufficiently insecure to renew King Robert of Naples' powers as
signor for a further four years. Given the Peruzzi's close relationship
with the king both in Florence and in Naples, the family and company would have supported the renewal. The commune's leadership
regained confidence in 1322, however, and allowed the king's man-
date to lapse, a decision apparently justified by the subsequent collapse of Lucca's alliance with Pisa. But Castruccio's shocking seizure
of Pistoia in May 1325 set the stage for the now independent Florence to embark on a new campaign, which will be discussed in the
following chapter.

There were signs of future trouble for the company as well, stem-
ming from an apparent tendency of certain shareholders to draw
heavily on company money for their personal needs. The only early
evidence is from one partner, but a very important one, Giotto
d'Arnoldo Peruzzi.[101] As far as can be ascertained, Giotto maintained
his capital investment in the company in full from 1300 to 1314, and
between 1308 and 1314 he kept a small running deposit as well.[102]
But from 1315 onward, he became increasingly indebted to the company, as shown by the fiscal year-end balances in Table 6.

[99] Peruzzi, *Storia commercio*, 402. The author provides costs associated with
Giovanni's participation in the Battle of Montecatini, but since he dates the
event 1335, he is probably referring to a different battle, which he has misnamed.

[100] See Louis Green, *Castruccio Castracani* (Oxford, 1986), for a useful account of
the complex political and military maneuverings of this period. Both sides also
contributed troops and money to the rival Guelf–Ghibelline forces in Lombardy
and Liguria.

[101] Giotto's behavior may not have been typical of family members. According to
the 1335 balances shown in Table A6, several non-Peruzzi shareholders were in
debt to the company, but only one other Peruzzi family member besides Giotto
was in debt.

[102] *I libri*, 419–26.

Table 6. *Balances owed company by*
Giotto d'Arnoldo Peruzzi (lire a fiorino)

Year at Nov. 1	
1315	7,638
1316	10,389
1317	16,272
1318	18,695
1319	19,508[a]
1320	10,710
1321	12,171
1322	15,196
1323	17,120
1324	22,018[b]

[a] Before interim dividend of li.11,000.
[b] Before final dividend of li.9,900 and
closing of company.
Source: I libri, 448–60.

These balances for a considerable period greatly exceeded Giotto's capital contribution of li.11,000. Thus, the dividends he received produced an outstanding return, despite the fact that he was charged interest at a rate of 8 percent per annum on his balances. Between 1312 and 1319, his actual investment was li.11,000 for less than three years. He received a dividend in 1319 of li.11,000 and was assessed interest on the capital shortfall compounding to li.4,250. He thus earned a net dividend of li.6,750 on his investment of two and two-third years, an excellent rate of return of 23 percent. Between 1319 and 1324, he did even better, earning a dividend of li.9,900 while being effectively charged li.5,200 in compound interest, yielding a net profit of li.4,700 on zero investment and thus a rate of return of infinity. Not bad!

When the books closed effective November 1, 1324, Giotto's account balance of li.22,018 was squared by crediting it with the dividend of li.9,900, a further dividend from the 1300 company of li.237, elimination of his capital contribution liability of li.11,000, and a cash remittance of li.881.[103] This cleanup has the look of what is now called the year-end "window dressing" applied by modern corpora-

[103] Ibid., 459–60.

tions and banks, and might imply that Giotto's normal deep indebtedness to the company was being hidden from the nonfamily shareholders.

This development has, of course, its positive aspects. It shows that the company's cash needs were increasingly being met by outside depositors and, therefore, that the enterprise was seen to be sufficiently successful to attract them. Even more gratifying, it confirms that the company's management of cash flow was effective and suggests that the branches may have been to a large extent self-financed. And finally, in theory at least, the shift from equity financing to borrowing from outsiders is of limited significance, given the fact that the company charged the shareholder interest on his shortfall and that all shareholders were subject to unlimited liability.

On balance, however, the withdrawal of equity capital must be judged a negative development for the company for several reasons. First, it signals increasing attention of a key partner on his personal affairs and a slackening of his commitment to the company's well-being. A large part of Giotto's borrowing from the company was for acquisition of property, often in tandem with other Peruzzi family members or on behalf of the family corporation that had been established in 1283.[104] Since the company charged Giotto only for his share of such acquisitions, it is probable that it handled the entire transaction and allocated appropriate shares to the other beneficiaries of the transactions. Similarly, the company handled allocations to the Peruzzi "family fund" established in 1292 and allocated charges to the individual concerned. It is therefore possible that other family members were in debt to the company at that time, although probably not to the same extent as Giotto.

As seen from these dividend data, Giotto's dividend income after interest netted to li.11,450, or less than li.1,000 per year over the twelve-year period. In addition to the property transactions noted, the company paid for several years the routine living expenses of Giotto and his family and billed him annually. Over the five years 1316 through 1320, these charges averaged almost li.1,500 per year, which means that he was living well beyond his earnings from the company and clearly relied heavily on the income from his private holdings. As a matter of interest, these figures, which exclude any expenses he may have paid for directly, show that he was indeed enjoying a princely standard of living. For perspective, the annual salary of the company's highest-paid employee reported in Chapter 3

---

[104] That is, the 1283 foundation discussed in Chapter 1.

was li.290, on which he could afford a house and servants, and could accumulate savings.

A second problem for the company with this situation is that its personnel – notaries, accountants, and buyers, for example – were being used extensively on shareholders' personal affairs. The living expenses for Giotto and his family included food, drink, clothing, the salaries of their servants, membership fees and donations to organizations to which they belonged, maintenance of horses, and "all other expense that the family has requested." Company personnel will have executed most of the transactions involved and accounted for them. Very likely there were many more services that went unrecorded. At the very least, these services were a distraction to company employees; more seriously, they added to the firm's overhead costs.

Finally, reliance on the deposits of outsiders for long-term financing would have committed the company to steady interest payments. These are easily borne when business is flourishing, but become a burdensome fixed overhead when business turns soft or less profitable. Whether interest costs were excessive in the years ahead cannot be ascertained, but they are likely to have been a contributing factor to the company's forthcoming decline and fall.

6

The decline begins, 1325–1335

The Fourth Company, formed effective November 1, 1324, marked a distinct change in the fortunes of the business. Its most immediately striking feature was the reduction of capital to almost half the level of the previous company, from li.118,000 to li.60,000. The reduction was not due, as in 1312, to the departure of shareholders, although two did leave the company. One outsider, Bencivenni di Folco Folchi, had died and was not replaced; one Peruzzi, Iacopo di Pacino, left for unknown reasons but was replaced by his brother Donato di Pacino. Most of the decrease by far stemmed from sharp cuts in the capital contributions of virtually all shareholders, including the charity share.

What were the reasons for this dramatic change? Sapori argues persuasively that the main motivation for the lower capital was tax avoidance.[1] The dictator of Lucca, Castruccio Castracani, had culminated months of intrigue in the internal politics of Pistoia with the sudden seizure of that city on May 5, 1325.[2] This alarming event created the need to revive the *estimo* or wealth tax, abandoned in 1315, to finance a military force to rescue the city. Affluent Florentines were expert at concealing the value of their holdings, but the capital of a company was easy prey for the city authorities to locate and tax.

Sapori says that the shareholders would have been aware in late 1324 of the likely imposition of an *estimo* and acted accordingly.[3] Here he seems to be assuming that the official establishment and dissolution dates of each company were those on which the actions took place. As we have seen in Chapter 4, the dates recorded in the books often were not the dates on which the actual entries were made. Realistically, the accounting for a company closing would take many months to complete before sufficient profit information was available on which to determine the size of a dividend, so that the date on

---

[1] Sapori, *Storia economica*, Vol. 2, 675–7.
[2] For details, see Green, *Castruccio*, 156–61.
[3] Sapori, *Storia economica*, Vol. 2, 675.

which the books were actually closed would have been much later than the stated closing date. Unfortunately, the accounts rarely show the date of the actual entry.[4] This is not a problem in calculating rates of return, because the company's internal accounting allocates credits to the shareholders and credits their interest as though the transfers were, in fact, made on the dates indicated. The curse of the lack of entry dates is that it robs historians of clues as to the motivation for certain actions. Fortunately, in this case Giotto d'Arnoldo provides an entry date in his Secret Book where he has formally reported the closing of the Third Company and the establishment of the Fourth Company.[5] The date is May 18, 1325, almost two weeks after the fall of Pistoia, when it would have been clear that the Florence commune must raise extra money for a major military campaign.[6]

Although this evidence lends support to Sapori's fiscal avoidance theory, the argument has a serious weakness. He points out that the company's capital was known not only to the authorities but also to the business community at large. If so, it would be obvious to all concerned what had happened, so that the calculation of the tax due could easily be adjusted to reflect the old capital level. Besides, such a blatant tactic would harm the Peruzzi's reputation at a time of grave crisis.

An equally valid reason for the reduction of capital is that the old company had far more subscribed capital than it needed. As discussed in the previous chapter, Giotto for long periods not only failed to contribute his capital, but also was able to borrow heavily from the company. Other shareholders may also have had shortfalls in their contributions, although it is unlikely that many of them would have been as deeply in deficit as Giotto. Another factor is that Giotto may have decided that he was paying an excessive amount of interest on his capital deficiency. By reducing his shareholding from li.11,000 to li.5,500, he realized a significant saving in his interest charge. Further support for an interest–cost motivation comes from a decision at around the same time to reduce the interest rate applicable to debit or credit balances from 8 percent to 7 percent per annum, a rate "good and permitted and blessed by God."[7] In any case, Giotto

---

[4] One exception is the report of the Bardi Company for the period July 1, 1330, to July 1, 1332, which was dated January 1, 1334. Lopez and Raymond, *Medieval Trade*, 372.

[5] *I libri*, 440.

[6] In late 1324, however, there was no circumstance that would have called for emergency taxation.

[7] Ibid., 441.

immediately went into debt to the new company, but for a much lower amount, due to the 1324 dividend of li.9,900 and his capital contribution reduction of li.5,500. His debt remained low – li.4,152 in November 1325, li.6,039 in 1326, and li.7,061 in 1327, the last recorded balance.[8] His interest cost in 1327 was li.438, a great deal less than the li.1,257 charged in 1324.

Another good reason for an interest-rate cut would have been to save money payable by the company to its depositors. Sapori's claim that the general knowledge of the company's capital reduction would have alarmed depositors does not seem to be borne out by their actions. The simultaneous reduction of interest payable to depositors suggests a company confident that they were not in a panicky mood.

While these changes were being made in the company, the Florence Commune was girding for war against Castruccio. It hired a captain who assembled over 2,400 horsemen, most of whom were mercenaries, and 15,000 citizen foot soldiers.[9] This force was soundly thrashed at Altopascio on September 23, 1325, a battle in which two Peruzzis were killed and two captured and later ransomed. The company as well as the family suffered from this catastrophe, one of the slain being a shareholder, Guido di Filippo. His son, Pacino di Guido, was one of the captives and, after his release, took Guido's place as shareholder.

After the defeat, followed by Castruccio's foray to the very gates of Florence, the commune felt obliged to look once again to the Angevin kingdom for help. In December of that year, Florence asked Robert if he would send his son and heir, the duke of Calabria, to be the city's regent and protector for ten years. The commune promised him 200,000 florins per year, the maintenance of 1,000 French knights, and the authority to nominate the podesta, the priors, and all other officials, and to exercise the right to decide on peace or war. The duke finally arrived in July 1326 and turned out to be both ineffective and extravagant. To add to Florence's worries, Emperor Ludwig of Bavaria crossed the Alps in 1327 and assisted Castruccio in the conquest of Pisa late in that year. Ludwig pushed on to Rome with Castruccio's help and received a less than convincing coronation in the following year.[10] During Castruccio's absence, the

[8] Ibid., 461.
[9] Green, *Castruccio*, 162. He cites Villani as indicating that 900 of the cavalry were Florentines and the balance mercenaries of mixed origin. The captain, Count Rugiero da Dovadola, was the same man who had dubbed Guido di Filippo Peruzzi knight in the preceding year.
[10] Ludwig received the imperial diadem in January 1328 from a representative of the Populus Romanus in a civil ceremony and was then consecrated by two bishops, both of whom had been declared heretics by Pope John XXII.

Florentines recovered Pistoia without the help of the duke, who had rushed to Naples when Ludwig marched on Rome. Castruccio returned from Rome to recapture Pistoia but died on September 3, 1328, shortly after successfully completing the siege. Two months later, the duke died in Naples.

The Florentines could well breathe a collective sigh of relief. By sheer good fortune, they were relieved of both their tormentor and their expensive and arrogant protector. Ludwig was forced to retreat from Rome to Lombardy and eventually to Germany. Pistoia was firmly under Florence's control and Lucca was weak and vulnerable. The Florentines celebrated by instituting yet another constitutional reform, broadening the basis of eligibility for high office and electing candidates by lot in an attempt to break the pattern of factional infighting. The centerpiece of the selection process was the creation of three committees of scrutators who were to present lists of suitable nominees for the approval of a scrutiny committee.[11] Several of the Peruzzi family were appointed to the first of these committees.[12] Priors selected by lot from the approved lists were to be advised by Twelve Good Men and nineteen *gonfalonieri* (heads of the administrative districts), comprising the *collegium*. Despite these well-intentioned changes and the seemingly democratic procedures, many of the same families, including the Peruzzi, continued to dominate public policy and foreign diplomacy over the next fourteen years.[13] Their policy was expansionist, with the financing of their machinations to be achieved through continued reliance on indirect taxes, the gabelles, supplemented by the *estimo* in the countryside only, and by interest-bearing loans secured by future gabelles. The inept execution of this policy over the next fifteen years brought Florence to crisis and contributed greatly to the bankruptcy of its super-companies.

The war with Castruccio had unquestionably been costly and disruptive to the Peruzzi and the business community as a whole. For a while, the sojourn of Duke Charles in Florence seemed beneficial to the Bardi, Peruzzi, and Acciaiuoli companies, which advanced him some 60,000 florins over a six-month period.[14] Much of the money was spent on entertainment and luxury goods, as well as arms, prob-

[11] See Najemy, *Corporatism*, 103–9, for an analysis of the complex procedures involved in the new system.
[12] Passerini, "Genealogica."
[13] Najemy, *Corporatism*, 118, points out that thirteen families, including the Peruzzi, held 20.9% of the key posts between 1328 and 1342, commenting that "perhaps at no time more than in the 1330s did the government of Florence approach the character of a true plutocracy."
[14] Yver, *Le commerce*, 315.

ably provided at least in part by the companies. Duke Charles' presence also gave the firms and their families added political prestige. For example, Giovanni Peruzzi was appointed provost of the prince's stables.[15] But Charles' excesses were becoming increasingly costly, alienating the people of Florence to the point of contemplating his ouster, had he not obliged with his timely death.

Further evidence of economic dislocation was the bankruptcy of the venerable Scali firm in August 1326, shortly after the duke's arrival in Florence. This collapse sent shock waves throughout western Europe. As an active participant in the commerce of southern Italy, England, and France and a favorite of papal princes, the company's fall created serious problems for the super-companies.[16] An indirect result was that it made depositors nervous and the Curia more cautious than ever in dealing with bankers. More directly, it put the super-companies under pressure to make good on the losses of their more prestigious clients. There is evidence that the super-companies felt obliged on at least one occasion to reimburse an ecclesiastical depositor for its eventual loss on a Scali default.[17]

Difficulties for the Peruzzi were also looming in France and England, as the two kingdoms began skirmishing over Aquitaine, following a brief period of unusual amity. The French had actually supported Edward's disastrous Scottish campaign of 1323–4 because the Scots had allied themselves with the Flemish.[18] This aberration ended soon after the accession of Charles IV, who provoked a brief war in Gascony, which was settled to his satisfaction in 1325. The antipathy of the French crown toward foreign merchants and bankers persisted long after the death of Philip the Fair, despite a succession of short-lived and relatively weak monarchs. The Peruzzi Company continued to ingratiate itself with the French kings by collecting indemnities in Flanders and especially by helping finance the 1328 campaign of their vassal, Count Louis, against the Flemish rebels (discussed later). Under these conditions, the Peruzzi operations in France remained profitable and

[15] Ibid., 316.

[16] Davidsohn, *Firenze*, Vol. 4, 1068–9. The company's origins date back to 1222, and in its final years the company had as many as twenty-five shareholders, only four of which were Scali. The losses on bankruptcy were no doubt considerable and widespread, but the figure of 400,000 florins cited by Villani (Book X, Chap. 4) should be treated with the usual caution applicable to his estimates. The settlement, which yielded creditors 44 1/6%, was accomplished in the remarkably short time of eight months.

[17] This is the deposit shared by the Bardi, Peruzzi, and Scali referred to in Chapter 3.

[18] N. Fryde, *The Tyranny*, 140.

were able to support the occasional fines as a "cost of doing business," but they were nevertheless neither very rewarding nor very secure.

Meanwhile, the Bruges branch came under great stress when that commune and Ypres joined a revolt of the free peasants of West Flanders in 1323. This turned into a particularly vicious class war, causing the rich merchants and patricians (the so-called *leliaerts*) to flee, mainly to Ghent, which had not joined the rebellion.[19] It is not at all certain that the Italians decamped along with them, because commerce in and out of Bruges continued at a reasonable level until November 1325, when the French severed commercial relations with Flanders. This action promptly caused a split in the rebels' ranks, resulting six months later in the Treaty of Arques, which was unfavorable to them. At that point, Count Louis named Donato di Pacino Peruzzi his General Receiver with responsibility for collecting the penalties assessed under the treaty.[20] Donato later arranged a loan to the count, apparently to help finance the campaign that led to the final crushing of the revolt at Cassel in August 1328. The acknowledged amount of the debt was the very large sum of lbr. 20,000 parisis, then equivalent to 33,333 florins, or nearly li.50,000. Under a contract signed in December 1328, the count assigned to the city of Bruges responsibility for repayment over a five-year period, with installments due monthly, presumably as a penalty for the city's participation in the uprising. As the managing partner of the Bruges branch at the time the contract was drawn up, Donato di Pacino Peruzzi, still the count's *receveur*, saw to it that the repayments were made directly to him.[21] The loan was apparently reimbursed by 1333.

In England, Edward II's incompetent but friendly regime was coming under increasing pressure, partly due to the king's attachment to Hugh Despenser, with whom the Peruzzi's relationship was now embarrassingly close.[22] By 1325, the English branch served not only as

[19] See H. Pirenne, *Histoire de Belgique*, Vol. 2 (Brussels, 1922), 75–100, for a more detailed account of this revolt. *Leliaert* would be roughly translated in today's terms as "lily-lover," i.e., a supporter of the fleur-de-lis of the French king.

[20] Kittell, *From* Ad Hoc *to Routine*, 151–6.

[21] De Roover, *Medieval Bruges*, 84–5, describes the contractual arrangements in detail, citing the Bruges municipal charters. A long, complex entry on this loan also appears in *I libri*, 164. It was written in 1345 after the firm's bankruptcy, acknowledging that the 1324–31 company owed Donato di Pacino one year's interest at 7%, because Donato had extended the remaining lbr. 8,000 parisis of the loan from February 1, 1332 to February 1, 1333, apparently out of his own pocket.

[22] Despenser referred to Bonifazio as "most beloved" and "my valet" in a letter written in late 1325 (Davidsohn, *Firenze*, Vol. 6, 719–20).

Despenser's deposit bank, but also as his purchasing agent and general merchant, dealing in all kinds of merchandise and services.[23] It is difficult to determine whether or not this was a profitable relationship for the Peruzzi. Given the frequent withdrawals, it is unlikely that the Peruzzi paid interest on much of the deposit balances.[24] At the same time, the cash was of limited use to the branch because it had to be available to Despenser at short notice, and the record confirms that payments were made with extreme punctuality.[25] Nor did this relationship bring to the company deposit business from other leading families of England; although data are too sparse to make a definite judgment, the consensus among English historians is that deposits from private individuals were not significant.[26]

Balances in the Despenser account declined precipitously by the end of 1324 due to large withdrawals and then eroded further over the next eighteen months as expenditures exceeded new deposits. By October 1326, when the Despensers were overthrown, the balance was actually a small deficit.[27] During that period, however, the prestige of the Peruzzi Company in England continued to rise. On September 13, 1326, Bonifazio, still head of the company's English branch, was selected by the government, along with Taldo Valori of the Bardi, to take charge of all the assets of the bankrupt Scali branch for eventual distribution to creditors.[28]

The Peruzzi fortunes in England were abruptly reversed eleven days later when Queen Isabella and Roger Mortimer invaded England with a small force, ostensibly to destroy the despised Despensers, but ultimately to overthrow Edward II. As they approached London, rioting broke out, and one of the looters' targets was the Bardi house. The Bardi personnel, and no doubt the Peruzzi, went into hiding. The Bardi Company, however, was quickly restored to grace, due to its generous funding of the queen during her sojourn in France and her continuing need for the Bardi's resources.[29] That company was

[23] Fryde, "Italian Bankers," 352.
[24] There is, however, a record of a five-month deposit by Despenser, with "interest" allowed through a favorable sterling–florin exchange rate. See Michael Prestwich, "Early Fourteenth-Century Exchange Rates," *Economic History Review* 2 series, 32 (November 1979): 476.
[25] Fryde, "Italian Bankers," 354.
[26] Ibid., 355; Lloyd, *Alien Merchants*, 197; Prestwich, "Italian Merchants," 96.
[27] Fryde, "Italian Bankers," App., 360–2.
[28] *CCR* E II 1323–7, 607.
[29] N. Fryde, *The Tyranny*, 193–4. Elsewhere, Fryde notes that Mortimer and the queen disposed of Edward II's accumulated treasure with astonishing speed (see 105).

therefore able to conduct business as usual with the regency and then with Edward III when the young king overthrew Mortimer in 1330.[30] The Peruzzi had been too closely associated with the hated Despensers to be fully reinstated, but it at least avoided expulsion. Bonifazio continued to act as a comanager in the Scali bankruptcy proceedings and conducted a business that was modest but not moribund.[31] But he departed for Florence early in 1328, leaving a factor in charge, confirming the relegation of the English business to a low-profile trading operation.[32]

In southern Italy, business seemed to be continuing as usual. Exports under the grain monopoly persisted at high levels between 1327 and 1331, as previously mentioned. There is no evidence to suggest that the commerce in the south was weakening; on the contrary, with gradually increasing emphasis on the manufacture of higher-quality textiles, Florentine penetration of this market with its own cloths may well have been improving.[33] But something must have been going wrong with this most important business, because the profitability of the Peruzzi Company had vanished.

Overall, during the late 1320s, the Peruzzi business had lost its earlier momentum. It had stopped growing in its established markets and had suffered setbacks in its attempts to expand into new territories. Not only had it lost ground in England, but it had also been rebuffed in its ambitions to develop business in Christian Spain. Its attempts to compete in the Kingdom of Aragon suffered from the close ties of the Peruzzi with the kings of Naples and France and finally ceased in 1331, after the king of Aragon's treasurer failed to pay 421 florins due on armor that the company had made in Florence on orders from the king.[34]

The Fourth Peruzzi Company closed its books effective June 30, 1331, after six years and eight months of not very satisfactory performance. It is not clear why closing took place on that particular date, but two possibilities come to mind. The first is that the long-serving

---

[30] See Fryde, "Loans to the English Crown."

[31] *CR* E III 1327–30, 40. A very long entry on the Scali bankruptcy confirms the role of the Bardi and Peruzzi as controllers of the Scali assets.

[32] Ibid., 372. This entry formalizes the appointment of Rinieri di Tommaso Peruzzi, a low-salaried factor, as attorney for Bonifazio and his experienced factor, Giovanni Giuntini, who were leaving the country. The appointment was renewed for a further two years in 1330 (*CPR* E III 1327–30, 492).

[33] Hoshino, *L'Arte della lana*, 74–5 and Table VIII. The data here, although far from precise, do show unmistakable evidence of a trend toward sales of higher-priced textiles.

[34] Sapori, *La crisi*, 42; *I libri*, 10. The entry recognizing the bad debt and charging it to the *mercanzia* company was made in 1337.

chairman Tommaso may have wished to tidy up his and the company's affairs in anticipation of his death later that year. The second is that the decision to close occurred *after* Tommaso's death with the date brought forward to July 1 to suit a new mix of operations. Perhaps the new date reflects a change of emphasis from grains to textiles, but there is no way of confirming this. It is worth noting, however, that the July 1 start for the Peruzzi's year was maintained throughout the remainder of the company's existence and that the Bardi Company, long a leader in the wool and cloth trades, had begun its year on July 1 at least as far back as 1318.

Irrespective of the reasons for the timing of closing the Fourth Company, the results were not good. There is no record of a dividend distribution until July 9, 1338, when accumulated collections of old debts permitted a payout to the 1324–31 shareholders of li.26,518. This is probably all the company earned, because, judging from the actions of the previous companies, dividends were only paid when the amount of surplus was significant or certain. A further distribution was made in 1345 as a result of the windfall recovery from Warden Abbey, but this came after the bankruptcy and no doubt ended up in the coffers of the creditors and so cannot be considered a profit for the shareholders. Realistically, therefore, the company can be considered as having earned a paltry li.4,000 per year over the life of the company. Given that the partners had to wait fourteen years for the dividend, their return on capital was a derisory 3 percent.

What was going wrong? The war with Castruccio and the upheavals in Florence in 1326 very likely played a part, with disrupted business and special taxes. The collapse of the Scali Company and the setback in England may have also dented the Peruzzi's profitability. But the flagship of the company's business, Angevin Italy, appears to have been thriving as never before. As has been previously mentioned, the grain export monopoly was operating at a sustained average rate of 110,000 *salme* per year between 1327 and 1331. Even though the Angevin rulers diluted the monopoly by including the Buonaccorsi in 1330, there remained plenty of business to go around. And the super-companies' penetration of the markets and administration of southern Italy appeared undiminished.

The most important cause of the poor results for the 1324–31 period is likely to be found in the weakening profitability of the Peruzzi's biggest business, the grain trade. Since the volume continued at a high level the problem must therefore have been lower profit per unit. Although direct evidence is difficult to find, there are clues to

Table 7. *Profit of the Bardi Company, 1330–2* (lire a fiorino)

	1330–1	1331–2	1330–2
General account	22,493	18,792	41,285
Wool business	22,491	17,463	39,954
Cloth business	3,911	3,910	7,821
Other	1,856	1,500	3,356
Total	50,751	41,665	92,416

Source: R. S. Lopez and I. W. Raymond, *Medieval Trade in the Mediterranean World*, 370–1; A. Sapori, *La Crisi*, 218–19.

support such a contention. The first is the very helpful profit analysis of the Bardi Company for the years 1330–2, as summarized in Table 7.

What is immediately striking about these figures is the enormous profitability of the Bardi Company, nearly twice that of the Peruzzi in its best years. There is no information on the capital subscription of that company, so that a return on capital cannot be estimated, but it must have been quite rewarding.[35] The next most noticeable feature is the lucrative wool business, which contributed almost half of the company's profit. By contrast, the contribution of the cloth business was minor. Within the "other" category were two items identified only by folio number, making it impossible even to guess what they represent. But one very important business is notable by its absence, the grain trade. Possibly it was too widely dispersed to be controlled as one profit center, but it is curious that this crucial business should have been relegated to a folio number or, more likely, to the general account catchall. What is clear is that grain sales, which we know were substantial during this period, did not account for a large share of Bardi profits.

The second clue provides a reason why profit on grain sales may have been low. This is the severe famine that struck Florence along with most of Italy in 1329, following two consecutive disastrous harvests, causing food riots in the grain market of Orsanmichele. The famous confraternity of the same name made extraordinary allocations of charity to the poor that year and, exceptionally, was appointed as the main agency of the commune for distributing government funds

---

[35] The capital of the 1331 Bardi Company was divided into fifty-eight shares held by eleven shareholders, but the value of each share is unknown. See Sapori, *La crisi*, 248–9.

to the population for the purchase of foodstuffs.[36] Villani's vivid description of the crisis and his estimate of the cost of subsidies to the commune may have been exaggerated, but Lenzi's lengthy day-by-day reports confirm a severe and unusual situation.[37] Villani pointed out that the wheat distributed by the commune came from Sicily. Puglia, however, remained the chief supplier of grain for northern Italy, even when there were riots from its own citizens over food shortages, which were blamed on the hoarding of wealthy merchants.[38] But the profiteering merchants in this case were probably not the super-companies. Instead, the latter were caught in a classic market squeeze, under enormous popular and government pressure to hold their selling prices down in Florence and other markets, while being forced by their suppliers to buy at premium prices. The famine, surprisingly, may well have driven the profit out of the super-companies' grain business.

Evidence for the profit squeeze appears in *Il Biadaiolo* price reports for 1329 and 1330. When the famine struck with full force in April 1329, the imported *grano ciciliano* disappeared entirely from the Orsanmichele for six weeks; the small amounts of *grano communale* available had to be mixed with barley or millet.[39] At the same time, the commune intervened to set a "political price" for grain several soldi per bushel below the market price and maintained these controlled prices right through the autumn of 1330.[40] The communal intervention may not have directly affected the super-companies' profit because the commune paid for the price differential. But the companies would have been under enormous pressure to keep their prices as close as possible to their costs, or even to sell at a loss.[41]

The reduced profitability of the Peruzzi Company was no passing phenomenon. The steady decline from low profits to severe losses that will be seen over the next several years was occurring at a time when the grain business was still the heart of the company's opera-

---

[36] J. Henderson, "Piety and Charity," 155.

[37] Villani, *Storia*, Book X, Chap. 118. Here he sets the cost to the Commune as 60,000 florins over the two years. For Lenzi's comments, see *Il Biadaiolo*, 292–354.

[38] Abulafia, "Southern Italy," 380–1.

[39] See Chapter 2 for a listing of the grades of grain.

[40] *Il Biadaiolo*, 68.

[41] As mentioned in Chapter 2, Davidsohn (*Firenze*, Vol. 5, 241) noted that guilds were expected, in times of scarcity, to buy grain abroad and sell it to the commune below cost, assigning their losses to the commune. Under such circumstances, it would be difficult for important guild members such as the Peruzzi to take profits on grain sales on a "business as usual" basis.

tions. Even the Bardi, although buffered by its strong participation in the wool trade, saw its profitability decrease sharply, suggesting that it too was losing money in its grain dealings. Sapori indicates that earnings for the 1332–4 period were low, with the eventual dividend probably not much more than 1 percent.[42] Specific reasons for these unfavorable results are offered later in this chapter. But it is worth mentioning at this point that the government involvement in the relief of the 1328–9 famine seems to have sparked a change in official attitudes toward the marketing of foodstuffs, directly affecting the super-companies' pricing policies. Although the Florentine Commune ceased its intervention during part of 1331 and all of 1332, it resumed this activity briefly in 1333 and continuously throughout 1334–5.[43] Further data after December 1335 are sketchy, but the record to that point suggests that political pricing would be imposed by the authorities whenever they deemed market prices to be unacceptable. Such actions were probably taken in 1336–7 and definitely during the next severe famine in 1339–40.[44]

It is unfortunate that Tommaso should have died at this time. Conservative in outlook, he built a powerful and prosperous business on the base of a long-term commitment to Angevin Italy and its grain trade. For twenty-eight years he steered the company firmly through wars and famines and established an effective system of control over its far-flung operations. He seems, however, to have shown only hesitating interest in capturing a leading position in the English wool trade. After an energetic start in the early 1320s, he left that business to the domination of the Bardi following the fall of Edward II. He recalled his son Bonifazio and appeared to show no further interest in rebuilding the Peruzzi's position with the English monarchy. Nevertheless, the business as a whole, although in decline, was still profitable and may well have remained so for several more years had his brand of cautious, close stewardship been continued by his successors.

The Fifth Company opened for business on July 1, 1331, still under the nominal leadership of Tommaso. After Tommaso's death later that year (the precise date is not known), the company under its new leader adopted the style Giotto d'Arnoldo de' Peruzzi e compagni. The new company registered a 50 percent increase in capital, from li.60,000 to li.90,000.[45] The additional money came partly from an

[42] Sapori, *La crisi*, 106.
[43] *Il Biadaiolo*, 68–70.
[44] Ibid., 95 n105, 102.
[45] See Tables A4 and A5 for details.

increase in contributions from existing partners but mainly from the addition of six new nonfamily shareholders who subscribed a total of li.22,250. One of the new partners was Francesco Forzetti, the company's long-serving manager of the Sicilian branch. The others were new associates – Baldo Orlandini, Piero Ubaldini, and three Soderini brothers – indicating that the Peruzzi Company still had the reputation and prestige to attract new investors. Only one minor shareholder, Giovanni Raugi, left the firm.

These changes meant that for the first time in its history, the majority ownership of the Peruzzi Company passed out of the hands of members of the Peruzzi family. Scholars have made much of this transformation, but in reality, the Peruzzi family leadership remained firmly in control of the business. One of the new shareholders, Forzetti, was a loyal company man and a permanent nonresident, unlikely to be influenced by any group of outside shareholders. The Baroncelli brothers were associates of such long standing that they could be regarded almost as family. The new partners were welcomed both for their cash and their particpation in the business; Orlandini served in England and Florence and his son worked as a factor in Bruges, while all of the Soderini brothers were active in Naples and Sicily.[46] And the capo remained a Peruzzi of towering prestige in the community. Giotto was an even more powerful figure in Florentine politics than Tommaso had been. Whether the new members were aware of the firm's lackluster performance over the previous few years is not possible to ascertain.

The four years of the Fifth Company, from July 1, 1331, to June 30, 1335, passed in relative peace under Giotto's stewardship. To be sure, Florence continued to be involved in the complex Guelf–Ghibelline conflicts in northern Italy, but without the cost in blood and gold of the ill-starred campaigns of the previous decade.[47] The company's good friend King Robert of Naples continued to make his kingdom a happy hunting ground for the super-companies. Pope John XXII's long crusade against the Ghibellines was winding down and ended with his death in 1334; his successor, Benedict XII, began his reign in a less aggressive style. England and France maintained an uneasy peace while the new king, Edward III, was bringing Scotland to heel and the still newer king, Philip VI of France, was consolidating his power. Altogether, this was hardly a placid period, but decidedly more orderly and felicitous for business operations than either the years preceding or following.

[46] *I libri*, 359–60 and 310 for Orlandini and 57 and 45 for the Soderini.
[47] G. Mollat, *The Popes of Avignon, 1305–1378*, trans. Janet Love (Paris, 1949), 106–7.

Nature was also reasonably cooperative. Although 1333 and 1334 were rainy and grain prices were somewhat above normal, there was no repetition of the severe shortages of the late 1320s.[48] But the one natural disaster to strike Florence in that period was catastrophic – the great flood of November 1333, the equal of which was not seen until 1966. The flood waters passed through the heart of the commercial districts, damaging or destroying not only buildings, furniture, and equipment, but also the great stores of merchandise of all kinds that were always present in Florence because of its role as a distribution center. Grain supplies were also affected; after a nine-day closure, the market reopened with prices up four soldi per bushel, a level that was sustained for several months.[49] Villani, as usual, offers a quantification of the loss, citing the city repair bill at 150,000 florins.[50] Whether this estimate is anywhere near the truth even as an order of magnitude is unimportant. The fact is that the Peruzzi, among all the entrepreneurs of Florence, will have suffered serious losses in damaged property and ruined merchandise. Moreover, they will have shared in some way the cost of the disruption and restoration of public services.

Aside from the losses associated with the flood, the Peruzzi business should have enjoyed in this benign environment about the same level of profitability as it did during the late teens and early twenties. On that basis, annual profit should have averaged in the range of li.15,000 to li.20,000 before flood damage. The actual results were losses averaging li.9,700 per year; thus, over the four years 1331–5, profits were almost li.100,000 to li.120,000 below what should have been expected. As we have seen in Chapter 4, there is no record of inventories in the surviving account books, so that it is impossible to make even a rough guess at the value of stocks exposed to flood risk, let alone any idea of actual losses. The total assets recorded in the Black Book and White Book on July 1, 1335 were li.295,000, and a significant portion of those assets may have been merchandise, so that it is theoretically possible for flood losses to have been as high as li.100,000. But a loss of anything approaching this magnitude is extremely unlikely without some mention of it somewhere in the company's records. A more credible scenario for the Fifth Company is a significant but not overwhelming flood loss and a deteriorating basic business. Flood damage no doubt also contributed materially to the Bardi's profit decline for 1332–4 cited earlier, but the next

[48] La Roncière, *Prix et salaires*, 716; *Il Biadaiolo*, 69–70.
[49] *Il Biadaiolo*, 491–2.
[50] Villani, *Storia*, Book XI, Chap. 1.

biennial balance, 1334–6, also reflected weak results, suggesting more deep-seated problems.[51]

With Giotto in charge, the basic business was not likely to receive much innovative stimulus. Giotto was very much preoccupied with communal and family interests and, far from being prepared to commit cash to the business, he continued to borrow consistently and heavily from the company. On July 1, 1335, Giotto's debt was li.8,216, suggesting that the previously reported arrears of over li.7,000 in 1327 were maintained during the intervening years.[52] Given his continued preoccupation with personal and political affairs, it is not surprising that Giotto would have let the company run very much as before, albeit without the close control exercised by his predecessor.

One important change was taking place in Florentine business during this period – the accelerating trend toward the local manufacture of top-quality cloth.[53] Whether the Peruzzi Company was a leader or follower of this movement is uncertain, but it undeniably was a participant. The Peruzzi accounts reflect an entry for legal expenses incurred in 1333 to obtain the favorable settlement of a lawsuit in Bruges. The expenses include the cost of four bolts of velvet made in Florence as a present for the countess of Flanders.[54] It is not known whether the cloth was of Peruzzi manufacture, but such a gift to a lady whose husband controlled Europe's finest fabricators of luxury cloth showed a level of confidence in the Florentine product that bordered on cheekiness. It must have been pleasing, nevertheless, because the lawsuit was eventually settled successfully.[55]

The Peruzzi participation in cloth manufacturing, however, was unlikely to have been significant. Members of the Peruzzi family had been enrolled, and exercised leadership, in the Calimala Guild since early in the company's history and, as such, would have been engaged in the redressing and finishing of imported cloth.[56] At a later

[51] Sapori, *La crisi*, 106, 230. There are no data for this or subsequent periods on Bardi results, except for a fragment that gives an apology for delays in getting figures because of lack of responses from branches. Sapori suspected that the Bardi began to incur losses, although probably not as great as those of the Peruzzi.

[52] See Table A6.

[53] Hoshino, *L'Arte della lana*, makes this point repeatedly in text and tables in Chaps. 2 and 3.

[54] *I libri*, 101. The cost of the cloth was an unidentified portion of the substantial sum of li.3,577, which included legal expense for the lawsuit and the cost of horses for Donato di Pacino Peruzzi's trip to Bruges.

[55] Ibid., 28.

[56] Filippo, Arnoldo, and Tommaso were all members of the Calimala Guild (Peruzzi, *Storia commercio*, 255, 257).

date, other family members also matriculated in the powerful Lana Guild of wool processors. The company definitely kept wool in its warehouses and shops in Florence, and although much of this raw material would have been for resale to other entrepreneurs, it would be surprising if the Peruzzi did not engage in cloth production for its own account.[57] Also, the company had enough activity going to justify having a full-time shearer on the payroll.[58] Finally, given that cloth making operated entirely on the putting-out system, with the entrepreneur providing capital and oversight, it would be an easy kind of endeavor for a super-company to enter.[59]

Why should the Peruzzi's involvement in cloth fabrication have been so limited? Hoshino makes an eloquent case that the typical cloth-making shop was of modest size, with production averaging between 80 and 100 pieces per year, consuming only eleven to four-teen English sacks of wool.[60] This is not to say that a super-company would shun a small business; the Peruzzi firm engaged in many small operations, including a furrier's shop in Florence.[61] Despite the logical expectation that companies such as the Peruzzi, and certainly the Bardi, would become large-scale cloth manufacturers, given their massive involvement in the wool trade, there are two reasons for believing that they would not. The first is that there are no significant economies of scale that larger firms could bring to the putting-out system. The second is that profitability was low because of the large number of small entrepreneurs and the stiff competition for market share discussed earlier. Hoshino argues that the manufacturers invested very little capital – from 500 to 2,000 florins – and were prepared to accept safe but low margins, leaving the big merchants and financiers to earn the big rewards and take the market risks.[62] The evidence from the Peruzzi accounts indicates that super-company avoided direct involvement in cloth manufacturing, participating instead through an association with two men described as "partners

---

[57]　*I libri*, 180. Here are several entries dealing with the rent of *fondachi* and *case* for storing wool.

[58]　Ibid., 65, 314. Entries describe Giovanni di Iacopo as a *cimatore*. But much of his time would have been spent on finishing imported cloth, and as noted in Chapter 3, he was absent for significant periods on assignments outside of Florence from 1335 onward.

[59]　A brief description of the putting-out system appears in Chapter 2.

[60]　Hoshino, *L'Arte della lana*, 203. The conversion rate for the number of pieces per English sack of wool is 7.26 (Table XX, 148). The English sack of 364 pounds is used throughout this book, rather than the smaller Italian sack of 220 pounds.

[61]　*I libri*, 312, refers to the company's *bottegha di nostra pelliccieria* (our furrier shop).

[62]　Hoshino, *L'Arte della lana*, 201.

in the *drapperia*."[63] The typical cloth-manufacturing shop in Florence at that time was a two-man entrepreneurship.

The conclusion of this analysis is that the shift to the manufacture of higher-grade cloth in Florence in the 1330s would not have added much to the Peruzzi's profit and more likely would have reduced it. The company, like other Florentine merchants, was in effect marketing fewer quality finished goods brought in from Flanders and Brabant, replacing them with more cloth from Florence, and shipping more wool to Florence and less to Flanders. Was this shift a positive action initiated by Florentine merchants to make more money or a reaction to preserve their markets in the Mediterranean and the Levant, following a production decline in Flanders? Hoshino has argued forcefully for the latter view, asserting that the decline in Flemish textile production after 1320 damaged the Florentines doubly, by simultaneously reducing the Flemish market for quality English wool and creating a scarcity of quality finished product.[64] The transport of English wool to Florence instead of Flanders was riskier and probably less profitable, and certainly, as we have seen, immobilized cash much longer.[65]

There are additional reasons for believing that the manufacture of high-quality cloth in Florence in the 1320s and 1330s was deleterious to the profit of the super-companies. Aside from the lower margins in the wool trade, the Florentine finished product would likely sell for less than Flemish goods of equivalent quality until the former's reputation had become established. Again, in the start-up phase, Florentine manufacturing costs would be high. But the effect on the super-companies' profit in the 1330s should not be exaggerated. Even Hoshino agrees that the decline in Flemish production was gradual and did not assume significant proportions until the second half of the fourteenth century.[66] Moreover, as reported earlier, the trade in raw wool remained very profitable for the Bardi as late as 1331–2. For the Peruzzi, the profits probably declined, but only moderately.

Except for its venture into quality cloth manufacturing, the pat-

---

[63] See Chapter 3 for a fuller discussion of this arrangement.

[64] Hoshino, *L'Arte della lana*, 139–40.

[65] Ibid. Also, Hoshino's estimate of profit on English wool landed in Florence is 5.3 florins (see table, 142), or £0.8 sterling per sack of 220 pounds, equivalent to £1.3 sterling per sack of 364 pounds. This compares with an average profit of at least £2 for the large sack, which Fryde calculated for wool shipped to Flanders ("The Wool Accounts of William de la Pole," 14). These are, of course, comparisons of very approximate data that may not really be comparable, but they tend to confirm Hoshino's intuitive judgment.

[66] Ibid., 137.

tern of the Peruzzi's business throughout the period 1325–35 would have been much the same as before, with continued reliance on the old standbys of a large grain trade, a small wool trade, marketing of cloth and other merchandise, and financial services. As far as can be told, the core enterprise was functioning normally. Yver notes that although the registers of the Angevin kingdom for the 1330s were incomplete, enough remained when he was doing his research to prove that relations between the super-companies and the Neapolitan court were as active and productive as ever.[67] There is no evidence from the company's markets in western Europe and around the Mediterranean to suggest a significant decline in business. Steadily draining out of the company, profits were meager between 1324 and 1331, and turned to severe losses between 1331 and 1335. Specific problems have been cited already, such as the setback in England, the famine of 1329, and the flood of 1333, but something more fundamental seems to have been sapping the company's strength. Three possibilities come to mind – the weakening of the company's leadership, rising transactions costs, and reduced profit on grain sales.

A company of the size and complexity of the Peruzzi required leadership of a special kind. Given the widely dispersed operations and poor communications, the chairman needed to possess an intuitive grasp of how far he should trust his branch managers to make decisions. Even more important, he had to pay intensive and continuing attention to day-to-day operations to make sure that all the moving parts of the company were working more or less in harmony. Tommaso appears to have provided such oversight during his first twenty years or so in running the business, but even he seems to have relaxed his grip during his declining years.[68] Giotto was already advanced in age when he took over the helm of the company and, as we have seen, had too many personal and political distractions to enable him to devote the intensive care that the company's affairs needed. Giotto's great prestige and his political acumen were important assets, but they did not seem to bring any noticeable benefits to the management of the firm. The company drifted along in the same old way, with the leadership seemingly unaware that the company was in de-

[67] Yver, *Le commerce*, 319. Yver completed his research early this century, long before the wholesale destruction of Neapolitan archives by the Nazis in World War II.

[68] The Peruzzi's overly close relationship with Despenser in England, for example, suggests that Tommaso had relied too much on Bonifazio's judgment of the political situation there, so that he failed to insist on the kind of hedging action that the Bardi took to reduce the company's vulnerability to a change in rulers.

cline or, if aware, unwilling or unable to do very much about its problems. These statements are, of course, speculative, but we do know that management neglect was a frequent cause of the failure of medieval as well as modern companies.[69]

Another of the problems that may have been contributing to the company's malaise is a rise in what John Munro and others have called "transactions costs." This term is usually narrowly defined to contain the costs of market information, contract negotiation, and property-right protection, but Munro has logically included those of transport and direct marketing to encompass all costs "ultimately involved in transferring goods between producer and consumer."[70] Because all of these elements contained very large fixed costs, he stresses the importance of economy of scale. The Peruzzi Company faced many fixed costs despite its avoidance of investment in buildings and transport equipment. Even the hired public carriers faced fixed costs that they had to pass on to their customers. And the company had its own direct fixed costs in the form of building rentals and the eighty-eight full-time factors employed in Florence and in the branches, despite its preference for hiring specialists only as needed.[71] The company's staff provided much of the market information, negotiation, and property protection services noted. Many of them, especially the accountants, served only the company's internal needs for information, communication, and control because of its size and complexity.

For the Peruzzi Company, therefore, fixed overhead costs were very large and required a steady volume of profitable business to absorb them. Merely taking into account the eighty-eight salaried factors on the payroll on July 1, 1335, who were paid an average of li.100 per year, and the rent of shops and warehouses in Florence at nearly li.2,000 annually results in a total annual fixed cost of almost li.11,000. The average annual loss of li.9,700 for 1331–5 indicates that the company failed to generate enough income to recover these overheads. But in those four years of relative stability, there is no evidence to suggest a significant reduction in the volume of general merchandise or wool business. Nor is there any indication that trans-

---

[69] One of the most clearly identified and spectacular medieval cases of management failure was the decline and fall of the Medici Bank.

[70] Munro, "Industrial Transformations," 110–48; see especially 120–1 for definitions and 121–30 for discussion.

[71] For example, on specialists, *I libri*, 552–3, shows that the company employed sixty-nine notaries in Florence and abroad for a variety of purposes but maintained only one full-time notary, Michele Boschi, on its payroll. For total factors employed, see Table 4.

actions costs had risen inordinately. Munro cites the impact of Mediterranean warfare between 1280 and 1350 as a prime cause of increases in costs, especially of transport and presumably insurance, but during the period of most intensive conflict from 1280 to 1328, the Peruzzi and other super-companies prospered. The reversal of Peruzzi fortunes was too abrupt to have been caused by the secular trends that Munro describes.

The third and most likely explanation of the company's problem is that the volume and profit margins in the grain trade had shrunk. Except for the fact that the Buonaccorsi gained admittance to the Neapolitan grain monopoly in 1330, thereby diminishing the Peruzzi's share of that trade, there is no evidence to suggest that the quantity of grain available from Puglia had declined.[72] Certainly, the monopoly of the Florentines appears to have persisted throughout the 1330s.[73] But, as suggested earlier, following the debacle of 1328–9, the grain companies may have been subjected to closer scrutiny by government authorities and constrained in their pricing practices.

We know that the Florentine government resumed setting official prices below market prices in 1334–5 after a brief respite resulting from the good harvest of 1331. At the same time that the super-companies' margins came under this renewed pressure, King Robert was making seemingly arbitrary and drastic changes in his export tax.[74] In November, 1333, the time of the Florence flood, he raised the export tax on wheat from 12 golden ounces (oz.) to 20 oz. per 100 salme, increasing the super-companies' costs by 2 soldi di piccioli per bushel (see Table A7 for the calculation of these relationships). He reduced it briefly in December 1334 to 10 oz. but promptly raised it again to 21 oz. in March 1335. But were such changes merely arbitrary? Renouard has stated that, in 1336, the export tax varied according to the season and the abundance of the crop.[75] If these adjustments had become policy, they suggest that Robert, to meet his growing needs, was returning to Charles I's practice of charging what the market would bear, leaving little profit for the super-companies.

As a decade of mostly mediocre or disastrous harvests wore on, a new problem emerged for the super-companies. Local government

---

[72] Yver, Le commerce, 309.

[73] David Abulafia, "Venice and the Kingdom of Naples in the Last Years of Robert the Wise, 1332–1343," Papers of the British School at Rome 48 (1980): 26–49. Although Abulafia does not confirm directly that the Florentine monopoly continued throughout the 1330s, the implication from his Venetian sources is that it did.

[74] Yver, Le commerce, 115.

[75] Renouard, "Une expédition des céréales," 812.

bodies increasingly negotiated directly with the Angevin king, by-passing the super-companies' monopoly or using the companies merely as expediters. Renouard describes the revealing case of a pa-pal purchase of about 5,000 *salme* of wheat for the relief of Christians in Cilicia.[76] The Bardi Company was employed to arrange the pur-chase and delivery, but appears to have "donated" its services as a goodwill gesture to the papacy. It may even have suffered a loss, be-cause it was left holding 4,000 *salme* of high-priced grain that it had bought in anticipation of the order. Extended negotiations between the papacy and the Naples government delayed the execution of the order until the new crop came in at a lower price. Another purchase was by Rome, which secured 10,000 *salme* from Naples in 1339.[77] And in 1341, Siena "pawned" several of its outlying communities for cash to import desperately needed wheat.[78] Overall, there is a high prob-ability of a reduction in the volume of the Peruzzi grain trade along with the likelihood of a narrowing of profit on that business. The grain trade, the engine of the company's earlier prosperity, was there-fore at the heart of the company's decline.[79]

One other possible explanation for the reduction in company prof-itability that deserves consideration is the effect of the well-known changes in the gold–silver ratio in the thirteenth and fourteenth cen-turies. Grossly oversimplified, this ratio was said to be important to Florentine businessmen because a significant part of their expense, especially wages, was incurred in silver or billon coinage, while their sales in the international markets were mainly in gold florins.[80] An increase in the price of gold relative to silver was thus expansionary and favorable to business interests, while a decrease was depressing and unfavorable to them. There is abundant evidence that the price of gold in terms of silver had been rising steadily in Italy from the middle of the thirteenth century until it peaked at around 14 ounces

[76] Ibid., 793–831.

[77] Yver, *Le commerce*, 118.

[78] Bowsky, *Finance of Siena*, 38–40.

[79] The depopulation of the Florentine *contado* before the Black Death documented by D. Herlihy in *Medieval and Renaissance Pistoia: The Social History of an Italian Town, 1200–1430* (New Haven, CT, 1967) and other works may also have been a factor affecting the grain trade. It is not a useful explanation here, however, because a secular depopulation does not help us understand the Peruzzi's sud-den reversal. Also, depopulation in the *contado* cuts two opposing ways, reduc-ing production as well as consumption of grain.

[80] See Cipolla, *Monetary Policy*, 20–9, for a fuller and more elegant account of this phenomenon. Billon is an alloy of silver and copper, with a high (at least 50%) copper content. Billon coins, usually of small nominal value, were often called "black money."

of silver for 1 ounce of gold (14:1) in Venice and Florence in the late 1320s.[81] Then the ratio began to move firmly in favor of silver during the 1330s and 1340s, provoking the severe coinage devaluations in Florence of 1345 and 1347. Lane and Mueller place the turning point in 1327, when the rulers of Bohemia and Hungary agreed to coordinate the coinage of silver groats.[82] The decline in the relative value of gold proceeded at different rates and timing around Europe – for example, 1331 in Venice, 1334 in Florence, 1337 in France, and 1344 in England.[83] In Naples, the decline was less severe, because, like most parts of the Mediterranean trading area, the gold–silver ratio never reached the peaks obtaining in western Europe.[84]

The relationship of the price of gold to silver was of course reflected mostly in currency rates of exchange, although it was just one of many variables involved in determining specific rates between different coinages in specific locations.[85] It is instructive, therefore, to review the relationship of the Florentine gold florin with various silver-based currencies (including the Florentine soldo) reported in Peter Spufford's *Handbook of Medieval Exchange* for the period 1300–45. Although some of the data are fragmentary and although each currency had its own peculiarities, some important generalizations can be made by indexing the exchange rates of Florence's major trading partners. The indices presented in Table A8 show that the Florentine florin strengthened against virtually all currencies between 1300 and 1330, directionally in line with the movement of the gold–silver ratio. The florin moved quite strongly against the soldi of Florence, Siena, Pisa, and Genoa, although much less so against the currencies of Naples, England, France, and Venice. Then, between 1330 and 1335, the florin weakened significantly against most currencies, but rallied or at least stabilized thereafter.[86] The modest recovery of the florin in Florence was attributed to the introduction of a new coin, the quattrino, equivalent to four denari piccioli. This coin, a

[81] See Spufford, *Money and Its Use*, 271, 354; Lane and Mueller, *Money and Banking*, Vol. 1, Chaps. 14–19.

[82] Lane and Mueller, *Money and Banking*, Vol. 1, 435.

[83] Ibid., 436–45, 460. In broad terms, the ratio dropped from about 14:1 to 11.5:1.

[84] Ibid., 442–3. The ratio averaged only about 12:1 before dropping to under 11:1.

[85] Other important variables included local supply and demand pressures such as trade imbalances, seasonality, warfare, and, occasionally, local government decisions to change the content of precious metals in their coinages. See Spufford, *Handbook*, xlvi–xlix, for a useful discussion of these variables.

[86] There were two important exceptions. Against sterling, the florin continued to rise until nearly 1340. However, the florin's weakness against the Neapolitan carlin persisted into the 1340s.

popular denomination for local use, contained only slightly more silver per lira than the piccioli, but much less than the silver grossi, both of which were left unchanged.

Lane and Mueller argue that the fall in the price of gold contributed importantly to the demise of the Florentine super-companies in three ways.[87] First, it worsened the terms of trade for both domestic costs and imported raw materials because the companies' sales were denominated mainly in florins and their costs in silver-based currencies. Second, and very important, the companies made large loans in florins when the price of gold was high and had to accept repayment (often only partial) when the price of gold was low. Third, the Florentines imported gold and exported the undervalued silver on a large scale in the early 1340s, intensifying an already ruinous deflation. In this connection, the Florentines, unlike the Venetians who were the prime silver traders in the Mediterranean, were not in a position to offset their losses by profitable trading in the Levantine silver markets.[88]

These arguments, while persuasive to a point, are seriously flawed as explanations for the downfall of the super-companies. First, the terms of trade expressed in exchange rates between Florence and its principal suppliers did not really change a great deal. As noted, most silver-based currencies in northern Italy moved in tandem with the florin's relationship to its own soldo. The currency of Naples, the source of so much of Florence's foodstuffs, actually *weakened* against the Florentine soldo between 1320 and 1335 and only modestly exceeded the 1315–20 average in 1335–40 (see Table A7). Remember that the period 1315–20 was very prosperous for the super-companies. And the exchange rate of the great wool supplier, England, continued to reflect the relatively high price of gold until the early 1340s.[89] Finally, it will be shown later in this chapter that the bulk of the Peruzzi Company business during the 1330–5 gold-price decline was concentrated in the Mediterranean, where, as we have seen, the price of gold never reached the peaks that it did elsewhere. Overall, then, the movement in terms of trade, while generally adverse, was not in a range that should have presented astute businessmen with insurmountable problems.

[87] Lane and Mueller's arguments are not laid out in the sequence followed here, but are expounded in a series of observations made in *Money and Banking*, Vol. 1, 439–55.

[88] Ibid., 442.

[89] The higher price of gold in England than that on the Continent is cited as one of the principal causes of the acute shortage of silver coinage there in the late 1330s and early 1340s. See Prestwich, "Exchange Rates"; Waugh, *England of Edward III*, 80–2.

The argument that the super-companies suffered from lending in expensive florins and recovering (partially) in cheaper ones leans heavily on the premise that the Bardi and Peruzzi companies' loans to Edward III were made in the late 1330s–early 1340s and were repaid from 1344 onward, when the florin was devalued against sterling. But the Peruzzi Company was already bankrupt in 1343. And in any case, very little of Edward's debt was repaid after 1343, as will be shown conclusively in Chapter 9, so that the exchange rate obtaining at the time is irrelevant as far as the companies' losses are concerned.[90] Regarding the third argument, it is probable that the price movements of the precious metals intensified Florence's problems. It is also true that the Florentines were not great international bullion traders like the Venetians. But Florentine companies did profit by bringing metals to the mints. Lane and Mueller point out that the mint in Florence relied exclusively on offerings of bullion and old coins by merchants and had to allow them acceptable profits to attract an adequate flow of metal.[91] The Peruzzi would have been important participants in this trade.

In summary, it is possible to justify the thesis that the reversal in the gold–silver ratio added to the problems of the super-companies, but not that it had a significant influence on their results. Certainly, it played little part in the heavy losses of the 1331–5 Peruzzi Company. We have already seen that exchange rate changes impinged only slightly on the cost of grain in the 1330s and were even directionally helpful up to 1335. At that time, the Peruzzi's involvement in the English wool trade was still too small to be a factor, and in any case, the ratios in northern Europe did not change materially until after 1335. And in the remaining eight years of the company's existence, the changes in gold–silver ratios pale to insignificance against the clearly identifiable causes of the company's eventual collapse that will be discussed in subsequent chapters.

At this point, it will be useful to reexamine the closing balances of the Fifth Company at June 30, 1335. These are extremely important because they provide a detailed picture of the company as it was just nine months before its first moves toward the ill-fated joint venture in England with the Bardi Company. The balances have already been discussed in Chapter 4 in the context of accounting procedures and

[90] Aside from the fact that the argument is inapplicable to the Peruzzi, the exchange rates between sterling and the florin on the company's huge transactions with the English government in this period were fixed at 1 florin equals 3 shillings. See Prestwich, "Exchange Rates," 478–9.

[91] Lane and Mueller, *Money and Banking*, Vol. 1, 447.

the calculation of profit. Now, we shall consider what they mean in terms of the size and health of the company, how it was financed, and what resources it had available for the English venture. To start, it will be helpful to condense and restate in balance sheet form in Table 8 the figures presented in Table 5:

The current assets in the Florence accounts reflect the cash, merchandise inventories, and accounts receivable reported in the White, Black, and Yellow Book totals. Although most of these assets are likely to have been located in or near Florence, we know that some were located elsewhere, even though recorded in the head office ledgers.[92] The foreign branches' asset total includes not only the usual cash, inventories, and receivables, but also loans to clients. As regards liabilities, the Florence accounts are primarily merchandise payables, including the small deposits and suppliers' advances linked to merchandise trade. Shareholders' capital has been extracted from the colored book totals and shown in the equity section. Foreign branches liabilities include not only merchandise payables, but also client deposits. The loans/deposits section deals with only loans and deposits recorded in the Florence books. The equity "asset" is the 1331–5 loss approximately as it would have been calculated at that time, that is, without the li.20,550 "interest" charge accumulated between 1335 and 1343.

These figures reveal a number of significant facts about the company. The first is that its working capital, that is, the excess of current assets over current liabilities in the Florence accounts, was financed primarily by the deposits of shareholders and of outsiders both in Florence and in the foreign branches. Less than 25 percent was financed by equity. The second is that over 42 percent of total company assets and nearly 50 percent of its liabilities were in the foreign branches. The third is that the foreign branches overall not only were self-sustaining, but also provided some surplus cash for the company. These data depict a loss-making company that was surprisingly highly leveraged with outside debt and poorly positioned to assume heavy additional borrowing that would later be needed for its English venture.

The balances of some of the foreign branches merit closer examination. As can be seen in Table A2, the individual organizations vary widely in size, composition, and strength. The June 30, 1335, balances for the most important branches are shown in Table 9.

These figures immediately highlight the importance of southern Italy to the Peruzzi Company, with 31.6 percent of all foreign assets

---

[92] For example, the fixed assets of li.2,539 recorded in the Florence Accounts were actually situated in Rhodes.

Table 8. *Balances at June 30, 1335* (lire a fiorino)

	Assets	Liabilities	Balance
Current assets/ liabilities			
Florence accts.	353,766	130,354	223,412
Foreign branches	328,871	382,421	(53,550)
Subtotal	682,637	512,775	169,862
Loans to/deposits from:			
Shareholders	27,260	66,375	(39,115)
All other	32,350	111,060	(78,710)
Subtotal	59,610	177,435	(117,825)
Equity	37,963	90,000	(52,037)
Total[a]	780,210	780,210	—

[a] This total omits the "unidentified" li.715.

Table 9. *Assets and liabilities of major foreign branches* (lire a fiorino)

	Assets	Liabilities	Balance
Naples	74,092	120,960	(46,868)
Barletta	30,124	32,997	(2,873)
Subtotal southern Italy	104,216	153,957	(49,741)
Sicily – Trading	37,191	43,083	(5,892)
– Royal loans	62,434	—	62,434
Subtotal Sicily	99,625	43,083	56,542
Paris	21,610	46,290	(24,680)
England	—	20,674	(20,674)
Bruges	—	593	(593)
Avignon	29,568	59,568	(30,000)
All other[a]	73,852	58,256	15,596
Total branches	328,871	382,421	(53,550)

[a] Rhodes, Cyprus, Majorca, Sardinia, Tunis, Venice, and Pisa.

and 40.2 percent of all foreign liabilities. They also bring into focus
the Mediterranean orientation of the business; bearing in mind that
the "all other" category consists entirely of branches in that area,
Mediterranean operations accounted for 84 percent of total branch
assets and 67 percent of total branch liabilities. To be sure, the figures exaggerate this bias because two of the northern European
branches, England and Bruges, reported their results on a net (*a
croce*) basis.[93] Judging solely on the basis of the manpower assigned to
these branches, they would be roughly comparable in size to the
company's Paris branch. But even after adjusting for this difference
in reporting, it is clear that the company's business in 1335 was predominantly Mediterranean.

The southern Italy balances deserve special attention. The assets
consisted of cash, merchandise, household goods, and a large number (239) of debts receivable.[94] The liabilities were entirely moneys
payable to 112 creditors.[95] The large credit balance and the high average payable per creditor (li.1,400) suggests that the liabilities included a number of important deposits, supporting the widely held
assumption that Neapolitan deposits were a significant source of financing for the super-companies. In contrast, the smaller assets total
spread over a large number of items implies that the company's loans
to the king and his courtiers were quite modest at that time. This is a
surprising situation, indicating that the company had its royal accounts
well in hand and possibly also that the grain trade was at a low ebb at
the time the books were closed.[96] The probable low loan balance in
Naples contrasts sharply with the large total of advances to the king
of Sicily, the Angevin king's long-time rival.

In the case of the Paris and English balances, the nature of the
excess of liabilities over assets appears to indicate that these branches
were operating at a loss and financing their bad debts by rolling over

[93] In the discussion of Table 5, we saw that most branches reported gross asset and
liability totals (the *a bilancio* system), but three branches, England, Bruges, and
Majorca, reported the net balance of assets minus liabilities (the *a croce* system). Majorca provided supplementary data to permit presentation on a gross
basis, but unfortunately Bruges and England did not. Worse, they did not even
indicate the number of debtors and creditors.

[94] *I libri*, 193. See separate entries for Naples and Barletta.

[95] Ibid., 8, 9. See separate entries for Naples and Barletta.

[96] It also suggests that government finances were in reasonably good shape, in
line with indications that Robert was rapidly paying off the regime's long-standing deficit to the papacy during the 1330s while continuing his established policy
of borrowing from the super-companies to meet his day-to-day needs (see Pryor,
"Foreign Policy," 46).

short-term deposits.[97] In Avignon, as in Naples, the liabilities are described as amounts due to creditors "assigned" to the period 1331–5, suggesting that at least some of them were of a longer-term nature, such as deposits.[98] It is, of course, risky to draw too many inferences from the sketchy data available, especially in the absence of information on the structure of intercompany accounts. The branch entries contain no references to the status of transactions between branch and parent and branch and branch, and there must have been many of these. Nevertheless, there is sufficient evidence to establish that overall the branches financed their working capital locally and had enough left over to enable the parent company to fund the large long-term loans in Italy as well as some of its needs in Florence.

The company that is depicted here in mid-1335 is one that was drifting steadily toward bankruptcy. When the accounts for the 1331–5 company were finally drawn up in 1343, the entries referring to the losses described them as the amount that the company "lost more than it gained."[99] Effectively, what this meant is that its core business in southern Italy was losing more money than could be made up by profits on general merchandise trading and financial services. Although there was no obvious way to turn this situation around, bankruptcy was far from an inevitable fate. The company was still strong enough to respond to sound direction and determined leadership, and could try again to enter new markets, despite its earlier rebuffs in England and Spain. But the reversal of its fortunes required a further period of relative calm, and this was not to be. The company in its weakened state was fated to enter a period of exceptional turbulence.

[97] Ibid., 7, 191, 192. These branches describe their liabilities as amounts due to creditors on June 30, 1335, and paid by the branch shortly afterward, indicating that none of the payables were of a long-term nature. But the branch deficits must have been financed somehow, at least partly by new deposits.

[98] Ibid., 7. There were eighty-one creditors in all, some of whom may have been suppliers, but more will have been clients giving funds to the company for transfer or deposit. The intriguingly round balance of li.30,000 is the coincidental result of several separate entries in florins translated into lire at differing rates.

[99] Ibid., 286, e.g., "che la detta compagnia perde piu che non guadangno in detto tempo."

7

The critical years, 1335–1340

The Sixth Company of the Peruzzi was formed effective July 1, 1335, again under the style Giotto d'Arnoldo de' Peruzzi e compagni. The motivation for establishing what turned out to be the last company, and the reasons for the timing of this event are not immediately evident. There was no hint of a dividend for the foreseeable future; the chairman was not about to die, and there is no evidence that any shareholders had passed away without heirs capable of taking over.[1] Most curious, there is no evidence that the new company was ever capitalized. As we learned in Chapter 4, the preceding company was not formally closed, and final distributions were not made to its shareholders until July 1, 1343, or later. The Sixth Company appears simply to have inherited the account balances from its predecessor without any infusion of fresh capital.

The most likely reason for the formation of the new company is the striking change in the list of its shareholders. Three outsiders (Gherardo Bonaccorsi, Catellino degli Infanghati, and Piero Ubaldini) and one Peruzzi (Rinieri di Pacino) departed without replacement. Earlier, two senior Peruzzi shareholders had died, bequeathing their shares to two heirs each.[2] As a result, the Peruzzi family achieved parity with outsiders at least in the number of shareholders.[3] Also, several other partners, both Peruzzi and outsider, had passed their shares along to heirs. The total effect of all these changes was a radical difference in the makeup of the Sixth Company compared with its predecessor, and even more so with the Fourth Company, which had closed a scant four years earlier. By April 1338, when

---

[1] One possible exception is Gherardo di Gentile Bonaccorsi, who simply disappeared from the record at the close of the Fifth Company after having been a shareholder since 1310. He may well have died sometime in the 1331–5 period, but what happened to his shares is a mystery.

[2] Tommaso was replaced by his sons Bonifazio and Pacino, Amideo by Niccolo and Ottaviano.

[3] See Table A2.

a further four senior partners had "passed from this life," only three remained who had been shareholders of the 1324–31 company, and none of them were Peruzzi![4]

The loss of so many experienced owner–managers and the infusion of so much new blood are bound to have affected the complexion of the company and the attitudes within it. Although shareholders old and new are unlikely to have known the bleak results of the Fifth Company at the time, they would have realized that all was not well. The Peruzzi Company had not paid a dividend in over ten years, nor were there prospects for one in the foreseeable future. Those shareholders who departed may have done so out of discouragement (we know that at least Infanghati and Ubaldini had not died), and the long-serving partners who stayed on may have simply hoped for the best. But the newer shareholders, recognizing that the company's business was stagnating, must have looked for a radical change in the direction of the firm.

Only two realistic options were available. One was to eliminate unprofitable operations and cut staff, what is commonly known today as downsizing. This would not have been a promising approach because the company lacked the analytical sophistication to determine which of its enterprises were unprofitable, especially where company and shareholder personal transactions were often so thoroughly intermingled. In any case, this alternative does not seem to have been tried, as there is no evidence that any lines of business were dropped or employees terminated.[5] The other option was to launch a large-scale expansion of business that would generate major new revenues and more fully utilize the company's resources. This the company attempted to do, targeting the English wool trade as the business opportunity most likely to restore its fortunes.

Historians have usually explained the motivations of the Bardi and Peruzzi for their massive lending to Edward III in terms of an expectation of direct profit on the loans, or of profit derived from privileges granted to market wool as a reward for the loans, or a combination of both. These are reasonable assessments of the perceived rewards and of the probable motivation of the Bardi Company, which was simply doing on a larger scale what it had already been doing in England for years. They do not, however, explain adequately what

---

[4] The four who had died were Giotto and Filippo Peruzzi and Gherardo and Tano Baroncelli. The three survivors were Ruggieri Silimanni, Filippo Villani, and Stefano Bencivenni.

[5] Employee enrollment did, however, begin to decline, but not significantly until after 1338. See Table 10.

prompted the Peruzzi to embark on this demanding new program in the face of the well-known risks of lending to an English monarch. Fryde was one of the few who recognized that the Peruzzi, driven by the need to "mend its fortunes," might have had an additional incentive to those of the Bardi.[6]

The conservative Peruzzi Company had to consider a number of problems before it was prepared to increase its risk exposure in England. The first was the effect on its resources of the probable outbreak of a new war over Lucca. The second was the need to face up to a decision on its French business, which was certain to be affected if the company opted for closer ties with the English monarchy. The third was the need to clear itself with the English monarchy regarding its old relationship with Hugh Despenser the Younger before exposing additional assets to the risk of seizure in England.

The city of Lucca had been left weak and vulnerable after the retreat of Emperor Ludwig from Italy in 1330. It was occupied by his unemployed German mercenaries, who sold it to the Genoese merchant Spinola, who sold it to John of Bohemia, son of Henry VII, who in turn sold it in 1334 to the Rossi of Parma, who turned it over to Mastino della Scala of Verona. Mastino attempted to negotiate the sale of the hapless city to Florence for 360,000 florins, but the talks collapsed, and the "war with Mastino" was decided upon at the beginning of 1336. Among the six leading citizens charged with the responsibility of obtaining alliances and prosecuting the war were Simone Peruzzi, Ridolfo Bardi, and Acciaiuolo Acciaiuoli, whose close family connections with Florence's top three enterprises ensured the financial support of these great firms.[7] A complex set of alliances, including an exceptionally costly one with Venice, was duly arranged by July 1336. To finance the war, an elected committee of ten merchants and company representatives decided to double many of the gabelles. The yield was estimated at 300,000 florins, 100,000 of which was to be anticipated by a forced loan on all businesses and citizens.[8] The big companies pledged to pay up one-third of the loan and to offer guarantee of repayment to those lenders distrustful of the commune's ability to repay the loan out of forthcoming gabelles.[9]

---

[6] Fryde, *William de la Pole*, 48.

[7] Simone Peruzzi, the family's leading diplomat, was, as we have seen, an important depositor in the company and owner of its main warehouse, although not a shareholder.

[8] Sapori, *La crisi*, 109–10. The loan was secured by the expected revenues from the gabelles.

[9] There is no evidence in the Peruzzi accounts of direct advances by the company to the commune on this loan, but there are numerous entries reflecting pay-

Those lending directly to the commune were promised interest at 15 percent per annum; those requiring a company guarantee would receive 8 percent and the companies would earn 5 percent for providing the guarantee.[10] At this point, the war, although threatening, does not seem to have been a strain on the company's resources.

The dilemma of the French business was a vexing one for the Peruzzi. The company had long run a generally successful branch in Paris and had enjoyed a long and for the most part productive relationship with the French monarchy. The latter's strong connections with other important clients of the company, especially the Avignon papacy, could not be ignored. Given the rapidly deteriorating relationship between the French and English monarchs, any attempt by the Peruzzi to enter into a closer association with the English would surely be met with hostility by the French.[11] And although, as Mollat emphasizes, the Avignon popes were by no means puppets of the French kings, an action offensive to the French monarchy was unlikely to sit well with the papacy.[12] Finally, the French–papal connection had recently become more valuable to the Peruzzi, as Benedict XII entrusted the bankers with the collection of papal revenues in northern France in 1334, an important break with previous practice.[13]

The event that may well have triggered the company's decision was an adverse judgment from the Parlement of Paris on a long drawn-out lawsuit. The origins and basis of the suit are obscure, as they dated back to the 1300 company. The claim concerned a large debt allegedly owed by the company to the Maghaloti firm of Florence.

ments made on behalf of shareholders, employees, and clients to the "Dieci sulla lega con Vinezia" ([committee of] Ten on the league with Venice) . See *I libri*, 46, 53, 68, 85, 86, 129, 201, 209, 210, 213, 343, 356, 357.

[10] Sapori, *La crisi*, 109–10.

[11] This concern was a real one for the Peruzzi. Two years later, when entering into a huge financial undertaking with Edward III, the Bardi and Peruzzi obtained from the king an agreement that he would compensate them for any damages incurred in France, because by entering into the agreement, the companies had "put themselves in rebellion with the King of France" (*CCR* E III 1337–9, 400, 412).

[12] Mollat, *The Popes of Avignon*, especially 249–54. Mollat acknowledges the close ties between Avignon and the French kings, but stresses that the objectives of the popes, in particular, Benedict XII, were distinctly independent. The strong attachment of Clement VI to the French monarchy, however, made it difficult for him to mediate the French–English conflict impartially when he became pope in 1342. See Diana Wood, *Clement VI* (Cambridge, 1989), Chap. 6.

[13] Renouard, *Les relations*, 126–9. France was by far the largest source of funds for the papacy, which traditionally used local collectors. The change to the use of the Italian bankers in 1334 applied only to northern France; the rest of the country continued to employ papal collectors.

The Peruzzi clearly felt strongly about the merits of their case, because they paid the expenses of a procurator for a period of over six years at a cost totaling at least li.1,000.[14] The judgment itself cost li.3,538, and "interest" accumulated over the years on all expenses added a further li.1,118.[15] All told, the suit cost the shareholders of the 1300–8 company li.5,706, a sum that was finally allocated to them in 1339.

The judgment was rendered by the Parlement of Paris on March 27, 1336. On April 15, 1336, the Peruzzi Company made a commitment to lend the very large sum of 5,500 marks to the English crown, its first loan of any size to that monarchy since 1322.[16] The proximity of these two dates may be coincidental, but there is good reason to suspect some linkage between the two events. Giotto, the chairman, was a prominent partner of the 1300 company affected by the French lawsuit and is likely to have invested much of his personal prestige within the company in its defense. At the same time, the English branch had undoubtedly been negotiating quietly with English officials for some time, presumably with the support of the company's more aggressive shareholders.[17] It is inconceivable that the branch would have obligated the company to a major loan that also constituted a profound change in policy without the approval of the chairman. The approval of the old and conservative Giotto would have been made easier by the disappointing outcome in France. To be sure, the dates are too close to have permitted a referral back to Florence for the approval, but it is entirely possible that the arrangements had been set up within the company to commit for the loan only on receipt of news of an adverse judgment from Paris.

The above analysis can be properly criticized as speculative, but it

[14] *I libri*, 115–19. The expenses, which included food, drink, and house rent in Paris for "our procurator," were incurred from January 1330 to July 1336.

[15] Ibid. The actual fine was 1,846 reales, 2 soldi, translated at s38 d2 per real.

[16] *CPR* E III 1334–8, 249. The king acknowledged receipt of £3,666 2/3, promising to repay £1,000 by Midsummer and the balance by Michaelmas or All Saints from the tax revenues of tenths and fifteenths. Also promised was what appears to have been a "gift" of £1,000 to be paid 500 marks on each of the upcoming and the following two Michaelmases.

[17] The agreement for a loan of this size, with a complicated repayment schedule, would have taken months to arrange. One indication that the Peruzzi was edging closer to the monarchy is an entry in the *Calendar of Close Rolls* (*CCR* E III 1333–7, 486) dated May 12, 1335, ordering the Bardi and Peruzzi to appear at York regarding the king's moiety of the clerical tenth and other items that had been agreed with Pope John XXII but interrupted by his death. The king expected that the advice of the companies "will be most opportune for the completion and happy disposition of the affair." Moreover, the first tentative step toward lending to the Crown occurred as early as November, 1335 (Fryde, "Italian Bankers," 347 n11).

does attempt to take into account the fact that decisions, including business decisions, are often influenced by the inclinations of leaders, which, in turn, are driven by their emotions as well as their experience, intuition, and intelligence. The importance of personalities would shortly become even greater, as Giotto died a few months later, to be replaced immediately as chairman by his nephew Bonifazio. There is no question as to the direction of the new leader's interests. Bonifazio had been in the forefront of the company's brief attempt at aggressive business-building in England in the 1320s and would have been among the "new men" anxious to restore the company's fortunes by vigorously expanding its participation in the English wool trade. His actions after becoming chairman left no doubt that England was where his priorities lay.

Whether or not this analysis of motivations is accurate, the fact remains that the Peruzzi determined to make a large-scale loan to the English crown and that this decision represented a change in direction of enormous significance for the company. From its earliest years, its political bias had been aligned with that of the Florence-Naples-Avignon-Paris axis, adapting to the many twists and turns within that axis. The company lent its financial support routinely to these polities and their clients, such as the Hospitalers and the count of Flanders. Its involvement in England in the 1320s occurred at a time when relations of that country with France were reasonably amicable, and its operations in Sicily raised no objections from Naples or the papacy. Now, lending to an English monarch who was patently hostile to the French and uncomfortable with the papacy represented a momentous break from the company's tradition.

The April loan, although large, was only a tentative step carried out by the Peruzzi under a hesitant Giotto. A closer and more lasting association with the crown awaited the release of the company from all claims relating to its business with Hugh Despenser a decade earlier. The first move came in June 1336, when the Peruzzi Company was discharged of liability on certain goods claimed from Despenser.[18] There followed several other "confidence building" agreements during July and August, which settled various claims regarding Despenser and clarified the assignment of revenues to repay the April loan.[19] The final exoneration of the Peruzzi from all Despenser liabilities was published in December 1336, freeing the company from this contingency for the first time since the overthrow of Edward II.[20]

---

[18] *CPR* E III 1334–8, 277. [19] *CCR* E III 1333–7, 519, 599, 608, 609.

[20] *CPR* E III 1334–8, 343. The announcement included a statement of the total of receipts and payments, which acknowledged that the company ended with a negative balance of £182 in its account with Despenser.

The death of Giotto, the last of his generation, on August 9, 1336, marked a genuine "changing of the guard," both for the company and the family. The leading lights were now three grandchildren of the founders of the firm – Simone, descended from Filippo's side, and Bonifazio and Pacino, sons of Tommaso, from Arnoldo's side. Simone continued to occupy himself with politics and diplomacy, while Bonifazio took over the reins of the company, and Pacino involved himself in both business and politics. The previous changes of chairman – Tommaso replacing Filippo and Giotto replacing Tommaso – involved men content to continue the policies of their predecessors. Bonifazio, in contrast, was charting a new course, and from this point onward a large part of the company's energies would be directed toward England. Historians accustomed to associating the Peruzzi with that country need to be reminded, however, that the company's preoccupation there took place only during the last seven years of its existence.

It is not the purpose of this study to struggle with the stupifying complexity of Edward III's financing of his early campaigns against France. Professor Fryde has analyzed the English king's war finance in great detail, and there is little to be gained by attempting to replicate his investigations. Fryde's valuable works, moreover, deal with the king's total financing resources and in most places couple the Peruzzi's involvement with that of the Bardi. It will be necessary, therefore, to extract relevant data on the Peruzzi alone from direct sources as well as his several studies.[21]

Because of the complexity of the company's dealings with the English monarchy, it is useful to break them down into manageable periods, which can be discussed separately in their appropriate place. Two periods will be dealt with in this chapter. The first, from April 1336 until February 1338, covers the company's early advances made independently before the joint venture with the Bardi came into force. The second, from March 1338 to October 1340, marks the arrival of Bonifazio on the scene and the launching of the Bardi joint venture. The final three years will be discussed in Chapter 8.

The first period is riddled with apparent anomalies. Here is a company weakened by persistent losses lending on a lavish scale to a monarch from whom it must gain prompt recompense to recover its fortunes. Mere lending to a prince for profit was entirely out of keep-

[21] The works of E. B. Fryde to be cited are "Edward III's War Finance, 1337–41"; "Materials for the Study of Edward III's Credit Operations, 1327–48," *Bulletin of the Institute of Historical Research* 22 (1949): Section A, 105–38, and 23 (1950): Section B, 1–30; "Financial Resources 1337–40"; and *William de la Pole.*

ing with years of company policy and made even less sense in a situation where the company was short of reserves. The Peruzzi must have expected a tangible reward, such as privileges in the wool trade. But just four months after the first large loan, on August 12, 1336, Edward III placed a total embargo on shipments of wool to the Low Countries to bring them to heel. At the same time, he was making plans to establish the English Wool Company in the following year under an agreement with a group of leading English wool merchants. This company, duly formed in July 1337, was to grant the king a loan of £200,000 out of the sale of 30,000 sacks of wool over which it had been awarded monopoly control, along with the power of forced acquisition from English growers. Simultaneously, customs duty on wool exports was raised from 6s 8d to 20s per sack, which would be used by the king to help repay the loan. The expectation was that after a year of embargo, the English Wool Company would be able to exact a premium price from the desperate Flemish cloth manufacturers and reap a handsome profit.

These machinations should have, in theory, shut the Peruzzi out of the wool trade. It appears, however, that although the embargo was strictly enforced, some shipments by foreign merchants were licensed for export to southern European destinations.[22] At the same time, there is evidence that the king had given orders in 1337 to confiscate the assets of all foreign merchants except the Bardi and Peruzzi, putting the latter firms in the position of monopoly exporters to southern Europe.[23] The value of sharing with the Bardi even a limited opportunity to export wool to cloth manufacturers in southern Europe was significant, given the shortage of quality finished cloth in the Mediterranean resulting from the Flemish embargo. The alternative of being turned out of England along with the other foreign merchants was no doubt added incentive to lend to the king.

During this early period, there is some evidence of connection between the Bardi and Peruzzi in their relationship with the monarchy, but the latter appeared to be making its loans independently.[24]

[22] Fryde, *William de la Pole*, 58.

[23] *CPR* E III 1334–8, 506. An entry dated September 1, 1337, gave a release to an officer of the crown to arrest, imprison, and take all valuables from all foreign merchants except the Bardi and Peruzzi. A subsequent order dated July 16, 1338 (*CPR* E III 1338–40, 123), granted the king's clerk, E. de la Beche, immunity from claims due to his actions against the foreign merchants.

[24] For example, protection and safe-conduct were granted jointly to the two companies in February 1337 (*CPR* E III 1334–8, 381); the assessment of "losses" reimbursable to the companies appeared in a single order in November 1337 (*CCR* E III 1337–9, 206).

The fixed allocation of loans between the two companies (60 percent for the Bardi and 40 percent for the Peruzzi), a notable feature of the joint venture, did not become established until the spring of 1338.[25] Between April 1336 and February 1337, the Peruzzi had run up an acknowledged credit of £11,733, identified as being for the Scottish war, possibly in deference to the company's sensibilities about France.[26] Most of these advances took place after Bonifazio's accession to the leadership of the company, and most after the imposition of the wool embargo, when the only means of repayment was the assignment of direct taxes. By September 1, 1337, the acknowledged debt of the king had risen to £28,000, and then increased to £35,000 the following day, apparently to reflect "compensation" for the company's services.[27] On October 15, the king issued a formal writ on the Liberate Rolls of the Exchequer commanding the treasury to pay the entire £35,000 promptly.[28] Then on November 5, the king reconfirmed the £35,000 total and ordered the treasury to pay the £9,000 "losses" included in that total, an order that also confirmed that no action had been taken on the October 15 writ.[29]

The *Calendar of Patent Rolls* and *Calendar of Close Rolls* are normally not a good source of loan data, as will be made strikingly clear later, but they are adequate for this early period of relative orderliness, especially as they provide figures of acknowledged cumulative debt. The net lending of £26,000 late in 1337 is a reasonable-looking sum compared with the later astronomical figures, but it is extremely large in relation to the Peruzzi resources we have seen just eighteen months earlier. Using the rough but convenient ratio of one pound equals ten *lire a fiorino*, the £26,000 translates into li.260,000.[30] Referring back to Table 8, the company showed little evidence of surplus cash. It had a small equity of li.52,000, net borrowing in Florence of

[25] *CCR* E III 1337–9, 349. This order to the Treasury specified £30,000 due to the Bardi and Peruzzi should be assigned £18,000 to the former and £12,000 to the latter.

[26] *CCR* E III 1337–9, 9. The largest single advance was for £8,000 in January 1337 (*CPR* E III 1334–8, 388).

[27] *CPR* E III 1334–8, 515, 517.

[28] Edward A. Bond, ed., *Extracts from the Liberate Rolls Relative to Loans Supplied by Italian Merchants to the Kings of England in the 13th and 14th Centuries* (London 1839), 320, extract 193. Russell was so impressed with the wording of the writ that he was convinced that the entire amount was reimbursed in one payment (see Russell, "Societies of the Bardi and Peruzzi," 114), which, of course, it was not.

[29] *CCR* E III 1337–9, 206. The same entry confirmed the Bardi's "losses" of £10,000.

[30] See the Introduction for the calculation of this ratio.

li.118,000, and net borrowing from foreign branches of li.53,000, all of which added to li.223,000, less than these new lending demands in England alone. The company would have to obtain all this money from long-term deposits, paying at least its standard rate of 7 percent. Where did it come from?

The first place to look is Florence, as most historians knowledgeable about the situation seem to concur with Villani's claim that the greater part of the funds for the English venture originated in Florence.[31] Florence, however, was unlikely to be awash with surplus funds for risky foreign investments. As we have seen, preparations for war with Mastino were very expensive, and the big companies, including the Peruzzi, were in the forefront of the financing. According to Villani, the war cost 600,000 florins over the thirty months until its effective termination at the end of 1338, a rate of 20,000 florins per month.[32] The figure may or may not have been accurate, but it was clearly far in excess of the funds available from the commune's taxes, even at their increased level, so that further forced loans were necessary. By the end of the war, the communal debt had risen to 450,000 florins.

The wartime cash needs of the city took precedence over investments in the super-companies, not only by virtue of their patriotic merit and obligatory nature, but also because of the superior return that the forced loans offered investors – up to 15 percent, versus the Peruzzi's 7 percent.[33] The Peruzzi's ability to attract Florentine cash for its English operations would depend entirely upon the amount of surplus funds that were available in the city after the wartime needs had been met. This question brings us to Villani's famous chapter on the greatness of Florence, which has attracted the attention of so many historians.[34] Even assuming that the key economic numbers are accurate for the 1336–8 period to which he refers, a questionable assumption, do they necessarily indicate a plenitude of cash? To be sure, the 1330s was a period of exceptional building activity – the completion of the third ring of walls, the Santa Maria Novella and Santa Croce basilicas; the reconstruction of the Ponte Vecchio after the 1333 flood; and the start of construction of the cathedral campanile and the loggia of Orsanmichele, to say nothing of private residential and industrial building.[35] Such activities may create a sense

---

[31] See, e.g., Sapori, *La crisi,* and Fryde, *William de la Pole,* 90.

[32] Villani, *Storia,* Book XI, Chap. 89.   [33] Sapori, *Storia economica,* Vol. 1, 237–8.

[34] Villani, *Storia,* Book XI, Chap. 94.

[35] Brucker, *Renaissance Florence,* 25. Note that Villani was directly involved in the construction of the city walls (see Appendix V).

of prosperity, but they absorb cash, not generate it. The consumption figures are also impressive, but they merely reflect a large, bustling population's daily necessities, which tend to be much the same whether times are good or not so good.[36] The production figures that he cites have, as we have seen, been seriously challenged.[37]

The most problematic aspect of Villani's glowing report on Florence is that the period described, 1336–8, falls between the years we have just examined and found to be lackluster commercially and the years 1339 onward, which are universally acknowledged to have been disastrous. Moreover, Sapori has conceded that in 1336 the main economic indicators were decidedly negative, pointing out that the enemy was near the gates, that the passes through the Apennines and Alps were closed or insecure, and that the capacity for the citizens to acquire goods was reduced by previous heavy taxes.[38] Under these circumstances, he expected foreign trade to be down and factories closed, but he insisted that Villani did not exaggerate Florence's opulence in those years. He has reconciled this anomaly by arguing that the prosperity Villani described was a transitory phenomenon caused by the war. Thus, jobs lost in industry and trade were recovered in military production and military service. But the huge sums in circulation, he said, did not constitute wealth, because the jobs were temporary and non-productive, replacing employment that had been permanent and productive, so that when the war ended and temporary employment ceased, the economy became very depressed.[39]

Sapori's scenario is reasonable as far as it goes, but it does not give adequate weight to the draining of resources from the commune during the period caused by the payment of large subsidies to allies and salaries and expenses to mercenary troops. Nor does it fit in well with Villani's statement that the mint was coining 350,000 to 400,000 florins per year, a figure that Sapori does not challenge. And the cloth industry was probably vibrant, although much smaller than Villani claimed.[40] As mentioned earlier, the cloth industry in Florence

---

[36] Villani's population estimate of 90,000 does have the support of most demographic historians.

[37] See comments in Chapter 6 on H. Hoshino's dispute with Villani's estimates of textile production.

[38] Sapori, *La crisi*, 110.

[39] Ibid., 112–13.

[40] Villani's statement that 200 shops produced 70,000 to 80,000 cloths per year results in an average production of 350 to 400 cloths per shop, about three times the average that Hoshino found in his meticulous searches of the records of the wool guild. Also, in examining the guild's register, Hoshino discovered that there were 626 matriculants registered in 1332, which would mean that

was probably receiving English wool through the Bardi and Peruzzi, so that it could make more of the superior product, for which there would have been an eager market in 1336 and1337, due to the English embargo on wool exports to Flanders.

To recapitulate, Villani's enthusiastic assessment of the level of business activity in Florence during 1336–8 appears exaggerated, and Sapori's explanation of how the level could be so high is unsatisfactory. But even if Villani's figures were somewhere near the truth, they would not lead to the conclusion that there was plenty of spare cash available for investment, because his estimates of the cost of the war and the taxes raised leave little in reserve. Nor would government borrowing have added significantly to the money supply. In medieval Europe, such borrowing had about the same effect as taxation, removing cash from the private sector and redirecting it for public purposes. A government's ability to create money was very limited, as only very low-value billon coins were fiduciary tokens, so that it could not borrow and simply manufacture the funds for repayment, as modern governments do. The preponderance of money coined at the mints was of an intrinsic worth close to the face value of the coins. Again, there was no evidence of inflation at this juncture; on the contrary, prices of most comestibles were comfortably below average for the entire period, a fact that perhaps contributed to the sense of well-being expounded by Villani.[41]

Finally, even if there had been surplus cash available, very little of it seems to have found its way into the Peruzzi's coffers. The surviving records of the company show no significant additions to the deposit balances of its shareholders or outsiders at this time. The only evidence of possible large deposits appears in the form of two expense items that might be of interest. The first is a series of entries crediting a Mazzo di Scrafana of Palermo with several amounts between September 1338 and September 1341, described as *per merito*.[42] If the expenses were interest at the usual rate of 7 percent, they would

    there were about 300 shops at the typical arrangement of two matriculants per shop. He concluded that there were more shops, but less total production than Villani estimated. See Hoshino, *Arte della lana*, 203.

[41] See La Roncière, *Prix et salaires*, 821–35; *Il Biadaiolo*, 95. Possibly Villani's attitude was colored by the two consecutive good harvests of 1336 and 1337, a rare event in the 1330s. Good crop years had a remarkable effect on Florentines during this period; mingled with chronicler Lenzi's reports on prices in 1321 was a sonnet of fulsome praise to God for the bumper harvests at that time (169–70).

[42] *I libri*, 185. The term *per merito* is an unusual one in *I libri* and might mean service, but Edler's *Glossary*, 179, defines the term as interest on a loan.

indicate a loan of about li.16,500 in 1338. The second is an item that forms part of a long entry, described as li.53,159 "in cash given at various times to several persons."[43] At least part of this payment may have been interest, but it is impossible to estimate the size of the relevant deposits because the expense covers the period 1335–41. If it were all interest at 7 percent, the deposits concerned might be at least li.100,000, equivalent to £10,000. These two possible deposit sources, if real, would have been a help in funding the Peruzzi's English loans.

Other possible sources are depositors in southern Italy, Avignon, and Flanders. Wealthy individuals in southern Italy had long deposited surplus cash with the super-companies, but there is no evidence that individuals in that country had large caches of unutilized funds to invest, even if special inducements had been offered, which they had not.[44] The same comment applies to the princes of the church at Avignon and elsewhere who would also be disinclined to lend money for use against the king of France, a powerful patron to many of them. The papal treasury itself was definitely not a source. As mentioned earlier, the quantity of money transferred by the Bardi and Peruzzi for the papacy was not impressive, and the policy of popes John XXII and Benedict XII was to avoid borrowing from or lending to their Italian financiers.[45]

Merchants in Flanders and Brabant might have had an accumulation of lendable cash because the embargo had prevented their buying wool, and they might have been prepared to lend some to powerful Italian concerns if they could be sure of retrieving the funds when the embargo ended.[46] In addition, some money may well have been transferred from the company's branch in Paris to minimize the

---

[43] *I libri*, 181.

[44] There is only one instance in *I libri* of interest paid to anyone at a rate higher than 7%. For reasons unknown, the company paid Iacopo di Bartolo Bardi 15% on a small deposit in 1339 (see 173).

[45] As noted in Chapter 2, annual transfers from England, the most important country handled by the super-companies for the papacy, averaged only 12,000 florins per year for the Peruzzi between 1332 and 1337. Transfers dropped sharply thereafter, due partly to papal caution and partly to lower revenues caused by the war with France. For papal policy on deposits and borrowing, see Renouard, *Les relations*, 188–90. The only continuing exception to the no-deposit policy occurred in Bruges, where deposits were allowed to accumulate to pay for vestments destined for the court at Avignon.

[46] They would not have been an acceptable source of funds for the Peruzzi, judging by their later dealings with Edward III. They were extremely predatory and demanded interest approaching pawnbroker rates of 1% per week. See Fryde, "Financial Resources, 1337–40," 1155, for examples.

company's assets there that would be vulnerable to seizure by the French king. All of these sources may have helped finance the English lending, but only partially, given the large amount needed and the even larger amount sought by the Bardi.

A substantial portion of the funds must therefore have been raised in England itself. A small part we know came from repayment of a debt of £1,333 by the prior of the Hospitalers in England.[47] Another part may have been received from Italian and other foreign firms eager to get their cash out of the reach of the English king's agents. Still another part might have been obtained from English merchants. Fryde has established that William de la Pole amassed a good portion of the huge sums he raised for the king by mobilizing the surplus funds of numerous smaller English merchant concerns.[48] If a parvenu merchant from Hull, however gifted, could do this, why could not a prestigious international firm also do so, at least among the merchants of London? In his excellent analyses of the documents and procedures of Edward III's administration, Fryde has pointed out that possession of letters obligatory under royal seal gave a creditor the best possible guarantee of repayment and that such letters were often pledged as security for borrowing.[49] The Peruzzi had obtained letters obligatory for £28,000 by September 2, 1337, and while there is no evidence that the Peruzzi pledged any of them, the mere existence, let alone the use, of these letters would have made the company's borrowing in England much easier.[50]

There is one further piece of indirect support for the argument that England was a significant source of funds for the super-companies' loans to the crown. This is the well-documented fact that England suffered severe price deflation and currency shortage in the late 1330s and early 1340s. Among the reasons advanced for this situation are the exports of specie by the king to help pay the expenses of his expeditions and subsidies to his allies.[51] If the super-companies' loans to the government had been sourced from abroad, the

[47] *I libri*, 195. The money was received in the London branch on May 1, 1337, and recorded in Florence on July 1, 1337.

[48] Fryde, *William de la Pole*, 30–2.

[49] Fryde, "Materials," Section A, 115–17.

[50] *CPR* E III 1334–8, 517.

[51] Other reasons include the excessive price of gold in England and normal coin wastage not made up by imports of silver. See N. J. Mayhew, "Numismatic Evidence and Falling Prices in the Fourteenth Century," *Economic History Review* 2 series, 27 (1974): 1–15; Mavis Mate, "High Prices in Early Fourteenth-Century England: Causes and Consequences," *Economic History Review* 2, series 28 (1975): 1–16; Prestwich, "Exchange Rates," 470–82; Waugh, *England of Edward III*, 76–89.

effect on the English economy would have been inflationary, or neutral at the least, had all their loans been used exclusively for foreign payments. The severity of the deflation suggests that the Italian super-companies as well as the English merchants borrowed locally to a considerable extent to secure cash for the king.

Although the royal lending to date imposed a great strain on the company's resources, it was perceived as short term and manageable, with specific repayment dates. Additional advances to the government between October 1337 and March 1338 were modest and partly conditional upon receiving licenses to export wool.[52] At this level, the company hoped to be able to roll over its accounts with the crown and with its creditors, gradually reducing the amounts with the cash flow generated by its share of the wool trade allowed by the king. In short, the company hoped to repeat its experience with the Angevin kingdom in southern Italy. Unfortunately, Edward's grand money-raising scheme with the English Wool Company came to grief early in 1338, and he was obliged to look elsewhere for finance for his plans to invade France.[53] At the same time, the English king was presented with a splendid opportunity when the Flemish cities, led by Jacob van Artevelde, rose in revolt. Edward's representatives quickly reached agreement that Flanders would remain strictly neutral in exchange for England's lifting the wool embargo. Shipments began to flow from stores held in Dordrecht in early March.[54] But the king needed money more than ever and was prepared to offer to those who could provide it huge quantities of wool. He promptly chose the Bardi and Peruzzi, concluding an agreement with them on March 11, 1338.[55]

This agreement initiated the second phase of the company's dealings with Edward III. Although it was modified somewhat in a new indenture two months later, its essentials were unchanged and represented a commitment vastly greater than anything the company had

---

[52] The licenses required the companies to pay both the higher rate of duty (30s per sack) imposed on foreign merchants and a loan of 20 shillings per sack (see Fryde, *William de la Pole*, 72). The Peruzzi evidently took advantage of the opportunity (see *CPR* E III 1334–8, 543; *CCR* E III 1337–9, 191, 200, 207, 217).

[53] For further information on the complex story of the English Wool Company and its collapse following the conference at Gertruidenberg in December 1337, see Fryde, *William de la Pole*, especially Chaps. 6 and 7; E.B. Fryde, "Edward III's Wool Monopoly of 1337: A Fourteenth-Century Royal Trading Venture," *History* new series, 37 (1952): 8–24; and Loyd, *The English Wool Trade*, Chap. 5.

[54] Henry S. Lucas, *The Low Countries and the Hundred Years' War, 1326–1347* (Ann Arbor, MI, 1929), 269–72.

[55] *CCR* E III 1337–9, 400. Giovanni Baroncelli and Tommaso di Filippo Peruzzi signed for the Peruzzi Company.

ever undertaken before.[56] Briefly, the two companies jointly agreed to lend the king £15,000 for his journey to the continent and a further £20,000 after his arrival there. The king would cause 4,000 sacks of wool to be placed at the disposal of the companies to fund the first £15,000 and give the companies the responsibility to sell a further 16,000 sacks after his arrival. Part of the proceeds of the sales would apply against the later debt, but the main recovery of this and previous debts was to come from the assignment of £30,000 to the companies from the tenth and fifteenth of the clergy and laity. To enable the companies to meet their marketing commitments, the king promised a monopoly on the wool sales on the continent until August 1, 1338. And as a further incentive, he gave the companies the right to sell 2,000 sacks of their own wool duty free and compensation for any damages inflicted by the king of France on their property in that country.

The companies had negotiated a very good deal for themselves, but they were well aware of the risks involved. Fryde has accused the companies of naivety as well as cupidity at this point, commenting that the companies had placed "excessive trust in the king's promises."[57] The companies had good reason to believe that their marketing skills and connections were equal to the task of disposing of the vast quantities of wool required by the agreement, but they realistically anticipated the probable antipathy of the English merchants that had now been bypassed. The Peruzzi firm was especially cautious. Not content with simply relying on the Bardi's long and successful experience in dealing with the English crown, the company took the unprecedented step of allowing its chairman, Bonifazio, to leave his post at the center of operations in Florence and take personal charge of the venture in Flanders and England. This was a staggering decision for a company with important widespread operations, the control of which depended so heavily on the close attention of a dictatorial chief at the center in Florence. It was clearly a tribute to the importance attached to the successful management of the English venture, rather than an act of desperation, as suggested by Russell.[58]

Both Sapori and Russell erroneously put the year of Bonifazio's arrival in London as 1339.[59] He apparently did spend time in Brabant and Flanders, which might have been necessary to establish confi-

---

[56] The modified version is dated May 11, 1338 (CCR E III 1337–9, 412).

[57] Fryde, "Public Credit," 460.

[58] Russell, "The Societies of the Bardi and Peruzzi," 112, 123.

[59] Ibid., 112, 123; Sapori, La crisi, 61. Here, Sapori stated that Bonifazio went to Brabant in July 1338 and stayed there until October 1339 before going on to London. Fryde repeated this comment in "Financial Resources," 1158.

dence in the company's new direction, given the Peruzzi's long-standing policy of consistent support for the count of Flanders and his liege lord, the king of France. But he may have reached England as early as the spring of 1338, which would have allowed him to be on hand for the framing of the agreements of March 11 and May 11, even though he was not a signatory to either document. He definitely was in England close to that time, because a letter in the Patent Rolls established him as a resident of England in June.[60] The timing of Bonifazio's appearance in that country is important, because his early arrival means that he was in control of the operation from the start.

The problem faced by Bonifazio was to feed cash to the English government with meticulous care, making sure that refunding was available from previous advances. He had to provide enough loans to maintain the company's standing with the crown but ensure that as little as possible was new cash. First, as we have seen, the company simply did not have access to the amounts of money agreed upon; and second, Bonifazio and his colleagues were well aware of the fate that befell the Ricciardi and Frescobaldi when they became overly committed in England. According to Fryde, the Bardi and Peruzzi together produced the initial £15,000 for the king by July 10, just prior to the king's departure for Antwerp.[61] During April and May, the government made several commitments to the companies that executed parts of the March and May agreements and that may have directly or indirectly helped them make these and later payments. The orders included assignments of £18,000 to the Bardi and £12,000 to the Peruzzi out of the clerical tenth and the lay tenth and fifteenth, as well as commands to customs officials to pay £4,483 and to permit the companies to export substantial quantities of wool.[62]

From here onward, the record becomes murky and unreal. Fryde has reckoned that in the two months between the king's arrival in Antwerp on July 22 and Michaelmas (September 29), the two companies paid the king's receiver in the Netherlands the astonishing sum of £71,522.[63] Why they should have felt obliged to lend such a large

---

[60] *CPR* E III 1138–40, 100. The entry, dated June 3, 1338, granted protection and safe-conduct to three members of the Peruzzi firm, including Bonifazio, noting that they are "dwelling in the realm." Numerous subsequent entries in the *Calendar of Patent Rolls* and *Calendar of Close Rolls* include Bonifazio among the members of the Peruzzi Society.

[61] Fryde, *William de la Pole*, 89. The Peruzzi's contribution was £5,979, in line with its agreed proportion of 40%.

[62] *CCR* E III 1137–9, 349 (April 5), 355 (April 15), 373 (May 11), 418 (May 24), 421 (May 2).

[63] Fryde, *William de la Pole*, 89–90. He notes further that the loans were "counterbalanced for the time being only by very scanty receipts from the king."

amount when their agreement called for further loans of only £20,000 is unclear. Where they were able to obtain this money in such a short time is not even mentioned. To put the size of the loans in perspective, the £86,500 reportedly advanced to the king between May and September corresponded to about 575,000 gold florins, equivalent to almost double the Florence commune's annual budget at the time, even using Villani's generous estimates.[64] The Peruzzi's 40 percent share would have been equivalent to li.346,000, an amount greater than its entire foreign branch assets just three years earlier. The cost of carrying these new loans, to say nothing of the previous ones, would be over li.24,000 per annum, an amount greater than the company's entire profit in all but its very best years.[65] The official English records, so painstakingly analyzed by Fryde, are incompatible with the records and capability of the companies. How can they be reconciled?

The possible sources of funds described earlier would have been largely exhausted by the end of 1337. Could the companies have generated additional funds through the creation of credit, lending money like modern banks through the use of fractional reserves? On the basis of today's criterion of a capital-to-loans ratio of 8 percent, the Peruzzi, even with its 1335 equity of only li.52,000, could tolerate total lending of li.650,000 or £65,000. However, the Peruzzi Company was not a bank, but primarily a marketing company, to which such ratios would not apply. More important, the creation of credit on a significant scale did not occur in medieval Europe. Lane and Mueller point out that deposit taking was merely a means of circulating capital and that real credit creation was a local phenomenon controlled by money changers dealing with people they knew.[66] Goldthwaite's investigations into the economic effects of banking in a somewhat later period revealed that some banks held less than 100 percent reserves some of the time but that the effect of fractional reserves on the Florentine economy was insignificant.[67] Day adds that "the creation of credit, the classic function of banking institutions, was considered an abuse of public confidence."[68] He notes that the use of fractional reserves by deposit banks did not occur until a somewhat later period. And, according to de Roover, bank money was not

---

[64] Villani, *Storia*, Book XI, Chap. 92, set the budget for 1338 at 300,000 florins.
[65] The figure used here assumes that the Peruzzi would pay its normal rate of 7%.
[66] Lane and Mueller, *Money and Banking in Venice*, Vol. 1, 62–4. Later (79) they emphasize the role of deposit bankers in creating credit but go on to explain that deposit and transfer banking were not important in Florence (81–2).
[67] Richard A. Goldthwaite, "Local Banking in Renaissance Florence," *Journal of European Economic History* 2 series, 14 (Spring 1985), 37–8.
[68] John Day, *The Medieval Market Economy* (Oxford, 1987), 150.

used extensively as a means of war finance until the sixteenth century.[69]

Another possible source of credit, discounting bills of exchange, was not regularly practiced as a means of raising cash, and in any case, since the bills originated in routine trade, they would not have produced anything like the volume needed.[70] Postan mentions the assignment of debts as a substitute for cash, whereby someone contracting an obligation would "set over" debts due to him in settlement, thus avoiding the use of coin.[71] But he suggests that the larger Italian houses would not have used this device often in England; and again, the amounts could not have been material. Finally, given the huge and inconvenient mass of coin that would have been represented by the loans, and in a foreign country as well, could the companies have made part of the advances in some form of scrip or promissory notes? Day refers to the use of scrip money among merchants in times of a sudden decline in monetary stocks.[72] The mobilization of so much cash so quickly presented acute physical problems of collection, movement, and rational deployment, and the use of scrip would have given the companies additional time to secure the cash.[73] But Fryde makes no mention of such instruments in his exhaustive examinations of the receipt and issue rolls.

The only remaining possible way to reconcile the records with reality is that the companies gave the king promises instead of money on several occasions in this period. In his analysis of receipt and issue rolls' procedures, Fryde acknowledges that the enrollment of loans on the receipt roll did not mean that the money had actually been been received by the government in cases where the officials were prepared to recognize the debt but were unable to repay at once.[74] In the summer of 1338, this would obviously have been the most common situation. Fryde goes on to say that the officials had to

[69] De Roover, *Medieval Bruges*, 321. This use first occurred in the Venetian Republic.

[70] The limitations on the use of bills of exchange for credit purposes, as described by Spufford, *Money and Its Use*, 255–9, were discussed in Chapter 5.

[71] Postan, *Medieval Trade*, 41. De Roover also notes that debts were assignable (*Medieval Bruges*, 51, 54, 68 n14), but that the "setting off" applied to bills of exchange.

[72] Day, *Market Economy*, 95.

[73] A useful illustration of logistics of hurriedly moving coinage is given by Sumption, *Hundred Years' War*, 569. Here he describes the frantic mobilization of cash to fund reinforcements for the siege of Calais in the spring of 1347, noting, "At Westminster, the cash was being laden onto the pack animals as soon as it was received."

[74] Fryde, "Materials," Section A, 128–9. In a footnote he quotes from McFarlane that the object of enrollment "was to entitle the creditor to repayment, not to prove that the amount had been received by the Exchequer."

be convinced that everything was in order before they enrolled a loan but that they could not be certain with regard to secret loans. At that time there were many such loans, which, he notes, were probably disliked by the officials, because they could not be sure whether the money had really been advanced by the financiers and could not control the way in which the funds were spent.[75] Specifically, Fryde writes, "When in the summer of 1338 the exchequer refused to recognize in this way a number of secret loans by the Bardi and Peruzzi, this so seriously alarmed the two societies that they threatened to cease to advance money to Edward III and, after repeated royal orders, the exchequer finally yielded and entered the loans in question on the receipt roll."[76] Thus, many of the recorded loans may not have been paid in at the time indicated, so that such loans, as well as the so-called loans that were really "gifts," did not involve any transfer of funds from the companies to the Exchequer.

If part of the loans attributed to the companies had been deferred or unpaid, then the possibility arises that the firms might have gained enough time to provide new loans from funds generated by the repayment of old ones and by the sale of wool. The mere addition of all moneys advanced over a period of time does not inform as to the peak lending at any one point because it does not factor in the repayments. Funding fresh loans by repayments of old ones creates the impression of very large totals in the same way that Emperor Toussaint l'Ouverture of Haiti is said to have created the impression of having a large army – by marching the same troops by the reviewing stand over and over again in different uniforms. Repayments were surely being made, even if late, and the goal of the company managers was to match their advances as closely as possible with their receipts. That they did not entirely succeed is evident, but the gap between loans and repayments over the longer term is not nearly as wide as suggested by the data in published sources. As will be shown later in this chapter, Fryde's detailed analysis of the period from May 1338 to March 1340 in his unpublished dissertation reveals a surprisingly small deficit in the Peruzzi Company's dealings with the English crown.[77]

One potential source of additional money for loans to the king is suggested by an item that formed part of an extraordinarily long entry of expenses in the Peruzzi accounts between 1335 and 1341 – the dispatch of a fast ship from Barletta to Rhodes.[78] Sapori has proposed

---

[75] Ibid., 113. [76] Ibid., 129.

[77] Fryde, "Edward III's War Finance," 333–5.

[78] *I libri*, 181. The item translates, "li.203 for the cost of an armed barc that was ordered from Barletta to Rhodes in October, 1338, to make known to our associates the news of the war by the King of England on the King of France."

that the reason for the order was to rush the news of Edward III's retreat from Buironfosse so that the Rhodes branch would have time to take measures to head off panic on the part of its depositors.[79] Fryde echoed Sapori's comment, saying that the ship was sent "to warn their factors in time against the danger of damaging rumours."[80] But Edward's failed campaign took place in 1339, not 1338; the late summer and early autumn of 1338 was taken up with a stately progress from Antwerp to Coblenz and back to Brabant in a successful but costly attempt to gather allies.[81] Then why should the Peruzzi send at substantial expense a fast ship to a minor branch, and why Rhodes? The answer must lie in the fact that the grand master of the Hospitalers resided there.[82] Two probable reasons for urgent communication come to mind. The first is the fact that the only important news on the war with France at that time was Edward's acceptance of the vicar-generalship of the empire from Emperor Ludwig, the pope's arch-enemy. The Peruzzi would have wanted to reassure the Hospitalers that this action of the company's new royal client did not affect its relationship with the papacy. The second is a request for money to help the company in its hour of need. A year earlier, Edward III had commanded the prior of the order in England to pay the Peruzzi all moneys due to it; perhaps the prior had not paid and needed prodding, but more likely the Peruzzi were asking for additional funds.[83]

The king's grand and expensive travels on the continent were increasing the pressure on the companies to find more money, some of which may have been made possible by a flurry of orders to customs between August and November 1338 to permit the export of large quantities of wool.[84] Some of these provided for outright grants of wool, which, for the Bardi and Peruzzi, totaled 2,513 sacks, 45 cloves, worth £17,221 after deduction of costs.[85] These generous grants

[79]   Sapori, *La crisi*, 66. Sapori also corrected a garbled account of the incident given by Peruzzi in *Storia commercio*, 454, which had included a wrong date.

[80]   Fryde, "Financial Resources," 1158–9; repeated in *William de la Pole*, 90.

[81]   See Lucas, *The Low Countries*, 290–3, for a colorful description of this diplomatic initiative.

[82]   Although the grand master, Hélion de Villeneuve, lived in Europe between 1319 and 1332 mending the order's finances, he was well settled in Rhodes by 1338, where he was described as "a very old and stingy man, who amassed great treasures," See Anthony Luttrell, "The Hospitallers at Rhodes, 1306–1421," in *A History of the Crusades*, ed. K. Setton III (Madison, WI, 1975), 290–1.

[83]   *CCR* E III 1337–9, 186. The order was dated October 4, 1337, and would have referred to money owed in excess of the £1,333 repaid in April of that year and noted earlier in this chapter.

[84]   See, e.g., *CPR* E III 1338–40, 441, 458, 460, 462, 499, 505, 545, 547, 561, 565, 570.

[85]   Fryde, "Financial Resources, 1337–40," 1162. Fryde says, "Between August and

of wool to his main financiers only partly reflected Edward's desperation during this period. He pledged the Great Crown and other valuable objects, and borrowed large sums under onerous terms from
the Portinari, Vivelin of Strasbourg, and several merchants of
Malines.[86] The earl of Derby, the king's cousin, stood surety for the
latter loan and was later held hostage for several months pending
settlement of the debt.

Fryde has described Edward's wool transactions as being completely
out of touch with reality, but his promises to the Bardi and Peruzzi in
Antwerp at the end of November were the stuff of cloud-cuckoo-land.
There, he solemnly committed to gifts of £30,000 to the Bardi and
£20,000 to the Peruzzi, to be paid promptly, along with substantial
awards to the wives of company officials and the daughter of
Bonifazio.[87] The companies knew that the agreement was a charade,
as they were well placed to understand the extent of the king's pre-
dicament. They no doubt cheerfully accepted the promises on the
basis of the leverage they might provide in their later dealings with
the monarch.[88] At this point, the companies were undoubtedly fully
stretched but were managing to keep solvent.

Back in Florence, the long, costly war with Mastino seemed to be
dragging on to a successful conclusion, when, in December 1338,
Venice signed a separate peace treaty without warning, leaving Florence exposed and without hope of victory. The companies, deeply
committed to the war and participating in its direction, quickly realized that they could not recover their investment by the seizure of
Lucca and reluctantly concluded peace with the Scagliero on January 24, 1339. Not much is known about the following two years, but
clearly the Bardi and Peruzzi, victims of two disastrous campaigns,
faced serious problems. Sapori asserted that the companies' ability

November 1338 Edward ordered the government at home to deliver 12,400 sacks
to the Bardi and Peruzzi, Pole, Duivenvoorde and Monte Florum [the king's
agent in the Netherlands]." The number of sacks eventually granted was 9,303,
of which the Bardi and Peruzzi share was 2,513 (see note 3 on that page).

[86] Ibid., 1154–5. The Portinari was a family of Florentine exiles resident in the
Netherlands.

[87] *CPR* E III 1338–40, 195. The entry is noted as "vacated because these bonds
were revoked and not delivered." The order, however, was reinstated in June
1339 (*CPR* E III 1338–40, 387, 392).

[88] These enormous gifts were supported by letters obligatory, and the Bardi did
not yield possession until the final settlement with Richard II in 1392. The
letter obligatory for the £30,000 was one of the four such documents given up
by the Bardi at that time. See Alice Beardwood, *Alien Merchants in England,
1350 to 1377* (Cambridge, MA, 1931), 4–9 and App. A.

to repair their situation was hindered by the deterioration of commerce in general, with trade with northern Europe virtually cut off by land and sea.[89] There was a very bad harvest in 1339, followed by famine and pestilence in 1340. The city vented its frustration with Venice by passing an act in March 1340 forbidding trade with Venice and her territories in the Levant, which of course redounded to the disadvantage of the companies.

In such grim times, there was no alternative for the companies but to trim sail and retreat, as Sapori put it, into a "modest life in harmony with the European economic and political situation and with the conditions of their city exhausted by the expense of an unsuccessful war."[90] Fryde too noted a sharp falloff in new loans from the companies to Edward III, commenting that between Michaelmas 1338 and February 1340 their loans to the king were "a mere £28,376."[91] Nevertheless, the companies managed to maintain substantial and vigorous business throughout their entire theater of operations. In England, as discussed, a part of the loans committed in the autumn of 1338 was probably not actually paid in until later, so that the drop in new loans executed was not as steep as the £28,376 figure suggests. Also, the companies were successful in shipping a very large quantity of wool to Italy in the years 1338–40, estimated to be at least 7,365 sacks.[92] The flow of so much quality wool must have helped Florentine manufacturing and maintained the companies' position as cloth suppliers to southern Italy. And although the trade embargo against Venice may have inhibited the flow of goods, Genoa would have been happy to fill the void. There is no evidence to suggest that the grain trade in that territory suffered unduly.[93]

The records left in the Peruzzi's accounts are not very revealing as regards the extent of the concern's business during 1338–40, but they do reflect considerable activity and travel around the branches by partners and factors.[94] There was even travel in and out of Paris, indicating that the Paris branch was still able to do business, al-

---

[89] Sapori, *La crisi*, 115. [90] Ibid., 117.

[91] Fryde, "Financial Resources, 1337–40," 1159.

[92] Fryde, "Italian Maritime Trade with Medieval England," *Recueils de la Société Jean Bodin* 32 (1974): 301.

[93] Yver, *Le commerce*. In spite of the lack of complete registers, Yver says on 319 that enough survived to prove that the association between the super-companies and the court was as active and prosperous as ever, right up to 1340. Also, he reports that King Robert continued to pledge jewelry and gold plate for loans from the Peruzzi as late as 1338 (see 390).

[94] See Chapter 3 regarding the abundant evidence of the monitoring of the company's business in Florence and abroad.

though not without risk to company employees.[95] Most definitely, there is no evidence to suggest any panicky cutbacks. The long list of expenses incurred between 1335 and 1341 are mainly of a routine nature, including interest, brokerage commissions, office supplies, fixtures, fines, and entertainment[96] Likewise, the account of warehouse rents during that period reflects routine renewals at unchanged rates, giving no indication of contraction.[97] And although there were staff reductions, they occurred gradually.[98] In short, the evidence suggests prudent husbanding of resources, more in the sense of skillfully riding out a storm, rather than preparing for eventual liquidation.

The English venture, which had been started with the object of recovering the Peruzzi's fortunes, was of course now the company's biggest problem. But despite the acknowledged reduction in the scope of the firm's loans to the king, the latter continued to favor both the Peruzzi and the Bardi. Edward's drastic order of May 6, 1339, revoking all assignments except those relating to Scotland and to the Bardi and Peruzzi illustrates dramatically how high the companies remained in the king's regard.[99] The reinstatement of the lavish promises to the companies and the wives of their personnel noted earlier was followed by an omnibus confirmation ceremoniously attested before an array of nobles that full satisfaction was to be given on all assignments and moneys due.[100] Nevertheless, both companies continued to back away gently from further commitments. They still managed to keep in the king's good graces by agreeing to some new loans, but at this stage the entries in the *Patent Rolls* and *Close Rolls* show that William de la Pole had become the predominant financier to the crown.

The year 1340 began in much the same vein, with the companies

---

[95] Two Peruzzi factors were imprisoned in the Châtelet in 1340 because of the company's loans to the king's enemies, but they were later released and their trading licenses restored (see Davidsohn, *Firenze*, Vol. 6, 642).

[96] *I libri*, 181.

[97] Ibid., 180.

[98] See Table 10.

[99] *CPR* E III 1338–40, 255. Despite the unequivocal language of this order excluding the Bardi and Peruzzi, along with supporting evidence from subsequent orders and actions, some historians have surprisingly interpreted it as meaning that the king was repudiating the Bardi and Peruzzi loans. See Peruzzi, *Storia commercio*, 471; Marvin B. Becker, *Florence in Transition*, Vol. 1 (Baltimore, 1967), 97.

[100] *CPR* E III 1338–40, 391. The statement, dated August 4, 1339, also noted fears for the solvency of the companies.

seemingly more intent on collecting against old commitments than making new ones. The *Patent Rolls* and *Close Rolls* are studded with entry after entry giving orders, repeat orders, and countermands regarding the disposal of various quantities of wool and payments due from promised taxes. Following his inconclusive campaign around Cambrai and the Thiérache in the autumn of 1339, the king began preparing for 1340 by negotiating a military and economic alliance with the Flemish towns. This he cemented by declaring himself king of France from Ghent in an elaborate ceremony on January 26.[101] On his return to England in February, he pressed the companies for new commitments for his next incursion into the continent in June of that year. New undertakings were eventually formalized in two agreements.[102] The first, dated May 28, provided that the companies would advance 2,000 marks per month of twenty-eight days for one year, totaling 26,000 marks in all for the upkeep of the king's household. In return, they were assigned the first year's proceeds from the ninth of sheaves, fleeces, and lambs from Gloucester, the second year's from Wiltshire, plus the clerical tenth.[103] In the second agreement on June 10, the companies agreed to pay three important royal debts on the continent, two of which involved the release of the earls of Derby and Northampton from their pledges as hostages of the merchants of Malines and Louvain, respectively.[104] In compensation, the two firms were to receive the first year of the ninth from six counties and the archdeaconry of Lincoln, estimated to be worth £20,915, plus the second year of the ninth from fifteen counties due for levy in 1341. As further incentives, the companies were awarded "gifts" (10,000 marks for the Peruzzi) and the promise of speedy accounting, the latter evidenced by a flurry of writs on June 15 and 16.[105]

Despite the king's remarkable naval victory over the French at

[101] Sumption, *Hundred Years' War*, 300–3. For a thorough account of the campaigns of 1339 and 1340 in the Low Countries and Gascony, see 239–369.

[102] The data for the two agreements shown in this paragraph are mainly from Fryde, "Edward III's War Finance," 570–83.

[103] The infamous "ninth," which was a tax in kind on agricultural produce, was similar to a clerical tithe. But it was complex, inequitable, and extremely unpopular, and its yield was well below expectations (Fryde, *William de la Pole*, 145–50). Until that time, the yields of Edward III's various direct tax levies had been remarkably close to assessments. See W. M. Ormrod, "The Crown and the English Economy," in *Before the Black Death*, ed. B. M. S. Campbell (Manchester, 1991), 149–83.

[104] The earl of Derby was Edward III's cousin, Henry de Grosmount, who later became duke of Lancaster. He was thus a very important hostage.

[105] *CCR* E III 1339–41, 418–20.

Sluys on June 24, his promises, so easily offered, were very slowly delivered. The Bardi and Peruzzi were therefore equally hesitant in executing their side of the bargain, notwithstanding the fact that the victory at Sluys greatly reduced the risk involved in shipping wool to Flanders and Italy. They did deal with the account that the king seemed to regard as the most important, paying off his debt of £10,500 to Simon de Mirabello, regent of Flanders and stout supporter of Edward III and the Flemish leader Jacob van Artevelde.[106] The companies were unprepared, however, to make any other payments until they received some of the promised revenues, and these were not forthcoming; the Peruzzi did not even pay its share of the Mirabello commitment until November.[107] For lack of funds, the king was forced to abandon his siege of Tournai, and on September 25 he concluded a truce with France in the village of Esplechin. As a result, the two earls were obliged to return to Malines and Louvain as hostages.

This phase of the Peruzzi's operations in England came to a sudden end on October 3, 1340, with the death of Bonifazio in London, allegedly of a broken heart.[108] The chairman had obviously been under continuous stress since his assumption of the leadership of the company, but his efforts to rescue it had been showing some signs of success. To be sure, the Peruzzi remained substantial creditors of Edward III, but Bonifazio had maintained a balancing act that enabled the company to control its exposure. Although there is no figure indicating exactly how much was still owed by the king at that time, the record shows that both the Bardi and Peruzzi had succeeded in obtaining substantial recoveries of their advances. Fryde has assembled tables giving the details of payments received by the two companies between May 1338 and March 1340. The total of these payments was £66,000 for the Bardi and £38,000 for the Peruzzi, £104,000 in all.[109] During a slightly longer period, the amount re-

---

[106] Mirabello, better known in the Low Countries as Simon van Halen, was also one of the guarantors of Edward III's debts in Brussels (Lucas, *The Low Countries*, 429). And despite his close connections with Edward III, he remained on good terms with Louis, count of Flanders, a loyal supporter of King Philip of France (438). He was also well known to the Peruzzi, having followed Donato di Pacino as general receiver of Flanders in 1329 (Kittell, *Ad Hoc*, 207).

[107] Fryde, "Edward III's War Finance," 592.

[108] While reluctant to refute the "official" Villani version, Sapori suggests that Bonifazio may have died of a recurrence of a throat ailment, for which he had had surgery in 1335 (*La crisi*, 61).

[109] Fryde, "Edward III's War Finance," App. B.

portedly advanced by the companies was £86,000 by the Bardi and £40,000 by the Peruzzi, for a total of £126,000.[110] These data show the difference between company advances and receipts to be significant but bearable for the Bardi and remarkably small for the Peruzzi. Fryde notes that the Peruzzi receipts may have been overstated by some £1,600, but even allowing for this item, the gap between reported Peruzzi loans and repayments over the critical period May 1338 to March 1340 was a mere £3,600.[111] And taking into account hidden interest in the loan totals and profit from 3,621 sacks of wool exported during that time, the Peruzzi company may have actually improved its cash position by as much as £8,600.[112]

Earlier in this chapter, we found that the Peruzzi had run up credits to the English government totaling £26,000 by late 1337. Allowing for the £8,600 improvement just cited, the company's net cash drain from the start of lending to Edward III would have been reduced to £17,400 by the spring of 1340. This is, of course, a rough and incomplete analysis, but directionally it is appropriate. It suggests a cash deficit in early 1340 in the range of £15,000 to £20,000, a substantial sum and one that could not be borne indefinitely, but not immediately overwhelming. And the deficit is unlikely to have changed much by the time of Bonifazio's death in October 1340. The king was in no position to repay old debts, and the companies, as we have seen, were prepared to honor their new commitments of May and June 1340 only partially and with much delay. The Bardi and Peruzzi even fell short in carrying out their promise to fund the king's household expenses.[113]

There is reason to believe that Bonifazio remained in England all this time because he judged that the company's survival depended upon the successful management of the English venture. Clearly, he

[110] Ibid., 333–4. The official schedule and receipt and issue roll numbers from which these figures are derived are given in Vol. 2, 175–6, nn424, 425. They date back to November 1337, but very little money was loaned between that time and May 1338. The totals exclude promises of "gifts" amounting to £72,000 during the period but do include certain less obvious elements of hidden interest, such as £4,917 reflected in letters obligatory but not reported as received by the king's agents (see 332).

[111] Ibid., 335. The £1,600 is the difference between losses claimed by the Peruzzi on certain wool deliveries and the losses apparently allowed.

[112] This very rough calculation reflects the hidden interest of £4,917 mentioned in note 103, plus £7,242 profit on the exported wool (3,621 sacks at £2 per sack), minus £3,600. The source for the number of sacks is Fryde, "Edward III's War Finance," Vol. 2, 173, n399.

[113] See Chapter 8 for further discussion on this issue.

went there in the first place to launch the Peruzzi into the heavy financing phase of the joint venture, not to salvage a company facing disaster. Possibly he felt that only he knew how to deal with the English nobility, having lived in that country for several years in the 1320s. On this basis, he may have reasoned that there were talent and experience aplenty in the company to run the bread-and-butter businesses in Italy and the Mediterranean but that the audacious English enterprise required the full and direct attention of the chairman. Whatever his rationale, he abrogated his central responsibility, delegating the management of the total business to a leading partner, presumably his brother Pacino.

The results of this key organizational decision must be judged as mixed. The figures cited suggest that the Peruzzi had been more successful than the Bardi in recovering their advances and that England may have been the right place for him to be stationed. But the cost to the organization as a whole must have been high, as indicated by the confused state of the accounts in Florence and the continued adverse trend in the overall business. Nevertheless, despite the stresses of the past three years and lack of central direction, the Peruzzi Company was still a going concern. Several more blows were required to bring this mighty organization to its knees.

8

The collapse, 1340–1343

The news of the death of Bonifazio reached the company's head-quarters in Florence on October 25. On the following day, those shareholders resident in Florence met and agreed to appoint as chairman Bonifazio's brother, Pacino di Tommaso, changing the name of the company for the third time in four years.[1] Pacino faced the unenviable task of taking charge of a company that was fighting for its very survival.

The new chairman was a very different type of leader from his brother. Unlike Bonifazio, who was inclined to take bold initiatives and whose interests lay abroad, Pacino appeared to be cast in the conservative mold of his father Tommaso. His were the "ink-stained fingers" that compiled the Assets and Secret Books of the Sixth Company.[2] His preoccupations were with local politics rather than foreign ventures, and he showed no interest in rushing to England to take up where Bonifazio left off. Thus, for the second time in succession, the appointment of a new chairman was accompanied by a sharp change in the direction of company policy.

The effect of the new management priorities was promptly felt in England, although the London branch headed by Giovanni Baroncelli continued to do its utmost to maintain the company's position there. For the first time, the Peruzzi began to back out of its obligations. Following England's truce with France, the Bardi and Peruzzi agreed to secure the release of the earls of Derby and Northampton within fifteen days of the receipt of 500 sacks of wool promised by the king's council.[3] The sacks had not arrived by the time the king had returned to England in November, which exonerated the companies from this liability. They were given £1,000 from the ninth but still felt unable

[1] *I libri*, 1. The name of the company became Pacino di Tommaso de'Peruzzi e compagni.

[2] Ibid. Sapori confirms this fact in his introduction and on photocopies of the manuscript pages.

[3] *CCR* E III 1339–41, 639–40. The indenture was dated October 19, between Bonifazio's death and the date the news reached Florence.

to oblige, as the amount required to release Derby had risen to £10,000. They were accordingly relieved of this responsibility and replaced by the Leopardi Company of Asti, which had a branch in Malines.

In commenting on this humiliating withdrawal, Fryde has noted that "the Bardi and Peruzzi, which of course were capable of paying this great sum, felt probably that the burden would be too great."[4] The statement is only partially accurate. The reduced interest in pursuing the English venture stemmed importantly from the change in Peruzzi leadership and even more from a new preoccupation of the Bardi Company with Florentine affairs. On All Saints' Day of 1340, just one week after Pacino's elevation, sixteen members of the Bardi family spearheaded a coup against the ruling *signoria*. The plot was nipped in the bud due to a leak by one of the conspirators, and the Bardi participants were fortunate to escape. The company did its best to dissociate itself from the conspiracy but could not help being seriously distracted by it.

The motivation of the plotters is not easy to discern. Villani apparently saw this eruption as just one more episode in the long-running conflict among the three main classes in Florence – the *magnati*, the *popolo grasso*, and the *popolo minuto*.[5] Sapori argued that such simplistic divisions did not fit the facts, noting that the capitalists often supported each other regardless of origin, citing the close collaboration between the *magnati* Bardi and the *popolani* Peruzzi.[6] The plot, he believed, had Ghibelline tendencies, with a wide range of adherents drawn from all sectors of society disaffected by famine, plague, and the policies of the *popolani*-dominated Guelf government. Moreover, he suggested that the Bardi plotters were driven by the desire for a new political orientation toward Emperor Ludwig, which would enable them to annul the huge debts owed the company's depositors in Naples and Avignon.

Professor Sapori's diligent researches have provided much valuable information and insight for this study, but his judgment in this instance lacks its usual acuity. In support of this startling statement, Sapori has argued that family and company were effectively one and

---

[4] Fryde, "Edward III's War Finance," 599.

[5] As discussed in Chapter 1, the *magnati* were a number of old, large, and violent families designated as dangerous to the commune in 1292 and subject to restrictions on their qualifications for public office, among other things. The *popolo grasso* were, of course, the wealthy merchant families currently dominating Florentine politics, and the *popolo minuto* were the artisans.

[6] Sapori, *La crisi*, 118. Further comments attributed to Sapori in this paragraph are drawn from ibid., 121–6.

the same, emphasizing that the Bardi family members dominated the firm, overriding the minority outside shareholders, including the powerful Taldo Valori. He treated with scepticism the company's attempts to dissociate itself from the conspiracy, in particular its termination effective October 31 of Piero di Gualtieri Bardi, the only plotter who had been a shareholder.[7] He also noted that five of the Bardi plotters had deposits in the company.

The argument that the family owners of the Bardi Company helped engineer the plot to repudiate their debts is out of character with the history of these merchants. It requires them to be so ruthless that they would trash their great company and its hard-earned reputation for fair dealing; so irresponsible that they would turn their backs on their associates, their employees, and their clients; and so naive as to expect that they could get away with such outrageous behavior. Sapori has also exaggerated the fusion of company and family. To be sure, family members controlled it, but the company, like the Peruzzi Company, was a separate legal entity subject to specific laws of the commune, responsible to all of its shareholders, employees, and customers. It was not a plaything to be disposed of at the whim of the family circle. Furthermore, it was not at all unusual for large Florentine families to be divided on political issues. As we have seen, the Peruzzi broke up into Guelf and Ghibelline branches during the previous century, and the Cerchi, Frescobaldi, and the Bardi themselves split into Black and White factions in the early part of the fourteenth century. Seen in this light, the termination of Piero's partnership can be construed as a repudiation of the conspiracy by the segment of the family that controlled the company. The fact that five of the plotters were depositors in the company is irrelevant; a company that accepted deposits from affluent people of all political stripes could hardly refuse members of its own family.[8] Finally, the financial condition of a company that was able to survive a further five years was not so desperate as to require such extreme measures.

The Peruzzi, as usual, maintained a low profile throughout. No family members were involved in the sedition, nor did any of them actively press for reprisals, given their close business relationship with the Bardi. Eventually, fines were imposed on the conspirators, rather than confiscation, and commercial life in Florence returned to an uneasy calm. Back in England, the joint venture continued as be-

[7] Ibid., 127. October 31 was, of course, the eve of the attempted coup.
[8] Two members of the family, Bartolo di Gualterotto and Bindo di Iacopo, maintained substantial deposits with the Peruzzi (*I libri*, 2, 183, respectively). One, Iacopo di Bartolo, had a small deposit briefly (173).

fore, but with increased caution. A stream of repeated orders from the government to various county collectors of the ninth of sheaves to accelerate payments to the Bardi and Peruzzi seemed to attest to the companies' continued unwillingness to advance more funds without a quid pro quo from the crown.[9] One pair of entries in the *Close Rolls* is particularly instructive. The first, dated April 1, 1341, ordered the treasurer to pay the Bardi and Peruzzi sums from various counties totaling £10,500 13s 4d, which the companies had paid to certain individuals in connection with the ransom of the earls of Derby and Northampton.[10] The second entry made it clear that the companies had yet to make the payment.[11] The companies did eventually pay up and were reimbursed, including an allowance for the suffering and imprisonment of certain of their employees who were held hostage along with the earls.[12]

Later entries in the *Close Rolls* suggest that the companies had again been lending faster than they had been receiving reimbursements. One order dated June 14, 1341, noted that the Bardi Company was still owed £2,370 on its share of the 26,000 marks the two companies had advanced over the previous year for the king's household expenses and demanded that certain counties pay up.[13] The second order was a very long one on the same date acknowledging that the companies had advanced a total of £29,257 "or thereabouts" for a variety of purposes, including the £10,500 to Simon van Halen (Mirabello).[14] The king urged the receiver of the subsidy of the ninth to deliver to the Bardi and Peruzzi all money received from a list of counties, as well as £2,000 from the triennial tenth of certain other counties. The order insisted on rapid payment because the companies had recovered only £6,492 of these advances. But the implication from these statements that the companies had given away a further £25,000 to the English government defies logic and fact. Under the circumstances obtaining in 1341, the companies' branch managers would not have been given the authority by their masters in Florence to lend additional money on this scale even if they had access to such quantities, which is doubtful. Moreover, Fryde repeatedly cites

[9] *CCR* E III 1339–41, 573, 591, 592, 593, 611. These orders are all dated between November 1340 and late January 1341.
[10] *CCR* E III 1341–3, 59. The sums assigned were from fines collected by the justices of the counties named.
[11] Ibid., 117.
[12] Fryde, "Edward III's War Finance," 604–5. The Peruzzi claimed £3,772 but received £3,389.
[13] *CCR* E III 1341–3, 164.
[14] Ibid., 171.

evidence that all merchants, including the Bardi and Peruzzi, were careful to avoid advancing funds without solid assurance of repayment in cash or wool.[15] And the companies were even delinquent in delivering the promised 2,000 marks per month for the king's household expenses; the official receipts of the Keeper of the Wardrobe add up to less than one-third of the total due.[16] As a result, we can be confident that a large part of any new loans would have been promptly repaid or funded by receipts from old debts carried over from 1340. Possibly the total outstanding credits to the king had risen, but not by much.

It is worth reiterating that the Peruzzi Company was very much a viable business during this first half of 1341, despite Villani's comments that the firm was in dire straits at least a year earlier.[17] Villani stated that the Peruzzi was unable to meet the claims of creditors in England, Florence, and elsewhere and lost its status in the commune. To this, Sapori sensibly responded that the company could not have refused such claims without provoking bankruptcy proceedings.[18] There was some alarm and embarrassment, he admitted, but they were not widespread, adding that the Neapolitans, whom he described as the best-informed capitalists in Europe, did not begin to pull back their deposits until 1342. Finally, the Peruzzi maintained status in the commune, as Pacino continued to receive appointments to high office.

In mid-1341, Florence was again threatened with a crisis. Mastino della Scala, faced with a rebellion in Parma and other problems, decided that Lucca had become too difficult to defend and returned to his old idea of selling it. Cunningly, he offered it simultaneously to Florence and Pisa, knowing that the acquisition of Lucca by Pisa would menace Florence's trade routes and hence be unacceptable to the Florentines. They accordingly prepared to fight and in July 1341 suspended the constitution and deputized a group of twenty citizens with full power for one year to offer Mastino 250,000 florins and to recruit mercenaries at a cost of 30,000 florins per month. If this new upheaval weren't distraction enough for the Peruzzi, the Twenty re-

[15] Fryde, "Edward III's War Finance," 606–9, 628.

[16] Ibid., 624–5. The Keeper's receipt rolls show only £3,552 as having been received from the Bardi and £1,593 from the Peruzzi, for a total of £5,145 out of the £17,333 promised. More may have been advanced to the king while he was abroad in 1340, but there is no record of any such receipts.

[17] Villani, *Storia*, Book XI, Chap. 87. The dates referred to in this passage are not indicated. The previous chapter touches on 1338, but the context of this one suggests a period around Edward III's unsuccessful campaign of 1339.

[18] Sapori, *La crisi*, 136.

sponsible for conducting the negotiations and war included their new chairman, Pacino. Although no Bardi was allowed to serve, Taldo Valori effectively stood for the Bardi Company on the committee. Iacopo Acciaiuoli was also a member, so that all three super-companies were represented in this powerful body.

Unfortunately, the Twenty was also an inexperienced, incompetent, and corrupt body of men, and their campaign was an inevitable failure. The Florentine forces tried to relieve Lucca, but were crushed by Pisa on October 2. The Twenty were accused of fraud by a populace that was angered and frustrated by defeat but were not subjected to an official enquiry until later.[19] Overlaying this unsatisfactory political situation was a fundamentally depressed economic environment. The severe famine in 1339–40 was followed by a plague said by Villani to have cost some four thousand lives.[20] After 1340, the Florentine economy was characterized by acute depression, high food prices, low wages, and general suffering, which persisted until 1347.[21] Funding to continue the war began to dry up as a result of this weakness. In November 1341, the gabelle was so reduced by low volume that an attempt was made to establish direct taxes and create new offices for the purpose.[22] Merchants who won the auctions for various gabelle farms found that they lost money on them. Then the artisans began to fail, as credit from the large merchant companies became scarce, depriving the former of the means to acquire raw materials. And the super-companies were directly affected in their international business; for example, all three were subjected to lawsuits in Sicily when the Florence Commune reneged on large debts for grain purchases there in 1341–2.[23]

The military defeat had indirect consequences that were even more damaging to the super-companies. On October 13, Benedict XII awarded a contract to the Nicolucci Company of Siena to receive and transfer all apostolic collections from Hungary, Poland, Romania, and Italy.[24] The loss of this strategic business, especially the Italian transfers, to an obscure Siennese organization was a shock to the super-companies and to Florence, as this action was a repudiation of both. The Acciaiuoli, which continued to be entrusted with the now

---

[19] Villani accused them of giving most of their thoughts to enriching themselves and their friends. *Storia*, Book XI, Chap. 130.

[20] Quoted in Brucker, *Florentine Politics and Society*, 9.

[21] La Roncière, *Prix et salaires*, 458.

[22] Sapori, *La crisi*, 138. The dispositions of the law, however, were not carried out.

[23] Trasselli, "Nuovi documenti," 191.

[24] Renouard, *Les relations*, 198.

minor flow of collections from England, remained the only Florentine company still doing business with the papacy. Papal business, as has been noted repeatedly, was valued less for its modest contribution to company profit than for the indirect benefits that it conferred. The papal collection network fit comfortably with and enhanced the companies' own financial networks. Being entrusted with the Curia's finances was not only a mark of papal favor, but also a declaration of faith in the companies' solvency by a very conservative adjudicator. Being dropped by the papacy was to the super-companies akin to a modern corporation's loss of its rating by Moody's and Standard & Poor's.

The reasoning behind Benedict's decision was partly financial and partly political. In the financial sense, it was typical of the papal treasury to change bankers whenever it had reason to believe that there was risk of insolvency among them. The entanglement of the Bardi and Peruzzi in the wasting English campaign and their deep involvement in the disastrous defeat at the hands of Pisa were sufficient evidence to make the Curia wary. But the abruptness of the change and the abandonment of its policy of spreading its risks among larger institutions at some cost in efficiency were clearly intended as a political message to the Florentines. The fact that other Florentine companies, much sounder and more competent than the Nicolucci, were passed over indicates that the papal insult was directed at the commune's regime.[25] Although Benedict's action was likely influenced by continuing pressure from the French king, it was mainly motivated by frustration with the repeatedly demonstrated ineptness of Florence's leadership.[26] Had the Florentines beaten Pisa on October 2, it is doubtful whether the papacy would have made such an abrupt change, if any, in its financial arrangements.

After the battle, the commune set about desperately to find help. The first of its great allies, the papacy, had made its attitude clear. Its other traditional source of support, the Angevin kingdom, was bogged down in yet another campaign in Sicily and was undisposed to provide any assistance. The *signoria* sent a long missive to King Robert later in October that attempted to put him in the position of either coming to Florence's aid or renouncing his protection of the city.[27] The king, well informed about the commune's desperate plight, was

---

[25] The Alberti Company, which later became official banker to the papacy, is an example.

[26] The French did their best to influence the Avignon popes against England and its allies, and were often successful (see Mollat, *The Popes of Avignon*, 251).

[27] Sapori, *La crisi*, 144–5.

not moved by this veiled threat and sent an embassy to Florence in November with the demand that he be given the possession of Lucca. Only on this condition, which he is alleged to have believed would be unacceptable to the Florentines, would he move his forces north.[28] To his surprise, the Florentines acceded with alacrity.

From this point, the story becomes extremely hazy, with three different versions of what happened. It is clear that Robert changed his mind about the possession of Lucca and sent no troops at all, but it is unclear when he made this decision known. According to Villani, the reaction to Robert's refusal came in the spring of 1342, when a secret delegation of certain leaders opened negotiations with Emperor Ludwig of Bavaria.[29] The emperor in this version promised that if Florence would receive one of his vicars, he would order armed aid and have the German mercenaries withdrawn from the Pisan army. The *signoria* as a whole, Villani said, disapproved of such contacts as contrary to the interests of the Guelf party and the church but failed to disavow them before Robert got wind of the negotiations. He flew into a rage at such perfidy, causing many of his barons, prelates, and other wealthy men to rush to redeem their deposits with Florentine merchant–bankers, precipitating the collapse of many companies. In a word, Villani claimed that the maneuvers of a few misguided citizens provoked the failure of the Peruzzi and Acciaiuoli and eventually the Bardi companies.

The Villani scenario, largely accepted by most historians, has been hotly challenged by two of them. Sapori argued that the priors of Florence dispatched a regular embassy to Ludwig, who ordered that a force of fifty knights and his vicar be sent to Florence.[30] This action was enough to upset Robert and cause him and the capitalists of his kingdom to withdraw their deposits. It was therefore not an ill-founded suspicion of King Robert that provoked the crisis but the official politics of the commune. The bankers, although in control of the public offices, blamed the politics. Realizing the significance of the disaster they had wrought, they promptly dismissed the embassy of the emperor. But they were too late, and as the alarm of the Neapolitans spread throughout Italy and abroad, the companies had to start refusing withdrawal requests as the run overwhelmed their resources. They were spared immediate collapse when Walter of Brienne, duke of Athens, assumed control of Florence.

The essential difference between Sapori's version and Villani's is

[28] Villani, *Storia*, Book XI, Chap. 137.
[29] Ibid., Chap. 138.
[30] Sapori, *La crisi*, 144–5.

that the former describes the negotiations with Ludwig as overt by the whole *signoria* rather than a covert effort by a few of the leading citizens. The end result, the run on the Florentine merchant-bankers, was the same in both cases. The third version, which appears in a recent study by Michele Luzzati, does not quarrel with the fact that there was contact with Ludwig or that Robert knew about it, but denies that Florence's "perfidy" caused the avalanche of withdrawals.[31] Luzzati points out that, during May 1342, the Florentines weighed the pros and cons of Ludwig versus Robert and opted clearly for the latter. They wrote to Robert on May 22 that they intended to take Walter of Brienne into their service as *capitano di guerra* and expressed hope that Robert would pledge aid, recognizing that Walter was one of his envoys.[32] On June 1, as noted by Villani, they elected Walter as their leader and so informed Robert.[33]

King Robert and his wealthy subjects, in Luzzati's view, had no reason to fear that Florence would opt for his enemy Ludwig and the Ghibellines and desert its traditional allies. They therefore had no reason to rush to remove their deposits. Luzzati notes that Villani is the only source for the claim linking the plot to the company failures, adding that Villani's list of companies bankrupted included the Cocchi, which had been in the hands of creditors' syndicates since April 1, long before the Neapolitan run could have started.[34] Another problem Luzzati finds with Villani here is that the latter attributed the Peruzzi collapse to the Ludwig plot after already having blamed Edward III back in 1339–40, using much the same terms.[35] In fact, Villani's own company, the Buonaccorsi, was the only one to flee Naples. The firm suddenly closed down on June 1, 1342, and disappeared from both Naples and Avignon, leaving a host of angry depositors. Thus, Luzzati concludes that Villani attempted to exonerate his company by creating a linkage between the Ghibelline plot

[31] Luzzati, *Villani e Buonaccorsi*, 62–9.
[32] Walter of Brienne was a French nobleman who was also styled duke of Athens, an empty title since his father had been driven from the Byzantine duchy of Athens many years before. Walter was brought up in the court of King Robert of Naples and married into his family.
[33] Villani, *Storia*, Book XII, Chap. 1.
[34] Luzzati, *Villani e Buonaccorsi*, 65.
[35] Ibid., 65–6. Luzzati aptly observes that the terminology in Book XI, Chap. 88, regarding the Peruzzi in 1339–40 and again in Book XI, Chap. 138, in 1342 is the same: "Fallirono di pagare . . . con tutto che non si cessassono per le loro grandi possessioni ch'aveano in Firenze e nel contado, e per la loro grande potenza e stato ch'aveano in commune."

and the collapse of so many firms and diverting the blame to the Florentine government.[36]

Luzzati's argument is persuasive; the sudden disappearance of a company of the size and stature of the Buonaccorsi would obviously have created deep concern in the minds of all depositors in southern Italy. Probably, many of them did withdraw their funds, while others, buoyed by the appointment of Walter of Brienne as military commander and later as dictator of Florence, may have been persuaded to keep their money with the super-companies for a while longer. Moreover, it is difficult to accept the idea that even the rather dim political leadership of Florence should have been so wrongheaded as to enter into really serious negotiations with the emperor. Ludwig was no longer a friend of England. He had unceremoniously dropped Edward III as his vicar in June 1341 after having formed an alliance with King Philip of France. And although this action should have put the emperor in better odor with the Avignon papacy, it would have made him an even greater threat to Robert. But whatever the real story, the events of mid-1342, following the loss of the papal business, left the big Florentine companies hanging on the ropes. It is quite possible that the Peruzzi and others would have failed at that time were it not for the relief afforded them by the new dictator.

At this point it would be useful to step back from the narrative of external events and look again at the internal workings of the Peruzzi Company. Despite the turmoil in Florence that was rocking the company to its foundations, business in the branches appeared to carry on, a tribute to the partially decentralized management system described in Chapter 3. The only evidence of discontinued operations was the closing of the tiny Chiarenza branch in 1342.[37] The branches in England and Bruges were of course exceptionally busy. Naples and Sicily, while no longer the dominant centers of the company's business, were still very active. Even the Paris branch remained open until the end in 1343, as did Avignon, where profitable business with individuals in the court continued after the cancellation of the papal transfer operations.

There can be little doubt, however, that the size of the company's active workforce was steadily shrinking, a clear signal that its overall operations were in irreversible decline. Specific numbers are difficult to establish, but a valid approximation can be obtained by comb-

---

[36] Ibid., 71.
[37] Peruzzi, *Storia commercio*, 420.

ing through the salary records and expense entries in the Peruzzi accounts to identify the dates on which named individuals were owed salary or expense.[38] Additional sources are the *Close Rolls* and *Patent Rolls* that often name specific officers of the English branch, albeit in anglicized forms that are sometimes difficult to relate to their Italian originals.[39] By these means, it is possible to construct three series of figures over the eight-year period between 1335 and 1343 that can provide insight into the decline of employment in the company. These are shown in Table 10.

The number of employees reported for the base year 1335 includes salaried factors and sons of shareholders working for the company without apparent salary, as shown in Table 4, but excluding the *drapperia* "partners." The second column represents the number of employees and shareholders' sons identified as being in the company's employ up to the years indicated. The third column gives the total number of employees that might have been working each year – that is, the total number from the previous year adjusted only for identified new hires, deaths, and departures. This is undoubtedly an excessive number, given the chaotic state of the salary ledger. As described in Chapter 3, the salary entries in the Secret Book were obviously of a "catch-up" nature, dealing with arrears of up to eight years. They show twenty-six employees due salary up to July 1, 1343, all of whom were on board for the entire period. But the fact that all others were due salary only up to earlier dates cannot be construed as meaning that they left the company on those dates, because other sources show that they were still employed in subsequent years. At the same time, the records are much too sketchy to permit the assumption that all personnel not specifically designated as having died or departed actually remained on board until 1343. Hence, there is need for a fourth column, which reflects the notion that some people remained in the company's employ but had their salary recorded elsewhere, while others not reported as departed had, in fact, done so.[40]

The resulting "probable" series is imprecise but provides a rea-

---

[38] *I libri*, 303–18, provides the salary data. Expense entries are scattered throughout the books, but Sapori's list of factors employed (*Storia Economica*, Vol. 2, 718–29) is a helpful guide.

[39] See note 23, Chapter 9, for an example.

[40] Certain employees, such as those seconded to the *drapperia*, some shareholders' sons, and others known to be working for the company did not appear in the salary ledgers. Some are known to have died or left the company. The "probable" column therefore tries to take into account the likelihood of both unreported people and unreported "wastage."

Table 10. *Total number of Peruzzi Company employees, 1335–43*

Year	Positively identified	Possible maximum	Probable
1335	96	96	96
1336	94	95	93
1337	86	94	90
1338	80	94	85
1339	72	87	77
1340	64	80	72
1341	57	76	66
1342	50	70	58
1343	40	69	47

sonable guide to what was happening to the company during this period. It was definitely downsizing, especially after 1339, but it was doing so gradually by attrition rather than by massive cuts. It also did very little hiring, adding only seven apprentices over the eight years, all but one before 1340. Interestingly, the company did not attempt to cut costs by reducing salaries or terminating its senior employees. There is not one reported instance of a salary reduction, while there were numerous cases of increases, and at the end, nearly all salaried personnel were long-service employees. All of this suggests that the company felt a strong sense of responsibility toward its people.

What parts of the business bore the brunt of these staff reductions, which amounted to one-third of the total workforce by 1340? Certainly England did not suffer until the very end, and even after bankruptcy there were at least six sons of shareholders still in the country. The smaller branches in the Mediterranean were probably allowed to run down. There is evidence to suggest that employees who died in Sardinia or departed from Tunis were not replaced.[41] The Paris branch was downgraded after 1337, as was that of Avignon after 1341, and undoubtedly some reductions occurred in the large branches in southern Italy and Sicily. But the biggest cuts had to come from the place with the most people – Florence. The areas of operations most likely to have suffered were those relating to recording and control, as suggested by the disorderly state of the accounts, but some of the company's basic merchandising and grain trading business must also have been dropped. The one exception to the cutbacks was wool trad-

[41] *I libri*, 309, 312.

ing, given the very large quantities of English wool controlled by the company. For the other businesses, it was probably a matter of doing more with less, bearing in mind that the "less" still amounted to a very large organization.

Over this same period, the shareholders' investment in the company was gradually declining. Data are available for each of the partners' personal accounts with the company, year by year, and these are presented for 1335 and 1343 in Table A6.[42] They show that certain family members increased their deposits with the company, while others decreased theirs. On balance, the Peruzzi family increased its investment by li.23,000, from li.27,000 to li.50,000. The nonfamily shareholders nearly all decreased their investments, most ending up in a net borrowing position. The only significant investors were the Baroncelli; at the other end of the spectrum, the Soderini brothers were heavy borrowers. Overall, the nonfamily shareholders reduced their investment by nearly li.48,000, dropping the grand total for all shareholders by li.25,000. These figures further undermine the argument that Florence was the main source of funds for the company's English venture.

By 1341 the company's greatest structural weakness had become the lack of coordination and control from Florence. With things going from bad to worse in Italy and with the chairman preoccupied with political affairs, the decentralized branches more or less had to fend for themselves. The Florence headquarters was obviously unable to put any more money or effort into the English operation, so that the branch was left with considerable latitude in the conduct of its affairs. Fortunately, the managers in England appeared to maintain a reasonably cordial relationship with their government counterparts, as royal orders continued to stream to the treasury, customs officials, and tax collectors to expedite payments to the Bardi and Peruzzi in fulfillment of agreements. Unfortunately, the responses to these demands were dilatory, as evidenced by frequent repetition of the orders. For example, because the subsidies from the ninth of fleeces promised in 1340 were inadequate, the king awarded the companies 20,000 marks, of which 15,000 marks should be paid in the form of 1,199 sacks of wool. The first order was dated June 14, 1341,

---

[42] This table shows the personal balances from the company point of view. Thus, the positive numbers are amounts *owed to the company by the shareholder*, i.e., borrowings by the shareholder and accounts receivable to the company. The negative figures are amounts *owed by the company to the shareholder*, i.e., shareholder deposits with the company. The grand total of negative li.39,115 agrees with the balance of the first line of Table 5 "Advances to/borrowed from shareholders."

and was followed by two more on June 26 and July 15, repeated with certain elaborations on October 2, on March 15, 1342, and on April 28.[43] Finally, on August 20, the king urged the treasurer to pay one portion of this debt speedily, noting that the Peruzzi cannot give the king any money unless the assignment is paid.[44]

Throughout the fifteen months from mid-1341 to the autumn of 1342, when company fortunes were deteriorating almost everywhere, the memoranda in the *Patent Rolls* and *Close Rolls* create the impression that the English had not grasped the significance of the events on the continent. They must have been aware of the papal decision to take its transfer business away from the Bardi and Peruzzi, although theoretically the Florentines had not lost the papal accounts in England until October 1342.[45] They must also have known of the increasingly strained relations between Florence and its protector, King Robert. Politically, these developments and the city's brief flirtation with Emperor Ludwig might have been welcome to Edward III, as they brought the Florentines more firmly into his camp. They may well have accounted for the courteous tone and continued support reflected in the kingdom's official orders, despite the fact that the Bardi and Peruzzi were no longer pulling much weight as financiers to the crown.[46] Notwithstanding the seemingly endless procrastinations, some money and considerable wool did change hands during this period of relative peace leading up to Edward's brief campaign in Brittany. The end result was probably a slight reduction in the king's debt to the company because there was no more money to lend, and the Florence head office was pressing for remittances to ease its own plight.

Back in Florence, Walter of Brienne was unable to reverse Florence's military fortunes, and Lucca fell to Pisa on July 1, 1342. Despite this setback, the confused and discredited leadership of Florence decided to follow the usual practice of the commune in times of crisis and increased Brienne's powers by making him dictator for

---

[43] *CCR* E III 1341–3, 172, 401; *CPR* E III 1340–3, 247, 263, 285, 454.

[44] *CPR* E III 1340–3, 507. The order dealt with the portion of the debt to be funded by the appropriation of fines collected by county justices, a source increasingly used by Edward at this time.

[45] The Acciaiuoli Company was used as late as April 1342 (Renouard, *Les relations*, 134, 138).

[46] But speculations on political motivations are very risky in this complex environment. Ludwig had revoked Edward's vicarship the previous year in a move to placate the French. And Walter de Brienne was no friend of the English, having commanded French forces against them and their allies in the campaigns of 1339 and 1340 (see Sumption, *Hundred Years' War*, 273, 310–11, 355).

one year. The duke had excellent credentials as a relative of King Robert and a friend of both the old and new popes. He was also well known to the Florentines, having served with distinction as vicar of duke Charles of Calabria when the latter was the city's dictator in the 1320s. The leading merchant families knew and trusted him, while the lower classes were so disenchanted with the rule of the Twenty that they were ready to try anything. So broad was Brienne's support that he was able to get his appointment extended to dictator for life on September 8, 1342.

His first acts brought welcome relief to the super-companies and merchant-bankers. In October, he reinstated the Bardi plotters of 1340, secured peace with Pisa by renouncing claims to Lucca for fifteen years, and granted immunity to all troubled companies from creditor claims for three years.[47] These actions did not necessarily mean, however, that the duke was a puppet of the great merchants. Sapori aptly suggests that these acts were all aimed at restoring peace and prosperity to the city. The return of the exiles was essential for peace among the citizens, the settlement with Pisa was necessary to terminate a wasting and hopeless war, and the debt moratorium was needed to head off financial chaos.[48] Given time, Brienne felt that he could bring back a modicum of prosperity to the city and regain the confidence of King Robert and his barons. In another confidence-building maneuver, he took the unusual step of appointing a judge with veto power over the syndicate charged with handling the bankruptcy of the Buonaccorsi.[49] The purpose of this and subsequent actions, Luzzati argues, was to prevent the syndicate from engaging in the usual Florentine tactic of excluding foreign creditors from sharing in the disposition of the fallen company's assets.[50]

These measures, enlightened as they may have been, came too late to restore the faith of foreigners in Florentine enterprises. On October 15, the new pope, Clement VI, eliminated all Florentine companies from participation in papal transfer transactions, appointing another obscure firm, the Malabayla of Asti, as collector for En-

[47] The immunity was decreed specifically to the company of Taddeo d'Antella, but was extended to all other companies in difficulty, provided that they gave adequate warning to their creditors.
[48] Sapori, *La crisi*, 149–50.
[49] Luzzati, *Villani e Buonaccorsi*, 48–9. The Buonaccorsi did not enter formal bankruptcy until November 7, more than five months after the flight from Naples.
[50] Ibid., 52. Foreign creditors were expected to make the bulk of their recoveries from assets located in their own locality. King Robert had already ordered the sequestration of all of the Buonaccorsi's assets in his kingdom and appointed a bankruptcy commission as early as June 9, 1342 (see Yver, *Le commerce*, 322).

gland.[51] During the same week, Edward III appointed a commission of oyer and terminer under Robert Wodehouse to "examine all accounts of the Bardi and Peruzzi touching wool, jewels, money, and other things of the king received as well beyond seas as within, for which they should account."[52] This is the first official evidence of a change in attitude of the English government toward the two companies. An earlier commission established in 1340 at the request of Parliament had as its brief an audit of the accounts of all merchants having done business with the king, including Monte Florum (the king's agent in the Netherlands), and Norwell, Keeper of the Wardrobe, and was not threatening to the Bardi and Peruzzi.[53] For the Neapolitan creditors, Brienne's debt moratorium was a double-edged sword, keeping the companies viable, but unassailable. And his attempt to obtain equal treatment for foreign creditors brought little comfort to those depositors familiar with the deviousness and tenacity of Florentine bankruptcy syndicates. Thus, increasing numbers of depositors are likely to have withdrawn funds from even the largest firms, especially after January 1343, when King Robert, the Peruzzi's old and valued friend over thirty-four years, passed away.

The honeymoon of Brienne and the super-companies was brief. Recognizing that the financial status of the city was indeed desperate, he suspended on November 20 all assignments for loan repayments that were to come from gabelle revenues. This decree was especially burdensome to the shareholders of the super-companies, who were important contributors to the war loans, and offset much of the advantage of the moratorium against their creditors. His greatest sin against the wealthy seems to have been his attempt to reorganize the administration of the commune with the object of increasing his revenues by much more rigorous application of existing laws. His minions conducted surveys of property holdings, enforced penalties for infractions formerly honored in the breach, and generally created difficulties for many of those who had been his original backers.[54] Whether Brienne actually squandered much of these revenues in festivities inappropriate for the time, as suggested by the chroni-

[51] Renouard, *Les relations*, 205. The Malabayla were also appointed transfer agents for all Christianity, following the Curia's unsatisfactory experience with the Nicolucci. The Malabayla also proved inadequate to the task (ibid., 200).

[52] *CPR* E III 1340–3, 558, dated October 19, 1342. A further order in January 1343 (ibid., 588) broadened and deepened the inquiry, increasing the size of the commission and extending the audit back to July 1326.

[53] Ibid., 87.

[54] See Becker, *Florence in Transition*, Vol. 1, 150–72, for a useful account of the administrative innovations introduced by Brienne.

clers, is not clear. But he did manage to antagonize enough of the *grandi* and *popolani* to provoke no less than three plots against him.[55]

The Peruzzi family and company actively supported the Brienne regime and, along with the Bardi, played an important part in the formulation and execution of its foreign policy.[56] Unlike the Bardi, however, the Peruzzi remained loyal to Brienne virtually to the end. While the Bardi joined the main conspiracy headed by Bishop Acciaiuoli, the Peruzzi and, surprisingly, the Acciaiuoli clan only became reconciled with the plotters after the rebellion had commenced. Sapori and Luzzati have voiced the suspicion that the Peruzzi leadership was motivated by the desperate situation of the company, which was likely to lose its protection from creditors under a new government.[57] This is a reasonable supposition, given that their allies in this affair, the Acciaiuoli and Antellesi, were also in dire financial straits.

In any event, the Brienne dictatorship fell after several days of rioting and was replaced on August 3, 1343, by a commission of fourteen citizens, seven *magnati* and seven *popolani*, presided over by Bishop Acciaiuoli. The members were almost all directors or shareholders of companies and included Ridolfo Bardi and Simone Peruzzi.[58] The commission, with full powers to rule until the end of September, appointed six men, again split evenly between important *magnati* and *popolani* families, to run collectively the office of the magistracy (*podestà*). Although historians have varied in their opinions of this new regime, it does appear to have been much more relaxed in its application of the law than its predecessor and to have favored the interests of the powerful capitalist families.[59] The nominations for the October–November period for the priorate and the principal administrative and justice offices promised more of the same, being strongly loaded with *magnati* representation. This was too much for the rising new families, artisans, and working classes. They erupted in revolt on September 24 and, after two days of de-

[55] Sapori, *La crisi*, 150–1. Sapori makes it obvious that he does not accept Villani's claims concerning Brienne's behavior.

[56] Becker, *Florence in Transition*, Vol. 1, 150.

[57] Sapori, *La crisi*, 152; Luzzati, *Villani e Buonaccorsi*, 54. Luzzati added that the Bardi, being in a sounder financial condition, could afford to risk the uncertainties of a new regime.

[58] The Peruzzi Company itself had no direct representative on the commission; Simone, the family's ace diplomat and a major depositor in the company, was still not a shareholder.

[59] Sapori, *La crisi*, 155–6, is cautious in his evaluation, suggesting that the government lacked a sufficient period of calm in which to work out its policies. Becker, in *Florence in Transition*, Vol. 1, 172–81, is highly critical.

structive fighting, triumphed. The burning and looting that accompanied the conflict included the destruction of a great deal of Bardi property, reckoned by Villani to have cost that family 60,000 florins.[60]

The rebels promptly formed a new priorate that excluded the *magnati* but included some of the old *popolani* families along with the men from the rising new families of entrepreneurs, the so-called *novi cives*. This government restored the old legal norms, recognized the public debt, and began to reorder the public accounts. This return to normal standards left the Peruzzi and other vulnerable companies, including the Acciaiuoli, unprotected from the claims of their creditors. On October 27, 1343, the company took the initiative of submitting itself "to the will of its creditors," declaring bankruptcy and depositing its books with the commune rather than waiting for the inevitable creditors' lawsuits.[61] The Sixth Company had endured for eight years, three months, and twenty-six days. The Peruzzi companies overall had existed without interruption for at least fifty-one years.

The Peruzzi Company ceased to exist – or did it? The head may have been severed in Florence, but as we shall see in the following chapter, the body parts continued to function for several more years in England and probably elsewhere. In any case, it is clear that the company was not brought down by any specific events in England, despite the claims of Villani and the initial declaration of the bankruptcy syndicate.[62] Most of the entries in the *Patent Rolls* and *Close Rolls* between January and October 1343 dealt with the specifics of the continuing audit of the Bardi, Peruzzi, and other foreign companies.[63] Although the Peruzzi in Florence may have been discouraged by the progress of the audit, the entries themselves were nonthreatening technical instructions, and the branch managers persisted in pressing their case with vigor. The company's continued good standing with the English government is evidenced by the fact that the name of Tommaso Peruzzi was included in the list of people acting as mainpernor to John Portinari.[64] The arbitrary treatment of the Peruzzi by the king did not commence until 1345, long after the firm's declaration of bankruptcy, and even then, as we shall see, it may not have been as heavy handed as it seemed.

[60] Villani, *Storia*, Book XII, Chap. 21.   [61] Sapori, *La crisi*, 160.
[62] This declaration will be discussed in more detail in the following chapter.
[63] *CPR* E III 1340–3, 588; *CCR* E III 1343–6, 45, 46, 59, 99, 160.
[64] *CCR* E III 1343–6, 106, 117, 224, 236. The unfortunate Portinari nevertheless languished several months in Flete prison despite these repeated orders to release him.

9

The aftermath

The situation following the bankruptcy as reported is replete with anomaly and even contradiction. In the first place, we are told that the declaration of bankruptcy came as a stunning surprise to the Florentine community and to company insiders alike. Sapori firmly backs this version of events, citing Villani's dramatic exclamations of surprise and arguing that as a practicing merchant, former shareholder, and brother of a current shareholder, Villani would have been "in the know" if anyone was.[1] He adds that the actions of the Peruzzi shareholders were atypical of the shrewd Florentine businessmen that they were – continuing to buy and sell property openly instead of taking steps to move their personal assets out of reach of their creditors and naively submitting the company's books to the commune instead of getting out of town.

Sapori's arguments are impressive but not really credible. Shock was indeed probable at the passing of this mighty institution, but not surprise, and certainly not to the shareholders who, as we have seen, were close to the business. Sapori claims that the myriad small transactions simply overwhelmed the bookkeeping system, rendering impossible a general accounting that would have produced a coherent statement of the condition of the company. It is true, as was made clear in Chapter 4, that the books had fallen into disarray, but the managing shareholders had every reason to realize that the company was in extreme difficulty. They were obviously aware that the business had paid only one tiny dividend since 1324 and that the 1331–5 company had made a loss, even though the accounts for that period had not been finalized. Even those partners uninvolved in the decisions to cut staff could not have helped noticing the steady decline in the number of employees. And it defies belief that they did not know of the problems in England, the loss of the papal business, and the withdrawal of deposits in Naples. They also understood that the company's survival beyond late 1342 depended upon the Brienne

---

[1] Sapori, *Storia economica*, Vol. 2, 686–7.

moratorium and that this stay of execution had lapsed with the coming to power of the new democratic government in September 1343.
Sapori himself recognized that once legality and normality had been
reinstated by this government, those companies that owed their survival to an exceptional regime could not be sustained one more day.[2]

It is possible that Villani had indeed been surprised. As shown in
Appendix V, he had plenty of problems to distract him. He faced
criminal charges in connection with the bankruptcy of the
Buonaccorsi Company a year earlier, and his brother Matteo's wife
had been imprisoned because of Matteo's debts. Also, he may not
have been as "in the know" as his writings suggest. His reputation in
the community had been sullied by the suspicion that he had taken
bribes while in public office and by his litigious tactics in defending
himself. His relationship with his brother Filippo was strained by a
long-standing family dispute. His connections to the Peruzzi Company and his knowledge of current conditions may therefore have
been slight. And yet, as we have seen, his writings reflect his suspicions over the health of the company as far back as 1339, when he
claimed that because advances to Edward III of 135,000 marks (over
600,000 florins) had not been repaid, the Peruzzi Company was de-
faulting on its payments.[3] Again in 1342, he stated that the Peruzzi
had failed to honor payment obligations, using exactly the same
words, but this time ascribing the cause to the withdrawal of deposits
in Naples as a result of the commune's flirtation with Emperor
Ludwig.[4] These statements lack the ring of truth not only because of
the use of identical wording, but also because either situation should
have provoked the immediate bankruptcy of the Peruzzi at the time.
Whether Villani was misinformed or had some special motive for
making these remarks is unknown. One piece of evidence, however,
does point to possible genuine concern about the company; in 1339
he appears to have withdrawn a deposit he had with the Peruzzi.[5]

This seemingly inordinate attention to Villani's writings and their
motivations is warranted because the public record on the Peruzzi
bankruptcy is equally mystifying, leaving the impression that we are
being presented with a charade. Shortly after the bankruptcy filing,

[2] Sapori, *La crisi*, 159.
[3] Villani, *Storia*, Book XI, Chap. 88.
[4] Ibid., Chap. 138. See also note 35, Chapter 8, this volume.
[5] *I libri*, 176, 228. These pages reflect the last entries relating to a deposit Villani
had kept with the Peruzzi for several years. They show interest accrued up to
July 1339 and a cumulative deposit total of li.249 s11 d6. There are no entries in
his personal account or charges in the expense section of the books beyond
that date, suggesting that the deposit had been withdrawn at that time.

the creditors chose delegates to examine the books. These quickly reported that the major portion of the liabilities consisted of huge sums of money due from debtors in England, France, Sicily, and other parts of the world, sums that could not be recovered because of the war.[6] This blanket statement is curious on two counts. The first is the cavalier acceptance of the nonrecovery of these allegedly huge amounts on the flimsy excuse of a "war" that was far from active at the time. It should not have interfered with returns from England and certainly not from southern Italy as long as the branch organizations remained in place. Sapori suspected that the declaration was meant to divert the blame for the bankruptcy on foreign sovereigns, deliberately failing to mention that the company was also owed substantial sums by the commune. These debts came to light publicly two years later.[7] The second oddity is that in the surviving Peruzzi Assets and Secret Books, there is no mention of advances of any kind to the commune or to any monarch except King Federigo of the island of Sicily.[8]

Sapori's supposition that the examining delegates were anxious to direct the blame to the foreigners is reasonable to a point. But it fails to explain why creditors anxious to recover their money should have given up so easily on the foreign debts. A more likely rationale is that they quickly found that most of the receivables from the kings had been financed by borrowings from abroad and decided that any repayments would be seized by the foreign creditors. If true, this would throw further doubt on Villani's assumption, already challenged in Chapters 7 and 8, that most of the financing of the Peruzzi loans to Edward III came from Florentine investors. At any rate, the creditors' syndicate promptly determined that all of the Peruzzi assets available in the commune would be allocated only among Florentine creditors.

Another puzzling event was the flight of Peruzzi shareholders after having apparently remained in Florence for a month after the collapse. On November 26, Filippo Villani was declared a fugitive

---

[6] Sapori, *La crisi*, 162. In this case, "Sicily" meant the Angevin kingdom of Naples, which still held to the name, despite its acknowledged loss of the island since 1302. Sapori mistakenly said that the money was due from creditors instead of debtors.

[7] Ibid.

[8] *I libri*. The only references to commune loans relate to small payments made on behalf of factors (78, 89, 91, 129) or collection of interest payments from such loans on behalf of a few individual shareholders (337–9, 355).

for having left the city, and his example seems to have been followed by most of the other shareholders. This assumption is supported by the publication of a safe-conduct for a list of twenty-two Peruzzi shareholders and eighteen factors on June 4, 1345.[9] The announcement stated that the individuals concerned would be free to reenter the city to defend themselves against charges of having transferred company or personal assets beyond the reach of the syndicate. Shareholders were of course personally liable for the debts of the company. Some of the names were of men from the foreign branches, but others, including chairman Pacino di Tommaso, were residents of Florence who must have fled the city at one time or another. What is strange is that so many shareholders, including the leader, were allowed to slip out of town when their objective must have been to frustrate the creditors.

The tortuous proceedings of the bankruptcy court and the legal adaptations of the commune to the collapse of the super-companies have been amply described by Professor Sapori, but the two main accords deserve some additional comment.[10] The terms of the first agreement, published in March 1345, established that creditors would receive four soldi (s4) per lira (i.e., 20 percent) and would retain the right to the remaining s16, which were to be obtained from the kings of England, France, and Naples.[11] This arrangement must have been greeted with derision by most of the Florentine creditors who sought more tangible redress. It is very likely, therefore, that the safe-conduct offered to the Peruzzi Company people in June 1345 was designed to encourage them to reveal and disgorge additional personal assets for the benefit of the claimants in return for restoration of their legal status. The cooperation of Peruzzi shareholders and factors was also essential to locating and wringing out maximum value for the creditors from the company books.

The second agreement, announced in June 1347 and ratified by the priorate of the commune on September 6 of that year, reflected the results of the efforts to assemble additional assets for the creditors. Claimants were offered two choices. The first was to receive s3 d3 per lira in addition to the previously agreed s4 in exchange for a quitclaim releasing the company and its shareholders from any further liability for the bankruptcy. The alternative was to accept the

[9] Sapori, *La crisi*, 160.
[10] Ibid., 158–206.
[11] Ibid., 167.

---

earlier accord, settling for s4 only, but retaining the right to seek the remaining s16. The agreement was underwritten for the company by ten shareholders, six from the family and four from the outside.[12]

The dispositions cited in the agreement were to have been carried out within four months for creditors from Florence and six months for those from outside the city. Unfortunately for the claimants, this timetable does not seem to have been met, as they registered complaints to the syndicate in November 1348 and again in October 1349.[13] By this time, the plague had disrupted proceedings further by causing the death of many of the people involved. Not all the creditors accepted the 1347 accord, especially foreigners and ecclesiastics, who continued to press their claims individually and collectively against the commune itself, using all the considerable forces at their command. This is further evidence that much of the company's funding for its English venture was drawn from foreign sources. The commune was apparently able to resist most of these claims by stalling and creating new legal criteria, but settled some in cases where the real threat of reprisal dictated special treatment.[14]

The princes and institutions of the church were conspicuous among the special pleaders, and a number of them, including Pope Clement VI, did evidently secure a modicum of satisfaction.[15] But papal support for a claim by the Hospitalers was not powerful enough, or perhaps was not vigorous enough to achieve success. In Chapter 5, we saw that the Hospitalers purportedly had accumulated by1343 the staggering sum of 360,000 florins in deposits with the three super-companies, which Anthony Luttrell linked to this papal-supported petition.[16] Such a claim should have attracted special notice and extraordinary effort on the part of the papacy, but there is no evidence of either. A further half-hearted revival of the claim occurred in 1351, but it too petered out. The conclusion from this evidence, or lack of it, was that the greater part of any deposits lodged by the Hospitalers with the super-companies had been routinely passed along to the papal treasury. The Hospitaler claim referred to here more likely related to the more modest but still significant debt of £3,000 ac-

[12] The Peruzzi family members who signed for the company were Pacino di Tommaso (the chairman), Donato di Pacino, Ottaviano di Amideo, Berto di Ridolfo, Lepre di Guido, and Bartolomeo di Giotto. Outside shareholders were represented by Gherardino di Tano Baroncelli, Baldo di Giovanni Orlandini, Guccio di Stefano Soderini, and Filippo Villani (*La crisi*, 168–9).

[13] Ibid., 169.

[14] Ibid., 182–201.

[15] Ibid., 198–9.

[16] A. Luttrell, "Interessi fiorentini," 319.

knowledged as owed by the Peruzzi to the English branch of the order in 1344.[17]

There are great gaps in the record, unfortunately, so that it is impossible to make even a wild guess at the extent of the losses that drove the company into bankruptcy. In view of the fact that the initial settlement was made while the shareholders were still in hiding, one can reasonably surmise that most of the distribution of s4 on the lira would have come from company assets. Thus, it can be assumed that there were enough net realizable assets remaining to cover one-fifth of the liabilities. But this does not yield a figure, and even if it did, the figure would be incomplete, as much if not all of the foreign data had been omitted. With regard to the final settlement, we can be sure that some of the money came from the personal property of the shareholders, but how much is a mystery. Moreover, it appears that the creditors did not even obtain full satisfaction for the distribution promised under the agreement, because the disposal of assets took place in a depressed market.[18]

Although there are no figures to guide historians to an estimate of the size of the company at the time of its bankruptcy, it is possible to arrive at a rough order of magnitude from the material that has been presented throughout this study. We know the balances at July 1, 1335, reported in Chapter 4, and we know from the review of the final eight years of the company's history that its business was generally shrinking. Loss of papal revenues, Naples deposits, and French business would result in lower balances in each of the branches concerned, and the decline in number of personnel would suggest reduced levels of business throughout the organization, including Florence. The great unknown is the size of the English branch, which would have been much larger than in July 1335. Overall, the increase in the English branch may have been greater than the declines elsewhere, but not by much. The Peruzzi business in total at bankruptcy is therefore likely to have been about the same as in 1335, although its makeup would have been radically changed.

The foregoing account of the post-bankruptcy events lends strong support to the argument advanced in Chapter 4 that a significant part of the surviving Peruzzi accounts was written after the bankruptcy and under the direction of the syndicate. The author of these books was Pacino di Tommaso, the last chairman. Many of the postings in

---

[17] CCR E III 1343–6, 356, records that the prior of the Hospitalers in England prosecuted the execution of a recognizance of £3,000 made to him by the Peruzzi in chancery in March, 1344.

[18] Sapori, *Storia economica*, Vol. 2, 687–8.

these books were of a catch-up nature and many more were dated July 1, 1343. It must be remembered that Pacino was an important participant in the political firestorm that engulfed Florence from July into October of that year, and he is unlikely to have found the necessary time and tranquility to have posted more than a fraction of these entries. From October 27 onward, the company books were in the hands of the commune and out of Pacino's control, but several of the entries recorded events that took place well after that date. Moreover, the fact that Pacino's name headed the list of shareholders granted the safe-conduct of June 1345 suggests that he was absent from Florence for much of the time between November 1343 and June 1345. It is therefore reasonable to assume that Pacino undertook the task of assembling the data and completing the accounts over the two years from mid-1345 to mid-1347.

If these speculations are anywhere near the truth, then the purpose of preparing the accounts would have been to help establish the basis for the 1347 settlement. Such a supposition is supported by the fact that so many of the entries dealt with adjustments of expense between the company and shareholders. In Chapters 3 and 4, I commented on these, expressing disbelief that shareholder–managers should have received no compensation for their efforts and expense in the company's service, especially in foreign branches. I suggested that this anomaly may be explained if the entries are understood as adjustments enforced by the bankruptcy court. It is probable that the company did normally reward its working shareholders by paying the living costs of themselves and families and other expenses. But in a bankruptcy accounting, such perquisites would have been reversed as easily identifiable shareholder assets to which the creditors could legitimately lay claim. Again, if the accounts had been prepared to meet the limited objectives of the bankruptcy court, then they may not have been intended "to lead up to a comprehensive financial statement or balance."[19] They would therefore not be an appropriate basis for judging whether the Peruzzi Company employed double-entry accounting.

Although the Peruzzi Company closed its doors on October 27, 1343, several of the branches appear to have continued operations well beyond that date. The news would have taken considerable time to reach some destinations; local legal formalities would have to be observed, inventories disposed of, and local creditors dealt with, if not satisfied. Of the nineteen factors included in the list of people

[19] This is one of the criteria advanced by de Roover for double-entry accounting noted in Chapter 4, this volume.

offered safe-conduct in Florence in June 1345, thirteen were men whose last known positions with the company were in foreign locations, suggesting that they had not yet returned from abroad.[20] The English branch remained fully operative, as the company men there struggled loyally to extract as much as possible from the crown, alongside the members of the still-functioning Bardi Company. The long-enduring truce of Malestroit of January 1343 had permitted at least a partial restoration of the king's finances, creating a constructive environment for settling his most pressing debts. During 1344 and early 1345, the orders recorded in the *Patent Rolls* and *Close Rolls* reflected some transactions in the wool trade, but dealt mainly with claims from the Bardi and Peruzzi challenging various findings of the audit commission.[21] The tone of these orders was not only correct, but even sympathetic, presenting the complaints in detail and commanding the commission to review the disputed accounts and report.

The situation changed suddenly in June 1345, when, coincident with the renewed outbreak of hostilities with France, the king ordered the arrest of six members of the Peruzzi Company and their detention in the Tower of London.[22] Although the Latin–English versions of the names are difficult to decipher, five of them are identifiable as members of the Peruzzi or other shareholder families.[23] What appears to have happened is that all but one of the previous members of the branch organization had been sent home and replaced by a team of shareholders' sons or nephews who were mostly new to England but experienced company operatives nonetheless. After the incarceration, there followed a peculiar and seemingly contradictory series of orders. First, in March 1346, the prisoners were required to remain in the Tower because of debts allegedly owed *by the company to the king* but were permitted to come and go freely to do business in the city.[24] Then in July of the same year, the treasury was ordered to

---

[20] Sapori, *La crisi*, 161. The locations of the men in the list can be found in *I libri* or more easily in Sapori, *Storia economica*, Vol. 2, 718–29.

[21] *CPR* E III 1343–5, 274; *CCR* E III 1343–6, 372, 406, 421–2, 438, 500.

[22] *CCR* E III 1343–6, 581.

[23] The names reported are Thomas Philipp (Tommaso di Filippo, shareholder), Robert Thomasy (Roberto di Tommaso, factor), Andrew called Amyday (Andrea di Amideo, factor), all from the Peruzzi family; Angelus Sutheryn (Angnolo d'Albizzo Soderini, a factor transferred from Paris), Peter Symon (Piero di Simone de Giovanni Orlandini, factor), and Andrew Forcet (the Italian equivalent should logically have been Andrea Forzetti, but there is no record of a Peruzzi employee of that name in England).

[24] *CCR* E III 1346–9, 53–4. The constable was also ordered to give the prisoners "decent chambers for their stay."

certify how much the Peruzzi owed the king and the king owed the
Peruzzi.[25] In the same month, the government granted three company members protection so that they could not be sued by creditors, as they were bound "in great sum" to the king.[26] This protection
was repeated in March 1347 and February 1348 in order that suing
creditors might not "pre-empt the crown's prerogative of priority."[27]
Meanwhile, on April 20, 1347, the king ordered Walter de Chiriton
to hold back three-quarters of the profit of the mint to pay for the
king sums due to a number of persons and "for other sums to the
merchants of the society of the Peruzzi or others for money lent to
the king for the time when William de Northwell, William de Cusancia
and William de Edyngton were keepers of the wardrobe."[28] And on
the same day a long indenture was enrolled between the king and
Walter de Chiriton and Gilbert de Wendlyngburgh testifying that these
men have undertaken, among other things noted in the indenture,
"to discharge the king of £20,000 due by him to the society of the
Peruches or other debts lent to him when Sir William de Norwell,
Sir William de Cusance and Sir William de Edyngton were keepers of
the wardrobe, for which bills were made under the seals of those
keepers."[29]

These various documents indicate that during the period following
the Peruzzi bankruptcy, the English government was attempting to work
toward some sort of agreement with the company while holding its creditors at bay on the manifestly false pretense that the Peruzzi owed the
king money. Overall, the company's recoveries were probably skimpy,
but it may have received a useful sum for the £20,000 receivable it sold
to Chiriton via Canaceon. Selling such obligations at a discount was
apparently fairly common, especially if they were backed by letters obligatory from the crown. Fryde offers numerous examples of large-scale discounting of various types of government debt instruments during this
period and cites Chiriton as one of the leading brokers.[30] The discounts
were deep, perhaps 90 percent, but even at that rate, the remainder in
ready cash would have been considerable for the Peruzzi.[31] The only

[25] Ibid., 143. [26] *CPR* E III 1345–8, 151.
[27] Ibid., 257; E III 1348–50, 6.
[28] *CCR* E III 1346–9, 204. Chiriton was a London merchant and farmer of the royal
customs 1346–9.
[29] Ibid., 260. Wendlyngburgh was a merchant. A memorandum added to the roll
states that the indenture was previously made to Matthew Canaceon, a Malines-
based Asti merchant, three years earlier and transferred to Chiriton and
Wendlyngburgh with Canaceon's consent.
[30] Fryde, *William de la Pole*, 184–5, 192–6, 204–5, 207.
[31] Fryde cites evidence that royal debts were often acquired at 2s to 2s 6d in the
pound.

amount actually known to have been collected by the Peruzzi was £100 given to Roberto di Tommaso on August 20, 1352, acknowledged as "in part payment of a greater sum in which the king is bound."[32]

How much money the Peruzzi actually lost in its dealings with Edward III is unknown. Although Fryde has acknowledged that the losses between early 1338 and 1340 were modest, he has also asserted that "much more serious losses appear to have been suffered by the two firms [Bardi and Peruzzi] as a result of loans advanced in 1340– 41."[33] We have seen, however, that both companies were unwilling to extend credit in those years and unable to do so thereafter. The *Close Rolls* entry of 1352 confirms that a significant sum remained unpaid, but the net loss to the Peruzzi, while serious, cannot have been overwhelming. Toward the end of Chapter 7, I estimated that the Peruzzi's net loss on its transactions with the English king by early 1340 was in a range of £15,000 to £20,000. The records since that time suggest that the Peruzzi had gradually chipped away at that amount by means of wool sales, repayments, and the discounting of the £20,000 receivable. In addition, there were the clamoring creditors mentioned in the rolls who presumably were left to a large extent unsatisfied.[34] The total amount owed to the creditors is unknown, and the extent to which the super-companies financed their English operations from local sources is a matter of disagreement among scholars.[35] But the total sum due to the creditors cannot have been insignificant. In all, therefore, the company's final loss in England may have been in the neighborhood of £10,000, or even less.

As noted at the end of Chapter 1, the Peruzzi family persisted and even prospered after the debacle. Various members were active in the business world, most notably Simone di Rinieri, grandson of Pacino, who was especially successful. Two Peruzzi even appeared in England in the 1370s, but unfortunately their claim to fame was a

[32] *CCR* E III 1349–54, 505. The entry included a note that Roberto came to the Chancery on September 16 to acknowledge the deed. This is the last entry in the rolls concerning the Peruzzi Company.

[33] Fryde, "Edward III's War Finance," Vol. 1, 335.

[34] One important creditor appears to have been the Hospitalers in England, who in the end were owed £3,000 by the Peruzzi (*CCR* E III 1343–6, 356), as discussed earlier in this chapter.

[35] For example, Postan thought that much of the capital employed by Italian companies originated from domestic sources (see *Medieval Trade and Finance*, 339– 40). But Prestwich said that in England "the Italians' role as deposit bankers was not considerable" (see "Italian Merchants in England," 96). Fryde's investigations give support to Prestwich's conclusion, but Fryde also warned that lack of evidence does not necessarily mean lack of deposits (see "Deposits with Italian Bankers," 359).

serious default on a wool transaction.[36] And the family remained an element to be reckoned with in Florentine politics as befitted its wealth and status, even though it never regained the political potency it enjoyed in the first half of the fourteenth century.[37]

Why was the family not utterly ruined financially by the collapse of the company, as would be expected under the doctrine of unlimited liability of shareholders and their immediate families and heirs? One reason is that not all branches of the family were owners of the company, although there were shareholders in most branches.[38] Another is that the losses were of course shared by the many nonfamily partners. But probably the most important reason is the skill with which the family members directly affected managed to shield their assets from prying creditors. As we have seen, most of the shareholders appear to have fled the city and arranged to shift property into safer hands. Such action seems to have been standard practice in Florence at the time, and many of the transfers would have been within the law.[39] At any rate, the Peruzzi were successful and, as early as 1348 and 1349, were again buying land.[40]

Superficially, the comments in the foregoing paragraph may be construed as suggesting that the family easily sacrificed the company in order to maintain its own well-being. To be sure, given the stark choice between the survival of the company and the preservation of the family's position, the priority would inevitably go to the latter. But the Peruzzi family's tie to the company bearing its name was a strong one emotionally. The family shareholders were not merely investors, prepared to abandon the business when it proved unprofitable. As we have already seen, they increased their investment in the company between 1335 and 1343. Had their interest been strictly economic, they should have closed it down in 1336, when it must have been clear that the business was steadily losing money. Instead, they took a huge risk, investing time, talent, and money in the English venture in a vain attempt to restore the company's viability.

---

[36] George A. Holmes, "Florentine Merchants in England, 1346–1436," *Economic History Review* 2 series, 13 (December 1960): 202.

[37] According to the 1427 *catasto* (a well-known tax survey), the Peruzzi clan was among the best favored in Florence, owning 1.1% of the total wealth of the city. See David Herlihy and Christian Klapisch-Zuber, *Tuscans and Their Families: A Study of the Florentine Catasto of 1427* (New Haven, CT, 1985), 100.

[38] See Figures A1–A3.

[39] Jones, "Florentine Families," 202. Some transactions were illegal. Jones notes that the Antellesi concluded fictitious sales to elude creditors, but Sapori denied that the Peruzzi used this device.

[40] Ibid., note 164.

Moreover, they stayed with the venture long after it was obvious that it was not a success and, after the bankruptcy, exposed their own kin to physical hazard in an attempt to salvage what they could from the wreckage. The company and family were closely entwined, and the final separation was reluctant and no doubt traumatic.

A word needs to be said about the fate of the other super-companies. The Acciaiuoli failed at the same time as the Peruzzi but was able to offer its creditors a more generous settlement of s10 per lira, or 50 percent.[41] Little more is heard of the company in England, but family members maintained an important presence in Naples. Niccolo Acciaiuoli, who began his career as a company employee in Naples in 1331, stayed on after the collapse and eventually became grand seneschal of the kingdom. As such, he was a man of great influence and wealth in both Naples and Florence, capitalizing on the continued trade links between those two polities.[42] But there is little further to be reported about the company itself.

The Bardi Company had a much longer history. Finally brought to its knees in April 1346, it agreed to a surprisingly swift settlement of s9 d3 per lira, or 46.25 percent, in August of the same year. The execution of the agreement took much longer, and Sapori reports that in April 1348 the bankruptcy syndicate was still busy.[43] In England, the Bardi Company branch continued in business after the collapse and then reorganized itself in 1357 under Philip de Bardi.[44] For the next three decades Philip, and then his son Walter after 1362, led a company of merchants and bankers that operated on a surprisingly substantial scale. For example, the company held very large deposits from Earl Richard of Arundel, who also bought up at a discount a sizable amount of the Bardi's old royal debts.[45] Moreover, Walter de Bardi was also master of the mint for both Edward III and Richard II at a time when the coinage was almost entirely concentrated in the Tower, putting him in close contact with the royal administration. He executed the final settlement of 1392, whereby all obligations on both sides were recorded and surrendered to the Ex-

---

[41] Ibid., 193. The settlement was also fairly prompt, being formalized on March 23, 1345.

[42] Sapori, *Storia economica*, Vol. 1, "Lettera di Niccolo Acciaiuoli a Niccolo Soderini," 133–53. See also Abulafia, "Southern Italy," 377.

[43] Sapori, *La crisi*, 174.

[44] Beardwood, *Alien Merchants in England*, 4.

[45] C. Given-Wilson, "Wealth and Credit, Public and Private: The Earls of Arundel, 1306–97," *English Historical Review* 106 (January 1991): 1–26. Deposits attained the level of at least 23,700 marks in the 1360s and 1370s (19); the largest loan discounted was one from the Bardi of £5,853 (11).

chequer for cancellation. Beardwood calculated that the net amount then due by the king to the company, recognizing repayments between 1345 and 1391 and sums owed by the Bardi, was £31,422.[46] The sum of 3,000 marks was originally granted by Richard II in consideration of the annulment but never materialized, although assignments worth £600 were recorded along with an annual pension for Walter.[47] Perhaps the king's treasurers decided that adequate justice had been done, bearing in mind that the Bardi total claim included Edward III's 1339 "gift" of £30,000. Taking that fact into account, the Bardi losses on its transactions with the English monarchy could be considered as close to zero. This is far too optimistic, given the losses the Bardi suffered from the rejection of expenses in the past and from the receivables sold to others at a discount. But here again, the net injury inflicted on the Bardi Company by its English business was not very great and clearly nothing like the calamitous 900,000 florins (£135,000) proclaimed by Villani.

Back in Florence, the Bardi remained a very large and prosperous family after 1350. Brucker cited it as "the wealthiest and the largest family in Florence" in 1364.[48] By 1427, the Bardi had fallen to second place behind the Strozzi, but was still enormously wealthy, holding 2.1 percent of the total net taxable capital of the city.[49]

In sum, then, although the main families associated with the super-companies undoubtedly suffered severe damage to their economic well-being and their social standing as a result of the debacle of the 1340s, they seem to have recovered both with remarkable swiftness in the years following.

[46] Beardwood, *Alien Merchants in England*, 8–9 and App. A. The total debts to the king registered in the documents proffered by the Bardi totaled £93,947, and the payments by the king and the sums owed by the Bardi totaled £62,525.

[47] Ibid., 9.

[48] Brucker, *Florentine Politics*, 21 n83.

[49] Herlihy and Klapisch-Zuber, *Tuscans and Their Families*, 100.

Conclusions

We have seen in the course of this study that the super-companies, unlike their smaller brethren, were separate and distinct from their eponymous families, despite their close connections. Here, the considerable mingling of company and personal affairs involved not merely family members, but all owners and, to a lesser extent, even the employees. Nonfamily members had the same access to the company's resources as did the Peruzzi family partners. If Giotto de' Peruzzi seems to have taken excessive advantage of his position in the company between 1315 and 1335, as reported in Table 6, so did the Soderini brothers between 1335 and 1343 (see Table A6). And if many members of the Peruzzi family remained wealthy after the crash, so did many of those of the other shareholders.[1]

We have also noted that the super-companies did not attain their great size through the normal process of gradual growth over an extended period.[2] In the case of the Peruzzi at least, they were *created large* to satisfy two special needs – large-scale supplies of foodstuffs and raw materials for the burgeoning industrial cities and large-scale cash for the ambitious rulers who controlled those commodities. For the Peruzzi and Acciaiuoli, the grain trade of southern Italy was the principal target and reason for being super-companies. The Peruzzi Company was not involved on the same scale in the other great commodity of medieval commerce, wool, until late in its history, while the Acciaiuoli was never a significant participant. The Bardi Company, the largest of them all, was unique in being a major player in both trades over a considerable stretch of time.

The wool trade, in itself, did not require the exclusive engage-

---

[1] Prominent Florentine families of the fifteenth century included the Baroncelli (see Goldthwaite, *Building Florence*, 306; De Roover, *Medici Bank*, 199), the Soderini (see De Roover, *Medici Bank*, 105; Herlihy and Klapisch-Zuber, *Tuscans and Their Families*, 101 n11), and the Orlandini (see De Roover, *Medici Bank*, 318).

[2] Contrast the Peruzzi evidence with the more normal gradual accretion of capital experienced by the Medici Bank between 1397 and 1451. See De Roover, *Medici Bank*, Chaps. 3 and 4.

ment of highly capitalized companies. Many small enterprises operated very successfully in this business. Large size became necessary only when rulers (Edward I and Edward III) determined to restrict the right of participation to those firms prepared to grant them large loans. The grain trade of the early fourteenth century was different in that it entailed the movement of vast quantities of a low-value material into a number of markets where both demand and price were extremely volatile. Small traders could and did participate at the fringes, but serious involvement required deep pockets and sophisticated organization in addition to the capability of satisfying the controlling ruler's need for cash.

Both of these businesses were lucrative. The case for the wool trade has been easily made by Fryde's analyses and the actual earnings reported by the Bardi Company in 1330–2.[3] The grain trade is more problematic because there are no direct reports of results and because profit margins were thin and prices volatile. It could, in fact, be argued that the grain trade was not really profitable at all and that the super-companies sought the grain monopoly as a means to secure the monopoly over the sale of cloth in southern Italy. But this thesis requires the strained assumption that the super-companies were willing to risk lending large sums to a spendthrift ruler to obtain the right to invest still more cash in a treacherous unrewarding business and thus secure the golden apple of a medium-sized cloth market. Again, the Bardi records show the total cloth business (not just for southern Italy) to have been attractive but not outstandingly rewarding. Large-scale grain trading was therefore likely to have been worthwhile in itself. For the Peruzzi it was undoubtedly healthy at least through 1324, judging by the overall profits reported by the company. The luster of the grain trade appears to have faded only from the late 1320s, when the intervention of various governments in pricing and procurement reduced both the scope of the business and the companies' room for maneuver within it.

Although the emphasis here has been appropriately on commodity trading, it is also important to acknowledge the enormous spread and variety of the super-companies' operations. One aspect of this fact that may have escaped the reader's attention is the amazing breadth of expertise required by the men who had to deal with operations of such geographic and product-line diversity.[4] The compa-

---

[3] See Table 7.

[4] The word "men" is used advisedly. Although there are numerous entries in the Peruzzi accounts involving women, often as property owners, all shareholders and employees were male.

nies had to have a corps of shareholder–managers and employees who were multilingual and numerate; knowledgeable in currency exchange systems, accounting, banking, legal systems, and logistics; expert in judging the quality and types of cereal grains, wines, spices, wool, tissues, dyes, precious metals, and stones; and who were personable, politically astute, enterprising, and physically courageous. Probably no modern corporation demands such a broad array of talents and acquired skills, for the scope of the super-companies' activities would be equivalent to something like those of Cargill, J. P. Morgan, and a modern trading company combined.

Three further conclusions can be drawn from this study, two of which are obvious and one less obvious. The first is the disposal of the myth that the super-companies were destroyed by their irrational dealings with Edward III. The myth has been fostered not only by Giovanni Villani's emotional and biased account, but also by the incompleteness and complexity of the surviving records and the history of earlier Italian companies, such as the Ricciardi and Frescobaldi, which did succumb to the reversal of their fortunes in England. Historians such as Sapori, Beardwood, and Fryde have recognized that English losses were not the only reason nor even the principal reason for the downfall of the Bardi and Peruzzi, but their conclusions were contradictory. They exonerated Edward III from maliciously reneging on his debts but accepted a level of losses on those debts that would have crushed the companies as early as 1339.

We have seen that the Peruzzi Company was heading on a downward path toward bankruptcy before it became involved in any way with the English crown. We have also seen that the company's English branch, although being audited, was still functioning more or less normally long after the head office in Florence ceased to exist. Finally, we have seen that the losses in England were significant, though not overwhelming, and were only one of several determinants contributing to the firm's demise.

This leads to the second conclusion and the demolition of the second myth, the exaggerated size and power of the super-companies. Careful examination of the Peruzzi business has shown that while the super-companies were very large indeed for their time, they were by no means the behemoths of historical fable. The magnification of their size has been nurtured by the oft-noted Bardi asset total of 875,000 florins in 1318, which has lured otherwise perceptive authors into making meaningless comparisons with unrelated data, such as the purchase price of certain territories or Edward III's annual revenues.[5] More important, the illusion of huge resources conjured up by this number has enabled historians to accept as a matter of faith the assumption that the companies had the financial strength to endure for years the freezing of massive amounts of money in unproductive loans to the English king. By studying the Peruzzi Company so closely, we have ascertained that a large part of such assets were widely scattered and reflected obligations rather than power. We have also discovered that the company had limited resources available on the eve of its English enterprise.

The less obvious conclusion that is drawn from this investigation is that the medieval super-company disappeared permanently with the dissolution of the three Florentine examples in the 1340s and that this was an important development. Up to that point, large Italian companies had evolved, prospered, collapsed, and been replaced by even larger organizations. After the 1340s, however, no new enterprises emerged even approaching the stature of the super-companies. As we have seen, members of the Bardi, Peruzzi, and Acciaiuoli families later operated successful businesses, but these were but a shadow of their predecessors. A few new companies rose to importance, most notably the Alberti, which reacquired the papal monopoly for Florence, but again they were only a pale imitation of the super-companies.[6] Even the heavily capitalized and highly profitable Medici Bank of a century later failed to match the size and reach of the fourteenth-century giants, despite its impressive manufacturing activity and substantial branch network.[7] This famous firm, although the larg-

---

[5]   See Brucker, *Florence: The Golden Age*, 88–9; Sapori, *Storia economica*, Vol. 2, 688; Fryde, "*Public Credit,*" 455; Renouard, *Les relations*, 60; Bolton, *Medieval English Economy*, 340; Kaeuper, *War, Justice, and Public Order*, 44, n84. Most of these comparisons were described in Chapter 4, this volume.

[6]   The Alberti employed a total of only nineteen factors – ten in Florence, six in Avignon, and three in the branches of Naples and Barletta. See De Roover, "The Alberti," 26–7. De Roover also notes in *Medieval Bruges*, 39, that the largest company of Lucca, the Guinigi, consisted in 1372 of twelve factors and seven shareholders spread over a number of small branches. In 1381, the number of factors had dropped to seven.

[7]   De Roover, *Medici Bank*. That company's capital was as high as 72,000 florins at the opening of the 1451 partnership (65–6), and profits averaged more than 18,000 florins per year between 1435 and 1451 (69–70). It had three manufacturing partnerships, eight foreign branches (83), and fifty-seven factors (95). Although a large company, it was smaller than the Peruzzi, except in its manufacturing endeavors, and it focused more on international banking than on trading.

est and geographically most extensive of the Florentine companies of the fifteenth century, did not enjoy a dominating position in Florence or in the foreign cities in which it had branches.[8]

Why did no new super-companies emerge? Part of the answer must come from reexamining why they appeared in the first place. At the beginning of this chapter, I had concluded that a few Florentine companies grew to the extraordinary size they did, and needed to do so, because of the opportunities presented by growing populations and cash-hungry rulers who controlled concentrated commodity sources. But in the late 1340s, two great changes took place, eliminating the effect of these criteria on business organization.

The first was the Black Death of 1347–50, which drastically reduced the population of western Europe, initially wreaking greatest havoc in the cities, especially the thriving, overcrowded cities of Italy. There is, of course, evidence of significant population decline in various parts of Europe, notably in Tuscany, well before 1348.[9] This trend may well have contributed to the erosion of the profitability of the super-companies' grain trade from the 1330s onward. But the Black Death was overwhelming in its sudden and devastating impact. Although estimates vary, Florence is said to have lost between one-third and one-half of the population that Villani had set at 90,000 in 1338. Demographers have given similar ranges of population losses for most other cities. Moreover, repeated outbreaks of various forms of the plague over the years ensured that population totals would remain depressed. Florence's numbers persisted in a range of 50,000 to 60,000 throughout the rest of the fourteenth century.[10] The result of this new fact was a greatly reduced grain trade. To be sure, food production in the areas surrounding the cities was also reduced by population loss, but the amount needed to make up for shortfall was normally much less than before. And in those years when large-scale imports were necessitated by famine, they were organized by the municipalities.[11] As a result, the grain trade was no longer the routine volume business it used to be and no longer required exceptionally large private organizations to manage it.

[8] Richard A. Goldthwaite, "The Medici Bank and the World of Florentine Capitalism," *Past & Present* 114 (February 1987): 3–31.
[9] Herlihy and Klapisch-Zuber, *Tuscans and Their Families*, 60–92.
[10] Ibid.
[11] For example, La Roncière, *Prix et salaires*, 563, reports a strikingly large value of wheat imports paid by the Florence commune in 1374–5.

The change in the second criterion was a break in the connection between the export demand for the great cash crops and the needs of the rulers that controlled them. In the case of Naples, Queen Johanna, successor to King Robert, was at least as financially profligate as her predecessor, but the strategic importance of her grain resources had diminished due to the drop in population. In England, however, the value of the wool crop persisted as demand for this commodity actually appeared to have increased in the years following the Black Death. English wool exports in the 1350s and 1360s reached levels not seen since the beginning of the fourteenth century and continued robustly into the 1370s.[12] Their decline thereafter was at least partly compensated by rising cloth exports. But the administrators of the English crown had become much more adroit in their handling of the king's finances, obviating the need for continuous financing by private companies, domestic or foreign. William Edington, bishop of Winchester, after his assignment as Keeper of the Wardrobe, became Edward III's treasurer between 1344 and 1356, and then chancellor from 1356 to 1363. During this extended period, he reformed the government's bookkeeping and financial information systems and its customs procedures, greatly improving the control of expenditures and enhancing revenues.[13] Thus, he gradually brought order into the financing of Edward's military campaigns, eventually releasing the government from the grip of private financiers.[14] Thereafter, the king's activities in France were less demanding of cash, and his needs could be managed on a reasonably orderly basis.[15] To be sure, Edward III and his successors continued to have frequent recourse to borrowing, but never again on the previous scale and never again with such concentration on one or two lenders.

The disengagement of the Florentine companies from the English

[12] E. M. Carus-Wilson and Olive Coleman, *England's Export Trade* (Oxford, 1963), charts, 122 and 138.

[13] Ormrod, *Edward III*, 86–90. Ormrod points out that, by the 1360s, the Exchequer was able to draw up statements of royal income and expenditure, "a feat unimaginable in the 1330s."

[14] Fryde, *William de le Pole*, 193. Customs were particularly productive, with the total revenue from that source exceeding £112,000 in 1353–4, a record for the reign of Edward III, and continuing at a very high level for the next few years. See J. H. Ramsay, *A History of the Revenues of the Kings of England, 1066–1399* (Oxford, 1925), 214–29.

[15] See G. L. Harriss, *King, Parliament, and Public Finance in Medieval England to 1369* (Oxford, 1975). And from 1352, Harriss notes, "War finance was henceforth to be dependent wholly on parliament and controlled by the Exchequer" (328).

monarchy may have been, as Professor Goldthwaite has suggested, a two-way street, as the Italians increasingly sought sources of wool closer to home and concentrated their efforts in the Mediterranean area.[16] The Florentine merchants had by no means abandoned the English wool trade, and there is evidence of their considerable continuing activity in that field between 1350 and 1376.[17] They had clearly lost position, however, and yielded the business, especially after 1376, to the now-dominant English merchants. In addition, the flow of credit, over which the Florentine had enjoyed such control, seems to have changed direction, moving from seller to buyer instead of from buyer to seller.[18] This was not necessarily a universal phenomenon, but it is noteworthy that the two Peruzzi defaulters of 1375 cited in Chapter 9 had acquired a large quantity of wool on credit from merchants of Lincolnshire.[19] Overall, the combination of all of these changes in commercial environment and the withdrawal from royal lending made a super-company with a large branch in London an anachronism.

A final and important reason for the nonrecurrence of super-companies in medieval Europe has to do with the nature of the companies themselves. As we saw in Chapter 3, the super-companies required an immense managerial effort to keep functioning coherently. They had become, as Goldthwaite has aptly observed, "abnormally large by standards of business organization of the time."[20] The communication and reporting technologies, barely adequate at the best of times, were simply not up to coping with the continuous disruptions caused by pestilence and extended warfare over the super-companies' market area. The increase in transactional costs cited by Munro was part of the problem, insofar as it altered trading patterns and distorted the super-companies' traditional markets.[21] But super-companies had been living with rising transactional costs since the beginning of the fourteenth century, and the continuing accretions merely reflected one of the additional adverse effects of an increasingly hostile environment with which smaller and nimbler organizations proved better able to cope. The main problem was that the effort and risks of running a super-company were no longer in bal-

[16] Goldthwaite, *Renaissance Florence*, 46, and idem, "The Medici Bank," 18.
[17] Holmes, "Florentine Merchants," 201–2.
[18] Postan, *Medieval Trade and Finance*, 9–11.
[19] Holmes, "Florentine Merchants," 202.
[20] Goldthwaite, *Renaissance Florence*, 45.
[21] Munro, "Industrial Transformations," 133–48.

ance with the potential rewards. In short, the game was no longer worth the candle.[22]

The game had also become much less interesting to investors badly burned by the multiple failures of the 1340s. Wealthy families were increasingly attracted to enjoying the fruits of their labors and putting their money into the adornment of their residences. They became more concerned about the safety of their investments and evolved into a *rentier* class, finding a ready outlet for their funds in the financing of the city's public debt. By 1427, the wealthiest segment of the city's population invested around one-third of its assets in public debt, leaving only one-third in commerce and industry and the remaining third in land.[23]

A last word needs to be said about the men who built the super-companies. I have attributed the *possibility* of super-companies to a unique confluence of population dynamics, commodity resources, and the cash needs of incipient nation-states. But the *actuality* of super-companies came about from the efforts of a handful of men with the vision to grasp the implications of the opportunity presented to them and the energy and skill to seize it. In the case of the Peruzzi, Filippo seems to have been such a man. His nephew Tommaso may not have been as gifted but possessed the administrative skill and an enormous capacity for work that kept this cumbersome giant of an organization functioning for almost thirty years. The rarity of the talent and single-minded effort required to create a company of great size is evidenced by the fact that nearly a century had passed before the organizing genius of Cosimo de' Medici raised the Medici Bank to its great heights. As soon as he passed away, the company went into decline. But the next true super-company did not emerge until the beginning of the sixteenth century. Then, Jakob Fugger found the same combination of forces – key commodities in great demand (silver and copper in this instance) and ambitious princes in need of cash – which he converted into Europe's last preindustrial super-company.

---

[22] The practice of partible inheritance also limited the family company's ability to amass capital for growth (see Goldthwaite, "The Medici Bank," 9–10), but the disinclination of the surviving brothers and sons to perpetuate the family business as a common property was decisive. The size and longevity of the Medici Company was a consequence, Goldthwaite notes, of the fortuitous combination of a series of exceptionally able men and the premature deaths of the less gifted heirs (12).

[23] Herlihy and Klapisch-Zuber, *Tuscans and Their Families*, 101–3. See especially the upper chart 4.2 on 102.

Appendixes

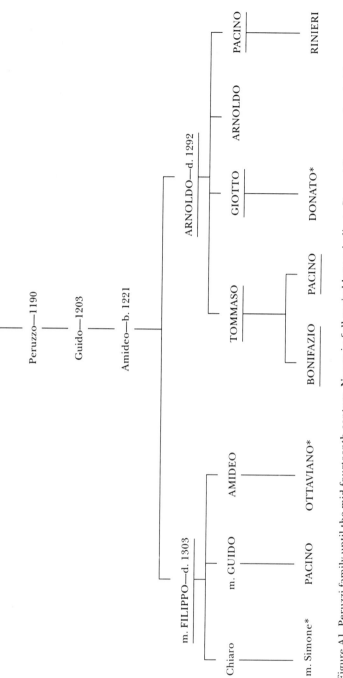

Figure A1. Peruzzi family until the mid-fourteenth century. Names in full capital letters indicate Peruzzi Company shareholders. Names in underlined full capital letters indicate company chairman at one time or another The "m." indicates the honorific title *messer*. The asterisk indicates died in the 1348 plague.

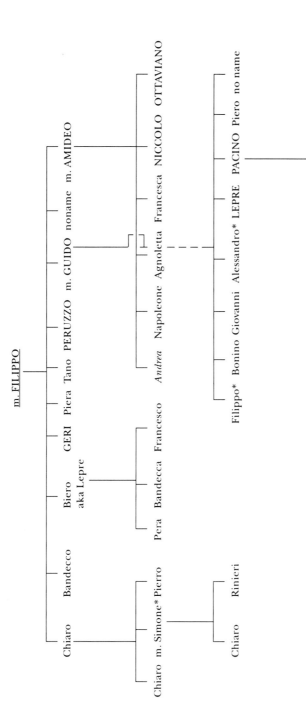

Figure A2. Early genealogy of the Filippo branch of the Peruzzi family. Names in Full capital letters indicate Peruzzi Company shareholders. Names in underlined full capital letters indicate company chairmen at one time or another. Names in italics indicate Peruzzi company factors. The "m." preceding a name indicates the honorific *messer*. The asterisk indicates died in the 1348 plague.

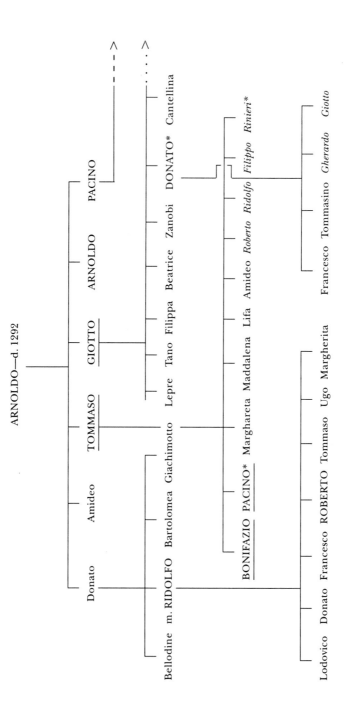

Figure A3. Early genealogy of the Arnoldo branch of the Peruzzi. Names in full capital letters indicate Peruzzi Company shareholders. Names in underlined full capital letters indicate company chairmen at one time or another. Names in italics indicate Peruzzi company factors. The "m." preceding a name indicates the honorific *messer*. The asterisk indicates died in the 1348 plague.

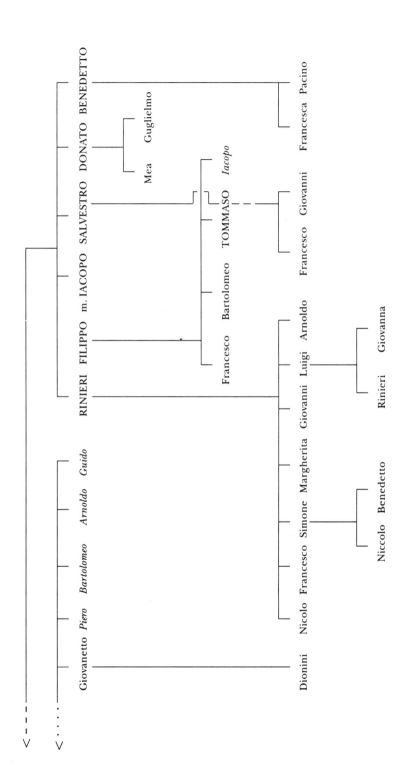

Appendix II: Peruzzi Company Balances at July 1, 1335

Table A1. *Detail of "others" balances at July 1, 1335* (*lire a fiorino*)

	Assets	Liabilities	Balance
Nonshareholder Peruzzi			
Simone & heirs	—	12,972	(12,972)
Others	893	9,356	(8,463)
Total	893	22,328	(21,435)
Hospitalers			
Florence Accts	12,193	28,636	(16,443)
English Accts	12,832	—	12,832
Total	25,025	28,636	(3,611)
Other church	208	22,260	(22,052)
Raugi family	484	16,892	(16,408)
All other	4,102	14,103	(10,001)
Grand total	30,712	104,219	(73,507)

Note: In this analysis "assets" are receivables to the company or loans to the individuals, and "liabilities" are the opposite. It highlights some useful information: (1) Non-shareholders of the Peruzzi family, especially Simone, were significant investors in the company. (2) Although the Hospitalers were net investors in the company in the Florence books, their large English borrowing (recorded separately from the English branch and controlled in Florence) largely balanced the Order's position with the company. (3) Other church-men, mainly bishops and abbots, were significant investors in the company. (4) the Raugi family, former shareholders, continued to invest in the company.

Table A2. *Detail of Peruzzi branch balances at July 1, 1335 (lire a fiorino)*

	Assets	Liabilities	Balance
Cyprus[a]	10,943	736	10,207
Bruges[b]	—	593	(593)
England[c]	—	20,674	(20,674)
Paris[d]	21,610	46,290	(24,680)
Avignon[e]	29,568	59,568	(30,000)
Pisa[f]	14,906	20,768	(5,862)
Venice[g]	—	11,481	(11,481)
Rhodes[h]	6,480	18,802	(12,322)
Naples[i]	74,092	120,960	(46,868)
Barletta[j]	30,124	32,997	(2,873)
Majorca[k]	13,709	—	13,709
Sicily Trade[l]	37,191	43,083	(5,892)
Loan[m]	62,434	—	62,434
Total	99,625	43,083	56,542
Sardinia[n]	16,108	430	15,678
Tunis[o]	11,706	6,039	5,667
Genoa[p]	—	—	—
Chiarenza[p]	—	—	—
Total Branches	328,871	382,421	(53,550)

Note: Because Cyprus, Bruges, and England branches provide essentially only net assets or liabilities, the figures give no indication of the level of activity of the branches and decidedly understate it.

[a]Closing date November 30, 1336; mainly balance of unstated cash, good debts, and merchandise, less payables. Currency is the bezant converted at B 1 = s6 d6.

[b]Closed September 1, 1335; balance of unstated payables less good debts and cash. Currency is libbra grossi tornesi converted at £GT 1 = li.30.

[c]Closed August 15, 1336; balance of unstated payables less good debts and cash. Currency is £ sterling converted at £ 1 = li.10 s10.

[d]Closed September 1, 1335; assets are good receivables from unstated number of debtors, and liabilities are payables to twenty-two creditors. Currency is £ buoni tornesi converted into florins at an average of £BT 2 s10 = fl 1, which were in turn converted to £ at rates ranging between fl 1 = 30s and 31s.

[e]Closed mostly August 15, 1335, but additional assets to October 15, 1335; assets are eighty good receivables plus a cash transfer, and liabilities are payables to eighty-one creditors. Currency is the florin converted at fl1 = 30s 3d to 31s.

[f]Closed September 5, 1335, for assets and July 26, 1335, for liabilities.

Assets are sixty-six good receivables plus cash, and liabilities are twenty-eight payables. Currency is the florin converted at fl 1 = 30s.

gClosed July 21, 1335; liability figure is a net of payables to eleven creditors less good receivables from twelve debtors and cash. The gross asset and liability figures are given in local currency in the entry. Currency is Venetian grossi manchi converted at £VGM 1 = li.15.

hClosed July 22, 1335, for liabilities, but asset closings occurred up to July 1, 1336. Liabilities are excess of amounts payable to fifty-one creditors over receivable from 114 good debtors, with details of each given in local currency in the entry. Assets are later closing entries for additional cash received attributable to the old company and confirmation of 50 additional good debtors. Currency is the bezant converted at B 1 = s4 d8.

iClosed July 20, 1335, for liabilities and December 10, 1335, for assets. Liabilities are payables to eighty-eight creditors and assets are money due from 137 good debtors plus household goods and cash. Currency is the Neapolitan ounce converted at oz. 1 = li.8.

jClosed July 25, 1335, for liabilities and December 19, 1335, for assets. Liabilities are payables to twenty-four creditors and assets are 102 good debts plus household goods, merchandise, and cash. Currency is the Neapolitan ounce converted at oz. 1 = li.7 s18.

kClosed September 22, 1335; assets are cash, good debts, and merchandise less payables. No details given. Currency is libbra maiolichini converted at £M 12 = li.17.

lClosed at September 1, 1335, for liabilities and December 6, 1335, for assets. Assets are receivables from sixty-eight good debtors plus cash, and liabilities are payables to thirty-nine creditors. Currency is the Sicilian ounce converted at Soz. 1 = li.6 s5.

mClosed at March 1, 1335, but accounted in Florence on *April 9, 1343*. Represents several loan contracts made with King Frederick up to June 30, 1335. Currency is the Sicilian ounce, converted on April 9, 1343, at Soz. 1 = li.5 s10. The choice of the conversion date is curious, as is the rate, which reflects a stronger Florentine currency at a time when it was weakening. Possibly the loans were actually settled by the date indicated at a lower amount, and the accountants chose the conversion rate as the means to reflect the shortfall.

nClosed September 1, 1335, for liabilities and November 25, 1335, for assets. Liabilities are payables to five creditors; assets are receivables from sixty-five good debtors plus merchandise and cash. Currency is libbra d'anfusini converted at £A 12 = li. 14 s14.

oClosed September 1, 1336, for liabilities and November 24, 1336, for assets. Liabilities are payables to twenty-one creditors and assets are receivables from fifty-four good debtors, plus merchandise and cash. Currency is the bezant converted at B 1 = s6.

pAlthough the Peruzzi had branches at Genoa and Chiarenza at this time, no balances were reported.

Source: *I libri di commercio dei Peruzzi*, 7–10 for liabilities and 191–6 for assets.

Appendix III: Peruzzi Company and Shareholder Data

Table A3. *Summary of capital and profit, 1300–35*

Company		Capital (li.)	Est. Annual return (%)[a] A	B	Avge. annual profit/(loss) (li.)
1	(1300–08)	124,000	15.4	11.0	23,000[c]
1A	(1308–10)	130,000	20.0	18.0	27,300[d]
2	(1310–12)	149,000	14.5	13.5	21,800[e]
3	(1312–19)[b]	118,000	14.0	11.0	16,500
3	(1319–24)	118,000	16.0	14.5	20,300
4	(1324–31)	60,000	N/A[f]	3.0	4,000
5	(1331–5)	90,000	N/A	NMF[g]	(9,700)[g]
6	(1335–43)	N/A	N/A	N/A	N/A

[a]Rates of return: Column A represents A. Sapori's calculations. Column B is "real" rate of return reflecting compounding.

[b]Interim closing. The company did not dissolve until 1324.

[c]Sum of dividends (lire a fiorino):1308, 124,000; 1314, 49,600; 1319, 25,548 (seems to include an unstated amount of sales of property and interest on cash tied up); 1324, 2,138; 1339, (5,706). The total was li.195,580, which divided by 8.5 years = li.23,009 (rounded to li.23,000).

[d] Reflects dividends of li.52,000 in 1310 and li.2,700 in 1312.

[e]Reflects dividends of li.43,061 in 1312 and li.620 in 1319.

[f]Results were not known, but Sapori suspected that they were not good, given the fact that the Peruzzi were prepared to open the next company with much increased outside shareholding, sacrificing majority control. However, there was a distribution of li.26,518 in 1338 from accumulated collections of bad debts, which would indicate that the business was close to breakeven when the accounts were made up in 1331. A later distribution of li.9,787 took place in 1345 as a result of a payment from Warden Abbey in England, but this occurred after the company had been declared bankrupt.

[g]Reflects operating loss of li.38,678 at July 1, 1335, as determined in Table 5. There is no meaningful figure (NMF) for a rate of return on the loss for the period 1331–5.

Sources: A. Sapori, *Studi di Storia Economica*, Vol. 2 (Florence, G. C. Sansoni, 1955), 665–78.

I libri, Secret Book of Giotto d'Arnoldo, and Secret Sixth Book.

Table A4. *Summary of shareholdings in the Peruzzi*
Companies, 1300–43

Companies	Peruzzi family		Outsiders		
	Number	% total	Number	% total	Total[a]
1300–8					
No. shareholders	7	41	10	59	17
Subscription (li.)	74,000	60	49,000	40	123,000
1308–10					
No. shareholders	7	41	10	59	17
Subscription (li.)	71,000	55	57,500	45	128,500
1310–12					
No. shareholders	10	45	12	55	22
Subscription (li.)	79,000	54	68,000	46	147,000
1312–24					
No. shareholders	9	50	9	50	18
Subscription (li.)	68,000	59	48,000	41	116,000
1324–31					
No. shareholders	10	56	8	44	18
Subscription (li.)	34,000	58	25,000	42	59,000
1331–5					
No. shareholders	8	38	13	62	21
Subscription (li.)	37,500	42	51,000	58	88,500
1335–43					
No. shareholders	11	50	11	50	22
Subscription (li.)	NA		NA		NA

[a]Subscription totals are slightly less than total capital shown in Table A3 because a small amount, ranging between li.1,000 and li.2,000, was attributed to the Charity Account.
Source: A. Sapori, *Studi di Storia Economica*, Vol 2, 665–70.

Table A5. *List of shareholders of the Peruzzi Companies, 1300–43*
(*shareholdings in lire a fiorino*)

First Company, May 1, 1300, to October 31, 1308

Giotto di Arnoldo Peruzzi	11,000
Tommaso di Arnoldo Peruzzi	11,000
Arnoldo di Arnoldo Peruzzi	11,000
Rinieri and Filippo di Pacino di Arnoldo Peruzzi	11,000
Filippo d'Amideo Peruzzi and sons	26,000
Geri di Filippo Peruzzi	4,000
Subtotal Peruzzi	74,000
Banco di Gianni Raugi	10,000
Tano and Gherardi di Micchi Baroncelli	13,000
Catellino di Manghia degli Infanghati	7,000
Gianni di Manetto Ponci	5,000
Bencivenni di Folco Folchi	4,000
Uguccione Bonaccorsi Bentacorde	3,000
Ruggieri di Lottieri Silimanni	3,000
Giovanni Villani	2,000
Giovanni di Ricco Raugi	2,000
Subtotal non-Peruzzi	49,000
Charity company	1,000
Total	124,000

First Company (A), November 1, 1308, to October 31, 1310

Giotto di Arnoldo Peruzzi	11,000
Tommaso di Arnoldo Peruzzi	11,000
Arnoldo di Arnoldo Peruzzi	11,000
Guido and Amideo di Filippo Peruzzi	18,000
Rinieri, Filippo, and Iacopo di Pacino Peruzzi	20,000
Subtotal Peruzzi	71,000
Banco di Gianni Raugi	10,000
Tano and Gherardo di Micchi Baroncelli	14,500
Catellino di Mangia degli Infanghati	8,000
Gianni di Manetto Ponci	5,500
Bencivenni di Folco Folchi	5,000
Uguccione Bonaccorsi Bentacorde	4,000
Ruggieri di Lottieri Silimanni	4,000
Giovanni di Ricco Raugi	3,500
Filippo Villani	3,000
Subtotal non-Peruzzi	57,500
Charity company	1,500
Total	130,000

Table A5. (*Continued*)

Second Company, November 1, 1310, to October 31, 1312

Giotto di Arnoldo Peruzzi	11,000
Tommaso di Arnoldo Peruzzi	11,000
Arnoldo di Arnoldo Peruzzi	11,000
Guido and Amideo di Filippo Peruzzi	18,000
Rinieri, Filippo, Iacopo, and Salvestro di Pacino Peruzzi	24,000
Ridolfo di Donato d'Arnoldo Peruzzi	4,000
Subtotal Peruzzi	79,000
Banco di Gianni Raugi	10,000
Tano and Gherardo di Micchi Baroncelli	14,500
Catellino di Mangia degli Infanghati	8,000
Gianni di Manetto Ponci	5,500
Bencivenni di Folco Folchi	5,000
Uguccione Bonaccorsi Bentacorde	4,500
Ruggieri di Lottieri Silimanni	4,500
Ghrardo di Gentile Bonaccorsi	4,500
Giovanni di Ricco Raugi	4,000
Filippo Villani	4,000
Stefano di Uguccione Bencivenni	3,500
Subtotal non-Peruzzi	68,000
Charity company	2,000
Total	149,000

Third Company, November 1, 1312, to October 31, 1324

Giotto di Arnoldo Peruzzi	11,000
Tommaso di Arnoldo Peruzzi	11,000
Guido and Amideo di Filippo Peruzzi	18,000
Rinieri di Pacino d'Arnoldo Peruzzi	7,000
Filippo di Pacino d'Arnoldo Peruzzi	7,000
Iacopo di Pacino d'Arnoldo Peruzzi	6,000
Salvestro di Pacino d'Arnoldo Peruzzi	4,000
Ridolfo di Donato Peruzzi	4,000
Subtotal Peruzzi	68,000
Tano di Micchi Baroncelli	8,500
Gherardo di Micchi Baroncelli	6,000
Catellino di Mangia degli Infanghati	8,000
Bencivenni di Folco Folchi	5,000
Ruggieri di Lottieri Silimanni	4,500
Gherardo di Gentile Bonaccorsi	4,500
Filippo Villani	4,000
Giovanni di Ricco Raugi	4,000

Table A5. (*Continued*)

Stefano di Uguccione Bencivenni	3,500
Subtotal non-Peruzzi	48,000
Charity company	2,000
Total	118,000
Fourth Company, November 1, 1324, to June 30, 1331	
Giotto di Arnoldo Peruzzi	5,500
Tommaso di Arnoldo Peruzzi	5,500
Guido di Filippo Peruzzi	4,500
Amideo di Filippo Peruzzi	4,500
Rinieri di Pacino d'Arnoldo Peruzzi	3,500
Filippo di Pacino d'Arnoldo Peruzzi	3,500
Salvestro and Donato di Pacino d'Arnoldo Peruzzi	5,000
Ridolfo di Donato Peruzzi	2,000
Subtotal Peruzzi	34,000
Tano di Micchi Baroncelli	4,250
Gherardo di Micchi Baroncelli	3,000
Catellino di Mangia deglli Infanghati	4,000
Ruggieri di Lottieri Silimanni	3,000
Gherardo di Gentile Bonaccorsi	3,000
Filippo Villani	3,000
Giovanni di Ricco Raugi	2,000
Stefano di Uguccione Bencivenni	2,750
Subtotal non-Peruzzi	25,000
Charity company	1,000
Total	60,000
Fifth Company, July 1, 1331, to June 30, 1335	
Giotto di Arnoldo Peruzzi	6,000
Tommaso di Arnoldo Peruzzi	6,000
Amideo di Filippo Peruzzi	5,000
Pacino di Guido di Filippo Peruzzi	5,000
Rinieri di Pacino d'Arnoldo Peruzzi	4,000
Filippo di Pacino d'Arnoldo Peruzzi	4,000
Donato di Pacino d'Arnoldo Peruzzi	3,500
Donato di Giotto d'Arnoldo Peruzzi	4,000
Subtotal Peruzzi	37,500
Tano di Micchi Baroncelli	4,750
Gherardo di Micchi Baroncelli	4,000
Catellino di Mangia degli Infanghati	4,500
Ruggieri di Lottieri Silimanni	4,000

Table A5. (*Continued*)

Filippo Villani	4,000
Stefano di Uguccione Bencivenni	4,000
Baldo di Gianni Orlandini	4,000
Geri di Stefano Soderini	4,000
Guccio di Stefano Soderini	4,000
Giovanni di Stefano Soderini	3,750
Francesco Forzetti	4,000
Gherardo di Gentile Bonaccorsi	3,500
Piero di Bernardo Ubaldini	2,500
Subtotal non-Peruzzi	51,000
Charity company	1,500
Total	90,000

Sixth Company, July 1, 1335, to October 27, 1343
(shareholdings unknown)

Giotto di Arnoldo Peruzzi
Bonifazio and Pacino di Tommaso Peruzzi
Donato di Pacino d'Arnoldo Peruzzi
Tommaso di Filippo di Pacino Peruzzi
Berto di Ridolfo di Donato Peruzzi
Donato di Giotto d'Arnoldo Peruzzi
Niccolo and Ottaviano d'Amideo di Filippo Peruzzi
Pacino and Lepre di Guido di Filippo Peruzzi
Gherardo di Micchi Baroncelli
Giovanni and Gherardino di Tano Baroncelli
Baldo di Gianni Orlandini
Filippo Villani
Geri, Guccio, and Giovanni di Stefano Soderini
Ruggieri di Lottieri Silimanni
Francesco Forzetti
Stefan di Uguccione Bencivenni

Sources: A. Sapori, *Storia economica*, Vol 2, 665–70; *I libri*, Secret Book of Giotto (436–41), for the first four companies, and the Sixth Company books for the Fifth Company (276–90) and the Sixth Company (1). The order in which the shareholders are presented has been taken from these sources.

Table A6. *Changes in company loan balances due (to)/from shareholders, July 1, 1335 to July 1, 1343 (lire a fiorino)*

	July 1, 1335	July 1, 1343	Change
Peruzzi family			
Giotto and heirs	8,216	9,989	1,773
Bonifazio, Pacino, and heirs	(10,507)	(11,398)	(891)
Donato and Salvestro di Pacino	6,442	857	(5,585)
Tommaso di Filippo di Pacino	(5,649)	(1,751)	3,898
Berto di m. Ridolfo	(1,817)	(2,193)	(376)
Joint heirs of m. Ridolfo	(4,284)	(18,930)	(14,646)
Donato di Giotto	(295)	6,102	6,397
Niccholo and Ottaviano di m. Amideo	(12,646)	(21,099)	(8,453)
Guido and heirs	(6,761)	(11,718)	(4,957)
Total Peruzzi family	(27,301)	(50,141)	(22,840)
Non-Peruzzi shareholders			
Gherardo di Micchi Baroncelli	(11,487)	(13,909)	(2,422)
Giovanni and Gherardino di Tano Baroncelli	(9,224)	(3,034)	6,190
Baldo di Gianni Orlandini	(2,179)	(1,363)	816
Filippo Villani	(461)	2,656	3,117
Geri, Ghuccio, and Giovanni di Stefano Soderini	5,100	24,788	19,688
Ruggieri di Lottieri Silimanni	684	5,348	4,664
Francesco Forzetti	1,149	7,396	6,247
Stefano di Uguiccione Benciveni	448	3,552	3,104
Catellino di Mangia degl' Infanghati	5,221	9,686	4,465
Piero di Bernardo Ubaldini	(1,065)	964	2,029
Total non-Peruzzi	(11,814)	36,084	47,898
Grand total	(39,115)	(14,057)	25,058

Source: I libri, individual accounts in the Secret Book of the Sixth Company.

Appendix IV: Exchange rate trends

Table A7. *Currency effects on Angevin wheat export tax, 1300–40*

Years	Carlins per florin[a]	Florins per oz.[b]	Soldi di piccioli per florin[c]	Soldi di piccioli per oz.[d]	Soldi di piccioli per bu.[e]
1300–10	13	4.6	50	230	2.5
1310–15	13	4.6	57	262	2.9
1315–20	13	4.6	65	299	3.3
1320–30	14	4.3	66	284	3.1
1330–5	13	4.6	60	276	3.0
1335–40	12	5.0	62	310	3.4

[a]Exchange rate from P. Spufford, *Handbook of Medieval Exchange*, 63.
[b]Column 2 divided by 60. There are 60 carlins to the ounce.
[c]Exchange rate from P. Spufford, *Handbook*, 3–4.
[d]Column 3 multiplied by column 4.
[e]Column 5 times 12 divided by 1,100. This assumes a "normal" tax of 12 oz. per 100 *salme* (one *salma* equals approximately 11 Florentine bushels). This rate, however, could and did vary considerably – from as little as zero to as much as 30 oz.

Table A8. *Exchange rate index – Florentine florin versus various silver-based currencies, 1300–45*

Years	Florence Soldi	Naples Carlin	Siena Soldi	Pisa Soldi	England Sterling	Venice Grossi	France Gr. tn.[a]	Genoa Soldi
1300–5	100	100	100	100	100	100	100	100
1306–10	106	100	106	107	90	100	N/A	117
1311–15	114	100	112	115	100	N/A	110	126
1316–20	126	104	118	116	110	105	104	132
1321–5	132	111	132	120	110	100	108	141
1326–30	132	108	132	124	110	100	104	153
1331–5	120	100	120	118	117	100	100	147
1336–40	124	92	126	120	115	100	100	147
1341–5	130	86	132	124	105	75	104	110
P. Spufford, Handbook, Page nos.	3–5	63	50–4	42–5	200	85–6	186	110

Note: These indices are derived from very rough averages of the rates quoted in Peter Spufford's *Handbook of Medieval Exchange* and are thus intended as approximations indicating general direction rather than an attempt at scientific precision.

[a] Gross tournois. French exchange rates in sous/denier are too volatile to index.

Appendix V: Giovanni Villani, his background and reliability

The most frequently quoted contemporary source of information on the Peruzzi and other great Florentine companies is Giovanni Villani. By and large, he is regarded as a reputable and knowledgeable chronicler of commercial affairs of the period. Jakob Burckhardt, in citing the 25 million florins in treasure reportedly left by Pope John XXII at his death, said the amount would be incredible on any less trustworthy authority."[1] Armando Sapori, while disputing some of Villani's claims, has supported most of his figures. He, along with Robert Lopez, regarded the chronicler's 1338 statistics on Florence as substantially accurate. Villani's reputation rests on a prominent business and political career in Florence spanning a period of almost fifty years. It is also buttressed by the fact that much of his data are supported by official records and the commentaries of others.

There are, however, dissenting opinions. German scholars, such as Werner Sombart, are so critical that Sapori has labeled them as obsessively suspicious of any data from any Florentine chronicler.[2] But a less critical German historian, Robert Davidsohn, disputes some of Villani's claims, such as the one accusing the Franzesi Company of inducing Philip IV to devalue his currency.[3] And the challenges of more recent scholars cannot be easily brushed off. Guillaume Mollat and Yves Renouard indeed found Villani's estimate of John XXII's treasure incredible, setting it at only 750,000 florins.[4] Michele Luzzati has charged that Villani deliberately distorted the story of the 1342 deposit withdrawals in Naples to exonerate his company, the Buonaccorsi (discussed later). Hidetoshi Hoshino has struck at the heart of Villani's Florentine statistics by persuasively challenging the latter's claim that 80,000 cloths were produced per year.[5] John Henderson discovered that even Villani's figure for charity distributions by Orsanmichele was greatly exaggerated.[6] And my own inquiries in this study have uncovered much questionable data, the most serious being his statement of the vast sums supposedly owed to the Bardi and Peruzzi companies by Edward III.

Given the conflicting opinions on Villani's reliability, a review of his personal history would be worthwhile. Villani is believed to have been born around 1280, although one source gives the date as early as 1276.[7] He be-

[1] Burckhardt, *Civilization Renaissance*, 98.   [2] Sapori. *La crisi*, 77.
[3] Davidsohn, *Firenze*, Vol. 4, 87.
[4] Mollat, *The Popes of Avignon*, 14.; Y. Renouard, *Les relations*, chart C opposite 32.
[5] Hoshino, L'Arte della lana, 203.
[6] Henderson, "Piety and Charity," 152.
[7] Green, *Chronicle into History*, 11.

gan his business career with the Peruzzi in 1300. Luzzati indicates that he served briefly as a factor in Bruges before attaining partnership status, but as is shown elsewhere, this would have been a most unusual progression; in any case, the Peruzzi records confirm that he was a shareholder of the 1300 company to the extent of li.3,000. This fact establishes Villani as a young man not only of means but also of social position.

In 1308 Villani withdrew his shareholding and was replaced by his younger brother Filippo, who served the company as partner and manager until its demise in 1343. Giovanni retained ties with the Peruzzi, as he was put in charge of a major Peruzzi property in Siena until 1312. There is a lacuna in his business history between 1312 and 1322, but it is likely that he had some connection with the Buonaccorsi Company because his relatives were closely involved with it and because we know from a 1322 family document that he was a partner in that year. The document was an agreement among the four Villani brothers – Giovanni, Filippo, Matteo, and Francesco – to pool their surpluses for the maintenance of their father. What is interesting about this agreement is the web of cross-company connection that it discloses within the family. Filippo was a partner and Francesco a factor of the Peruzzi; Giovanni was a partner and Matteo a partner-employee of the Buonaccorsi.

During most of this period and on up to 1331, Giovanni was very active politically. He held many prestigious offices, including the priory (three times) and was often consulted on a wide range of affairs. In 1331, however, he was alleged to have taken bribes on his leaving the office of chamberlain of the Mura, overseer of the completion of the third set of walls around the city. Although he does not seem actually to have been formally convicted, his legal delaying tactics caused his reputation to suffer, and from 1331 onward he was rarely in the limelight and his name appeared in affairs of only minor importance. His attitude shows up in Chronicles X and XI, which are studded with laments about "perfidious Florentines." His personal and commercial relationships were also clouded by extensive litigation with his brothers over the 1322 agreement already mentioned.

The company with which he was most closely associated, the Buonaccorsi, was large and important, but was not among the movers and shakers of Florence at the commune level. It derived much of its influence from its strong position with King Robert in Naples and later Walter of Brienne, who became dictator of Florence in 1342–3. Thus, the Buonaccorsi and its representatives were regarded as "outsiders." Luzzati describes the company as a newcomer established in 1307, although there were references in Neapolitan state documents, which mention the Buonaccorsi as far back as 1278.[8] Whatever its origins, the company expanded rapidly throughout the 1320s and became probably the fourth-largest concern in Florence. Unfortunately, it appears to have become overextended, and on June 1, 1342, its representatives quietly disappeared from Naples and Avignon, leaving substantial debts.

From this point onward, the stories of the Buonaccorsi and Giovanni Villani are closely intertwined. The company was to be cited by the Florence tribunal on September 1, 1342, but was saved by the advent of Walter of Brienne as despot. Bankruptcy was formally acknowledged on November 7, but Brienne appointed a judge and a foreign noble with veto power over

---

[8] Yver, *Le commerce*, 292, for example.

the bankruptcy syndicate, forestalling action. This unusual procedure was designed, Luzzati believes, not to save the Buonaccorsi, but to enable the Neapolitan creditors to share in the disposal of the company's Florentine assets. All these delays suited Villani, who feared criminal prosecution for fraud in connection with the bankruptcy. Eventually, the case was processed, and on February 4, 1346, Villani was incarcerated. The final concordat between the commune and the company, which also annulled penal sentences to the shareholders, was reached on March 29, 1349 – too late for Giovanni Villani, who died of the plague in 1348.

Did these dramatic events in the life of Villani the businessman influence the writings of Villani the chronicler? We know one instance in which they did and can suspect that there were others, especially during his late years. Referring to the Naples deposit withdrawals already mentioned, Villani stated that they were provoked by a plot by the commune in May-June 1342 to enlist the help of Emperor Ludwig and the Ghibellines in its struggle with Lucca. This desperate, ill-advised action, he asserted, angered the papacy and the king of Naples causing a run on the deposits of all Florentine banks and contributing to the collapse of many of them, including the Bardi and Peruzzi. Luzzati has challenged this construction by showing that one of the companies Villani said was ruined by the withdrawals was the Cocchi, which had already been in the hands of its creditors before the withdrawals were alleged to have taken place. In fact, the only company to have fled Naples was the Buonaccorsi. Finally, he notes that Villani is the only source of the Ghibelline plot story and concludes that Villani felt the need to create a diversion from a dangerous truth by pointing a finger at the commune.[9]

This little history also suggests that Villani may not have been the well-informed insider that he would have his readers believe. Since 1331, his connections, never powerful, were weakening, and his relations with his brother Filippo were becoming strained. For example, S. L. Peruzzi has noted that Filippo, as one of the executors of the estate of John XXII at Avignon, was an impeccable source for Villani's estimate of the value of the papal treasure at John's death.[10] But, as we have seen, Villani's figure was wildly off the mark.[11] His estimates of the Bardi and Peruzzi losses on their loans to Edward III are probably the stuff of rumor emanating from the bankruptcy syndicate's first look at the Peruzzi books. He was actually in prison at the time of the Bardi collapse.

Overall, most of his figures appear to be exaggerations on close inspection, but this does not mean that they are worthless or misleading. And some, such as his estimate of Florence's population, have stood up to the test of modern analysis. His great contribution is his brilliant attempt at a macroeconomic analysis of his city. His figures may be exaggerations or

---

[9] But see 219–20, this volume, for Sapori's version of events, which confirms Florence's flirtation with Ludwig.

[10] Peruzzi, *Storia commercio,* I 64.

[11] Peter Partner, however, sensibly warns us to view all medieval papal statistics with caution, as they are often incomplete. See P. Partner, "Camera Papae: Problems of Papal Finance in the Later Middle Ages," *Journal of Ecclesiastical History* 4 (1953): 55-68.

even rough guesses, but they provide a compendium of medieval urban
amenities and consumption patterns, along with a sense of their relative
importance, if not their absolute size. And in general, despite their short-
comings, his chronicles are usually directionally apt and provide valuable
insights into the attitudes of the commercial elite of fourteenth-century
Florence. They deserve to be treated with respect, albeit with caution.

Bibliography

Published primary sources

Bond, Edward A., ed. *Extracts from the Liberate Rolls Relative to Loans Supplied by Italian Merchants to the Kings of England in the 13th and 14th Centuries.* London: Communicated by Charles George Young, 1839.

Calendar of Close Rolls. Edward I, II, and III.

Calendar of Patent Rolls. Edward I, II, and III.

Compagni, Dino. *Chronicle of Florence.* Translated by D. E. Bornstein. Philadelphia: University of Pennsylvania Press, 1986.

Lenzi, Domenico. *Il libro del Biadaiolo* [di Domenico Lenzi]: *Carestie e annona a Firenze dalla metà del '200 al 1348.* Edited by Giuliano Pinto. Florence: Leo S. Olschki, 1978.

Lyon, Mary, Bryce Lyon, and Henry S. Lucas. *The Wardrobe Book of William de Norwell, 12 July 1338 to 27 May 1340.* With the collaboration of Jean de Sturler. Brussels: Commission Royale d'Histoire de Belgique, 1983.

Pegolotti, Francesco B. *La pratica della mercatura.* Edited by Allan Evans. Cambridge, MA: Medieval Academy of America, 1936.

Sapori, A., ed. *I libri di commercio dei Peruzzi.* Milan: S. A. Fratelli Treves, 1934.

Villani, Giovanni. *Storia di Giovanni Villani.* Florence: Filippo e Iacopo Giunti, 1587.

Secondary sources

Abulafia, David. "Venice and the Kingdom of Naples in the Last Years of Robert the Wise, 1332–1343." *Papers of the British School at Rome* 48 (1980): 26–49. Reprinted in *Italy, Sicily and the Mediterranean, 1100–1400.* London: Variorum Reprints, 1987.

"Southern Italy and the Florentine Economy, 1265–1370." *Economic History Review* 2 series 33 (1981): 377–88. Reprinted in *Italy, Sicily and the Mediterranean, 1100–1400.* London: Variorum Reprints, 1987.

"Crocuses and Crusaders: San Gimignano, Pisa and the Kingdom of Jerusalem." In *Outremer: Studies in the History of the Crusading Kingdom of Jerusalem.* Jerusalem: Yad Izhak Ben-Zvi Institute, 1982, 227–43.

"The Crown and the Economy under Roger II and his Successors."

Dunbarton Oaks Papers 37 (Washington D.C. 1983): 1–13. Reprinted in *Italy, Sicily and the Mediterranean, 1100–1400.* London: Variorum Reprints, 1987.

"Sul commercio del grano siciliano nel tardo Duecento." *La societa mediterranea all'epoca del Vespro: XI Congresso della Corona d'Aragona, Palermo-Trapani-Erice, 25–30 aprile 1982.* Vol. 2. Palermo: Academia de Scienze Lettere e Arti, 1983, 5–22. Reprinted in *Italy, Sicily and the Mediterranean, 1100–1400.* London: Variorum Reprints, 1987.

"The Anconitan Privileges in the Kingdom of Jerusalem and the Levant Trade of Ancona." In *I Communi italiani nel Regno crosciato di Gerusalemme* (Colloquium Jerusalem, May 24–8, 1984). Edited by G. Airaldi and B. Z. Kedar. Collana di Fonti e Studi Genoa, 1986, 523–70.

"A Tyrrhenian Triangle: Tuscany, Sicily, Tunis, 1276–1300." In *Studi di storia economica toscana nel Medioevo e nel Rinascimento in memoria di Federigo Melis.* Pisa: Biblioteca del Bolletino Storico Pisano, Collana Storica 33, 1987.

"Les Relacions commercials i politiques entre el Regne de Mallorca." *XIII Congress of the History of the Crown of Aragon, Palma, 1989–90,* Vol. 4, 69–79.

"The Problem of the Kingdom of Majorca (1229/76–1343): 2. Economic Identity." *Mediterranean Historical Review* 6 (June 1991): 35–61.

Baker, Evelyn. "Images, Ceramic Floors, and Warden Abbey." *World Archaeology* 18 (February 1987): 363–81.

Bayley, C. C. *War and Society in Renaissance Florence: The* De Militia *of Leonardo Bruni.* Toronto: University of Toronto Press, 1961.

Beardwood, Alice. *Alien Merchants in England, 1350 to 1377: Their Legal and Economic Position.* Cambridge MA: Medieval Society of America, 1931.

Becker, Marvin B. *Florence in Transition.* Vol. 1, *The Decline of the Commune.* Baltimore: Johns Hopkins University Press, 1967.

Florence in Transition. Vol. 2, *Studies in the Rise of the Territorial State.* Baltimore: Johns Hopkins University Press, 1968.

Bischoff, John Paul. "Pegolotti, an Honest Merchant?" *Journal of European Economic History* 6 (Spring 1977): 103–8.

Blomquist, Thomas. "The Castracani Family of Thirteenth-Century Lucca." *Speculum* 46 (1971): 459–76.

"Commercial Association in Thirteenth-Century Lucca." *Business History Review* 45 (Summer 1971): 157–78.

"The Dawn of Banking in an Italian Commune." In *The Dawn of Modern Banking* (Selected papers delivered at a conference held at UCLA, September 23–5, 1977). New Haven, CT: Yale University Press, 1979, 53–75.

Bolton, J. L. *The Medieval English Economy, 1150–1500.* London: J. M. Dent, 1980.

Bowsky, William M. *The Finance of the Commune of Siena, 1287–1355.* Oxford: Clarendon Press, 1970.

A Medieval Italian Commune: Siena Under the Nine, 1287–1355. Berkeley and Los Angeles: University of California Press, 1981.

Bresc, Henri. *Un monde Méditerranéen: économie et société en Sicile, 1300–1450.* 2 vols. Rome: École Française de Rome, 1986.

Brown, Richard, ed. *History of Accounting and Accountants (1905).* London: Frank Cass, 1968.

Brucker, Gene A. *Florentine Politics and Society, 1343–1378.* Princeton, NJ: Princeton University Press, 1962.

Renaissance Florence. New York: Wiley, 1969.

Florence: The Golden Age, 1138–1737. New York: Abbeville Press, 1984.

Brush, Kathryn. "The Recepta Jocalium in the Wardrobe Book of William de Norwell, 12 July 1338 to 27 May 1340." *Journal of Medieval History* 10 (December 1984): 249–70.

Burckhardt, Jakob. *The Civilization of the Renaissance in Italy.* New York: Modern Library, 1954.

Burke, Peter. "Republics of Merchants in Early Modern Europe." In *Europe and the Rise of Capitalism.* Edited by J. Baechler, J. A. Hall, and M. Mann. London: Basil Blackwell, 1988, 220–33.

Campbell, Bruce M. S., ed. *Before the Black Death: Studies in the "Crisis" of the Early Fourteenth Century.* Manchester: Manchester University Press, 1991.

Carus-Wilson, E. M. *Medieval Merchant Venturers.* London: Methuen, 1967.

Carus-Wilson, E. M., and Olive Coleman. *England's Export Trade, 1275–1547.* Oxford: Clarendon Press, 1963.

Cipolla, Carlo M. *The Monetary Policy of Fourteenth-Century Florence.* Berkeley and Los Angeles: University of California Press, 1982.

Codell, Julie F. "Giotto's Peruzzi Chapel Frescoes: Wealth, Patronage, and the Earthly City." *Renaissance Quarterly* 41 (Winter 1988): 583–613.

Cuttino, G. P. *English Medieval Diplomacy.* Bloomington: Indiana University Press, 1985.

Dameron, George W. *Episcopal Power and Florentine Society, 1000–1320.* Cambridge, MA: Harvard University Press, 1981.

Davidsohn, Robert. *Storia di Firenze.* 7 vols. Florence: Sansoni 1956.

Day, John. *The Medieval Market Economy.* Oxford: Basil Blackwell, 1987.

De Boüard, Michel. "Problèmes de subsistances dans un état médiéval: le marché et les prix des céréales du royaume angevin de Sicile (1266–1282)." *Annales d'Histoire Économique et Sociale* 53 (September 1938): 483–501.

Delaville le Roulx, Jean. *Les Hospitaliers à Rhodes (1310–1421).* Paris: Ernest Leroux, 1913.

De Roover, Raymond. "The Commercial Revolution of the 13th Century." *Bulletin of the Business Historical Society* 16 (1942): 34–9. Reprinted in *Enterprise and Secular Change.* Edited by F. C. Lane and J. C. Riemersma. Homewood, IL: Irwin, 1953, 80–5.

Money, Banking and Credit in Medieval Bruges. Cambridge, MA: Medieval Academy of America, 1948.

"New Interpretations of the History of Banking." *Journal of World History* 2 (1954): 38–76. Reprinted in *Business, Banking and Economic Thought in Late Medieval and Early Modern Europe*. Edited by Julius Kirshner. Chicago: University of Chicago, 1974.

"The Development of Accounting Prior to Lucca Pacioli According to the Account-Books of Medieval Merchants." In *Studies in the History of Accounting*, edited by A. C. Littleton and B. S. Yamey. Homewood, IL: Irwin, 1956, 114–74. Reprinted in *Business, Banking and Economic Thought in Late Medieval and Early Modern Europe*. Edited by Julius Kirshner. Chicago: University of Chicago, 1974.

"The Story of the Alberti Company of Florence, 1302–1348, as Revealed in Its Account Books." *Harvard Business Review* 32 (Spring 1958): 14–59. Reprinted in *Business, Banking and Economic Thought in Late Medieval and Early Modern Europe*. Edited by Julius Kirshner. Chicago: University of Chicago, 1974.

The Rise and Decline of the Medici Bank, 1397–1494. New York: Norton, 1966.

di Camugliano, Ginevra M. *Chronicles of a Florentine Family, 1200–1470*. London: Jonathan Cape, 1933.

Edbury, Peter W. *The Kingdom of Cyprus and the Crusades, 1191–1324*. Cambridge University Press, 1991.

Edler, Florence. *Glossary of Medieval Terms of Business: Italian Series, 1200–1600*. Cambridge MA: Medieval Academy of America, 1934.

Edwards, J. R. *A History of Financial Accounting*. London: Routledge, 1989.

English, Edward D. *Enterprise and Liability in Sienese Banking, 1230–1350*. Cambridge, MA: Medieval Academy of America, 1988.

Fiumi, Enrico. *Storia economica e sociale di San Gimignano*. Florence: Leo Olschki, 1961.

Forey, A. J. "The Military Orders and the Holy Wars against Christians in the 13th Century." *English Historical Review* 104 (January 1989): 1–24.

Fryde, E. B. "Edward III's War Finance, 1337–41: Transactions in Wool and Credit Operations." Ph.D. diss., Bodleian Library, Oxford, 1947.

"Materials for the Study of Edward III's Credit Operations, 1327–48." *Bulletin of the Institute of Historical Research* 22 (1949): 105–38 and 23 (1950): 1–30.

"The Deposits of Hugh Despenser the Younger with Italian Bankers." *Economic History Review* 2 series, 3 (1951): 344–62. Reprinted in *Studies in Medieval Trade and Finance*. London: Hambledon Press, 1983. Reprinted in *Studies in Medieval Trade and Finance*. London: Hambledon Press, 1983.

"Edward III's Wool Monopoly: A Fourteenth-Century Trading Venture." *History* new series 37 (1952): 8–24.

"Loans to the English Crown, 1328–31." *English Historical Review* 70 (1955): 198–211. Reprinted in *Studies in Medieval Trade and Finance*. London: Hambledon Press, 1983.

"Financial Resources of Edward I in the Netherlands, 1294–98: Main Problems and Some Comparisons with Edward III in 1337–40." *Revue Belge de Philologie et d'Histoire* 40: 2 (1962): 1168–87. Reprinted in *Studies in Medieval Trade and Finance*. London: Hambledon Press, 1983.

"Public Credit with Special Reference to North-Western Europe," in *The Cambridge Economic History of Europe*. Vol. 3. Edited by M. M. Postan, E. E. Rich, and E. Miller. Cambridge University Press, 1963, Chap. 7.

"The Wool Accounts of William de la Pole." *St. Anthony's Hall Publications* 25 (1964): 3–31. Reprinted in *Studies in Medieval Trade and Finance*. London: Hambledon Press, 1983.

"Financial Resources of Edward III in the Netherlands, 1337–40." *Revue Belge de Philologie et d'Histoire* 45: 2 (1967): 1142–1216. Reprinted in *Studies in Medieval Trade and Finance*. London: Hambledon Press, 1983.

"Italian Maritime Trade with Medieval England." Recueils de la Société Jean Bodin 32 (1974): 291–337. Reprinted in *Studies in Medieval Trade and Finance*. London: Hambledon Press, 1983.

William de la Pole. London: Hambledon Press, 1988.

Fryde, Natalie. The Tyranny and Fall of Edward II, 1321–26. Cambridge University Press, 1979.

Galvani, Conte Francesco. *Sommario storico delle famiglie celebre Toscane*. Vol. 3. Florence: Ulisse Diligente, 1864, 1–4.

Given-Wilson, C. "Wealth and Credit, Public and Private: The Earls of Arundel, 1306–97." *English Historical Review* 106 (January 1991): 1–26.

Goldthwaite, Richard A. *Private Wealth in Renaissance Florence: A Study of Four Families*. Baltimore: Johns Hopkins University Press, 1968.

"Schools and Teachers of Commercial Arithmetic in Renaissance Florence." *Journal of European Economic History* 1 (Fall 1972): 418–33.

"Italian Bankers in Medieval England," review of *Bankers to the Crown* by R. A. Kaeuper. *Journal of European Economic History* 2 (Winter 1973): 763–71.

The Building of Renaissance Florence. Baltimore: Johns Hopkins University Press, 1980.

"Local Banking in Renaissance Florence." *Journal of European Economic History* 14 (Spring 1985): 5–55.

"The Medici Bank and the World of Florentine Capitalism." *Past & Present* 114 (February 1987): 3–31.

Green, Louis. *Chronicle into History: An Essay on the Interpretation of History in Florentine Fourteenth-Century Chronicles*. Cambridge University Press, 1972.

Castruccio Castracani. Oxford: Clarendon Press, 1986.

Grendler, Paul F. *Schooling in Renaissance Florence: Literacy and Learning, 1300–1600*. Baltimore: Johns Hopkins University Press, 1989.

Harriss, G. L. *King, Parliament, and Public Finance in Medieval England to 1369*. Oxford: Clarendon Press, 1975.

Harte, N. B., and K. G. Ponting, eds. *Cloth and Clothing in Medieval Europe: Essays in Memory of Professor E. M. Carus-Wilson.* London: Heineman, 1983.

Heers, Jacques. *Family Clans in the Middle Ages.* Translated by Barry Herbert. Amsterdam: North Holland, 1977.

Henderson, John S. "Piety and Charity in Late Medieval Florence: Religious Confraternities from the Middle of the Thireenth Century to the Late Fifteenth Century." Ph.D. diss., University of London, 1983.

"Religious Confraternities and Death in Early Renaissance Florence." In *Florence and Italy: Renaissance Studies in Honour of Nicolai Rubenstein.* Edited by P. Denley and C. Elain. London: University of London Committee for Medieval Studies, 1988, 383–94.

Herlihy, David. Medieval and Renaissance Pistoia: The Social History of an Italian Town, 1200–1430. New Haven CT: Yale University Press, 1967.

Medieval Households. Cambridge, MA: Harvard University Press, 1985.

Herlihy, David, and Christian Klapisch-Zuber. *Tuscans and Their Families: A Study of the Florentine Catasto of 1427.* New Haven, CT: Yale University Press, 1985.

Hewitt, J. H. *The Organization of War Under Edward III, 1338–62.* Manchester: Manchester University Press; New York: Barnes & Noble, 1966.

Holmes, George A. "Florentine Merchants in England, 1346–1446." *Economic History Review* 2 series, 13 (December 1960): 193–204.

The Good Parliament. Oxford: Clarendon Press, 1975.

Florence, Rome and the Origins of the Renaissance. Oxford: Clarendon Press, 1986.

"A Letter from Lucca to London in 1303." In *Florence and Italy: Renaissance Studies in Honour of Nicolai Rubenstein,* edited by P. Denley and C. Elain. London: University of London Committee for Medieval Studies, 1988, 227–33.

Hoshino, Hidetoshi. *L'Arte della lana in Firenze nel basso medioevo.* Florence: Leo S. Olschki, 1980.

Housley, N. *The Italian Crusades: The Papal–Angevin Alliance and the Crusades against Christian Lay Powers, 1254–1343.* Oxford: Clarendon Press, 1982.

Hughes, Dorothy. *A Study of Social and Constitutional Tendencies in the Early Years of Edward III.* London: University of London Press, 1915.

Hunt, Edwin S. "Multinational Corporations: Their Origin, Development, and Present Forms." In *Research in Economic Anthropology.* Vol. 8. Edited by B. L. Isaac. Greenwich CT: JAI Press, 1987.

"A New Look at the Dealings of the Bardi and Peruzzi with Edward III." *Journal of Economic History* 50 (March 1990): 149–62.

"The Great Medieval Merchant-Bankers: A Study of the Peruzzi Company of Florence." Ph.D. diss., University of Cincinnati, 1992.

Hyde, John K. *Padua in the Age of Dante.* Manchester: Manchester University Press; New York: Barnes & Noble, 1966.

Society and Politics in Medieval Italy. London: Macmillan Press, 1973.

Johnson, Paul. *Edward III*. London: Weidenfeld & Nicolson, 1973.

Jones, P. J. "Florentine Families and Florentine Diaries in the Fourteenth Century." *Papers of the British School of Rome* 24 (1956): 183–205.

Kaeuper, Richard W. "The Frescobaldi and the English Crown." In *Studies in Medieval and Renaissance History*. Vol. 10. Edited by Wm. Bowsky. Lincoln: University of Nebraska Press, 1973, 41–95.

Bankers to the Crown: The Riccardi of Lucca and Edward I. Princeton, NJ: Princeton University Press, 1973.

War, Justice, and Public Order. Oxford: Clarendon Press, 1988.

Kedar, B. Z. *Merchants in Crisis: Genoese and Venetian Men of Affairs and the Fourteenth-Century Depresssion*. New Haven, CT: Yale University Press, 1976.

Kent, Francis W. *Household and Lineage in Renaissance Florence*. Princeton, NJ: Princeton University Press, 1977.

Kent, D. V., and Kent, F. W. "A Self-disciplining Pact Made by the Peruzzi Family of Florence (June 1433)." *Renaissance Quarterly* 34 (Fall 1981): 337–55.

Kittell, Ellen E. *From* Ad Hoc *to Routine: A Case Study of Medieval Bureaucracy*. Philadelphia: University of Pennsylvania Press, 1991.

Knowles, David. *Religious Orders in England*. Vol. 1. The Old Orders, 1216–1340. Cambridge University Press, 1950.

Krekic, B. "Italian Creditors in Dubrovnik (Ragusa) and the Balkan Trade, Thirteenth through Fifteenth Centuries." In *Dawn of Modern Banking*. New Haven, CT: Yale University Press, 1979, 241–54.

Krueger, H. C. "The Genoese Exportation of Northern Cloths to Mediterranean Ports, Twelfth Century." *Revue Belge de Philologie et d' Histoire* 65:4 (1987): 722–50.

Kuehn, Thomas. *Law, Family and Women*. Chicago: University of Chicago Press, 1991.

Ladis, Andrew, and Taddeo Gaddi, *Critical Appraisal and Catalogue Raisonné*. Columbia: University of Missouri Press, 1982.

Lander, J. R. *The Limitations of the English Monarchy in the Later Middle Ages*. Toronto: University of Toronto Press, 1989.

Lane, Frederic C. "Double Entry Bookkeeping and Resident Merchants." *Journal of European Economic History* 6 (Spring 1977): 177–91.

Lane, Frederic C., and Reinhold C. Mueller. *Money and Banking in Medieval and Renaissance Venice*. Vol. 1, Coins and Moneys of Account. Baltimore: Johns Hopkins University Press, 1985.

Lansing, Carol. "Nobility in a Medieval Commune: The Florentine Magnates, 1260–1300." Ph.D. Diss., University of Michigan, 1984.

The Florentine Magnates: Lineage and Faction in a Medieval Commune. Princeton, NJ: Princeton University Press, 1991.

Larner, John. *Italy in the Age of Dante and Petrarch, 1216–1380*. London: Longman, 1980.

La Roncière, Charles M. de. *Prix et salaires à Florence au xive siècle, 1280–1380*. Rome: École française de Rome, 1982.

"Indirect Taxes or 'Gabelles' at Florence in the Fourteenth Century." In Florentine Studies: *Politics and Society in Renaissance Florence.* Edited by Nicolai Rubenstein. London: Faber & Faber, 1968, 140–92.

Lestocquoy, J. *Aux Origines de la Bourgeoisie: les villes de Flandre et d'Italie sous le gouvernement des patriciens (xi^- xv^ siècles).* Paris: Presses Universitaires de France, 1952.

Lewis, Archibald. "The Islamic World and the Latin West, 1350–1500." *Speculum* 65 (October 1990): 833–44.

Lloyd, T. H. "The Movement of Wool Prices in Medieval England." *Economic History Review* Supplement 6 (1973).

The English Wool Trade in the Middle Ages. Cambridge University Press, 1977.

Alien Merchants in England in the High Middle Ages. Sussex: Harvester Press; New York: St. Martin's Press, 1982.

Lopez, Robert S. "Italian Leadership in the Medieval Business World," review of *Studi di storia economica medievale* by A. Sapori. *Journal of Economic History* 8 (May 1948): 63–8.

"Majorcans and Genoese on the North Sea Route in the Thirteenth Century." *Revue Belge de Philologie et d'Histoire.* 29 (1951): 1163–79.

Lopez, Robert S., and Irving W. Raymond. *Medieval Trade in the Mediterranean World.* New York: Columbia University Press, 1955.

Lucas, Henry S. *The Low Countries and the Hundred Years' War, 1326–1347.* Ann Arbor: University of Michigan Press, 1929.

Luttrell, Anthony. "Interessi fiorentini nell'economia e nella politica dei Cavalieri Ospedalieri di Rodi nel Trecento." *Annali della Scuola Normale Superiore di Pisa: Lettere, Storia e Filosofia,* 2d series, 28 (Pisa, 1959): 317–26. Reprinted in *The Hospitallers in Cyprus, Rhodes, Greece, and the West, 1291–1440.* London: Variorum Reprints, 1978.

"The Hospitallers in Cyprus after 1291." *Acts of the First International Congress of Cypriot Studies* 2 (Nicosia, 1972): 161–71. Reprinted in *The Hospitallers in Cyprus, Rhodes, Greece, and the West, 1291–1440.* London: Variorum Reprints, 1978.

"The Hospitallers at Rhodes, 1306–1421." In *A History of the Crusades.* Edited by K. Setton III. Madison: University of Wisconsin Press, 1975, 278–313. Reprinted in *The Hospitallers in Cyprus, Rhodes, Greece, and the West, 1291–1440.* London: Variorum Reprints, 1978.

Luzzati, Michele. *Giovanni Villani e la compagnia dei Buonaccorsi.* Rome: Istituto della enciclopedia Italiana, 1971.

Luzzatto, Gino. *An Economic History of Italy from the Fall of the Roman Empire to the Beginning of the 16th Century.* London: Routledge & Kegan Paul, 1961.

Machiavelli, Nicolo. *History of Florence.* Introduction by Charles W. Colby. New York: Colonial Press, 1905.

Masschaele, James. "Transport Costs in Medieval England." *Economic History Review* 2 series, 46 (1993): 266–79.

Matc, Mavis. "High Prices in Early Fourteenth-Century England: Causes and Consequences." *Economic History Review* 2 series, 28 (1975): 1–16.

Mayhew, N. J. "Numismatic Evidence and Falling Prices in the Fourteenth Century." *Economic History Review* 2 series, 27 (1974): 1–15.

Mazzaoui, Maureen F. *The Italian Cotton Industry in the Later Middle Ages, 1100–1600.* Cambridge University Press, 1981.

Melis, Federigo. *Storia della ragioneria.* Bologna: Zuffi, 1950.

Miller, Edward. "War and Taxation and the English Economy in the Late 13th and Early 14th Century." In *War and Economic Development: Essays in Memory of David Joslin.* Edited by J. M. Winter, Cambridge University Press, 1975, 11–31.

Miskimin, Harry A. *Money, Prices, and Foreign Exchange in Fourteenth-Century France.* New Haven, CT: Yale University Press, 1983.

Mollat, G. *The Popes of Avignon, 1305–1378.* Translated from the 9th French edition by Janet Love. London: Thomas Nelson, 1949.

Muendel, John. "The 'French' Mill in Medieval Tuscany." *Journal of Medieval History* 10 (December 1984): 215–47.

Munro, John H. "Industrial Transformations in the North-west European Textile Trades, c1290–c1340: Economic Progress or Economic Crisis?" In *Before the Black Death: Studies in the 'Crisis' of the Early Fourteenth Century.* Edited by B. M. S. Campbell. Manchester: Manchester University Press, 1989, 110–48.

Muré, Giuseppe. "Note sulla gestione bancaria e sul fallimento della Compagnia mercantile dei Peruzzi." In *Studi in memoria di Federigo Melis.* Naples: Gianini, 1978, 147–58.

Najemy, John. *Corporatism and Consensus in Florentine Electoral Politics, 1280–1400.* Chapel Hill: University of North Carolina Press, 1982.

Nelson, B. N. "The Usurer and the Merchant Prince: Italian Businessmen and the Ecclesiastical Law of Restitution." *Journal of Economic History* supplement (1947): 104–22.

Nicholas, David. *The Metamorphosis of a Medieval City: Ghent in the Age of the Arteveldes, 1302–1390.* Lincoln: University of Nebraska Press, 1987.

The Van Arteveldes of Ghent. Ithaca, NY: Cornell University Press, 1988.

Ormrod, W. M. *The Reign of Edward III: Crown and Political Society in England, 1327–1377.* New Haven, CT: Yale University Press, 1990.

"The Crown and the English Economy." In *Before the Black Death: Studies in the "Crisis" of the Early Fourteenth Century.* Edited by B. M. S. Campbell. Manchester: Manchester University Press, 1991, 149–83.

Ottokar, Nicola. *Il commune di Firenze alla fine del dugento.* Florence: Vallechi, 1926.

Partner, Peter. "Camera Papae: Problems of Papal Finance in the Later Middle Ages." *Journal of Ecclesiastical History* 4 (1953): 55–68.

"Florence and the Papacy." In *Europe in the Middle Ages.* Edited by J. R. Hale, J. R. L. Highfield, and B. Smalley. London: Faber & Faber, 1965, 76–121.

The Murdered Magicians: The Templars and Their Myth. Oxford: Oxford University Press, 1982.

Passerini, Luigi. "Genealogica e storia della famiglia dei Peruzzi." MSS folios 41 and 156 in the Biblioteca Nazionale Centrale, Firenze.

Storia degli stabilimente de beneficenza e d'istruzione elementare gratuita della città di Firenze. Florence: Tipografia le Monnier, 1853.

Storia e genealogica delle famiglie Passerini e de' Rilli. Florence: M. Cellini, 1874.

Peruzzi, S. L. *Storia del commercio e dei banchieri di Firenze, 1200–1345.* Florence: M. Cellini, 1868.

Postan, M. M. *Medieval Trade and Finance.* Cambridge University Press, 1973.

Power, Eileen. *The Wool Trade in English Medieval History.* Oxford University Press, 1941.

Prestwich, Michael. "Italian Merchants in Late Thirteenth and Early Fourteenth Century England." In *Dawn of Modern Banking* (selected papers delivered at a conference held at UCLA September 23–5, 1977). New Haven, CT: Yale University Press, 1979, 77–104.

"Early Fourteenth-Century Exchange Rates." *Economic History Review* 2 series, 32 (November 1979): 470–82.

The Three Edwards: War and State in England 1272–1377. New York: St. Martin's Press, 1980.

Edward I. London: Methuen, 1988.

Prienne, Henri. *Histoire de Belgique.* Brussels: Lamertin, 1922.

Pryor, John. "Foreign Policy and Economic Policy: The Angevins of Sicily and the Economic Decline of Southern Italy, 1266 to 1343." In *Principalities, Powers and Estates* (studies in Medieval and Early Modern Government and Society). Edited by L. O. Frappell, Adelaide, 1978.

Pullan, Brian. *A History of Early Renaissance Italy: From the Mid-thirteenth to the Mid-fifteenth Century.* London: Allen Lane, 1973.

Ramsay, J. H. *A History of the Revenues of the Kings of England, 1066–1399.* Oxford: Clarendon Press, 1925.

Raveggi, Sergio, Massimo Tarassi, Daniela Medici, and Patrizia Parenti. *Ghibellini, Guelfi, e Popolo Grasso: il detentore del potere politico a Firenze nella seconda metà del dugento.* Florence: La Nova Italia, 1978.

Renouard, Yves. "Une expédition des céréales des Pouilles en Arménie par les Bardi pour le compte de Benoit XII." In *Mélanges d'Archéologie et d'Histoire.* Rome: École française de Rome 53, 1936, 287–329. Reprinted in *Études d'Histoire Mediévale.* Vol. 2. Paris: S.E.V.P.E.N., 1968, 793–824.

Les relations des papes d'Avignon et des compagnies commerciales et bancaires de 1316 à 1378. Paris: Bibliothèque des Écoles françaises d'Athènes et de Rome 151, 1941.

The Avignon Papacy, 1305–1403. Translated by Denis Bethell. Hamden, CT: Archon Books, 1970.

Reynolds, Robert L. "Origins of Modern Business Enterprise: Medieval Italy." *Journal of Economic History* 12 (Fall 1952): 350–65.

Rhodes, W. E. "The Italian Bankers in England and Their Loans to Edward I and Edward II." In *Historical Essays by Members of the Owens College.* Edited by T. F. Tout and James Tait. London: Longmans, Green, 1902, 137–68

Rostow, W. W. *The Stages of Economic Growth.* 2d ed. Cambridge University Press, 1971.

Runciman, Steven. *The Sicilian Vespers.* Cambridge University Press, 1958.

Russell, Ephraim. "The Societies of the Bardi and the Peruzzi and Their Dealings with Edward III." In *Finance and Trade Under Edward III.* Edited by G. Unwin. London: Longmans, Green, 1918, 93–135.

Salvemini, Gaetano. *La dignità cavalleresca nel Commune di Firenze e altri scritti.* Milan: Feltrinelli, 1972.

Sapori, Armando. *La crisi delle compagnie mercantili dei Bardi e dei Peruzzi.* Florence: Leo S. Olschki, 1926.

Studi di storia economica medievale. Florence: G. C. Sansoni, 1947.

"The Culture of the Medieval Italian Merchant." Abridged translation by Raymond de Roover and Florence Edler. In *Enterprise and Secular Change.* Edited by F. C. Lane and J. C. Riemersma. Homewood, IL: Irwin, 1953, 53–65.

Studi di storia economica. Vols. 1 and 2. Florence: G. C. Sansoni, 1955.

Sayles, G. O. *The King's Parliament of England.* New York: Norton, 1974.

Schevill, Ferdinand. *History of Florence.* New York: Harcourt Brace, 1936.

Seward, Desmond. *The Hundred Years' War: The English in France, 1337–1453.* New York: Atheneum, 1986.

Spufford, Peter. *Handbook of Medieval Exchange.* London: Royal Historical Society, 1986.

Money and Its Use in Medieval Europe. Cambridge University Press, 1988.

Staley, Edgcumbe. *The Guilds of Florence.* London: Methuen, 1906.

Strayer, Joseph R. "Italian Bankers and Philip the Fair." In Economy, Society, and Government in Medieval Italy: Essays in Honor of Robert L. Reynolds. Edited by D. Herlihy, R. S. Lopez, and V. Slessarev. Kent, OH: Kent State University Press, 1969, 113–21. Reprinted in *Medieval Statecraft and the Perspectives of History: Essays by Joseph R. Strayer.* Princeton, NJ: Princeton University Press, 1971, 239–47.

The Reign of Philip the Fair. Princeton, NJ: Princeton University Press, 1980.

Strayer, Joseph R., ed. *Dictionary of the Middle Ages.* S.v. "Textile Technology" by John Munro. New York: Scribner, 1988.

Sumption, Jonathan. *The Hundred Years' War.* Vol. 1, Trial by Battle. London: Faber & Faber, 1990.

Swetz, Frank J. *Capitalism and Arithmetic: The New Math of the 15th Century.* La Salle, IL: Open Court, 1987.

Takayama, H. "Familiares Regis and the Royal Inner Council in Twelfth-Century Sicily." *English Historical Review* 104 (April 1989): 357–72.

Tintori, L., and Eve Borsook. *Giotto and the Peruzzi Chapel.* New York: Abrams, 1965.

Trasselli, Carmello. "Nuovi documenti sui Peruzzi, Bardi, e Acciaiuoli in Sicilia." *Economia e Storia* 3 (1956): 179–95.

Tuchman, Barbara. *A Distant Mirror: The Calamitous Fourteenth Century*. New York: Knopf, 1978.

Usher, Abbot P. *The Early History of Deposit Banking in Mediterranean Europe*. Vol. 1. Cambridge, MA: Harvard University Press, 1943.

Vale, Malcolm. *The Angevin Legacy and the Hundred Years' War, 1250–1340*. Oxford: Basil Blackwell, 1990.

Van Egmond, W. "The Commercial Revolution and the Beginnings of Western Mathematics in Renaissance Florence, 1300–1500." Ph.D. diss., Indiana University, and University Microfilms, Ann Arbor, MI, 1976.

Veitch, John. "Repudiations and Confiscations by the Medieval State." *Journal of Economic History* 46 (March 1986): 31–6.

Veseth, Michael. *Mountains of Debt*. New York: Oxford University Press, 1990.

Victoria History of the Counties of England. Bedfordshire. "Warden Abbey." Microfiche 409: 359–66.

Waley, Daniel. "The Army of the Florentine Republic." In *Florentine Studies: Politics and Society in Renaissance Florence*. Edited by Nicolai Rubenstein. London: Faber & Faber, 1968, 70–108.

Waugh, Scott L. *England in the Reign of Edward III*. Cambridge University Press, 1991.

Weissman, Ronald F. E. *Ritual Brotherhood in Renaissance Florence*. New York: Academic Press, 1982.

Wood, Diana. *Clement VI*. Cambridge University Press, 1989.

Yamey, Basil S. "Scientific Bookkeeping and the Rise of Capitalism." *Economic History Review* 2 series, 1 (1949): 99–113.

"Notes on Double-Entry Bookkeeping and Economic Progress." *Journal of Economic History* 35 (Winter 1975): 717–23.

Yver, Georges. *Le commerce et les marchands dans l'Italie méridionale, au XIIIe et au XIVe siècle*. Paris: Librairie des Écoles françaises d'Athènes et de Rome 88, 1903.

Index

Abulafia, David, 39n, 46n, 70
Acciaiuoli, company, 1, 4, 39–40, 47, 61, 135, 217, 243; bankruptcy of, 229, 241
Acciaiuoli, family, 33, 90, 94, 228, 246; Acciaiuolo, 186; Iacopo, 217; Niccolo, 241
accountants, training of, 5, 104–5
accounting, (see also Peruzzi Company, accounting anomalies, etc.); accruals, 110, 113; bad debts, 106; closing, 109, 156–7; double-entry, 101–3, 109, 122, 123, 236; fixed assets and depreciation, 114; inventory valuation, 169; receivables, 110–11; religious invocations, 108; single-entry, 102–3; units of account, 7, 111
Acre, destruction of, 22
Adimari family, 25, 30–1
Alberti, company (see also de Roover, Raymond), 96, 99, 136, 218n, 246
Alberti, family, 33, 90
Alexandria, 55, 134
Altopascio, battle of, 26, 28, 32, 158
Anagni, 24, 131
Ancona, 50
Angevin kingdom of southern Italy (see Naples, kingdom of)
Antellessi, company, 228, 240n
Antwerp, 200, 204, 205
Aragon, 46, 71, 163
arithmetic: abacus, 104–5; arabic system, 104, 112; roman numerals, 104, 112;
Artevelde, Jakob van, 198, 209
Arundel, Earl Richard of, 241
audits, by English government, 102, 227, 229, 237, 245
Avignon (see also Peruzzi Company, branches), 28, 30, 31, 34, 54, 62, 66, 72, 97, 121, 269, 270; depositors at, 213, 220

banking (see also Edward III, financing; papacy, money transfers; Peruzzi Company, banking and lending), 3, 48, 201
Barcelona, 55, 87
Bardi, company, 38, 39, 60, 106, 148, 164, 237; bankruptcy of, 1, 242; charitable donations of, 83; English venture with Peruzzi, see Peruzzi Company, joint venture with Bardi; exaggerated size,121, 245–6; factors, 12, 88, 96; in England before joint venture, 60, 162,199: in England after joint venture, 241–2; papal business, 81, 175; profitability of, 65, 78, 116, 165, 167, 169–70, 172, 244
Bardi, family, 11, 14, 33, 94, 214, 229, 242, 246; 1340 coup attempt, 12, 213–14, 226; Piero di Gualtieri, 214; Ridolfo, 228, Walter, 241–2
Barletta, 49–50, 87
Baroncelli, family, 25, 92, 130, 224, 243n; Gherardino di Tano, 234n, 264, 265; Gherardo di Micchi, 32, 97, 168, 185n, 261–4, 265; Giovanni di Tano, 97, 198n, 212, 264, 265; Tano di Micchi, 32, 168,185n, 261–3
Beardwood, Alice, 242, 245
Bencivenni, Stefano, 262–4, 265
Benedict XI, pope, 130
Benedict XII, pope, 168, 187, 196, 217–18
Bentacorde, Uguccione, 25, 135, 261–2
Biada, "six of the," 50–2
Biadaiolo, il libro del, 51n, 52, 166
bills of exchange, discounting of, 202
Black Death, 3, 6, 28, 35, 234, 247, 252–5, 270
Black-White dispute, see Florence
Blomquist, Thomas, 18, 19
Bolton, J. L., 121
Bonaccorsi, Gherardo di Gentile, 97, 119, 184, 262–4